Writing Lough Derg

D1597530

Irish Studies
James MacKillop, *Series Editor*

Lough Derg, Co. Donegal. *Courtesy of the National Library of Ireland.*

WRITING LOUGH DERG

From William Carleton to Seamus Heaney

PEGGY O'BRIEN

SYRACUSE UNIVERSITY PRESS

Syracuse University Press, Syracuse, New York 13244–5160
Copyright © 2006 by Peggy O'Brien
All Rights Reserved

First Edition 2006
06   07   08   09   10   11   6   5   4   3   2   1

The paper used in this publication meets the minimum requirements of
American National Standard for Information Sciences—Permanence of
Paper for Printed Library Materials, ANSI Z39.48–1984.∞™

Library of Congress Cataloging-in-Publication Data

O'Brien, Peggy, 1945–
Writing Lough Derg : from William Carleton to Seamus Heaney / Peggy O'Brien. 1st ed.
p. cm.
Includes bibliographical references and index.
ISBN 0–8156–3073–5 (alk. paper)—ISBN 0–8156–3098–0 (pbk. : alk. paper)
1. English literature—Irish authors—History and criticism. 2. English literature—20th century—History and
criticism. 3. English literature—19th century—History and criticism. 4. Saint Patrick's Purgatory (Ireland)—In
literature. 5. Christian pilgrims and pilgrimages in literature. I. Title.
PR8755.O27 2006
820.9'9417—dc22   2006020327

Manufactured in the United States of America

This book is dedicated to Harriet O'Donovan Sheehy, my Virgil

Do not fear, for no one can take from us our passage,
by such an One is it granted us; but wait for me here,
and comfort your every spirit and feel it with good hope,
for I will not forsake you in the nether world.

—Dante, *Inferno*
canto viii, 104–8, translated by Charles S. Singleton

PEGGY O'BRIEN teaches in the English Department at the University of Massachusetts, Amherst. For the first half of her career she taught at Trinity College, Dublin. She is the author of a collection of poems, *Sudden Thaw,* and the editor of the *Wake Forest Book of Irish Women's Poetry.*

Contents

Acknowledgments

PURGATORY IS LONG and so was the writing of this book. Its inception, however, could not have been more spontaneous and presageful. Over a decade ago in a casual conversation with Seamus Heaney about his poem "Station Island," he suggested that I take a look at the work of other writers who had tussled with Lough Derg. I think he mentioned William Carleton and Denis Florence MacCarthy. Furthermore, I received this nudge into the underworld on a narrow, winding staircase between two stories, a liminal site, as we say now. That the eighteenth-century house in Pelham, Massachusetts, where Heaney was visiting was the home then of Paul Muldoon and his wife, Jean Korelitz, was also portentous, given the bearing of Lough Derg, I maintain, on contemporary Irish poetry. (And was it merely coincidence that the family who enjoyed the boatman's sinecure at Lough Derg for generations was none other than the Muldoons?) Since that hesitant start, countless people have assisted me on my tortuous way. Seamus Heaney himself has been unstinting in his help and kindness, not least in the matter of granting permission to cite his poetry and prose. Paul Muldoon has been similarly accommodating about quoting his work. My fear right now is that I will fail to recall all those who were forthcoming with their knowledge and encouragement. If I do omit someone, I hope he or she will chalk this oversight up to the human fallibility on which this book dwells.

Fortunately, for memory's sake, most of the people named below live and work in one or both of my spiritual homes: the United States and Ireland. First, I wish to single out those who live and work in this rarefied corner of western Massachusetts, all of whom, as it happens, are attached to one of the many institutions of higher learning here. The following are both close friends and colleagues. At the University of Massachusetts, Amherst, I wish to thank: Anne Herrington, Deborah Carlin, Laura Doyle, Nick Bromell, Randall Knoper, and Madeleine Blais, and former colleagues Margo Culley and Kathleen Swaim; at Amherst College, Daniel Hall and Susan Snively; at Mount Holyoke College, Brad Leithauser and Mary Jo Salter; at Holyoke Community College, Deborah Fairman. I owe special scholarly debts to two local colleagues: Catherine Ciepiela at Amherst College, who introduced me to Brodsky's theory about the relationship between the Magdalene poems of Pasternak and Tsvetaeva, and Fred McGinness at Mount Holyoke College, who introduced me to Le Goff's history of purgatory. Further afield, I wish to thank Elizabeth Cullingford at the University of Texas, Austin, Natalie Anderson at Swarthmore College, Lucy McDiarmid at Villanova University, Vera Krielkamp at Pine Manor College, and Robert Faggen at Claremont McKenna College. I am especially grateful to busy Jack Harrison at the University of Massachusetts Press for his informed advice about publishing and to both him and his wife, Mary Irwin at the Smith College Library, for being my loyal, abiding friends: family really.

Throughout the years my staunch, stimulating colleagues in Dublin have been both a constant prod and an endless source of bibliographical information, ideas, and lifesaving humor. Kevin Whelan at the University of Notre Dame in Dublin simply refused to let me not complete my chosen penance. Conversations with Luke Gibbons, also at Notre Dame, over the years have proved crucial in forming my views on Irish culture. I wish also to thank Anne Whelan and Dolores Gibbons for great kindness. And the poet Nuala Ní Dhomhnaill, when I had my doubts about this book, never wavered in her belief in it. I also thank James Lydon at Trinity College, Dublin, for introducing me long ago to Picard's translation of the *Tractatus de Purgatorio Sancti Patricio*. Indeed, my faithful retinue of Dublin friends have chivvied and cheered me on for years. Special thanks to Tony Glavin, Adrienne Flemming, Marie Heaney, Anne Kelly, Mary Ellen Fox, and Mimi Tatlow. I must also recall my recently deceased friend Kate Slattery, who actually drove me to Lough Derg and urged me to go to the island. (My soul sank as I looked out on a tiny wafer of land weighed down by a stone basilica and waterside dormitories.)

I could not have completed this work, given the pressures of teaching, without the lavish research and writing time afforded by two fellowships that came at critical periods. First, in 1994, when I was beginning research, the Institute for Irish Studies at Queens University, Belfast, awarded me a senior fellowship. I would like to thank in particular at Queens Brian Walker and Sophie King. Medbh McGuckian, a fellow fellow that year, proved the author not just of celestial poems but of fiendish fun. Another fellow, Jane Leonard, accompanied me to Donegal on my first trip to view Station Island from a safe distance. Other friends in Belfast, particularly Michael and Edna Longley and Denise and Brian Ferran regularly provided sustenance for body and soul with fantastic food and great conversation. Finally, I need to thank my sister Christine and her husband Michael Leckey for all their hospitality in Lough Gall, County Armagh, during that year. I also want to recognize the efficient and always genial staff at the Linen Hall Library in Belfast and the National Library of Ireland in Dublin.

The second fellowship, enjoyed in the spring of 2002, was at the Liguria Study Center outside Genoa in Italy. There, I was able largely to complete a first draft. I urgently need to thank everyone at Bogliasco, who made my stay one of the most productive and comfortable, indeed luxurious, writing periods in my life. I am especially grateful to Anna Maria Quaiat, Ivana Folle, Gianni Migone, Rita Abbis, and Alan Rowlin. I will never thank Mary Jo Salter enough for pointing my body in the direction of the balmy Golpho Paradiso, when my mind was frozen in Celtic Purgatory.

I owe a special debt as well to the various editors, readers, agents, and professional contacts who have made the onerous final task of assembling this book as easy and civilized as possible. In this regard, I especially want to thank Glenn Wright at Syracuse University Press for his flexibility and patience. I wish also to salute James MacKillop at Syracuse, who initially asked to see my manuscript, and Audrey Eyler, one of my first and most astute and appreciative readers. I am also indebted to D. J. Whyte, Therese Walsh, and Fred Wellner, indeed to the staff at Syracuse University Press in general.

For granting permission to cite the many authors in this book I wish to thank especially for their generosity: Andrew Rynne acting for Alice Curtayne's estate; John Deane for Denis Devlin's; and Desmond Leslie for Shane Leslie's. Permission to quote Patrick Kavanagh has been kindly granted by the trustees of the estate of the late Katherine B. Kavanagh, as represented by the Jonathan Williams Literary Agency. I thank also Maurice Harmon, Maurice Craig, and Jim Mays for helping me untangle knotted matters pertaining to permissions. Also, Maggie Evans at the Wylie Agency and Andrew Lord at Faber and Faber in London, plus Victoria Fox at Farrar Straus and Giroux in New York, could not have been more attentive and expeditious. Above all, I owe an incalculable debt to my courteous, canny, and erudite agent, Jonathan Williams. Further, I want to thank Nancy Doherty, my sophisticated and sensitive editorial consultant, who prepared this manuscript for print. She has saved me from large and small embarrassments. All those venial and mortal sins still extant are mine. I alone must pay.

Finally, since the lesson carried by all Lough Derg writing is the perpetually unfinished business of spiritual regeneration, let me add a personal note on this subject. As my shame-faced words above indicate, I have been to Pettigo in County Donegal twice. I have ventured out to Lough Derg, stood on the shore and peered out over that gray, infamously inhospitable slab of bog lake and shivered with ambivalence. I still have not done the pilgrimage. The dormant demons of my Catholic childhood might come rampaging back to life given half a chance. That the pilgrimage has this power over me may go some distance to explain why I chose this subject, kept pursuing it, and above all am fascinated by those over whom it has had a much more potent and creative sway. As my dedication of this book reveals, I have had the wisest and truest of friends at my side through my adulthood, sharing both my long travails and moments of grace: Harriet O'Donovan Sheehy. I have also had the pure blessing of my daughter, Kristen Kennelly Murphy, and her daughters, Meg, Hannah, and Grace Murphy, angels all (and not to forget my highly literate and good son-in-law, Peter Murphy). Finally I have had my dear husband, Wynn Abranovic, at my side daily: joy after a long pilgrimage. My friends and family are my heaven.

Peggy O'Brien   Amherst, Massachusetts   Febrary 2006

Introduction

FROM VERY EARLY ON, one's view of Lough Derg is refracted by how others have seen it. Our first glimpse of the lake in William Carleton's story about his youthful pilgrimage there is through the eyes of someone else, not our author:

> The lake itself was certainly as fine as rocky shores and numerous islands could make it: but it was encompassed with such dreariness; it was deformed so much by its purgatorial island; the associations connected with it were of such a degrading character, that really the whole prospect before me struck my mind with a sense of painfulness, and I said to myself, "I am already in purgatory."[1]

The speaker in this excerpt seems to be approaching a place that he is seeing for the first time but has already fully imagined. Alluding to "the associations connected with" this site, he unwittingly reveals how draped in myth even the most barren Irish landscape can be, if the human imagination has settled on it repeatedly. This process of gradually domesticating a place is accomplished in the Irish tradition usually by means of successive poems and stories. There is even a collection of tenth-century Irish place lore, the *Dindshenchas*, where each entry celebrates a site, particularly its history and the origin of its name. Even such venerable, pristine sources from geographical history, however, carry with them complication. For example, Croagh Patrick, the mountain in County Mayo associated with Saint Patrick, is commemorated by such a story, relating how Crom Derg murdered his nephew Aigle there, thus explaining how the mountain originally came to be called Aigle. Peter Harbison, who has studied pilgrimage in Ireland, speculates that the name Croagh Patrick indicates a Christian overlay on a pagan source.[2] This isolated act represents a linguistic appropriation with a sweeping colonial agenda, one not unrelated to the later Anglicization of place names. It is not surprising, therefore, that my opening quotation, which relates to a second, even more famous Patrician landmark in Ireland, displays analogous, historically determined, implicit narrative layers. William Carleton quotes the speaker, the Reverend Caesar Otway, as a way of introducing a story that more conventionally opens with Carleton's own account of approaching the lake as a young, fervent Catholic.

The particular story I am writing here, another layer of inscription, is on its most accessible level about the destination that Otway and Carleton at separate times both approached: Lough Derg, a bog lake in the northwest corner of Ireland, the destination like Croagh Patrick of a still active penitential pilgrimage. "Doing Lough Derg" is the common expression in Ireland for performing this pilgrimage. The site, also known as Saint Patrick's Purgatory, has been a destination for pilgrims in Ireland for probably more than a thousand years and, what is more, it enjoyed widespread European fame in the Middle Ages. My story, however, is not primarily about this place but rather about a long and complicated conversation concerning it, overheard for the most part between the lines of poems but also of some prose—fiction; letters; a play; scholarly, devotional, and polemical writings. The dense intertextuality of this conversation is merely hinted at by the nesting of Carleton's originally Catholic voice in that of the arch-Protestant Otway. The topic that creates a thread of common preoccupation among all these related works is ostensibly Lough Derg; however, the concerns that bind these writers, whose connection with one another constitutes more a web than a line, are much more far-flung. Indeed, the participants in this conversation, which rises above the actual desolate place in County Donegal, extend far beyond Ireland. They include a number of medieval European pilgrims, who left us their accounts of the underworld, and a range of modern and contemporary Irish writers with rich, deep European connections.

Catholicism, the cultural force that, particularly with Irish independence, came to center and epitomize a constructed Irish identity in the twentieth century, is, ironically, also the force that links insular Ireland intimately with the larger and more diverse continent. Europe represents a powerful challenge to the specific brand of conservative Catholicism associated with post-Famine Ireland, at least until very recently. The literary writers who contribute to the text of this extended Lough Derg conversation all share a concern with the way literature, especially poetry, both responds to and creates culture, and the way Catholicism inflects, for better or worse, the world they inhabit and the worlds they create. These authors also have in common a concern for poetics because the principles of operation behind a literary creation seek alignment with one's beliefs about first and last things. The underpinnings of religious response and the exercise of the literary imagination both involve a negotiating of external and internal pressures, for example, culture and temperament, history and metaphysics. A coherent strategy for relating style and content relies on a truthful reflection of often unspoken principles that bear on matters of belief and morality far beyond the margins of a poem, certainly of an earthly nation.

In keeping with the centrifugal nature of this implied conversation, I will begin my retelling of it *in medias res.* Let me initiate a narrative ostensibly about Ireland, which threads eventually through the Lough Derg writings of William Carleton (1794–1869), Denis Florence MacCarthy (1817–1882), Denis Devlin (1908–1959), Patrick Kavanagh (1904–1967), and Seamus Heaney (1939–), with a poem by Polish poet Czeslaw Milosz, who died in 2004. I risk this digression because even a glance at Milosz's poem, "A Treatise on Poetry," discloses the landscape of aesthetic and religious questions through which Heaney is moving on a long journey, which only begins with his trek through purgatory on "Station Island." I see that poem as pivotal in Heaney's career, a penitential exercise to expiate certain self-perceived poetic and moral lapses, which leads to the affirmation of "Clearances" (*The Haw Lantern*) and the renewed but refined doubt of "Squarings" (*Seeing Things*). This metaphysical exploration on Heaney's part will accomplish a definitive wresting of the soul of the individual artist both from Catholicism and from nationalism without diminishing the gravitas of religion. Further, around the time of the composition of "Station Island," Heaney is absorbing Milosz, who on many occasions compared Ireland to Poland, seeing both as self-identified Catholic countries on the edges of Europe, and both as victims of serial conquests.

Milosz's long, only recently fully translated "Treatise" opens in belle époque Kraków, a bijou, medieval city described as being "tiny as a painted egg / Just taken from a pot of dye on Easter,"[3] a patently Christian image. Milosz quickly zooms in on a specific location, a café; a specific person, a poet; and specific objects, a pair of gold or silver cufflinks as prominent and indelible against white cuffs as one metallic tooth in a mouth. His anonymous human subject, a stylish flaneur who sits reading a paper, an image of ephemera, is one of a foppish band:

> In their black capes poets strolled the streets.
> Nobody remembers their names today,
> And yet their hands were real once,
> And their cufflinks gleamed above a table.[4]

That brilliant and slightly sinister flash of jewelry not only arrests and focuses the reader's attention but serves, because it seems so true to a vivid present, to mitigate the effacement of human life through time, to redress faulty historical memory. This monumental poem, which Helen Vendler viewed retrospectively as "the most comprehensive and moving poem of this half century,"[5] opens with the figure of a poet because the poem's task is to interrogate the efforts poetry has made to do justice to the horrors of the last century in Poland and in Europe overall, and to take an accurate toll of the damage done to human civilization. Far from resorting to tricks of light, the sensory stimulation generally that poetic resources can muster, Milosz is bent in this poem on serious argument about how morality and metaphysics impinge on one's poetic. In the preface he laments the inheritance of a belle époque hedonism that still hobbles poetry, disabling it as a too-generous trust fund can hobble a young person, determining a pursuit of pleasure only, a skirting of the weighty, the painful:

> You often ask yourself why you feel shame
> Whenever you look through a book of poems.
> As if the author, for reasons unclear to you,
> Addressed the worst side of your nature,
> Pushing thought aside, cheating thought.[6]

The "worst side of your nature" has an almost Jansenist ring to it, suggesting that the appeal only to the senses, to pleasure, is debasing. And yet Milosz, a poet of titanic intellectual strength and passionate love of beauty, refuses to let thought and pleasure simply divorce in order to accommodate a diminished poetry. His preface, while stating clearly that poetic language "should contain more than images," also sounds levels of apprehension deeper than reason, locating the springs of poetry in a subconscious or perhaps, at the opposite pole, transcendent place: "Singsong lured it into being, / Melody, a daydream. Defenseless, / It was bypassed by the dry, sharp world."[7] Milosz's project for poetry entails the synthesizing effort of holding onto, indeed protecting, this necessary, evanescent, but sensuous "day-dream" by deploying new defenses not always associated in our age with poetry: argument, moral accountability, intellectual rigor. These seeming opposites of the frail but persistent "daydream" are all enlisted to preserve an inseminating "melody."

Milosz completed "A Treatise on Poetry" in the spring of 1956, a time when, having defected from a People's Poland under Soviet domination, he was living in Paris. There he was confronted daily with a climate of intense philosophical debate, dominated by Sartrian existentialism and European Marxism. Milosz's poetry does not flinch before this assault, as he regarded it, on the link between poetry and hope, always tied for him to religious faith, always the content of his "daydream." Hope is the first substantiating word that attaches itself to this wisp of "melody." Godless, albeit idealistic and, therefore, seductive philosophies, all nonetheless associated with the "dry, sharp world," were coming at Milosz antiphonally from east and west, Moscow and Paris, at this historical juncture. His poetic had to involve a way to engage muscularly in this combat, yet not injure in the process the vulnerable, human heart of poetry as he conceived it. His "Treatise on Poetry" both argues discursively for a way to negotiate this purgatory of twentieth-century literature and lodges an exultant affirmation through its very praxis. Therefore, those "gleaming cufflinks" are not a gratuitous touch; rather, they represent imagery used with sober responsibility. At a lesser level, however, where style takes its cue from poetics, they also function as a way of centering and framing the reader's attention and the poem's field of operation. The poem will range over so much history and so many centrifugal repercussions to events that both the magnetic pull inward and the radiance outward of this gleaming image are required equally to fix the reader's attention and leave it open to the diverse, often apparently conflicting, meanings created by the poem's cumulative language.

Only this balance of both cohering and diffusing meaning can prepare the reader for the paradoxes of history the poem will reveal. For example, although opening with a Christian presentation of Kraków, the ancient seat of Polish Catholic culture, the poem quickly through its imagery makes us see Poland as religiously mixed. Another arresting image soon pairs itself with the cufflinks, themselves tellingly a pair. A hatpin, also an appurtenance, as easily overlooked as the ethnic divisions that simmer underneath the exquisite, cosmopolitan, thin-as-aneggshell surface of this city, is associated by the rhetorical logic of the poem with what is opposite to but interdependent with everything represented by the cufflinks. The hatpin belongs to a woman identified as a muse, but most of all lightly sketched as Jewish. Milosz also wrenches the reader from the public space of the café, where self-presentation has already been accomplished, as it is in a finished poem, to an interior, private space where that perfection is being wrought by means of a deliberate yet nonchalant act of self-creation:

> Muses, Rachels in trailing shawls,
> Put tongues to lips while pinning up their braids.
> The pin lies with their daughters' ashes now,
> Or in a glass case next to mute seashells
> And a glass lily.[8]

Milosz, writing in the middle of the twentieth century and drawing uncritically on the cultural precedent of using race and gender as shorthand, renders the female and the Jew as emblems without hesitation, so legitimating to him seems this historical imprimatur. We will see, later in this study of Lough Derg literature, Denis Devlin, albeit with painful self-consciousness, drawing on the Christian icon of the Virgin, an ideal embodiment of the feminine, to facilitate personal transcendence. Milosz's Rachels collectively serve both as a muse to the poet, hence a vehicle for transport, and, it is implied, as the face of Judaism, the necessary other half of a Janus-faced, heterogeneous culture, a reminder of an unresolved, earthbound history. These binaries like male and female, the logic goes, need each other for the vitality of poetry, which depends on the whole complex truth to thrive. By observing the twinning of this symmetrical, symbolic object from the female toilette with the cufflinks from the male, the reader experiences a further level of wholeness. Having penetrated a secret, hidden life, traditionally presented as female, the flat, official image of society represented by the newspaper and on display in the fashionable café is effectively rounded out. This appearance of the feminine also prepares us to consider certain other obscured but integral mysteries, certainly sex, associated with the bedroom, but also death, associated with hidden or nonexistent graves. The name Rachel ("Rachel weeping for her lost children") hints ever so slightly in this introductory moment of mass burial graves and the lost, dispersed ashes of Polish Jews. Milosz creates all this meaning in the space between those gleaming cufflinks and the tip of that hatpin: an accumulated sense generated like electricity crackling between two points.

These Jewish women, young in the 1890s, might have had daughters, the poem speculates, who perished in Auschwitz, "the pin lying with their daughters' ashes now." The poem, beginning in turn-of-the-century Kraków, an idealized Christian city exposed as having a less visible but crucial Jewish population, will have to delve into actual conflict and appalling devastation, above all into the phenomenon of the Holocaust, which may be cast as a battle between absolute good and evil. The way poetry deals with such an inheritance of rupture, suffering, and shameful collusion is implied by the second speculated destiny of the pin. It becomes an object in a glass case, along with other attenuated, excessively precious art deco objects, summed up in that "glass lily," an example of art as a travesty of life. This lifeless image registers as a warning about the consequences of a poetic, the ever-mediated, ever modulated relationship (especially under the aegis of Modernism) of art to reality. In the face of great tragedy, the stark choice can seem to be between diametrical yet echoing opposites: unmitigated loss or retrieval through an inviolate aesthetics devoid of life. Milosz will say elsewhere that there is no poetry that is not about eschatology. The opening stanza to the "Preface" of his poem announces boldly the kind of poetic he will strive to embrace:

> First, plain speech in the mother tongue.
> Hearing it you should be able to see,
> As if in a flash of summer lightning,
> Apple trees, a river, the bend of a road.[9]

Despite the simplicity, the "plain speech," Milosz, by means of this seemingly deliberate affront to the ontological ins and outs of modernism, describes a profound and miraculous relationship between language and reality: simple speech producing visionary experience, the ordinary world made extraordinary, shot through with the numinous. This is the poetic Patrick Kavanagh arrived at after his own prolonged contemplation of historical suffering, a poetry of personal transformation that carries with it political redemption. Although Yeats cautions us that, on a metaphysical level, tragedy is tragedy and "cannot grow by an inch or an ounce" ("Lapis Lazuli"), the quantitative, historical losses for Poland and Ireland do not equate; however, a particular loss on the Irish side inflicts a deep wound for poetry, the loss, that is, of language itself. "Plain speech in the mother tongue" is not a plain matter over the course of Irish literary history.

Kavanagh is one of the four writers I investigate in the first section of this book, a study of a mere fragment of the long, pan-European tradition of writing about Lough Derg. My concern is specifically with Irish writers using English and writing after 1800. This study culminates in a close and extensive examination of Seamus Heaney, including a lengthy comparison of him with Milosz, as the latest and most substantial contributor to this segment of Lough Derg writing. Heaney makes this contribution not simply through the addition of his long poem "Station Island" but through the metaphysical poetry that flows from this breakthrough in his career, sequences like "Squarings" and "Clearances," a sonnet sequence that stands in symmetry with and is an implicit response to the "Glanmore Sonnets," written before "Station Island." Heaney's Lough Derg poem is critical in his oeuvre, a fact that is true to a greater or lesser extent of the Lough Derg works by all the writers discussed here. Like "A Treatise on Poetry," which interrogates the response of Polish poetry to moral truth, "Station Island" proceeds by means of a selective inventory of previous attempts to confront the complex meaning of Lough Derg, especially the convergence of politics and religion. The actual pilgrimage takes

place on an island, in fact Station Island, a synecdoche for an island nation idealized and sanctified as "Holy Ireland." Like Catholic Poland over the course of the
twentieth century's two great wars, the idea of the Irish nation presents a tight knot
of moral, political, philosophical, religious, and aesthetic problems for the artist.
Heaney and Milosz have found an affinity by means of a shared problem, namely
how poetry, with that "daydream" about hope at its beating heart, should conduct
itself in a world where violence, moral failure, and human tragedy have prevailed.
"Station Island" becomes Heaney's way of thoroughly examining his moral
conduct, specifically in relation to the carnage of the recent, decades-long, still
unresolved Northern Troubles.

Lough Derg, the place reputed from medieval times to be an entrance to purgatory, is also a particularly Northern Irish shrine (three out of the five writers featured here hail from the ancient province of Ulster). In the twelfth century, a cave on
an island in Lough Derg, perhaps Saints' Island, was a place where penitents, often
self-described spectacular sinners, saw ghoulish visions that amounted to a premature, first-hand experience of hell. Lough Derg, as Jacques Le Goff identified it in
his book *The Birth of Purgatory*,[10] also plays a key role in the history of a doctrine that
came into being slowly, evolving out of rumor and tradition. The very name Saint
Patrick's Purgatory not only denominated a cosmological site between heaven and
hell, but also gave this remote location the beginnings of a geography and a morphology. Moreover, as a site between worlds, where the metaphysical and physical
meet, purgatory is a natural conceit for poetry itself. As well, the discernment behind the theological fine-tuning of purgatory as a doctrine mirrors the discernment
behind the establishment of a poetic, where similar questions press about the relationship of language to reality. Does language, the word, deliver vision, figure, fact,
or wholesale falsification? Purgatory, too, like a poem with a strong moral back-
bone, is the place where good and evil are exposed and cleansed but not erased
from conscience. It is apt that Milosz's poem, which asks how adequate poetry can
be in the face of the Holocaust, begins with a vision, because the poetic Milosz
comes to deploy will bear a remarkable affinity to medieval Christianity with its
lambent simplicities, its reliance on beatific vision, and its unsullied belief in the existence of those dangerous concepts, good and evil.

The "dry world" for Milosz can be any world view that cuts off the sources of
irrigating hope. That essential emotion for survival has been, after all, the great gift
for the Christian offered by purgatory, that next-door-to-heaven place, site of the
second chance. Its further attraction for the poetic imagination is that it embodies
paradox, for example that its hope rests on a firm confession of every cause for despair. For Milosz at this stage of his life the "dry world" is specifically any comprehensive vision that categorically rules out metaphysical intervention in a reality
limited to materiality alone. Such arid certainty is repugnant to him; existentialism
and Marxism both leave Milosz thirsting for more. For the contemporary reader of
poetry, this "dry world" can seem the product of the application of certain strains of
literary theory (especially certain premises of cultural history) to desiccating effect

on the living matter of literature. When such approaches fail to stop, for example, at illuminating the incontrovertible dependence of poetry on culture, but rather make culture the determiner, the progenitor of poetry, they deprive it of vitalizing mystery. For the Irish poet who is reading it as a cumulative text, Lough Derg sets up a cognate problem because Saint Patrick's Purgatory, a putatively spiritual place, has been, to say the least, overly determined by culture. Lough Derg can readily be exhibited as a consummate example of a social construct, especially the Lough Derg of the last two centuries, the monolithic icon of a gradually merged nationalism and Catholicism. All the poets who encounter Lough Derg and wrestle with this Laocoön of nativism, to borrow with deliberate irony Patrick Pearse's image for British domination,[11] participate in the creation of a template for the final, albeit qualified, independence of the creative imagination.

Far from reductionist, all these artists predicate at some level a dialectic between the genetic inheritance of culture and the genesis of unique human expression, a balance that today's reader can translate into a recognition both of cultural determinism and a contingent artistic autonomy, the literary equivalent of free will. By finding a place for the individual and an agency for poetry in a context overwhelmingly determined by culture, these works collectively override the despotism of any "dry world" where the flow of free expression is choked. For this reason these works are centrally implicated in the final phase of inner, personal liberation delineated by Franz Fanon. The securing of a nation's political independence creates only the potential conditions for this individual freedom. One of the much-noted ironies of this specifically Irish saga of a liberation gradually expanding from politics to the personal is that the very freedom of religion curtailed by the English was one of the first freedoms to be eroded by the theocratic Irish Republic. Irish artists, since the creation of the independent state, have exposed this irony and exerted resistance against first actual, then residual, repression of the freedom to be anything other than Irish Catholic. The literary imagination has taken upon itself the effort of ensuring that religious belief or its lack remains the private, ineffable matter it ideally is for a free person. Heaney's metaphysical poetry comes at a point in history where the rejection of faith as a Joycean demonstration against an overweening nationalism is as tired and constricting a posture as the militant retention of faith once was against an opposing but cognate tyranny, British colonialism.

My story about this cumulative effort at liberation, centered on a site consummately associated with the repression of heterodoxy, is not the first to ascribe a subversive power to the literary imagination in the face of nationalist orthodoxy. This is largely David Lloyd's story about James Clarence Mangan, who was both a mirror of his times and one whose genius smashes that mirror. My contention is that studying the history of an iconic Lough Derg becomes a way both of confirming and challenging certain accepted premises of post-colonial theory, specifically the collaborative and collusive interdependence of imperial and native cultures. Lough Derg as a constructed idea embraces a litany of paradoxes that both bear out and interrogate the larger paradoxes that by now are axiomatic to the study of both colonial and postcolonial cultures. Let me give one example of how this further paradox of confirming and questioning theory works. Lloyd in his preface to *Nationalism and Minor Literature*, his study of Mangan, explains:

> The larger argument of this book is that while nationalism is a progressive and even a necessary political movement at one stage in its history, it tends at a later stage to become entirely reactionary, both by virtue of its obsession with a deliberately exclusive concept of racial identity and, more importantly, by virtue of its formal identity with imperial ideology. Ultimately, both imperialism and nationalism seek to occlude troublesome and inassimilable manifestations of difference by positing a transcendent realm of essential identity.[12]

A historical moment in relation to Lough Derg, which illustrates Lloyd's central, illuminating insight, is the establishment in 1795 of Maynooth College, a national Catholic seminary supported by British funds. No institution was more instrumental in inculcating the stifling and mechanical devotionalism that came to inform Lough Derg ritual at the turn of the nineteenth century.[13] Lawrence Taylor, an anthropologist who has studied rural Irish religious practice, speculates that, although diocesan structures suffered as much as monastic ones in Ireland under the Penal Laws, by the end of the eighteenth century "the British government finally saw the advantage of a strong Catholic Church. It might achieve, if not the conversion, at least the *"embourgeoisement"* or the pacification of the peasantry, or both. It may be further supposed that the English preferred an episcopally dominated Catholic regime, less thoroughly connected to the power centers of Catholic Europe than were the religious orders."[14] Maynooth, the font of Catholic teaching in Ireland, therefore the life force behind the Romantic nationalist myth predicated on Holy Ireland and underwritten by capitalism, was a British construct further built on, solidified, even sanctified by the Irish. Further corroboration of Lloyd's premise may lie in the fact that many of the Lough Derg writers I will examine here react to a conformist Catholic nationalism by at some level endorsing the founding values of the Reformation, particularly the sanctity of individual conscience. William Carleton, who actually converted to Protestantism, echoes the most strident Protestant attacks against Lough Derg mounted throughout the eighteenth century and extending into the nineteenth, just after Maynooth was established. Somehow, for the stability of the status quo to be maintained, these exercised critics need the bulwark of the diocesan system, as the rebellious generally need a wall of orthodoxy against which to kick. Although other writers do not convert, they court values associated with what Heaney, in the title of one his most anthologized poems, calls "The Other Side." They do this by acting not just as slavish mimics but as deft deconstructors of a debilitating monolith. In a sense, therefore, these tight oppositions, so collusive as to constitute the fused hemispheres of one impregnable sphere of normative cultural response, provide both an expanded and a circumscribed cultural vocabulary for the born Catholic. What Lloyd dubs "minor" or oppositional literature, which sets itself up to subvert both halves of this globalizing system, may be revealed more simply, however, as an example of the resistance mounted by the individual imagination in the face of any totalitarianism. I make this distinction because I believe that Milosz's free-floating and untethered "melody" is ultimately the force that demands realization and that cries out for original language, something far beyond rebellion, something fueled by an energy that is healthier, freer, more mature.

Like finding the explosive energy within the atom, Lough Derg, too, must be split open along the many seams it conveniently offers. As a dense and discrete symbol of all that both enables and disables the artist, for example faith and the annihilation of the individual, Lough Derg affords an efficient, available means of detonating cultural determinism to release an autonomous, individual act of creation. Perhaps the greatest Lough Derg paradox is that, while the ritual performed there has always involved submission to total self-effacement, the resulting experience can be an increased sense of both new-found isolation and reaffirmed selfhood. The Lough Derg exercise has been modified, indeed mollified, over the last two hundred years. Whereas in medieval times it centrally featured enclosure for days in a cave or cavelike structure, more recently it has come to center on staying up all night in a church, the relatively humane replacement for the cave. This symbolic incarceration takes place after a day of fasting and praying as one walks barefoot over rings in the ground of jagged stones, the famous Lough Derg "beds," or *turas* in Irish. Whereas medieval pilgrims regularly reported seeing visions in the cave, modern pilgrims under this mitigated regime have been known to experience a spiritual purging. They have also experienced fatigue, cold, hunger, and a flat but threatening sense of meaninglessness. These extremes, and everything in between, are contained in the Lough Derg writing under inspection here.

For modern Lough Derg writers, however, even these ameliorated rituals of self-mortification and self-hypnosis, aimed at eroding personality and easing assimilation into a collective identity, produce the opposite effect: the determination to fight even more aggressively for an inviolate individuality that resists any form of imperialism. In addition to this paradox—of individuality emerging from collectivism, autonomy from contingency—Lough Derg also appears both to conjure the soul out of the body and the reverse. The effects of systematic mortification of the flesh can be equally a release into spirituality and a sinking into intractable carnality. Further, a pilgrimage that is penitential rather than healing in purpose gives rise to extreme questions about the place of pleasure in redemption. For the artist, the fundamental question arises of whether poetry is possible at all within this programmatic pursuit of pain, a morphology that for the Irish can seem like a metaphor for the projected teleology of a self-punishing but pure Holy Ireland. This fusing of Jansenist Catholicism and nationalism is blown apart when the artist encounters Lough Derg and uses all his strength to maintain these dyads as separate questions. This deconstructive energy is quite distinct from the usually synthesizing zeal associated with Romantic fusions (which is not to say that the two cannot coexist, as they do typically in Devlin).

Finally, Lough Derg, as the joint product both of imperialism and nativism has an ancient, ultimately uneradicated monastic pedigree, which represents the opportunity for escaping the vice of these dichotomies altogether. This link between Ireland and continental Europe is forged not just by means generally of Catholicism but specifically by means of the most independent manifestation of institutional Catholicism, the monasteries that medieval Ireland was instrumental in fostering. The Augustinians were the first caretakers of Lough Derg, establishing a monastery there in the twelfth century and remaining until the English routed them in the early seventeenth century. The evocation of monasticism, therefore, helps mitigate not just the effect of British imperialism but also that of the diocesan system by gesturing toward a more cosmopolitan and intellectual European Catholicism with palpable Irish roots.

My overriding concern in the succeeding chapters is to try to reconstruct the cultural and historical conditions in which the individual writer, often in this instance a poet, is operating and to show where in this context originality finds an opportunity, "a look in," as one might say in Ireland. Heaney manages to reconcile the longstanding antithetical strains of visionary and penitential experience at Lough Derg. More deeply and specifically, he revives transformative possibilities while not endorsing the tradition of Romantic, violent nationalism and while reversing a staid nationalist position that ironically mimics Reformationist objections to the site. Heaney's efforts at creating new syntheses and conflicts have enabled a new discourse about religion in Irish poetry, free of a nationalist taint. Paul Muldoon, for example, who wrote an early Lough Derg poem, in later poems enhances and hybridizes his own highly metaphysical poetry by means of Judaism. This act in itself rectifies an entrenched nationalist, racialist preoccupation with Catholic purity identified with Lough Derg and centered on Saint Patrick, the putative founding saint. Lough Derg, as I have said, is the place where the pressure of conformity clashes most violently and productively with the pressure of individualism. At their most trenchant, all these writers attempt, in ways that reflect very different metaphysical leanings and religious beliefs or nonbeliefs, to wrest the idea of transcendence from the nationalist realm of identity and return it to the spiritual domain, where it belongs. My most cherished goal is to reveal how poetry has advanced this search for an ever-elusive independence.

Writing Lough Derg

I

The History

"Purgatory—what a grand thing."
—*Saint Catherine of Genoa*

THE TRANSMISSION OF CULTURE, as we now know, is an extraordinarily complex process, the study of which is always inexact. The five Irish Lough Derg literary writers extensively considered here all possess a lens through which they see this highly refracted site. In each case that lens is both a cultural and a personal product, the result of a single life, starting in a specific place, though often ending in another, and occurring in a discrete span of time, which nonetheless can connect with other times, past and future. William Carleton, the son of a storyteller, born at the very end of the eighteenth century, would have had direct access to the pagan Lough Derg of myth, a fragment of the Fenian cycle. As a protégé of the Protestant evangelist Caesar Otway, Carleton also would have been made familiar with the weight of dissenting Protestant opinion since Cromwellian times against Lough Derg, the very apogee of Irish Catholic superstition. The contemporary writer most extensively examined here, Seamus Heaney, given his rural Northern, mid-twentieth-century upbringing, is both distanced and not entirely severed from Carleton and his oral sources. As well, like Carleton in his time, Heaney has experienced his share of cosmopolitan exposures. Indeed, Heaney, an omnivorous scholar by means of being a markedly erudite poet, would be almost fully apprised of the history and especially the poetry that now mediate Lough Derg. My aim is to try to reconstruct without any claims to minute thoroughness the reception of culture, popular and high, that each of these writers has experienced and then transformed into his view of Lough Derg, his confrontation with Catholicism and the nation.

The discipline of history as distinct from cultural tradition, for example, can seem like theology as distinct from religion: both appear as arcane bodies of privileged knowledge which we, the laity, rely on our not impartial high priests to elucidate. Culture has a more slapdash and democratic reputation than does history. It includes the fruits of reading and systematic study, but it is equally, if not more, the result of the unconscious absorption of a mixture of fact and fiction: the stories, traditions, rituals, and the shared meanings attached to place and time. We tend to associate this kind of transmission with an oral tradition, receiving it by word of mouth, as instinctively as an infant sucks. The problem for the Irish literary imagination in relation to Lough Derg in the twentieth century is that the shrine had become so much an icon of Irish Catholic and nationalist culture that detachment from it loomed as socially both difficult and dangerous. The discomfort of cultural claustrophobia could be matched by the anxiety of alienation. Gaining a distance on Lough Derg could be felt even toward the end of the last century as akin to usurping the role of the priest or denying your mother. While this double anxiety in the face of hubris and loss may appear to have become obsolete after James Joyce, in fact such a sweeping reactive gesture of usurpation and renunciation may have appeared, especially to the rural imagination in even the recent past, as treacherous. To urban and rural minds alike it is by now an anachronistic stance in need of revision.

Bishop Joseph Duffy in his preface to *On Lough Derg,* a compendium of verbal and visual snapshots of pilgrims in the late 1980s, builds a warning around this distinction between culture and history: "It must be said that Lough Derg is not easily understood by observers who are not pilgrims. The journalist or historian or tourist as such will not have a rewarding time in this extraordinary place. . . . The historian will get plenty of reminiscence from older pilgrims but will soon discover here an indistinguishable mixture of fact and fancy which has been a special feature of Lough Derg since earliest times." Bishop Duffy goes on to declare, "Lough Derg has a secret, which it reveals only to the believing pilgrim. It is a secret which transforms this inhospitable rock into a haven of peace, a secret which removes the barriers of sin and fear, of ill-fortune and misery."[1] The not very hidden message is "Historians, journalists and tourists, stay out. Believers welcome." But believers in what? "Fact and fancy" apparently, which is associated with an old-style faith, while accuracy and reason belong to a new skepticism, which creates an impermeable barrier between the soul and Lough Derg. Skepticism is made to seem incompatible with elusive secrets, and what is more, a single secret, an essential, hidden truth. What journalists, tourists, and historians have in common is a necessary detachment. I would also include artists, for all their immersion in culture.

To dip even randomly into the variety of testimonies that we have of pilgrimages to Lough Derg, not only by literary artists but also by a range of ordinary pilgrims, is to discover how complex for everyone the response to it is, drawing as much on rational as suprarational faculties, approaching understanding by both conscious and unconscious routes, by study and received tradition. Let me give two examples spanning the poles of culture from high to low: a poem and a recorded conversation. A mid-sixteenth-century poem, "The Song of Tuileagna Mac Torna," translated here into prose by Shane Leslie, begins, "Lough Dearg, Eire's chief shrine and ever called Eire's Pilgrimage, is a lake which none other can rival; so I find in the old lore. . . . Of Saint Patrick's Cave I read that, for one who would cleanse his soul, no better penance-cell exists; it ceases not to wash away his sins."[2] Two phrases stand out: "so I find in the old lore" and "Of Saint Patrick's Cave I read," one phrase pointing to a passive reception of Lough Derg culture, its "lore," the other to an active pursuit of information through reading about "Eire's chief shrine." Two truths, however, emerge from both phrases. The first, now obvious and proved, is that Lough Derg's history predates the sixteenth century. The second, more subtle, is that self-consciousness about the Lough Derg legacy, an awareness of other texts oral and written, exists even at this juncture. Likewise, the motivation to explore this resource is a critical part of composing a full, individual response to the place. This one poem illustrates the conversation between disembodied voices that constitutes culture at its deepest, most enduring level.

This phenomenon, a stream of intensely private, spiritual experience at Lough Derg flowing from and winding back into a common cultural reservoir, is present in the observations of a Christian Brother from New York, whom Deirdre Purcell, the author of *On Lough Derg* (1988), interviewed on Station Island. John Prior, the Brother who was based at the time in a tiny mission in the Andes, begins his account by dispassionately comparing the ritual of Lough Derg to other spiritual practices he has come to know in the rest of the world. These, too, may be regarded as extreme by western urbanized man. He speaks of ritualized journeys into the desert in Peru, whirling dervishes, and mantras: "So I think that for humans to express ourselves to God in human ways, many things should be common between the Hindus and the Buddhists and ourselves."[3] The hint of vagueness in his words seems symptomatic of the searching, unresolved character of his thoughts.

Toward the end of the account of doing the station, however, Prior lands accidentally on a memory that gives shape to this circuitous process, centering his cosmopolitan analogies in a particular culture, Ireland's, and even a particular family, his own: "I didn't expect to be here at all. I had heard some people commenting on the existence of Lough Derg and I understood from them that if you want to touch some part of the soul of the Celt, you really had to come here. But while I was doing the rounds, it came to me. I remembered my mother telling me she 'did' Lough Derg. It's really something extraordinary to me to realize that I am walking in my bare feet on the very stones that my mother walked on her bare feet."

It is possible to chart the advent of illumination by watching Prior's speech leave behind a New Age notion that happens to coincide with nativist and cultural nationalist piety, "the soul of the Celt," to arrive at a precise recollection, as verifiable as any official history. This memory literally grounds Prior but also vaporizes materiality and mortality, making his feet his mother's feet and her time his, likewise merging New York, Donegal, and Tyrone, his mother's old home. Conflating space and time, this is an almost mystical insight prompted by history—more, maternal history—a rich channel flowing outside the margins and beyond the page of written culture. Notice, too, the way self-realization, a higher degree of autonomy, emerges as Prior arrives at his discovery of this vibrating tuning fork of two Lough Derg experiences in his mind, a mother tongue speaking through and separate from his own. Before he has his epiphany, he offers no strong reason for being there.

He relates casually, even lackadaisically, that other people thought he should "do" Lough Derg to learn about that fabricated entity, "the soul of the Celt." Lack of self-direction seeps from his words. Compare, however, "I understood from them" and "you really had to come here," conveying reliance on unidentified others, with the individual authority and excitement in the verb "realize" and then with the vividness and simplicity of "I am walking in my bare feet on the very stones that my mother walked on her bare feet."

We use the expression "if the stones could talk," referring to places resonant with history. The cliché, like most, a part of oral culture, may contain a kernel of truth about the informal transmission of culture outside books, maybe even below the level of consciousness. We do know from books, however, of the distinct possibility that the transmission of a substantial part of this Lough Derg oral inheritance actually happened in the early part of the twentieth century in a place not far from the birthplace of John Prior's mother. Shane Leslie in *Saint Patrick's Purgatory: A Record from History and Literature,* a compendium published in 1932 of Lough Derg writings from medieval to modern times, includes a passage from E. Evans Wentz's book *Fairy Faith in Celtic Countries,* written in 1909. Wentz, who would go on to relay both the Fenian and Patrician legends about how the lake received its name (Lough Derg in Irish perhaps translates to "red lake" in English), explains first the authoritative oral source of these tales: "The following weird legends, which during the autumn of 1909 I found surviving among the Lough Derg peasantry, explain how the Lough received its present name."[4] One story is told to Wentz by James Ryan of Tamlaght in Donegal; the other by Arthur Monaghan, who lived three miles away from Ryan. If these legends were intact in oral culture in 1909, so much more must have been available to Carleton through his *shanachaí* father in the 1780s in nearby west Tyrone. The Lough Derg of the mind is a plethora of cultural associations from history and folklore, from spiritual practice and social custom. To analyze the cultural issues that the artist confronts in "doing the station," it is necessary to try to reassemble the mosaic of Lough Derg that might be in his possession, thus seeing how the various tesserae connect and clash and leave gaping black holes.

The Lough Derg legend, as distinct from the history, which disputes a pre-Christian provenance for the site, runs from pagan times to the present. Any literary imagination encountering the legend can theoretically, depending on the extent of one's accidental points of entry into this legacy, focus on any or all of the different layers: pagan Lough Derg, patrician Lough Derg, medieval Christian and European Lough Derg, Penal Law and Famine Lough Derg, cultural nationalist and post-independence Lough Derg. I would like to look briefly at these first three layers in preparation for discussing Carleton, the forerunner of all relatively modern and Irish Lough Derg writers. I will also include in this overview an indication of the tenor of Protestant opposition from the seventeenth century on, surveying this colorful debunking as preparation for the section on Carleton.

Following discussions of Carleton and Denis Florence MacCarthy, I will insert an analogous survey of the cultural context of post-independence Lough Derg. While laying out this inherited framework and thereby indicating how Lough Derg is a perfect peephole for the cultural historian onto the last two hundred years in Ireland, I will also examine how each Lough Derg writer performs a Houdini-like feat of extricating himself from this limiting frame: Lough Derg writ small as Ireland. My study, therefore, is also one of poetic magic, of the sort wielded by Prospero on his island, as distinct from that ascribed to Lough Derg. That little lake in Donegal, with an island in it and a cave on it that was thought to be the entrance to the other world, hence the synonym "Saint Patrick's Purgatory," is the entrance not only into the fascinating, still insufficiently charted but nonetheless mundane territory of Irish cultural identity but much more into the purgatory of modern poetics, where human despair and redeeming revelation vie for supremacy.

First, consider the pagan layer. There is a Fenian tale set in Lough Derg, the story Wentz mentions, used traditionally to explain the name. There are many versions of the tale but most include an episode in which the hero Fionn drags his mother's corpse the length and breadth of Ireland, ending up at the lakeside. In one version the severity of this physical ordeal leaves the corpse mutilated, severed at the waist with only the lower half remaining and seriously decomposed. A maggot is lodged in the maternal shin and, according to one version, Fionn's son sees the worm and throws it into the lake. The maggot transforms itself, bloated by the water, into a gargantuan monster with a maw wide and powerful enough to suck in men and cattle. The Fenians have to slay the serpent to be free and safe. The blood of the transmogrified body of Fionn's mother turns the water red, hence Lough Derg.

The above retelling is a crude, synoptic mishmash of many versions, but my point is the potential and flexibility of narrative to serve any number of ideological and polemical ends, be they feminist or Freudian. The end this myth most directly and immediately served was evangelical, as a means of allegorizing the triumph of Christianity over paganism. Saint Patrick, the founder of Christianity in Ireland, is woven by time into this legend, seamlessly assuming the place of Fionn. Saint Patrick becomes the hero who redeems Ireland from the pagan, implicitly feminized dark. These versions of the foundational Lough Derg tale dramatize this forlorn site in Donegal as the place where the final battle between the Druids and Saint Patrick took place. The maternal serpent appears to have been just waiting in the shin of history to be converted into the symbolic snake of paganism subdued and banished by Saint Patrick. All these versions of the tale implicitly illustrate through their narrative inclusion of pagan and Christian elements a tumultuous, rending turning-point in Irish history tenuously made whole by this newly spliced legend. In another version, Fionn's son flings the maggot into the lake deliberately to feed the vile creature, make it bigger. It takes Saint Patrick to kill it. In yet another, Conan, a Fenian, is swallowed like Jonah by a water monster and it takes Saint Patrick, the midwife of Christianity in Ireland, to cut Conan out of the pagan mother's belly. In still other versions, Saint Patrick banishes the serpents on Croagh

Patrick and they end up for their final slaying in Lough Derg, having traveled through a mythical *souteraine* like a birth canal. These ingenious revisions of earlier myth above all point not just to the universal use of the story in making disruptive history whole, but more particularly to the status of Lough Derg from early on as a pressure point demanding such assuaging, artistic response.

All these stories, the purely pagan ones and the Christian overlays, interpret progress as a reinscribing of male authority on raw female energy, this domination being most often concretized as a mutilation of a female body inflated with fantasized magnitude and ferocity. Feminist theory, adducing, as Julia Kristeva does in "Stabat Mater," that men attach to women an originating power, which for the male constitutes an "idealization of primary narcissism," may help to explain the continuing threat the site appears to present to male autonomy.[5] Approaching the historical shrine from this point of view may help to account for these reigning misogynist, founding myths and even aid speculation surrounding the origin of the Lough Derg ritual as a male initiation rite; but this will always remain just that, speculation. What we cannot codify or explain fully is the way that cultural work appears to be done incrementally by one generation after another, rewriting the same story in different ways, adding a fresh gloss on an unsolved mystery. Postcolonial theory posits rupture as a corrective to the fantasies of continuity that dominate nativist historical narratives. Lough Derg, with its layered, only partially fused identities that both echo and differ from each other, offers a mediating example between these two extremes: one of interrupted but substantial continuity. It is often this unfinished subject of a male battle with the powers of the female that imposes an unresolved, abruptly terminated quality on Lough Derg narratives, which typically leave the reader of culture waiting for the next, incomplete installment. As it turns out, Heaney's consummate Lough Derg work hugely advances but does not fully resolve these vexed gender problems that somehow inhere in the pilgrimage. As we have seen, John Prior's experience at Lough Derg was intimately connected with a female source, his mother. This wrestling with the female, more with gender than with nationalist politics, is perhaps the hidden heart of "Station Island." A reckoning with female sexuality, which is still taking place in Irish culture, seems to be a part of the subtext of every Lough Derg text read here.

Neither postcolonial nor feminist theory used alone or even in tandem, however, is sufficient to comprehend the pilgrimage and the implicit conversation from Lough Derg writer to writer over time. Nonetheless, it can be instructive to pursue one angle, say that of gender, to see how quickly it becomes entangled with other issues. For example, the myth of Saint Patrick's relationship with Lough Derg prefigures to some degree every relationship with the site that we will examine here, all involving male artists. Each exercises a defense mechanism that distances him, to a greater or lesser degree, from the associations of female blood and erotic guts that the pagan stories bestow on the site. Perhaps the best proof of the surpassing purity Saint Patrick came to represent comes from the pen of someone not Irish, the seventeenth-century Spanish playwright Pedro Calderón de la Barca, who wrote a play about Lough Derg, *Purgatorio de San Patricio*, translated by a nineteenth-century Dubliner, Denis Florence MacCarthy, the second Lough Derg writer in the story being told here. This instance of overlap, this meeting of Ireland and continental Europe, displays the integral link Lough Derg constitutes for the insular Irish imagination with the continent. It also indicates the tendency, especially of the urban Irish artist, to avail himself of this roundabout route to Lough Derg, so close to the heart of rural Irish Catholics, so alienating often to urban Catholics. Saint Patrick's life, according to Calderón, predicting the Jansenist slant of much of this erudite intellectual, Catholic rewriting of Lough Derg, embodies allegorically a Christian denial of the flesh. Speaking of his conception and making it as immaculate as possible, Saint Patrick, as drawn by Calderón, assures his listeners,

> My pious parents,
> Having thus the debt exacted
> From all married people paid
> By my birth, retired thereafter
> To two separate convents, where
> In the purity and calmness
> Of their chaste abodes they lived,
> Till the fatal line of darkness,
> Ending life, was reached, and they
> Fortified by every practice
> Of the Catholic faith, in peace
> Yielded up their souls in gladness,
> Unto Heaven their spirits giving,
> Giving unto earth their ashes.[6]

As an expression of ethereal purity, Lough Derg will appeal to certain transcendentally inclined poets, especially those who seek such transformation through language, as MacCarthy, a Young Irelander, began to do through an eschewal of politics for poetry, and as Devlin attempted just after Irish independence through his modernist experiment with language. Calderón's Saint Patrick sets an exacting, impossible standard for human behavior, a moral absolutism and successful sexual repression, that is central to the Lough Derg "secret" Father Duffy touts.

The fact that Calderón wrote his *Purgatorio* at all indicates the prominence of the pilgrimage site in the European Christian imagination. The Renaissance playwright draws on a widespread medieval, continental familiarity with, and belief in, Lough Derg. Next to Rome and Santiago de Compostella in Spain, it was one of the most famous pilgrimage destinations in medieval Europe, a prime site for penitents. The most famous of these medieval narratives, Calderón's ultimate though indirect source, is the twelfth-century story of Knight Owen's experiences at Lough Derg as told by the English monk known as H. of Saltrey. Containing motifs that perhaps influenced Dante, not least an infernal architecture, the twelfth-century otherworld tale takes Owen through several rooms with many often ingenious scenes of torture and terror as, for example, this grotesque fountain of fire: "And suddenly he saw in front of him a horrible flame stinking of foul sulfur which shot up as if from a well. It seemed to hurl people of both sexes and all ages, naked and blazing like sparks of fire, high into the air and as the flames lost their driving force, they kept falling back into the well and the fire."[7] The reader is tempted to read this as allegory, emblematic of the power of evil; but the text quickly corrects such an assumption. The medieval narrator adds a cautionary postscript, as though anticipating that his own inclusion of conditioning language ("as if" and "seemed") may prompt a distancing reaction in the reader. H. of Saltrey's reflexive postscript consists of the warning issued by his fellow monk, amanuensis to the original eyewitness, Knight Owen, and the source for our narrator, who confides in us:

> One day the oft-mentioned Gilbert was relating these things to a large assembly—I was there listening—"as he had often heard them told by the knight," when a man in the audience said he doubted that these things had actually happened. Gilbert said to him: "There are people who say that when they enter the hall at the beginning they fall into ecstasy and they see all these things in their minds. But the knight denied adamantly that this had happened in his case; on the contrary, he testified very consistently that he had seen these things with his own bodily eyes and that he had endured the torments of the flesh."[8]

Our narrator's point is that all these things really happened, that it was not merely imagined: Owen's body literally entered a different space, another order of reality, hell. This anticipated question of whether or not true transformation from the physical to the metaphysical can occur is the crux in an ongoing, contemporary, infinitely sophisticated but still basic debate in poetics that Heaney highlights in his 1995 Nobel Prize acceptance speech, "Crediting Poetry." It is a question, with an obvious religious dimension, that Heaney begins to ask openly in "Station Island."

In the Middle Ages there appears to have been widespread belief, disseminated largely by the Knight Owen text, that Lough Derg was the literal place on the medieval map, in fact on an actual map that survives from the sixteenth century, where the entrance to hell was located.[9] An indication of the extensive medieval fame of the shrine is the recently uncovered fourteenth-century fresco in an Umbrian church in Todi depicting the Lough Derg cave and Saint Patrick beside it. In this representation, the cave is divided into chambers housing the seven deadly sins. This elaboration of the cave into hell's mansion is a medieval convention, which provided the architecture for the more than 150 European underworld narratives indebted to the Lough Derg story. The deeper, more historically based reason, therefore, for making Milosz a substantial part of the present-day story of Lough Derg is that Europe was from this early point central to the creation of the site's aura, a legacy I believe Heaney is drawing on in his use of Lough Derg as a way to break down the calcified dichotomy of Anglo-Irish conflict. While I have found no narrative of a Polish penitent traveling across Europe to Donegal, there is such a record among the documented visits of many French, Italian, and a smattering of Spanish, Dutch, and Swiss pilgrims, and one Hungarian. The following, originally in Latin, is drawn from an official certificate drawn up in 1358 and citing the words of King Edward III in relation to one "Maletesta, a Hungarian nobleman and Knight of Arminium." Note the defensive tone, even from the English king, as though anticipating rebuttal:

> We, therefore, considering the dangers and perils of his Pilgrimage and though the statement of so great a nobleman stands, yet we are informed by letters and other clear evidence from our faithful and beloved Knight Almarick of St Amande our Justice in Ireland and from the Prior and Convent of the said Purgatory and from others of great credit that the aforesaid nobleman hath duly performed his Pilgrimage and we have thought heartily fit to give the favorable testimony of our authority in addition to the same: and to take away all doubt of the premises and to leave the truth clear to all we have thought right to concede these our letters signed under the Royal Seal. Given in our Palace of Westminster Oct. 24th.[10]

Considering the effort that clearly went into securing this certificate, it must have bestowed on its recipient considerable leverage in this world. The granting of this imprimatur most certainly brought monetary advantage to its royal author, but also a liability, should the pilgrim's testimony or the pilgrimage itself come under dispute.

That is just what happened through the offices of another European visitor, the fabled Dutch monk from Eymstadt who made a visit in 1494 and subjected himself to the full Lough Derg treatment: "He sat in the Pit terrified and trembling all night: but offering fervent prayers to the Lord in his horror of the momentary approach of demons." In the end he was "much astonished because he had seen nothing nor heard anything nor suffered any discomfort or affliction."[11] This Dutch monk also "meditated much on what he had read and heard about this Purgatory."[12] He no doubt reflected on the fact that the long and arduous route he had traveled, from ecclesiastical authority to authority, up and up the hierarchical ladder in search of permission to enter the cave, had nearly ended in frustration, the denial of his request. As a mendicant, apparently he lacked the funds required to grease a series of clerical palms. All this, the simony and spiritual inconsequence of finding cold and hunger rather than visions at the end of his trial, led him to conclude that "once the Faith had been established the ancient miracle had ceased."[13] Furthermore, not only was miracle defunct at Lough Derg, the local Catholic authorities were fully conscious of this truth and, cynically, publicly denied it: "As a matter of fact it was on account of quest of money that local inhabitants asserted to strangers that their sins could be purged therein."[14] Pope Alexander VI ordered the cave closed in 1497.

By 1519, however, a skeptical papal nuncio, Chiercati, was visiting the site, undergoing its tortures with other penitents and recording these results: "Of those who entered the cave when I was present, two saw such fearful things that one went out of his mind and when he was questioned, declared that he had been beaten violently, but he didn't know by whom."[15] Restored to operation, however tainted by official Rome's censure, the pilgrimage displayed an irrepressible vitality, refusing to expire. As a perverse testament to its power, Oliver Cromwell regarded it as necessary to raze the old Augustinian monastery that stood on the site. This destruction was accomplished in 1632 under the direction of Bishop Spottiswoode, who, claiming to find no notorious cave, nonetheless personally oversaw the leveling of everything aboveground, most of which was already beneath contempt: "I undermined the Chapel, which was well covered with shingles and brought all down together. Then we brake down the Circles and Saints' beds which were like so many coalpits and so pulled down some great Irish houses. Thus when I had defaced all saving one Irish house: I came out of the Island myself and left one half of my men behind to pull that down also so soon as they should see me landed not sooner."[16]

By 1648 another papal nuncio, Rinnucinni, was determined to redress the evil in his eyes of "Calvinists in their rage leveling the ground" and "filling up the cavity as one can scarce discover any vestiges of the place," meaning the cave, which Spottiswoode claimed not to have even detected. Rinnucinni dedicated himself to the restoration of the pilgrimage: "I should have in some measure fulfilled my career, if in this place covered as much by the insults as by the earth thrown on it by the puritans it had been granted to me again to plant there the Cross."[17] By 1714 Bishop Hugh MacMahon, Catholic bishop of Clogher, was able to write: "Though everywhere else throughout the kingdom the ecclesiastical functions have ceased, on account of the prevailing persecution; in this Island, as if it were placed in another orb, the exercise of religion is free and public, which is ascribed to the special favor of Divine Providence, and to the merits of Saint Patrick."[18]

Perhaps the phoenix-like longevity of the pilgrimage owes its impetus to human needs that predate Christianity, indeed appear ahistorical, and extend spatially far beyond one specific culture or religion. Anthropology offers a way of understanding such attributes of a religious site and the almost seamless transition from pagan to Christian shrine and all the further vicissitudes. Victor Turner, in his book *The Ritual Process,* offers the concept of liminal zones, places set on boundaries between one world and another, sites from primitive times of rituals that transport the individual into unfamiliar territory, be it death, a dormant sexual identity, or the other world.[19] Such theory creates a way to splice the early maternal narratives, where emergence from a female-dominated to a male-identified self occurs, with these tales of purgatory, where a journey to hell and back happens. The idea of purgatory itself is a liminal concept, concretizing the threshold between a known and unknown world. Such theory, however, offers a coherent interpretation only to someone unattached to the specific religion that claims Lough Derg exclusively as its domain. Curiously, if a person is so affiliated to Catholicism and Lough Derg fails for him, it fails on every level. Again, theory may explain a phenomenon to the detached scholar, but genuine penitents need to believe in the spiritual efficacy of the ritual, and with regard to Lough Derg even belief very often is not enough.

While medieval Europeans were having their visions at Lough Derg, we are not entirely sure, since there is no absolute proof, whether or not the site was equally venerated and frequented by the Irish, although, as Peter Harbison remarks in *Pilgrimage in Ireland*, there is no good reason that this should not be the case.[20] We have seen that the most publicized quality of the experience gained in the cave in this period was ecstatic and visionary, a matter literally of transport, of one thing becoming another, if only temporarily: earth the other world, mortal man an eternal soul. We do, however, have evidence of Irish experience at the site from the seventeenth century in the form of several examples of Baroque, bardic poetry that refute the miraculous strain of European narratives of the pilgrimage. Tadhg Ó Dúshláine, in an essay on Lough Derg poetry in Irish, begins with this critical premise:

> Native Irish Literature in general, and bardic poetry (c. 1250-c. 1650) in particular, is usually regarded as being traditional, insular and untouched by the main literary currents of Europe until comparatively recent times. The exception to this rule is the religious poetry of the bards and many of the religious conceits and apocryphal legends in the works of Donnacha Mór Ó Dálaigh (1175–1244), Philib Bocht Ó hUiginn (+ 1487) and Aonghus Ó Dáliagh (1520–1570) come directly from continental sources.[21]

This remains true in the seventeenth century when "Lough Derg comes sharply into focus as a place of pilgrimage and repentance."[22] Ó Dúshláine makes the crucial point, however, that these poems are informed by the postures struck in a devotional prose coming out of Europe, although composed largely in the Irish colleges in Rome and Louvain and concerned with controversial Catholic practice at the time, predominantly the sacrament of penance. In a disquisition published in 1618 from Louvain, Lough Derg is mentioned in reference to its Calvinist suppression: "God of Glory, many an Irish soul is in the clutches of the devil today because of a prohibition on this divine, angelic Lough."[23]

As interesting for my own narrative as the early, tight connection between Irish religious poetry and European Catholicism may be, perhaps even more arresting is the fact that most of this religious poetry is not, in keeping with the above prose snippet, rapturous about the miraculous effect of Lough Derg. In most instances, transformation fails and a recalcitrant, unregenerate flesh is lamented. The most famous poem in this vein is Donncha Mór Ó Dálaigh's "Truach Mo Thuras go Lough Derg" translated by Thomas Kinsella as "Vain My Journey to Lough Dearg":

> In my narrow hard stone cell
>   after all my proud foul acts
> I can find, for shame, no tear.
>   I am buried in a grave alive.[24]

Ó Dúshláine comments: "This poem is shot through with that metaphysical anxiety which is the hallmark of all great religious poetry. The poet's frank and unconcerned admittance of his unsuccessful pilgrimage becomes, paradoxically, a sincere statement of true contrition and strikingly reveals man's contrary nature and the conflict of body and soul."[25] It is this same conflict between body and soul that will resurface most dramatically in Devlin, who forges his own modernist, tortured, and tortuous poetic to accommodate the struggle.

For all this evidence of intelligent doubt on the part of native poets, however, native practice seems to have flourished because of the popular, unblemished, holy aura around the site and may perhaps have already constituted a threat to British dominance. Claims of visions were as outlandish to Puritan ears as the doctrine of transubstantiation. Basically, however, no place as potent spiritually to Catholics could leave Protestant church leaders from the seventeenth century forward unengaged in vigorous protest. The convenient thing about Lough Derg as a peephole through which to view Irish cultural history is that, despite first impressions, its legacy is not, as I have said, homogeneously Catholic. Protestant influence plays a major role in defining its composite image. Indeed, the Protestant perspective is not confined to Protestants, as I have suggested, but echoes in any number of skeptical views of the ritual. Actual Protestant spokesmen generally are exercised about the superstition they see abounding at Lough Derg. We have observed Bishop Spottiswoode of Clogher personally seeing to the razing of all physical evidence of the pilgrimage site, but no such easy erasure of conflicting, yet interdependent, curiously collusive versions of Lough Derg proved tenable. Bitter controversy has surrounded Lough Derg periodically since its papal closing. This disputatious atmosphere affects the artist, because the seductive, visionary promise attached to Lough Derg clashes with a faithful account of its full history, the value Milosz is defending in the opening to a "Treatise on Poetry." Reason on both sides of the sectarian divide has insisted, for example, that demons and torture chambers are phantoms of the mind induced by hunger, sleeplessness, and fear, whereas both faith and the unquestioned urge to transcend reason have supported the achievement of an altered reality. To indicate the degree of contention occasioned by Lough Derg, I will look at a few examples of vitriolic attacks on it from the eighteenth and nineteenth centuries, the period that produced the most frequent and furious Protestant diatribes.

Perhaps the most famous, indeed infamous, objector is John Richardson, rector of Belturbet, who in 1727 made his views known in a pamphlet with the verbose but unequivocal title *The Great Folly, Superstition and Idolatry of Pilgrimages in Ireland; especially that to Saint Patrick's Purgatory, together with an Account of the Loss that the Public Sustaineth thereby truly and impartially represented.* Richardson states, not mincing words:

Everybody knows how excessively the Irish are addicted to Pilgrimage, there being few Parishes in the Kingdom in which there is not some Thing or other to which they frequently resort on a superstitious account. Of this the Parliament thought fit to take Notice, very justly and wisely observing that the Corruptions of Popery are thereby greatly increased and upheld. The invocation of Saints, worshipping of Relicks, the Delusions about Purgatory, Works of Supererogation and Transferring of the pretended merits of one to another, being apparently kept up and propagated by this Practice. Their Devotion at these places of imaginary sanctity is founded upon ridiculous Fables and Legends, and made up of many foolish and absurd Rites, which are recommended to the credulous people as effectual means of Salvation, and the whole is very much polluted with Idolatry.

In addition, the issue of simony was a salient one and continued in a basic sense to be a concern with later born-Catholic yet skeptical visitors. Carleton makes the venality of a priest the somewhat forced, clinching evidence of Lough Derg corruption. Kavanagh regards the materialistic aspirations of a philistine, gombeen, middle-class pilgrim as symptomatic of the ritual's spiritual poverty in the 1940s. These earlier, virulent Protestant critics of Lough Derg see in its mythical connection with purgatory an opportunity for blackmail, to extort money from a faithful living in universal terror of perdition. Samuel Dillon of Sligo, as late as 1818, remarks, "Thus in the dark ages of superstition and ignorance was Saint Patrick's Purgatory established, to work upon the hopes and fears of the people and fetter their minds with religious terrors."[26] The Reverend Philip Skelton, rector of Fintona, in the late eighteenth century condemns particularly the exchange of money at the shrine for spiritual favor, from paying the boatman to paying another human being to do your penance for you. He claims that of the hundreds he observed on the island, most were remunerated surrogate penitents.[27] Abuse upon abuse of true spirituality is indexed, all coming under the rubric of deviation from the correct path laid down by scripture; but perhaps the most targeted error in spiritual practice at the Purgatory is the mortification of the flesh, corporeal abuse aimed at spiritual advancement. These critics allege that such depleting of the vital force makes the Christian less able to carry out the genuinely strenuous moral injunctions of the Christian way of life. In short, Lough Derg inspires, as they see it, delusion and perversion.

One of the most remarkable inclusions in at least two of these arguments, that by Skelton and another by a Reverend Reilly, is a retelling of the ancient pagan legend already mentioned. The use to which these revisions are put is the point. Skelton rehearses the narrative to underscore its pagan gothic excesses, implying the absurdity of a religious practice founded on such an outlandish fiction. He locates the myth's origins in a lewd, female genital image, probably an example of a *Sile na gig* or pagan fertility symbol. He claims that this graven image was inscribed on a stone in the church on the island, evidence of a persistent paganism shamelessly defiling a Christian present. While uncovering the legend's heathen heart, he also exposes his own dark fantasies, projecting unconscious fears and fetishes onto the tale through his grotesque embellishments. His minute intimacy with the myth further gives the lie to positing any firm cultural and sectarian division in pre-Famine Ireland. Skelton's projection of his own animus onto native myth is mirrored by Carleton's use of Protestant dissent as a ready vehicle for his own skepticism. Skelton employs a standard opening to the tale. He begins with the water monster, who is the devil's mother, and moves to Fionn MacCool's grandson, who was swallowed by this leviathan in a self-sacrificial gesture to appease the voracious female avatar, whose power Skelton greatly exaggerates. The vengeful vampiric monster agrees "to abstain from her customary depredations, on the condition of having one annual victim chosen by lot, placed on the top of a mountain about three miles from the lake, from whence, such was the force of her suction, she drew him into her mouth and at one gulp swallowed him."[28] It is not a large stretch of the imagination to see what Skelton calls, again with cultural intimacy, the Keeronagh blooming in his mind as the demonic Catholic Church, which in his view also kills moral vitality, devouring an entire people

The Reverend Mr. Reilly, author of the pointed *Hindooism in Ireland, or a succinct Account of the Celebrated Saint Patrick's Purgatory at Loughderg and a similar Station, lately established, at Coronea, In the County of Cavan* a title implying the exotic benightedness of the native religion, recounts the legend, again beginning with the devil's mother, implying that she is still the reigning anti-deity at Lough Derg. His story ends, however, as so many we have seen do, with Saint Patrick killing the beast in a gruesome, sadistic scene, which is much more exaggerated than other versions: "The victorious saint pressed upon her and repeated the blows until the water became red with her blood, and by blessing the water of the lake, changed it into wine for the refreshment of the pilgrims."[29] Again, using narrative for ideological ends, Reverend Reilly allies the sacrilege of transubstantiation with the horror of the death of the devil's mother, replacing the blood of Jesus Christ with that of this vile, female avatar. Above all, however, he inadvertently reveals to our more psychologically attuned consciousness a blatant conflation of racism and sexism, which is not unrelated to a budding nativism and longstanding misogyny also apparent in Catholic uses of the myth to justify Saint Patrick. Here, significantly, the founding saint is the axis around which Protestant justification also revolves.

The preceding historical survey brings us up to the time of William Carleton, whose contribution to the Lough Derg tradition I will outline here, then go on to introduce those further contributors whose Lough Derg works will be examined in detail, along with Carleton's "Lough Derg Pilgrim," in the first half of this book. I will also preview my explorations of Heaney, the central focus of the second half. Some readers see the narrow but roaring stream of Protestant dissent just described as flooding William Carleton's "Lough Derg Pilgrim," the first story he wrote, the wellspring of his masterpiece, *Traits and Stories of the Irish Peasantry*. All Carleton's writing, however, partakes of at least two worlds, his inner life occupying both sides of the border between native Irish and Anglo-Irish culture. Carleton's literary imagination straddles this line to such a degree that as a man of unadulterated native Irish origin, the child of two Irish speakers, he can appear to have no home as an adult other than his own head. So fierce and noble does Carleton seem, so removed for us from the familiar, that he can loom as a magnificent predator at Ultima Thule coping with the breakup of the icecap, falling through any number of cracks and yet surviving. Carleton, the youngest of fourteen children, born in 1794 near Clogher in County Tyrone, was a child when the failed 1798 Rebellion took place. As a young man he experienced, in contrast to the liberal enlightenment principles of Emmet and Tone, stressing unity rather than division,[30] the effects of O'Connell's narrower brand of nationalism, which Carleton regarded as both priest-ridden and sectarian, in short, to use that word he connects with Lough Derg, "degraded."[31] Not only as a child did Carleton live through the reimposition of direct English rule by means of the Act of Union in 1801, but also as an adult he witnessed from the sideline the beginnings of even greater racial suffering in the series of famines that led up to the Great Famine. What is more, at the same time he observed the revived idealism of Young Ireland, the Republican movement emerging under Thomas Davis in the 1840s. Pushed and pulled in a number of directions, buffeted by a seeming repugnance toward and love of his native culture, he encounters at Lough Derg, yet more in himself than anywhere else, an almost intolerable anxiety in both owning and disowning his origins.

Doubly distanced from his native Tyrone, mentally by a conversion to Protestantism and espousal of English and physically by a move to Dublin, Carleton nonetheless delivers to the reader the rapidly evaporating world of rural Ireland before the Great Famine, just as Milosz summons Poland's prewar innocence through those forever brilliant cufflinks. Also, as Milosz punctures lost privacies with that hatpin, Carleton penetrates with his powers of observation and recollection the domestic life of this lost Ireland, exposing the intimate habits and speech of the people who accompanied him in 1813 at the age of nineteen to Lough Derg. He comes to write about that pilgrimage as a crisis, a head-on collision with the juggernaut of a mind-numbing devotionalism. He would manage from the later remove of Dublin to recover a sense of the overwhelming moral and mental danger to which he felt exposed in doing Lough Derg, plus the sheer excitement of that early experience, especially the motley, fascinating crew he encountered on his way there. Carleton achieves this resurrection by means of his flawless ear for dialogue and eye for particularity, physical details so mimetic and mnemonic that they outweigh his rote anti-Catholic bombast. Yet Carleton's images are not mere grace notes that cheat the reader of a deeper, broader meaning, one in fact striven for but eluded by that rant. So integral to an entire way of life is each image, it is like a sudden, vibrant stab of light in a Dutch interior, allowing us to see an otherwise shrouded scene acutely and in detail.

There is one particular image from "The Lough Derg Pilgrim" that is as indelible as Milosz's cufflinks, but more vital because it is something ephemeral that has been made permanent: a mark on the human body like the brand of history on a living culture. The image is a blister on the foot of young Carleton, who in company with other pilgrims has been walking to Lough Derg. That is not the full mnemonic reach of the image, however, because its lasting power lies in the depiction of a close social interaction, of one person administering physical assistance to another, of the transmission of survival skills through the still-open channels of a healthy culture. We see a female innkeeper pass a soapy length of thread on a needle through the blistered skin and leave the thread in place, presumably to palliate and promote healing. This simple gesture in print not only immortalizes a folk remedy; it also provides the thread by which we, and Carleton too, can retrieve an entire world through a culturally healing act. Further, a remnant of that basic image from Carleton, as though pulled through the generations, surfaces as "blistered corn-fields" in Heaney's "Station Island" just before the shade of his Tyrone precursor appears as a ghost. Carleton's images avoid the antiquarian feel of museum specimens, of Milosz's example of the "glass lily," not just because they enjoy this documentary immediacy but also, from the opposite temporal perspective, because they so clearly emerge from a memory that is also living in a separate present. By crossing his antipapist vituperation, felt in this present on a fully recovered past, Carleton delivers a sense of lived, ongoing history.

Carleton will evolve through *Traits and Stories of the Irish Peasantry* a narrative approach dependent on the inclusion of competing, ultimately discordant voices and modes that accurately depict both an inner and outer confusion. His way of telling a story conveys more than anything, however, the storyteller's search for an integrated voice. For example, at moments he can sound slavish and ingratiating toward the literate, English-speaking reader, in fact his only reader, one far removed from his illiterate but accomplished, famously articulate Irish-speaking father. Such rhetorical moments make the reader register the sorrow implicit in the brutal separation effectively forced on the ambitious and brilliant Carleton with regard to his paternal, and for that matter maternal, legacy. More often Carleton, for all his fulminating and vivid evocations, can sound detached from two worlds, one by reason of birth, the other by reason of adult experience. Tess Hurson points to the vacuum at the center of this hitherto uninhabited linguistic space we now call Hiberno-English, a locally specific mixture of the two languages: "Those who spoke the dialect would not or could not read it, those who could read it could not or would not speak it."[32] So, when Seamus Deane, after calling Carleton's writings "miscellanies of prose styles," further asserts that "the linguistic instability and the wavering political and sectarian loyalties endemic to the Irish situation are themselves insufficient to account for these variations,"[33] I have to agree, but, perhaps not for Deane's exact reason, rather because a full accounting of Carleton must include, in addition to these demanding and fragmented external pressures, a complex internal life. Carleton is coping not only with the breakup of the ice cap of history but with rapidly shifting architectonic plates within himself, huge psychic conflicts. Resisting binarisms, one can regard his magpie indiscriminacy in art and life as a sign of everything from a decentered, ever-shifting, shallow pragmatism to quite the reverse, a self-directed, ever fluid adaptability that protects an inner complexity, the gestational space of Milosz's "melody." I believe Heaney in "Station Island" authoritatively credits Carleton with the latter: the single-minded determination of the artist. Working at this profound and personal level, Carleton's narrative strategy enables him to conduct a conversation between parts of himself as much as between cultures and classes. Writing a prose that floats halfway between a digressive tale from oral culture and the more thematically honed, formally shaped and centered story required by print, Carleton attempts to translate not just Irish experience into English and vice versa, but one self into another. The resulting text is never perfect. Its imperfection, however, identifies its value. Carleton's flawed artistry is like a chronic blister forever benefiting from an ingenious, indigenous form of treatment.

Lough Derg in the nineteenth century was dealt a nearly fatal blow to its many lives. The Famine was catastrophic for the pilgrimage, naturally, for subtle and obvious reasons, from moral and spiritual despair to the absurdity of a people who had just starved then choosing to fast for spiritual preferment. For decades after the Famine the pilgrimage languished. Yet it was during this period that MacCarthy translated Calderón's play about Lough Derg and published his version, along with the rest of Calderón's major plays, in 1887. That this Lough Derg text is completely a translation seems apt at many levels. MacCarthy, who began his professional life as a considerable figure in Irish culture, close to the center of Young Ireland and the Catholic hierarchy, soon found himself at a distance from Ireland in self-imposed exile abroad. Translating Calderón's *Purgatorio* in many ways became a way of restoring an idealized Ireland to himself, an Ireland dashed by the premature loss of Davis, who died in 1845 at the age of thirty-one from tuberculosis, and by the Armageddon of the Great Famine. MacCarthy's translation of a Renaissance Spanish playwright's imaginary rendering of Ireland parallels the emergence after the Famine, in part as a reaction to that catastrophe, of a compensatory, Romanticized Ireland. It makes further sense, given the way a post-independence, sanctified Ireland emerges eventually as an urban superimposition on an objectified rural west, that MacCarthy, cut off by geography, but more by disillusionment and tragic events, from Ireland in the flesh, constructs his myth. This product, in contrast to Carleton's ever impure, ever fluid re-creations, bespeaks a loneliness and alienation far in excess of Carleton's and, above all, a prophetic fetishizing of Ireland by means of Lough Derg.

MacCarthy spent much of his pre-Calderón literary energy as part of the cadre of poets and scholars attached to *The Nation* and the *Dublin Magazine*—"Davis, Mangan, Ferguson" in Yeats's triad—who were engaged in the first phase of the recovery of a native Irish culture. This effort was for historical reasons necessarily centered on translation. MacCarthy will be attracted to Calderón in part for the way that playwright's exacting assonantal prosody has a jarring effect, not unlike Irish prosody, both syllabic and accentual, on English ears. This very discomfiture provides an invitation for a show of both fidelity to Ireland and rebellion against England. MacCarthy, by faithfully translating Calderón, compensates for a failure of translation on a large scale closer to home, essentially of a lost past into a present. In addition, Calderón's use of a form referred to as an *auto* involves a swift transformation of reality suggestive of surrealism or, to the religious mind, revelation. This formal attribute appeals to the believer in MacCarthy, but his use of it also unwittingly anticipates the visionary, nationalist politics that will underlie Yeats's poetic.

It is instructive to compare the public lives of Carleton and MacCarthy for key similarities and differences. As we have seen, Carleton, a pragmatist and an isolated survivor who was suspicious of and curried favor with every quarter, did not pretend to make full sense of the public political sphere. In Deane's words, "Carleton wrote for everybody,"[34] for publications with radically divergent, even openly opposing political and religious agendas. Carleton lived on the social and political periphery, indeed moved closer to the edges, according to Deane, by distancing himself from O'Connell, who identified himself with the people from whom Carleton came. MacCarthy, a thoroughly urban being, experiences none of these overt tensions because his cosmopolitan circle of associates appears to embrace difference. Yet MacCarthy evokes a Lough Derg more symbolic of a purified and purist Ireland than any previous representation. He also conjures the diametric opposite: a demonic, evil place. Paradoxically, the enigmatic MacCarthy, both conventional and anarchic, manages to idealize and complicate. The moral seems to be that the more removed one is from a culture that has been objectified, the harder it is to revivify that artifact through an accuracy bred of familiarity. Lack of direct experience at this source seems to increase the need to impose a false unity and then, perhaps, to dissect it into false but unyielding binaries. All this energy may be directed toward what may be irretrievably fragmented. Then again, to use this irreparable loss as the beginning and end of one's art may involve a pain that is so extreme, it is palliated only by distancing falsification.

MacCarthy, born in 1817, a generation after Carleton, was a well-to-do Dubliner who appeared poised to play a central role in the forging of a native identity from the center outward. Like Carleton, who once thought of the priesthood but then thought better of it, MacCarthy nonetheless was awarded a hieratic role in Ireland in the form of the first chair of literature at the Catholic University. MacCarthy, however, a complicated and very private man, appears indirectly from his poems and prose in addition to the reports of others to have been torn on many levels by competing allegiances, such as art versus religion, the wider world versus Ireland. While politically committed to the resurgence of a nonsectarian Republicanism, MacCarthy remained a fervent Catholic. This commitment is critical, since he appears to have lived on the fault line between a time, such as Carleton's, when religion and the nation were separate, often equally passionate, matters and a time when these passions would be immeasurably intensified by being fused. While

both a devoted Catholic and a Republican, at some level MacCarthy was still able
to remain detached about, and yet committed to, what would become cultural nationalism. It is crucial to see MacCarthy as a literary gentleman and member of
Young Ireland, not anticipating any political or cultural reprisals for his skepticism
and independence. Not surprisingly, when he felt such a rebuke even lightly, his
poetry registered a growing longing for a far-off, exotic dream place free of conflict.
We also hear guilt for that or some other veiled, adulterous fantasy or act in his
poem "To the Bay of Dublin." There he confesses a complicated love not unlike
Carleton's for both home and an exotic other:

> My native Bay, for many a year
> I've lov'd thee with a trembling fear,
> Lest thou, though dear and very dear
>   And beauteous as a vision,
> Shouldst have a rival far away,
> Whose sparkling waters ever play
>   'Neath azure skies elysian.[35]

MacCarthy's critical essays, for example his preface to *Poets and Dramatists of
Ireland*, reflect both an Anglo-centric and an independent-minded suspicion of a
touted Gaelic Ireland, a distrust of its advertised but then unproved literary distinction,[36] reservations that led to his compensatory composition of Irish ballads in
English, and retellings of major myths and stories.

A secretive man, MacCarthy finds voice for violent and anarchic human acts
and emotions, which we now know to be indigenous to the brutal and frank world
of Irish myth found, for example, in the *Táin*.[37] MacCarthy unwittingly echoes this
all-but-extinct, robust, violent world through the ventriloquism of translating a
Spanish playwright with a fantastical, founding story to tell about Ireland. More
than just indirectly recovering a lost Ireland, MacCarthy manages to complicate
that concept through the expression of feelings and fantasies quite illicit in the increasingly prudish, actual place. MacCarthy, by means of translation, manages to
speak and stay silent, sin and abstain. In his lifetime the recovery and burnishing of
the Patrician legacy in confluence with Victorian prissiness was having a marked
effect also on Lough Derg. For example, the naked bathing, albeit of men and
women separately, a feature of the ritual during the seventeenth and eighteenth
centuries, disappeared in the nineteenth. We have already heard how Calderón's
Saint Patrick, via MacCarthy, is the soul of chastity. The compelling persona of the
play, however, as in *Paradise Lost*, is the villain, Saint Patrick's alter ego, Luis Enius.
In the early scene from which I have quoted, where both men tell their stories,
Luis's biography stands in shocking and obvious contrast to the saint's. Luis Enius
is an embodiment of evil, endlessly inventive and insatiable. In his speech he confesses, without a sign of remorse, to killing several men and women, to living by
the rule of lust, and to raping a nun, a cousin, abducting her, and then attempting to
profit by being pimp to her prostitute. By exposing these outrageous sins, Mac-

Carthy mines that earlier layer of Lough Derg culture deposited by hair-raising medieval narratives.

MacCarthy lived much of his life in England and on the Continent. When he returned to Ireland in 1881 to die in the arms of his daughter, a nun, his obituaries commemorated only the man who wrote deceptively pious but subversively nationalist ballads. One obituary claimed, "I believe I am quite safe in saying that during his chequered career no word escaped his pen that could wound the most sensitive modesty." [38] "Chequered" verges on censure, although still it is doubtful that this squeamish elegist ever read MacCarthy-Calderón on Lough Derg, or even heard of Knight Owen's graphic tortures in the cave. In a sense, the closing of the Lough Derg cave, like the corking of an evil genie in a bottle, presaged a sealing off of the most volatile, disrupting, and potentially liberating meanings carried by the shrine's cultural heritage, meanings that are intensely human and, in the subliminal sense of Victor Turner, universal.

Lough Derg was being cleaned up, readied for the more antiseptic, parochial role it was to play in the assertion of a morally correct, de Valerian, independent Ireland, which finally and ironically achieved its Cromwellian purgation. What this superficial purging could not achieve was a healing of deep rifts in Irish culture. As history (rather than any narrative design on my part) would have it, these first four Lough Derg writers alternate between originally rural and urban men, between writers with an inborn native perspective and those more naturally cosmopolitan: Carleton and MacCarthy first, followed by Kavanagh, the ploughman-poet, and Devlin, the diplomat-poet. What this initial survey also reveals is how each man is sui generis, enjoying both unlikely alliances with and differences from each other, and with and from the prevailing culture. Each struggles through Lough Derg to realize that paradox necessary for self-realization: being part of society and enjoying self-possession.

The 1930s and 1940s in Ireland represent a time of never greater pressure to conform to an ideal of Irishness and of equal and opposite assertions of vigorous individuality. I will first set the cultural stage by surveying the writings that surround such struggles through art. Inspecting the roots of a pious nationalism, I will look at D. Canon O'Connor, Shane Leslie, and Alice Curtayne, all Lough Derg scholarly or devotional writers, or both, all Catholic, yet all very particular and different from each other in ways that from this distance complicate a time dominated by a myth of homogeneity. O'Connor, a countryman priest, writing from the priorship on Lough Derg in the 1880s, paves the way for what would become the independent but obediently Catholic Ireland. This prophetic role is best confirmed by the reprinting into the 1930s of the 1903 edition of his book *The Pilgrimage of Saint Patrick's Purgatory.* Consciously repudiating Caesar Otway's slurs on Catholicism through insults heaped on the Lough Derg landscape, O'Connor rhetorically asks, "What wonder is it that the eye of the pilgrim is charmed, his heart elevated, nay even his love for holy Ireland increased when Lough Derg first meets his view?" [39]

Shane Leslie, a cousin of Winston Churchill, wrote primarily between the two great wars from his desk at Castle Leslie in Glaslough, County Monaghan. This castle was the home of the Leslie family, who had their hunting and fishing domain in nearby Donegal, the land on which Lough Derg rests, land once owned by the routed McGrath family. Leslie demonstrates how Lough Derg, known to Ernest Renan and implicated in his fetishizing of Celticism, is increasingly of interest to an Ascendancy imagination romanticizing a peasant West. An Anglo-Irish aristocrat who claimed to be related by blood to the British royal family, Leslie performed the opposite transition in his life from Carleton's. Leslie was a Protestant who converted with a vengeance to Catholicism. Unlike Yeats, who may have written the short poem "The Pilgrim" about Lough Derg but who, despite his Celticism, limited his rebellion against his inherited religion and class by affecting to espouse Theosophy, Leslie went over completely to Rome. And yet we glimpse Leslie's Lough Derg through a Yeatsian mist: "It is a long passage of time since the men of Ireland first felt the mystery of those quiet little hills and looked for the unseen waters that lie at their feet, for the spiritual history of Derg stretches back into the dimmest ages of legend."[40] Despite the sincerity, there is a ring of propriety off this landlord's words that make his cultural nationalism, in keeping with Yeats's, hardly revolutionary in intent. So, while Leslie's pride, and O'Connor's, may seem to serve the same obfuscating, rhapsodizing end, they have radically divergent origins and politics.

The early twentieth century produced a rash of born Catholic apologists for the site who mirrored, that is to say, who replicated in their zeal and reversed in their convictions, the host of Protestant essayists in the seventeenth and eighteenth centuries who derided Lough Derg. These modern apologists were particularly urban-identified writers, who, benefiting from cultural recovery performed for the previous hundred years, were aware of and could boast about Lough Derg's European pedigree. Alice Curtayne is the prime example of this new Irish cosmopolite. A prolific and prodigious writer of Christian hagiography, particularly of women saints, and translator of religious literature, she imparts to her writing on Lough Derg a new-found Irish confidence but also a sectarianism. She, however, while using Lough Derg to promote a pan-European Catholicism, is quite distinct from the contemporary but more provincial Bishop Duffy, who is bluntly direct about the iron link between the sacred and the political made stronger by Lough Derg. Referring to the building in 1930 of the basilica on Station Island, he asserts, "The Basilica expresses accurately the extraordinary revival and spirit of the Lough Derg pilgrimage in the present century. It became an intensely Irish institution and was part of the revival of Irish nationalism, which eventually effected political changes."[41] When poets Kavanagh and Devlin, along with prose writer Seán O'Faoláin are presented with this range of equally powerful threats to individuality, each finds a strategy for survival. All the Lough Derg publicists, as distinct from artists, together constitute a phalanx of conformist pressure and yet each one is subtly different from the next. Each, therefore, under the cover of tribal pride advances a personal and national agenda.

It is up to the artists to hack through this enthusiasm and hypocrisy to uncover a truth, not necessarily sublime. Yet each of them also falls foul of his own needs and fears, which Lough Derg has the habit of uncovering. It is not just the prose advocates for and against the shrine who display bias. The poets and fiction writers still have to negotiate between culture and self, and are warped to some degree by contingency. Seán O'Faoláin's story "Lovers of the Lake," for example, reveals under the author's usual patina of urban polish an atavistic attachment to Holy Ireland cleverly veiled by an ambiguous conclusion. This masterful story features a bourgeois Dublin doctor, someone from MacCarthy's class, who follows his ambivalent mistress to Lough Derg where, he fears, she is trying to summon the courage to break off their adulterous affair. O'Faoláin's characters justify their behavior and mitigate their Catholic guilt by means of their savoir faire, their adherence to European Catholic social and sexual mores, an alternative law. In a sense the doctor, Bobby, sums up all the layers of sophisticated, acquired, superior culture which are suppressed by nationalist, devotionalist, peasant Lough Derg by displaying a scientific skepticism and feigned detachment akin to Carleton's when he speaks as a Protestant, plus, ironically, a fetishized pagan intimacy with nature and sex. Doing Lough Derg means relinquishing all these sources of pleasure, privilege, and evasion. As his lover, Jenny, observes, "She was among people who had surrendered all personal identity, all pride. It was like being in a concentration camp."[42] Yet the end of the story leaves the reader unsure whether or not Bobby has also submitted to this leveling of his ego, yielding to a stringent spiritual truth still extant at Lough Derg and awakened in this proud, humbled skeptic. It is Jenny's comment, however, that alerts us to perhaps the most sinister crack in the public image of an inward-turning Ireland. Her apparently casual mention of the concentration camps plumbs a cultural guilt the way a tossed-off joke illuminates murky depths. For the reader of Lough Derg as a text, her quip threads back to Shane Leslie's Celticism, openly celebrated as Aryanism, therefore weaving Ireland into Europe indeed, but not the medieval Europe of saints and beatific visions, rather the Europe of gas chambers and Christian collusion, the contemporary history with which Milosz has had to contend morally.

Kavanagh and Devlin both wrote poems in the early 1940s entitled "Lough Derg." Both works are substantial, Kavanagh's the length of "The Great Hunger." Both poems occupy critical positions in the canons of each writer, as "Station Island" does in Heaney's. For each of these earlier poets, a confrontation with Lough Derg means delving into material that, if it does not kill the imagination, will revive it and send it out into new territory (which is really old territory rediscovered). The distinctly different fates of Kavanagh's and Devlin's poems predict, in very different ways, the public reception each poet would enjoy. Devlin's "Lough Derg" was instrumental in securing critical recognition of him, a respect until recently enjoyed more abroad than in Ireland. Kavanagh's poem was never published while he was alive (it came out first in 1978) because he deemed its scathing view of a scheming, mercenary Irish piety too iconoclastic for exposure. And yet the grounded spirituality wrested in that poem from the observation of such impure spiritual posturing would play its part in making Kavanagh the widely loved poet he is today in Ireland. Kavanagh is inveterately the plain-speaking poet Milosz calls for, but not unlike the opinionated Carleton, Kavanagh suffered not only as a person but also as an artist for his directness, often as a poet insufficiently transforming bile into art. His "Lough Derg," however, despite the ploy of using others' failings to brag about his own accomplishments, contains a truly purgatorial insight. Kavanagh learns in this poem how simplicity comes only through seeing and naming every aspect of an apparently intractable complexity. The poem, often lacking in minimally transcendent language, is as close to sociological fact as the Lough Derg pilgrim's bare feet are to the ground. This sustained nontranscendence, very much in keeping with the honesty of "Vain My Visit to Lough Derg," serves as the springboard for Kavanagh's best mature poetry where, with no less plain speaking, a luminous world unfolds out of this dark, given one.

Kavanagh's pilgrimage to Lough Derg metaphorically predicts the many pilgrimages he made in his life, not just from the country to the city, but from the plane of matter to that of spirit. What makes Kavanagh unique as a poet is this eschewal of a middle ground, his capacity for leaping from clay into light in ways presaged by medieval, visionary Lough Derg. Without any European pretensions or trappings, Kavanagh recovers this early lambent, redemptive spirit. This is above all a triumph of the individual soul over the soul of the nation. And yet the restoration of the nation is advanced by the spiritual affirmation of this one man. True, Kavanagh disowns the abuses of spirituality he observes at the site, almost exactly echoing earlier Protestant objectors. He also knows firsthand the inroads on personal fulfillment paved by sexual repression and, its flip side, crazed fantasy life: in sum, the rampant hypocrisy sanctioned by Lough Derg. Kavanagh has a very wide Carletonesque vein of disgust, but he bravely directs it as much at his neighbor as at the obvious target of the Church. What makes Kavanagh's spiritual breakthrough beneficial to his neighbor, however, is its grounding in empathy. Speaking of himself, Kavanagh admits in a moment of hard-won communal and personal identity:

He too was one of them. He too denied
The half of him that was his pride
Yet found it waiting, and the half untrue
Of this story is his pride's rhythm.[43]

This feeling of inclusiveness is almost beyond Devlin's reach, so far removed is he, through his elite education and career, from the multitudes herded at Lough Derg. Significantly, Kavanagh executes his sociological incision into the tradition by means of Carleton's tactic: separate, sharply delineated characters who together act as his scalpel. For Devlin no such differentiation is possible. And yet, for all the class differences that pervade his poem and make the people figure in it as an abstraction, it, too, ends on a moment of qualified empathy. Devlin eventually sees the mass of pilgrims as a living presence expanding beyond the mechanical boundaries of the exercises. He sees it, however, largely by means of a poetic that aims to find wholeness and reconciliation among wildly diverging opposites. Devlin, as an official representative of the Irish Republic's government, the new Department of Foreign Affairs, traveled the globe armed with an official image of this new nation among nations. His privileged status, regarding the actuality of Ireland from a height, imposes a remoteness and distance on his voice, the equivalent of Mac-Carthy's in the mufti of translation. Devlin forges a Modernist style that demands nothing less than patient translation by the reader. No less difficult a style, however, seems adequate to the impossible syntheses to which his poetry aspires. Moved less overtly by fusing an imperfect Catholic Church with an imperfect Ireland, he takes the mysteries of the constitutionally embedded, national religion and tests them through words on the infinitely various and ineffable flux of consciousness. Devlin's purgatory is that of endlessly elliptical, ambiguous, never absolute language. The purgatory of modernism, exemplified by the metaphysical trials of Wallace Stevens, is Devlin's site of suffering. He applies this minute attention to language and the impact of faith and philosophy on it to the world of Irish letters. As a diplomat, he brought Ireland to the outside world. As a poet, he brought that world back to Ireland by applying the skeptical questions posed by Modernism to the set text of Irish Catholicism. Yet, in the way that Kavanagh's miscellany of styles and forms, the mirror in poetry of Carleton's in prose, instinctively grasps the modernist problem, so Devlin, in his overweening striving for a unity, betrays a yearning for a simplicity not unrelated to that Kavanagh achieved with great difficulty. Almost echoing Kavanagh, who finds empathy in himself for the despicable "faithful" offering up their paters and aves for a child's good examination result, a promotion, or a good price for a bullock, so too Devlin can register repulsion for the masses in the opening lines of his "Lough Derg":

> The poor in spirit on the rosary rounds,
> The jobbers with their whiskey-angered eyes
> The pink bank clerks, the tip-hat papal counts
> And drab, kind women their tonsured mockery tries.[44]

Having located in his "kind women" an emotional pivot that eventually enables a countervailing compassion, he can end his poem with, "This woman beside me murmuring My God! My God!"[45]

As we will see, Kavanagh lets sonnets, as moments of vision, happen as they will, studding his formally uneven, eclectic, early long poems. This practice, echoing unconsciously the insertion of prophetic *roscs*, bursts of poetry, in the prose narrative of the *Táin*, anticipates the way his later epiphanies will break unplanned into the ordinary. Devlin seeks this intensity of vision throughout, attempting to weld it to a style not unlike Hart Crane's, designed like specially alloyed, twisted cables made to carry a high voltage. He aims by means of this style to find ecstasy consistently. It is an attempt reminiscent of one by Yeats, who tries to cure the fleet-ingness of symbols by attaching them to timeless Irish myths.[46] Kavanagh and Dev-lin demonstrate how radically different but related strategies emerge in response to the spiritual legacy and challenge represented by the same Lough Derg. Although Kavanagh had finished his poem when he read Devlin's for the first time, I will treat Devlin's first, not just because his poem was published first, but also because Kavanagh's poem, published in the 1970s, leads more directly into a discussion of Heaney, his scion.

In anticipation of exploring in this preliminary way how Heaney handles the entire legacy, I would like to review briefly the questions, conflicts, and helpful tips that emerge when these four writers, who constitute the first half of the book, are set side by side. First, the paramount question at the core of poetics arises of how much transformation of material reality an artist seeks to achieve either through statement or enactment in language. Carleton, regarded essentially as a poet by ac-tual poets descended from him, at first glance plumps for untransformed fact, Dev-lin, for the opposite. Carleton observes the caution of guarding against any dangerous idealizations, deleterious for one's psychic and political independence, since transformations in Irish literature are traditionally attached to religious and patriotic rapture. On the other hand, a genuine legacy of visionary religion local-ized in Lough Derg is an integral part of Irish history; this energy is the very life force of a transcendental poetic like Devlin's, for all its modernist attributes. A re-spect, therefore, for both belief and skepticism enjoys precedents in Lough Derg writing. Devlin, MacCarthy, and Kavanagh, in his iconoclastic way, all display a vital or vestigial faith. Carleton may even have apprehensions of ecstasy, but jetti-sons them for the sake of self-possession. This question of the degree to which ma-terial reality is transcended relates to the question of how much fragmentation, the failure of unity, is acknowledged and reflected in style and content separately or to-gether, or transformed to a seamless uniformity. The permutations of recognizing and repairing rupture by means of style and content seem endless, and yet a curi-ous paradox appears to emerge consistently. Writers such as Carleton, who use het-eroglossia, a play of many voices, also seem for the most part to cleave to mimesis, the presentation of the material world as unmitigated fact. The more modernist the writer, the more, one would think, a broken condition would be acknowledged at all levels, and yet the more, too, is fragmentation apparently transformed by a pre-siding, consistent, transcendent style. As this style interjects a striving for simplic-ity into the complex cogitations of modernism, so the realist Carleton often in his conclusions enters a psychological state approaching psychosis, where all conven-tionally accepted surfaces are transformed.

At the bottom of such abstract questions of poetics lie the most basic human ones, such as, how close can the writer bear to be to his material? Lough Derg, after all, is about walking barefoot on jagged stones. Carleton's realism, however, can read both as a sign of intimacy and of chill detachment. Devlin's pyrotechnics can come off equally as narcissism and a feverish struggle to connect. There seem to be no rules for solving the basic problem of how to reconcile a sense of belonging with a sense of self-possession, not just belonging to one's family but to the human family, not just to oneself but to God, not just to things but to words. On and on the antinomies proliferate. Lough Derg, standing, as we have seen, on the line between physics and metaphysics, begs the most profound questions involved in the search for a poetic; but local questions, particularly about Ireland and Irish identity, also press. The inheritance created by writings about Lough Derg again offers no solution. Cosmopolitanism can be as easily crossed on piety, as it is with Devlin and MacCarthy, as it is on dissent, as with Carleton. Even the question of sensual pleasure and its renunciation is complicated. For Carleton, the robust countryman, the mortification of the flesh is absurd, counterproductive. For Kavanagh, with similarly impeccable rural credentials, the ascetic carries great appeal and realizes great benefits. For all these writers, the price of finding an individual strategy for confronting these endlessly complex and endlessly related matters seems to be a troubling alienation from their living, communal source, where the solutions range from pat to subliminal and wise but not personal.

The challenge for Heaney appears to be, once again, the problem of reconciling the artist with society. But to see this problem through the lens of Lough Derg, a site that history has had to reckon with repeatedly, rescues the extreme self-centeredness and reflexiveness in "Station Island" from charges of narcissism. Lough Derg poses both the threat of extinction and the promise of redemption, certainly the possibility of hope. Not only does its persistence through history as recorded in words ameliorate the ruptures wreaked by colonization, but also the resolute individuality of each Lough Derg writer mitigates the pressure for uniformity, the self-conscious search for a tradition that is part of postcolonial identity and equally threatening to the artist. It is finally, therefore, the genuine combination of continuity and separateness represented by this series of writings about this one site that provides a present-day writer with both support and the imprimatur for daring.

It is above all significant that the chief legatee now is a Northerner. The Lough Derg problem has come to rest with him, as the colonial legacy of the island came to lodge in the North. Ethnic and religious polarization, in addition to an increased self-consciousness in both Northern Irelands about the continuity of tradition, contributes to the pressure created by Lough Derg to conform, belong, relinquish individuality. What is more, Heaney has had to go over all the old, barren, but still sacred ground of the Jansenist Catholic conscience, around and around like the *turas* themselves. He recalls in "Station Island" an early feeling of arousal on glimpsing a woman's bare back through "the wide keyhole of her keyhole dress"; but he also recalls almost in symmetry a later nightmare, corresponding to Carleton's vigil at Lough Derg, when the poet sees a shed breast float down a foul stream of guilt. The iconography, especially that of mutilation, reiterates gruesome details from medieval Lough Derg writing. The pagan and the European layers of the shrine's cultural history, however, will offer Heaney liberation, just as an overview of recent Lough Derg writing gives him courage. Section 11 of the poem contains a translation of a poem by Saint John of the Cross, an echo of MacCarthy's deployment of Calderón. Heaney homes in on the Spanish mystic's image of the eternal fountain of faith, a source without beginning or end, always irrigating and clear, never sere and turbid like Heaney's soul on Lough Derg, under the stern dispensation of a northern Catholicism. The fountain dispenses forgiveness, the precursor of hope.

This renewal is what Heaney seeks not just for the North but for a poetry responding to it always, it seems, inadequately. He will mentally flagellate himself throughout for his selfishness, the self-absorption of the poet, which has kept him from being the friend and relation he ideally should have been to others, especially those who have suffered more than the "lucky poet." Since so many of these omissions of word, or thought, or action constitute in his mind the betrayal of someone who has directly suffered because of the Troubles, the nationalist influence of Lough Derg is felt acutely once again, this time in a predominantly northern context. Bishop Duffy, reporting on the resurgence of Lough Derg in the 1930s and 1940s, remarks that "During these years Lough Derg became a truly national pilgrimage with pilgrims coming in large numbers from all over Ireland, rather than from the counties in the vicinity."[47] The existence of Heaney's poem and its centrality in the contemporary Irish poetic canon suggest that the cultural expansiveness applauded by Duffy through the example of Lough Derg gave way to a contractile countermovement as the twentieth century ended, concentrating an important question of identity in a corner of the larger island that contains the small but symptomatic Station Island.

By now it should be apparent that I regard the cumulative text of Lough Derg as an ecosystem through which the evolution of Irish literature in the last two centuries may be studied. The pilgrimage for a believer, or even a half-believer, poses the most profound and vexed spiritual questions a human being can face and, for someone Irish, questions only marginally less pressing of national identity. Above all, the still-trying ordeal begs, especially at the close of the twentieth century, the overarching problem of whether these two sets of questions, though related, can remain discrete. These are especially pertinent inquiries for a Northerner. Heaney tries to achieve this careful, painful separation of issues, while leaving room, too, for the aesthetic matters about poetics that underlie the entire interrogation. Lough Derg, particularly if the station is sincerely done, almost always ends in painful separations: the soul felt in its shivering isolation, the faulty conscience ripped from the warmth of human fellowship. "Station Island" may be read as the capstone conversation among all those, each unique, who explore Lough Derg, not just as a desolate spot in a bog but as place of painful growth, the steward of separations. Heaney will conclude his poem with an image that circles right back to the earliest Lough Derg text from oral culture, the tale about Fionn's mother. Heaney's closing image, which echoes this founding text, is placed in the mouth of Joyce, the final father figure among a host of father figures, all somehow compensating for a rupturing from an original, actual father and ultimately the far removed, mythologized body of the mother. Joyce urges Heaney toward the psychic separation that the original pagan myth centering on that singular maggot might have been describing through allegory. Joyce refers, significantly in the plural, to eels, the way their very bodies inscribe a calligraphy that produces a new, mysterious and as yet indecipherable script. Joyce advises,

> It's time to swim
>
> out on your own and fill the element
> with signatures on your own frequency,
> echo soundings, searches, probes, allurements
>
> elver-gleams in the dark of the whole sea.

The next lines read anticlimactically:

> The shower broke in a cloudburst, the tarmac
> fumed and sizzled. As he moved off quickly
>
> the downpour loosed its screens round his straight walk.[48]

Joyce's wide-open phrase, "the whole sea," invites the contemporary Irish artist to enjoy the freedom offered by the whole world, not just one island or an even smaller island within it. Yet Joyce is immediately enclosed, separate, hidden behind sheets of rain, "screens" like confessional screens. We are left with the impression that concluding the Lough Derg conversation is as impossible as Joyce's escaping Ireland for the wide world. Exile may be the other side of home. If feeling "lost, / Unhappy and at home," as Heaney writes in "The Tollund Man," is a propitious condition for art, Lough Derg is likely to be one of the stations an Irish Catholic artist performs in his life.

2

William Carleton

A Poet, but Not a Fanatic

CARLETON, AS WE HAVE SEEN, begins "The Lough Derg Pilgrim" with an odd, apparently slavish narrative gesture. He abnegates authority, ceding it in fact to two other authors: Caesar Otway and Bishop Henry Jones, prominent Protestants who have already recorded their stern disapproval of Lough Derg. Indeed, Carleton credits his emergence as an author to Otway, who suggested that the young writer commit to paper his abidingly negative memory of doing the station in the summer of 1813. This recovery became the record of an experience, which, according to the hindsight he no doubt obligingly confessed to Otway, put Carleton off the Catholic Church forever. As though sealing his apostasy with the tale, Carleton gives over the first few pages to Otway's vituperation that speaks of "Lough Derg, with its far-famed isle, reposing there as the monstrous birth of a dreary and degraded superstition, the enemy of mental cultivation, and destined to keep the human understanding in the same dark unproductive state as the moor land waste that lay outstretched around."[1] Carleton presents himself at the formulaic beginning and ending of his tale as roundly concurring with Otway. Taking up those evangelical cudgels, Carleton even rails intermittently throughout his story about the insults to the human spirit perpetrated by Catholicism. Beneath this rant, however, in the practice of his art, Carleton reveals himself as serving fully neither his Catholic past nor his Protestant present.

The retrospective narration operates by means of an ironic contrast between these two levels of time and two casts of mind: the benighted Papist and the enlightened Protestant. Carleton begins by humorously recalling himself, when he made the pilgrimage, as an impressionable, vain, romantic youth, a natural for the excesses of devotion. He even relates a self-revealing anecdote of extreme credulity: an attempt on his part to walk on water with nothing buoying him other than the presumption of his own sanctity. He sinks, a prediction of the direction in which his faith will eventually travel. Meanwhile, back in his naïve past, en route to Lough Derg, near Lough Erne, he notes his temptation then to relieve penitential self-examination with visual treats, indulging, as he calls it, the "lust of the eye."[2] Trying to be pious, a protopriest, he chastises himself and turns his vision inward, becoming increasingly morose. He concludes that the mortification of the flesh ironically creates an obsession with it, that such a penitential exercise is more a barrier than a route to transcendence: "I never felt the infirmities of humanity more than in this ludicrous attempt to get beyond them."[3]

This jaundiced backward look climaxes in a demeaning comparison of Lough Derg to Rome. The sardonically honed, sharp-edged comparison conveys both the inflated reputation of Lough Derg in the suggestible pilgrim's mind and the diminished value of the site in the adult Protestant's estimation. Today's reader, however, knows that Lough Derg once was as famous and popular a pilgrimage destination as Rome, but this medieval level of the Lough Derg past is unavailable to Carleton, whose historical memory has been harmed by colonization. Furthermore, for him, Rome, the seat of Antichrist, the pope, is not a spiritual center but rather the center of classical civilization, a symbol of mental freedom. Rome, therefore, is the apogee all that Lough Derg challenges and the Enlightenment spirit the United Irishmen originally championed. In its undercurrents, "The Lough Derg Pilgrim" participates as a lament for the loss of these egalitarian and rational principles after the failed 1798 Rebellion.

Carleton is bent on presenting himself as a model of rationality and proportion, despite his engaging in deliberate disproportion to advance his reductio ad absurdum argument. The superior narrator, in contrast to the young pilgrim approaching Lough Derg, refers to a hypothetical cultivated person, an alias for his mature self, approaching Rome. That mature author, in cahoots with an ideal, indisputably Anglo, reader, is "a poet not a fanatic."[4] The logic is that Lough Derg, in its insistence on a denial of the flesh and of reason, threatens to eliminate the very sources of literary creation: impressions picked up on the senses and processed by the mind. The problem, however, which Carleton does not acknowledge, is that his imagination works by more than reason and the senses in tandem. It also draws on intuition, that more Romantic endowment, which Carleton has in abundance about his culture but which he regards as a questionable gift. Intuition is too close a neighbor to faith; and all suprarational faculties and experiences menacingly portend a flooding of ego boundaries, a dubious transcendence. As Carleton slips into the anti-Enlightenment ritual of Lough Derg, ambiguity suffuses his recollected account. In the midst of the vigil in the church then known as "prison" (the cave was closed in 1790), Carleton begins to drift in and out of reason. What little rationality he has left reassures him that these alterations in perception are due to physical causes, but this clarity wears away, eroded by hallucination. Outside the chapel, he has a quasi-mystical experience, which nearly amounts to a vision of purgatory. Carleton, however, swiftly reminds himself, as much as the reader, that the cost of such transport may be extreme, even fatal. Before we know it, a young man leaps to his death from a balcony to the chapel floor. The climactic, prophetic passage that comes before this spectacle of suicide is a sustained evocation of an underworld on earth, of a vertiginous, altered sense of reality, certain doom. The critical point is that in his recounting of the catastrophe, which is cited in full later, Carleton holds on, like someone crazed but reluctant to leap to his death, to words like "mind" and "idea." The author, utterly identified with his doomed doppelgänger, knows that such retention of rationality is a matter of physical and mental survival. Knowing what is chimera and what is material reality is crucial, since insanity, not ecstasy, is the risk of losing track of this distinction. As though running for cover in the reasonableness of the brand of Protestantism he espouses, Carleton ends the story with a standard jibe at simony, exposing, with all the high moral coloration of melodrama, a priest trying to take the last penny off a sick old man and his sick son. This conclusion appears to confirm the sway of Protestantism over Carleton, particularly the evangelical, angry Protestantism that emerged after the failure of 1798.[5] The stock anti-Catholic ending, however, is also a run for cover from the traumatic episode that takes place in "prison." As such, the conclusion betrays perhaps even more the vestigial power of ancestral religion. Carleton's narrative stance, itself a purgatory, occupies a site somewhere between these two magnetic poles.

Carleton's story does not end, however, on this note of spurious moral triumph. Bewilderment is more the tone, especially because this confusion is kindled not just by a religious crisis but by one of identity. The intimacy he develops both by having been with and then writing about his fellow pilgrims blazes into a raging conflict of love and hate with his own people, those he has depicted with devilish and passionate accuracy. To study Carleton's impressive gift of portraiture is also to see how he uses even this talent to protect himself against psychic pain. In the beginning of the story, two characters appear who are drawn in such bold strokes and rich colors that they are as unforgettable as that historic blister. They are two women of the roads dressed in incongruous, androgynous clothes and possessing a social manner that is insinuating and irresistible. The young Carleton absorbs their blandishments and old wives' wisdom as though it were mother's milk. They will turn out to be, of course, seasoned hucksters, not remotely intent on a Christian exercise. They represent the wily, seductive pull of the culture, which their author, if only by means of attempting to stereotype it, is determined to resist. He is bested, however. In the night the women steal his clothes, the black, smooth garments aspiring to clerical sartorial status, and leave him with their theatrical, sexually unspecific bits and pieces. Humiliation, confusion and an increased sense of humor will be the lasting souvenirs he takes home from Lough Derg. For the reader, the entire narrative remains retrospectively both shadowed and illuminated by this parable of gender confusion, illustrating the internalized power of the female and of native Ireland. The old woman of the pair may as well be the hag (the *cailleach*), the devil's mother supposedly killed by Saint Patrick, but alive and well and ripping off unsuspecting young men in the Age of Reason. Therefore, despite his protestations, as it were, a still-unreconstructed, more fertile self remains.

Carleton, despite his management of an ambivalent rootedness, reveals a Lough Derg of legend so charismatic that all his adult powers of reason, an Enlightenment commitment to banishing the past, must be mustered to counteract a spell laid down in childhood: "Ever since my boyhood, in consequence of the legends which I had heard from my father about the far-famed Lough-derg, or Saint Patrick's Purgatory, I felt my imagination fired with a romantic curiosity to perform a station at that celebrated place."[6] What is more, in the opening words to the tale, Carleton begins to bow in the direction of a future use of the site as a symbol for Irishness, telling us that to understand the Irish one must study Lough Derg: "In describing the habits, superstitions, and feelings of the Irish people, it would be impossible to overlook a place which occupies so prominent a position in their religious usages, as the celebrated Purgatory of Saint Patrick."[7] Kevin Whelan, in his study of the United Irishmen, points to that body's philosophical commitment to the annihilation of history, all reminders of the ancien régime, in favor of the fresh start that marked the idealism inherited from the French Revolution.[8] In the narration of this tale, with its chasm of irony created between the naïve Catholic protagonist and worldly Protestant narrator, Carleton can be seen as emulating this sleight-of-hand with regard to his past. Yet the inadequacy of this tabula rasa approach in coping with the inheritance and losses of culture is patent in Carleton. He is perhaps the first native writer in English to reveal the individual psyche as the site of the nightmare of history Joyce will locate. Carleton may reject the role of cultural enthusiast in favor of scientific anthropologist studying his own people, scrupulously detailing their remembered ways, but his way of accomplishing these resurrections reveals how the past haunts.

It is also important to stress that these interior dramas are occluded in the narration, indicated only through thick clouds of irony or strategic blanks in that dense cover. Carleton, because of both his temperament and his place in history, does not frontally deliver to us the subjective experience of doing the pilgrimage, its implications for identity, as Heaney will. Reading these examples of Lough Derg literature in sequence yields the impression that the various writers perform cultural labor for each other, that they carry out an incremental act of writing with various tasks implicitly apportioned. For example, Heaney's introspective poem illuminates some somber nuances only glimpsed beneath the surface of Carleton's insistent cheer. Even though the order of the exercise has become less severe over the years, Carleton's story remains our best guide yet to the physical implications of doing the station, the rigmarole involved. By the time Kavanagh comes to his "Lough Derg," he can afford to insert only snatches of description in the poem: "The middle of the island looked like the memory / Of some village evicted by the Famine."[9] This simile, appealing to memory, distances the reader from concrete reality, asking us to compare a fabled place to a remembered racial tragedy. (After the Famine, we also see a radical departure in Irish culture from this Enlightenment tendency to jettison the past.)[10] Foregoing fact, Kavanagh provides instead an unrivaled sociological analysis of the ritual. Heaney includes almost no documentary evidence in his meditative, somnambulist account. Significantly, Carleton's story, as it nears conclusion, highlights the cumulative, phantasmagoric effect of the rite, the sensation of a loosening of anchors in the objective world. It is as though Heaney has the luxury of exploring this consequence exclusively. Self-consciousness increases as the genre evolves, but the corollary is that interiority is latent in Carleton's originating text, waiting to be brought to the surface of expression.

Each author, through the agency of Lough Derg, undergoes a realignment with his past, advancing at once his personal development and that of the genre and the culture. The result for Heaney is an adjustment in the balance between artistic and social responsibility, shifting toward personal autonomy, accountability, and artistic assertion. This experience goes straight back to Carleton, who, referring to his story, declared, "The description of that most penal performance . . . not only constituted my début in literature, but was also the means of preventing me from being a pleasant, strong-bodied parish priest at this day; indeed, it was the cause of changing the whole destiny of my subsequent life."[11] From Carleton's story, we feel sure that Lough Derg not merely discouraged the priest in him but encouraged the poet. The psychic buoyancy essential to the artist in him surfaced there in a battle waged against the self-abnegating, downward tug of culture. As previously noted, a convention of the genre is to approach Lough Derg as an epitome of culture. It is equally typical eventually to question this essentialist assumption, entertaining the possibility that separateness need not exclude one from a culture less homogeneously defined. This process makes the experience a maturing one, akin to separating from powerful parents. Not only does Carleton free himself from the rule of reason through his fearful, partial yielding to the numinous, he also subverts the tyranny of Catholicism through a prolonged, discriminating analysis that breaks the unitary Church into manageable, nontranscendent parts. In short, the story rails against the Church on the surface, a gift to his Protestant readers and his patron, Otway, but in its fast-running and turbid undercurrents, through its very telling, it risks a highly individual realignment with his native faith and culture.

Carleton asks throughout his tale what precise values Lough Derg represents, other than tribal togetherness. This in an interrogation that, as I have maintained, all these Lough Derg writers mount to different degrees. Mirroring, again in a manner that both prefigures and reverses, the scholastic scrupulousness of Devlin, Carleton brings the revisionist spirit of the Reformation to bear on the Catholic heart of Lough Derg. As such, he lays the ground for subsequent, often less thorough and gleeful, dissections. Ironically, however, he also succeeds in revising a devotionalism that opposes the sacramental, transformational heart of a more experiential Catholicism, another target of Enlightenment rationalism. It is worth rehearsing the range of disparate questions lodged by the "Lough Derg Pilgrim" because Carleton's discernment creates a paradigm for subsequent inquisitions of the penitentiary.

The Church is deconstructed implicitly by these writers into its liturgical, doctrinal, and ecclesiastical parts. Clericalism becomes an automatic target to a greater or lesser extent, but all invest equal energy in confronting the repercussions of beliefs and practices. It is hard to avoid the problem of narcissism, which this exercise in self-immolation ironically exacerbates. In general, these writers face the question of pride, whether to celebrate the self or to efface it. All have to question the relationship between imagination and religion, considering, for instance, the role pleasure has in an act of penance that pivots on a recognition of one's unworthiness. They may ask whether or not the religious transcendence promised by self-denial bears any resemblance to the sublimity of art. Contingent on the answer to that question, they may consider how to reconcile the loss of individual identity produced by mystical ecstasy with the earthed egotism of the artist. Further, how does one retain the independence, even anarchy, of imagination in a church and culture that demand conformity? Asking whether or not one can submit on these levels raises the more general question of whether one belongs or not. Scrutinizing how one relates to other people—neighbors, relations, the rest of the tribe—becomes a pressing, painful task. The ritual of Lough Derg seems designed to provoke this question, as the lonely endurance required to do the station prompts the need to huddle into the crowd for comfort. Finally, this duality of being both a needy animal and a questing soul raises urgent questions of mode and invites options ranging from realism to surrealism, image to allegory. Not all these questions are answered by every Lough Derg writer or are present, directly or indirectly, in Carleton. He does, however, introduce the basic pattern of cultural interrogation.

"The Lough Derg Pilgrim" is quintessential Carleton: funny, observant, and worldly. As I have said, it contains an abundance of realistic description of what it meant to do Lough Derg in his time: how the island looked from a distance and up close, what one did by way of penitential acts and for how long, how one's body felt performing these, and what the people around one looked like. It is very physical. Yet even as Carleton begins the story, complicated feelings and thoughts expand the narrative beyond a narrowness of material concerns, eventually beyond even realism. Almost every sentence operates on at least two levels, one communicating the nervous anticipation of his young mind, the other the ironic detachment of maturity. He is skeptical above all of the superstition that sustains his juvenile romanticism. Trying to provide a sense of just how agitated he was moments before seeing this long-gestated symbol as fact, he launches into that apostrophe where he asks an imagined, urbane reader to remember how he felt on his first trip to Rome. The apostrophe itself reinforces a collusion between reader and author that creates its own sad, colonial meaning. Yet we also observe Carleton both standing back from his frenzied, blinkered youth and coolly relegating such immoderate enthusiasm to the human condition. He rhetorically asks the reader, "Have the monuments of the greatest men and the mightiest deeds that ever the earth witnessed . . . excited a curiosity amounting to a sensation almost too intense to be borne?"[12] He seems to want both to humanize a predisposition toward a sacramental Catholicism and to distance himself from it. He goes on to take a direct swipe at the Church, urging the prudent visitor to keep his Protestant good sense about him, guarding against the popish miasma. He tells his reader it is lucky "you awoke in good time from your shadowy dream, to escape from the unvaried desolation and the wasting malaria that brooded all around."[13] Disease and Catholicism equate and further equate with Lough Derg. Carleton's studied realism is an effort to escape from the pathological "shadowy dream" of his religious heritage, for which in fact he has too much sympathy and firsthand knowledge for his own comfort. It is not just a matter of fitting in with the cosmopolitan Anglo-culture of the "reader" but of inhabiting his own skin without terror of "unvaried desolation," which for him is overpowering and omnipresent.

Priests for their venality, brutality, and greed arouse his rage, but one of the main sources of ironic tension comes from having the young pilgrim mistaken for a priest. The older author gently mocks his young self for being flattered by the mistake. Furthermore, his emergence from the self-perpetuated disguise measures his growth beyond the baneful influences of the past. So intense is his anti-clericalism that toward the story's end, the narration loses the detached quality of its realism and becomes quite fevered when Carleton taps into this red-hot channel. Anger pours forth uncontrolled by judgment as he relates the circumstances that fuel his feelings. This anger is so uncontainable, it explodes into the melodrama of the priest who demands the last shilling from that poor, sick father accompanied by his also ailing son. The priest goes so far as to threaten them with harm when they refuse payment. The ostentatiously noble narrator gives the father the money he needs to guarantee his son's survival. This perfect virtue makes the reader suspect an evasion of difficult, deeper issues about Catholicism. The theatrical passage is a set piece for the benefit not just of his audience but of Carleton. It is intended to convince himself that a proscenium arch separates him from these people. Lough Derg, however, has a way of stripping the self-conscious, self-protective element from the creative process, thereby revitalizing it.

The story unlocks Carleton's urgent personal psychological reasons for his decision to become a Protestant, one of the more obvious being that superstition and fanaticism are not just repellent but perceived as dangerous. He also often appears to present these affronts to reason in an amusing light, because outright condemnation of anything connected with the people and not the priests challenges his deepest, most integrative loyalties. Yet he laughs at himself almost too loudly when displaying such atavisms, for instance that water-walking episode. For all the defensiveness of the self-mocking tone of the mature author, when the spindly pretender promptly sinks, so does the narrative bravura. This literal comedown sends a subtextual message to the reader that perhaps the nonrational part of Carleton is not unrelated to the robustness of his imagination. The narrator, who describes an earlier self taking "a tremendous stride, planting my right foot exactly in the middle of . . . [a] water-lily leaf"[14] is much more winning than the sober, self-conscious author moralizing about "what a strong authority vanity has over the principles and passions."[15] Carleton feels compelled to demonstrate, however, that he hates superstition for the way it robs reality of proportionate meaning, filling it with amorphous and misleading suggestion. Everything objective and clear is turned into the subjective and turbid. Feelings of immense foreboding flood even the most innocuous encounters. At the beginning of his pilgrimage, a hare crosses his path. The innocent animal instantly becomes the devil in camouflage. While on one level Carleton is mocking an earlier self, he is also revealing his abiding temperament. The debilitating result of such distorting perception worries the grown-up Carleton because it seems to threaten his sanity, masculinity, and art. Speaking of the sophisticated visitor approaching Rome but really of himself, he gloats, "You were not submitted to the agency of a transcendental power. You were, in a word, a poet, but not a fanatic. What comparison, then, could there be between the exercise of your free, manly, cultivated understanding, and my feelings on this occasion, with my thick-coming visions of immortality, that almost lifted me from the mountain-path I was ascending, and brought me, as it were, into contact with the invisible world?"[16] Levitation is ludicrous, the transcendental treacherous, the invisible dangerous, but not, mark, fallacious. Despite the conditioning interjection, "as it were," enforcing the idea of mere illusion, the remainder of this sentence, which in its very syntax simulates the pilgrim's classic ascent, rises in fact to a consummately divided peak. The poet, according to Carleton's too-protested Enlightenment paradigm, is a self-possessed being not enthralled by any power greater than himself, except a God amenable to and approached by reason. Our author's potency depends on a freedom gained by rational detachment from excitable emotions; Catholicism impedes this distancing. It is also the springboard for all these artistic feats, and somewhere in him Carleton knows it.

A pervasive and unshakeable sense of sin, however, thwarts the liberation he seeks. Constant introspection about the imperfect state of one's soul seems to be an involuntary, chronic posture. One of the first things Carleton notices about his fellow pilgrims is their sad distractedness. A vaporous self-involvement appears to be the doom of true believers: "there was a shade of strange, ruminating abstraction apparent on all."[17] Carleton finds himself suffering from the same funk, which indicates again that the melancholy and superstition he abhors stubbornly inhere. Nobody can draw him out in conversation. As they near Lough Derg, passing by Lough Erne, the moroseness and solemnity increase, but Carleton makes a bid to save himself, drawing back from despondency by rejecting the sway of sin. He believes that his salvation from punitive cerebrality is the beauty of the world: "How . . . was it possible for me to register the transgressions of my whole life, heading them under the 'seven deadly sins' with such a prospect before me as the beautiful waters and shores of Lough Erne?"[18] He wants to convince us that a racial propensity for self-punishment is matched, if not exceeded, by an appetite for pleasure. But the contemporary reader recognizes Carleton's mental condition in the beginning as depression, a numbness rather than a sadness: "It was not pleasure, nor was it pain, but a chilliness of soul which proceeded from the gloomy and severe task which I had undertaken."[19] No wonder he begins to interrogate the value of penitential exercises. He parades the conviction that self-mortification is perverse and counterproductive, leaving the penitent ironically less able to resist sin because so weakened by torture. Talking of the elusive sadness that results from self-inflicted pain, Carleton maintains, "It was this gloomy feeling that could alone have strangled in their birth those sensations which the wisdom of God has given as a security in some degree against sin."[20] All that an overpowering sense of sin solipsistically produces is more sin.

Carleton's most apparent reason for defending the natural over the supernatural is the preservation of a psychic balance, even more than the maintenance of abstract Enlightenment principles. A proportionate view of externals guarantees personal equanimity. The benefits of this outlook are to be seen throughout the text where there is self-irony, narrative self-consciousness generally. The water-walking episode, for instance, is a secular miracle in unraveling the interwoven threads of thoughts and feelings that compose the mania: "My heart beat high with emotion, my soul was wrapt up to a most enthusiastic pitch of faith, and my whole spirit absorbed in feelings, where hope—doubt—gleams of uncertainty—visions of future eminence—twitches of fear—reflections on my expertness in swimming . . . and on the depth of the pond—had all insisted on an equal share of attention."[21] His art appears to spring from an equipoise produced by counterbalancing a "spirit absorbed in feelings" with an intelligence bent on analysis. Enumerating the distinct emotions involved, "hope-doubt" and so forth, he checks qualitative rapture with quantitative thought. The humor arises both from the exaggerations of an unchecked fancy and from the uncanny exactness of analysis. Irony is the result of the juxtaposition. Further, the division between the knowing author and the misled boy is repeated in a division within the youth, who is as much a budding empiricist, worried about the depth of the pond, as he is a vainglorious fanatic bent on strolling by faith alone across its surface. However much balance and the tension of opposites give Carleton's art its distinction and may even provide its genesis, as a narrator he does not call attention to these contradictions. He publicizes the consistent, rational, moral pragmatist in himself, blissfully free of Catholicism's hocus-pocus.

The reader, however, is on to his game. Often, as I have suggested, he protests too much. The dispassionate adult does not entirely eclipse the excitable youth. Implications of authorial superiority, produced by irony, are intense and intensely suspect when he confesses to but really boasts about a sacrilegious propensity to indulge the "lust of the eye": "I found my heart on the point of corruption, by indulging in what I had set down as the lust of the eye, and had some faint surmise that I was plunging into obduracy. I accordingly made a private mark with the nail of my thumb on the 'act of contrition' in my prayer-book, and another on the Salve Regina, that I might remember to confess for these devilish wanderings."[22] We are meant to see it as almost literally crazy to call the sane need for relief "devilish." Underneath the irony made possible by recovery from this madness, however, there is the worry of a man still wracked by scrupulosity, still Catholic. This qualm comes out in a second passage where the pursuit of relief is defended with too much arrogance. The tone is so arch, it sounds insecure: "I broke away, too, from several 'acts of contrition' to conjecture whether the dark, shadowy inequality which terminated the horizon, and penetrated, methought, into the very skies far beyond the lake, were mountains or clouds: a dark problem, which to this day I have not been able to solve."[23] The preciousness of the diverting problem is meant to throw the gravity of the religious ritual into doubt. We are supposed to see a civilized aesthete too preoccupied with the fine points of beauty in this world to get lost in contemplation about the vague horrors of the next.

The text, however, contains the suggestion that the author is not providing a full self-disclosure, just the flattering angle on himself he wishes us to glimpse. To be sure, the phrase "lust of the eye" goes far toward describing the verve of Carleton's style. He devours the physical world with extraordinary gusto and savor. Dialogue and description are his forte. He is gifted at landscape and portraiture both, but the human form stimulates his appetite for anomaly and eccentricity. He has, indeed, a Rembrandt-like talent for exposing every mole, wrinkle, and stray whisker in the unforgiving light of his concentrating eye. Take, for example, this incidental portrait of a man "who struck him as a remarkable figure; his back was long, his legs and thighs short, and he walked on the edge of his feet. He had a pale, sorrowful face, with bags under his eyes, drooping eyelids, no beard, no brows, and no chin; for in the place of the two last, there was a slight frown where the brows ought to have been, and a curve in the place of the chin."[24] The style derives its strength from sinewy particulars, but the inordinate detachment of the viewer and his insatiable hunger for detail create an inadvertent irony. He wants to appear scientific, but the excesses of the stance contradict the pretense of being disciplined. The "lust of the eye" is given full permission, for lust it is, this consuming of another physical being with his gaze, a replication of an imperial appropriation of another's subjectivity. Carleton's comedy is borne out of a compulsion. The feared disproportion that comes from fanaticism is converted to comedy, but the disproportion remains. Most of his ploys for countering religion operate by this ironic principle: he disguises in art those same postures that he labels as Catholic and elsewhere exposes as vile.

For example, the tendency toward eviscerating abstraction attributed to Devotionalism is transferred to the ostensibly secular operation of seeing and describing. Certain thumbnail sketches contain swift, allegorical implications, where the author is so eager to equate corporeal peculiarities with essential character traits, he seems to fear rather than relish the multifarious splendors of life. His voice takes on the censorious tone of a prelate: "There were . . . countenances in which a man might almost read the histories of their owners. Methought I could perceive the lurking, unsubdued spirit of the battered rake, in the leer of his roving eye, while he performed, in the teeth of his flesh, blood, and principles, the delusive vow to which the shrinking spirit, at the approach of death, on the bed of sickness, clung, as to its salvation."[25] Despite the preacherly tone, there is more than a whiff of terror about the flesh in this passage where speculation exceeds observation. The reader thereby suspects that a haunted rather than a liberated author is ascendant. Perhaps Carleton deploys his best description, where the beam from the eye is bright and steady, as a defense against his own tenebrous interior and the dark hearts of others. Sometimes, when confusing data overly stimulates him, the defense fails.

The best evidence of such failure is found in the most successful description in the story, so much is the quiddity of his art a mixture of strengths and weaknesses. In "Station Island" Heaney meets Carleton's ghost at a place the younger writer designates with this reminder to his elder: "Round about here you overtook the women."[26] Heaney is referring to the two outlandish crones the young pilgrim meets en route, who latch onto him. The vividness of the portraits is, again, a virtue of particularity. The older of the two women is made unique for the reader, if only by the oddity of her attire, which is utterly unpredictable and absolutely right: "She then drew out of a large four-cornered pocket of red cloth, that hung at her side, a hare's skin cap, which, in a twinkling was on her own cranium. But what was most singular, considering the heat of the weather, was the appearance of an excellent frieze jacket, such as porters and draymen usually wear, with two outside pockets on the sides, into one of which she drove her arm up to the elbow, and in the other carried her staff like a man."[27] The details of dress and carriage are bizarre, incongruous and authentic. Together they create an image that is indelible because credible. They appear to be the outgrowth of glorious life, not an extravagant fancy. Surely no author straining to be believed would go to such extremes. Only life itself is this surprising. Yet this is art. It is Carleton's genius to be able to deliver the excitement of unmediated reality. Appreciating how close he brings life to the reader, we assume that is how close it came to him. His descriptive talent delivers the world to him, makes him on some level belong. Nevertheless, he embraces this world selectively, controlling the way intimacy occurs, as he omits from description what he does not want too near.

Although we know in detail how these singular females dress, walk, and talk, we do not see their faces, as great an oversight of essential humanity as any imperial gaze has ever committed. What sets Carleton's omission apart, however, is the reader's sense that, if the loyal author looked his subjects in the face, his courage to separate from the culture would fail him. Tellingly, given the release words provide for the young Carleton, we infer the characters of these women not by their physiognomies but by their speech. In every hilarious curlicue of blandishment and insinuation, their talk tells us who they are. Consider this calculated speech to the mistress of a "dry lodgin" house within earshot of the vain young pilgrim: "Here's a clargyman, and you had betther lose no time in gettin' his Reverence his breakfast. . . . Avourneen, if you have anything comfortable, get it for him; he is generous, an' will pay you well for it; a blessed crathur he is too as ever brought good luck under your roof; Lord love you, if ye hard him discoursin' uz along the road, as if he was one of ourselves, so mild and sweet!"[28] These formidable rural opera-tors fleece the gullible young man by flattering him into a priestly piety that demands an appropriate dispensation of charity; that is, buying breakfast for them. Carleton can't sketch their faces not just because such wiliness makes him nervous for the way it evades all moral law, but also because they rob him of what he values most, autonomy. To hear their manipulative talk and not see how they look accords exactly with the way other people are apprehended under the pressure of anxiety, when they impinge but cannot be fully seen. Of course there is irony here: the mature author is deliberately letting us watch without interference the boy being conned by rogues, but the bafflement, signaled by the defensively pat use of stereotype, extends into adulthood. His normal facility in portraiture is hobbled. Carleton is most adept at drawing faces when his subjects are more like objects, faces in a crowd, where the artist remains concealed and unthreatened. Maybe the lust of Carleton's eye, like lust generally, functions best without emotional involvement. Human interaction makes dispassionate appraisal difficult.

This lacuna indicates an unresolved part of Carleton's character, which is related to the depression he manifests at the beginning, and his continual wariness of the sadness all around him. Carleton has a notable tendency to court solitude, a perch from which to observe but also a corner in which to protect himself, bursting forth occasionally in spasms of self-assertion. The numbness and the anger may have deep roots. In the introduction to *Traits and Stories* he writes about the typical Irishman, and we have to wonder if his knowledge of the race might be based on knowledge of an intimate, a mother or father, someone who had great influence on his development. Despite the stereotypical, imperial tenor to these remarks, anticipating Matthew Arnold on the subject of the Celt, there is also the unmistakable ring of intimacy off such particularity:

> The national imagination is active and the national heart warm, and it follows very naturally that he should be, and is, tender and strong in all his domestic relations. Unlike the people of other nations, his grief is loud and lasting, vehement but deep; and whilst its shadow has been chequered by the laughter and mirth of a cheerful disposition, still in the moments of seclusion . . . it will put itself forth after half a life with a vivid power of recollection which is sometimes almost beyond belief.[29]

Carleton, preferring to displace awkward aspects of his own temperament onto his race, predicts the theoretical penchant in our time to explain away the idiosyncratic and individual in literature in exclusively cultural-historical terms. Knowledge of abiding pain may be what Carleton turns away from in the sunnier directions of comedy, sensuous description, and satire. These big bright patches on the surface of his prose, which is in tone "chequered by the laughter and mirth of a cheerful disposition," appear to cover depths of personal suffering, as well as cultural sorrow.

The dormancy of this grief is critical; it can erupt anytime, particularly in moments of seclusion. It may be the surfacing of this enormous emotion, the magnitude of which appears to terrify him ("with a vivid power of recollection that is sometimes beyond belief"), that occurs in the climax of "The Lough Derg Pilgrim" when the all-night vigil in the chapel takes place. Fear of going crazy becomes an idée fixe. A rational explanation may be that, robbed of the usual external stimuli, which keep these rampaging, black feelings at bay, there is a fear of being ruptured by their violent birth. He reports with trepidation the superstition that if pilgrims fall asleep, "they will not only be damned in the next world, but will go mad, or incur some immediate and dreadful calamity in this."[30] He is furious that the sheeplike masses can be so deceived, taking the temptation to sleep as the devil's work, rather than the natural result of exhaustion. Despite this rage at irrationality, he fears a mental breakdown for sound scientific, psychological reasons: "By stretching the powers of human sufferance until the mind cracks under them, it is said sometimes to return these pitiable creatures maniacs . . . sunk for ever in the incurable apathy of religious melancholy."[31] The voice speaking recognizes the potential for this fate in himself and will do anything to avoid it.

The threat of insanity posed by Catholicism makes it responsible for the author's probing of the mind's hidden chambers, where those unruly emotions bound up with religion and race live. Even a mechanistic devotionalism can induce the black magic of transformation. The richest, least intended irony presented by Carleton is that what produces the most fear and anger also produces the most creative energy, probably a truism of the imagination, and that the devil of real life is the angel of art. Carleton's imagination exerts its greatest resistance from within precisely at that point on the surface of consciousness where the pressure from without is most felt. Given this dynamic, Carleton is certainly more opposed to Catholicism than to colonialism, but this very opposition is a recognition of the enemy's power. A paradox results: Carleton's best hatred creates his best work. While he maligns a reduced religion, his real energy is reserved for the sacramental heart of Catholicism that still pumps within this diminished, doctrinal frame. His attacks, therefore, serve a restorative purpose in relation to the Church, recalling it from a cramped Devotionalism to its real power. The emotional resonance and psychological subtlety of Carleton's prose, as distinct from its brio, flows directly from this obscure, denied center, what Melville called in relation to Hawthorne a "great power of blackness." Carleton's description, the product of an unflinching, self-delighting eye, has a mimetic flatness compared to the fathomless inner world he illuminates in the self-conscious stretches of his prose. His highest art is in connecting sense impressions and outside occurrences to the vibrations they cause within.

Carleton's narration of the endless hours in the "prison" comes to focus on the theme of the loss of conscious control, the breakdown of an ability to make skepticism conquer Catholic mesmerism. Distinguishing with certainty between real and unreal, subjective and objective, is no longer possible; his mind is arrested and divided. He speaks of the queer, schizoid state of mind he finally enters, holding onto reality with one hand and reaching out to Lethe, his intimation of "easeful death," with the other: "I experienced . . . that singular state of being, in which, while the senses are accessible to the influence of surrounding objects, the process of thought is suspended, the man seems to enjoy an inverted existence, in which the soul sleeps, and the body remains awake and susceptible of external impressions."[32] Prohibited, in a way reminiscent of being colonized, a self-determination over basic matters of bodily integrity—mobility, sustenance, sleep—this symbolic gesture of obedience makes the mind preternaturally susceptible to sense impressions. The irony in this climactic section of the story is that the sensory appetite, which fed the "lust of the eye," is nourished now only by the appurtenances of religion. The same faculty that was stimulated by the wonders of the earth is hypnotized by the paraphernalia of Catholic ritual. This inversion nearly prompts an ultimate tumble into madness, or faith. The coruscating light of candles, their deliquescent smell, the undulating sound of murmuring penitents are all soporifics. The ultimate somersault, performed under the stress of doing the station, is the conversion of matter to menacing energy. When he rises hungry, in darkness, after the first night spent on a hard pallet, Carleton views a material world suffused with ethereal intimations:

> There was just sufficient moon to make the "darkness visible," and to show the black clouds drifting with rapid confusion, in broken masses, over our heads. This, joined to the tossing of the billows against the shore—the dark, silent groups that came, like shadows, stooping for a moment over the surface of the waters and retreating again in a manner which the severity of the night rendered necessarily quick, rising thereby in the mind the idea of gliding spirits—then the pre-conceived desolation of the surrounding scenery—the indistinct shadowy chain of dreary mountains which, faintly relieved by the lurid sky, hemmed in the lake—the silence of the forms, contrasted with the tumult of the elements about us—the loneliness of the place—its isolation and remoteness from the habitations of men—all this put together, joined to the feeling of deep devotion in which I was wrapped, had really a sublime effect upon me. Upon the generality of those who were there, blind to the natural beauty and effect of the hour and the place, and viewing it only through the medium of superstitious awe, it was indeed calculated to produce the notion of something not belonging to the circumstances and reality of human life.[33]

He is transported to a domain of "spirits" where darkness, both the mystery in himself and its mirroring correspondence without, is, to use Milton's word, "visible." Suddenly he is in the "shadowy dream," now a lurid nightmare that he has been determined to avoid. Or is he? The ending is ambiguous, telling us both that he is "wrapped" in "deep devotion" and experiences awe, a "sublime effect," but at the same time is different from the enchanted masses who were "blind to the natural beauty and effect of the hour and the place," being victims, unlike him, of "superstition." Is he one of the people or not? Do his roots strangle or sustain? When the religion he denounces enables him to evaporate substance into the atmosphere of mood, it is not unrelated to the work of the romantic imagination. The hallucinatory heart of Lough Derg is a source of artistic vitality: the surreal provides no less of Carleton's lifeblood than the real does. His denials of this truth are made in a bid primarily for safety, however much reader approval he gains simultaneously.

Catholicism, like the waters he tried to walk on, is always there and can drown him. He propels himself forward, he thinks, on the wings of good sense.

It is this paradoxical blend of dialectical reasoning and helpless empathy that determines the use of diverse voices in his more elaborate tales, for instance, "The Hedge School." There the narration, like the guiding, bouncing ball above song lyrics, drops into one center of consciousness after another, for example inhabiting intermittently the interiors of a hybrid narrator, native schoolmaster and English observer. In addition, a chorus of native voices, each identified by the shorthand of "a peasant," presents a single, parodic view of native culture, a distancing device to shore up the author's protection from this esurient source. Multiple-point-of-view narration provides Carleton with a means of orchestrating the various, potentially discordant, separately despotic voices in himself. There are circumstances, however, that appear to induce a panic, routing reason and multiplicity and resulting in projection and polarization. A companion piece to "The Lough Derg Pilgrim" for the way it shares key images, especially the infernal, is "Wildgoose Lodge." This story, if anything, intensifies the hellishness of "The Lough Derg Pilgrim," for "Wildgoose Lodge" contains no comic relief and bears on an even weightier subject than the dangers in Catholic superstition. It exposes the herd instinct: the consequences of such group conditioning when used to perpetrate sectarian violence. "Wildgoose Lodge" locates the site, in this far-flung web of Lough Derg-related writing, where the underworld conceit is used to express a sense of racial doom.

"Wildgoose Lodge," which has a direct bearing on recent paramilitary activity in the Northern Ireland, is a story about the group coercion behind violent land agitation at the turn of the nineteenth century. In fact, in this story the destruction of human life and razing of property is tellingly committed not against an Anglo "other" but against a native informer. Carleton applies his own demonization to the anarchic, depersonalized energy that leads to such absurdities as self-destruction and the endless circularities of a revenge culture. He displaces the conflict, which his own collusion with this behavior creates within him, onto his portrait of the ringleader, "The Captain." This man's surreal mien is the clear product of the self-divided mind viewing it: "The Captain's look had lost all its calmness, every feature started out into distinct malignity, the curve of his brow was deep, and ran up to the root of the hair, dividing his face into two segments, that did not seem to have been designed for each other."[34] A plethora of antitheses suggest themselves as these "two segments": body and soul, Protestant and Catholic, England and Ireland, Church and Nation, the self perceived from within and without. It is possible to read this story as yet another example of the colonized internalizing an image of themselves as diabolical and bestial, so that the Protestant diatribes we heard earlier actually became converted in Carleton's heart to racial self-loathing. Without categorically excluding this possibility, another level of the story seems to be genuinely about a fear of the everlasting consequences of sin, a story about the anguish of individual conscience.

As in "The Lough Derg Pilgrim," Carleton presents us with a protagonist (Carleton himself did not participate in such agrarian violence) who is prone to over-stimulation, anxiety, and what we once again recognize as depression. Again, he places his persona in a past as a way of rooting out psychological torture in the present. There are many similarities of mood between these two stories, both of which record a trauma. The vague malaise, a summarizing of dread, which Carleton ascribes to his protagonist, is easily recognizable as panic. Describing how he felt after receiving a summons to attend a secret meeting of his local chapter of Ribbonmen, the protagonist confesses:

> I felt a sense of approaching evil hang heavily upon me: the beats of my pulse were languid, and an indefinable feeling of anxiety pervaded my whole spirit; even my face was pale, and my eye so heavy, that my fathers and brothers concluded me to be ill; an opinion which I thought at the time to be correct, for I felt exactly that kind of depression which precedes a severe fever. I could not understand what I experienced, nor can I yet, except by supposing that there is in human nature some mysterious faculty, by which in coming calamities, the dread of some fearful evil is anticipated, and that it is possible to catch a dark presentiment of the sensations which they subsequently produce. For my part I can neither analyse nor define it; but on that day I knew it by painful experience, and so have a thousand others in similar circumstances.[35]

He admits that, whatever this "presentiment" is, it eludes rational understanding, and that it still haunts him. Once again, therefore, reason is clung to like a life raft to prevent drowning in sensations and feelings that overwhelm. Trying to allot this condition that swamps all rational faculties either to nature or to nurture, to psychology or to history, is futile. Clearly it is both personal and political, just as that moment Carleton delineates so precisely, when the individual is drawn in by his own weakness to a dubious group activity, is both personal and political. Carleton has the narrative genius to make the stone of doom roll with the touch of just a feather. Further, he has the psychological acuity to make this very slight pressure merely a brushing appeal to vanity. Our protagonist reads the notice he receives and is flattered to discover that the meeting to be held is not "general" but "select." The tragic irony is that an evil group endeavour is initiated by making each recruit feel special.

Carleton, although painting his narrative in the thickest applications of sooty blacks and fiery reds, counterbalances all his rampant demonizations with pin-pricks of sharp, illuminating realism, an alternation that mimics the battle in the individual for self-possession over group identity. This unholy fusion of the individual conscience with political necessity is heightened by the impending fusion of Catholicism and nationalism hinted at in the story. Much of the anxiety produced in the early scenes results from the fact that the meeting is held in, and therefore desecrates, a chapel. For example, recruits, upon taking an oath to violence in direct and diabolic parody of legitimate rituals—weddings, funerals, and confirmations—are committing sacrilege. A perversion of the Eucharist is suggested by their being exhorted by the Captain, an antipriest, to consume a draft of whiskey. Carleton, however, resisting the very unifying diabolism of his story, lets some of the men consume this poison draft and others resist. Even the egregious but clever Captain has the shrewdness to devise an accommodation, letting the squeamish take their unifying draft outside, on the chapel steps.

As the action of the story mounts, as its doom gathers, the infernal projections increase:

> Their gleaming eyes were fixed upon him with an intensity of savage and demon-like hope, which blazed out in flashes of malignant triumph. . . . I saw the satanic expression of which his face, by a very slight motion of its muscles was capable. . . . The countenances of these human tigers were livid with suppressed rage; their knit brows, compressed lips and kindled eyes, fell under the dim light of the taper, with an expression calculated to sicken any heart not absolutely diabolical.[36]

Periodically the narrator will step back from his own dualistic, demonizing formulations and insert reason and realism into the scene, much as he did in "The Lough Derg Pilgrim," eschewing the fantastical for the empirical:

> The chapel, I should have observed, was at this time, like many country chapels, unfinished inside, and the pigeons of a neighbouring dove-cot had built nests among the rafters of the unceilinged roof; which circumstance also explained the rushing of the wings, for the birds had been affrighted by the sudden loudness of the noise. The mocking voices were nothing but the echoes, rendered naturally more awful by the scene, the mysterious object of the meeting, and the solemn hour of the night.[37]

Put side by side, these are the two Carletons, the "two segments" of himself "that did not seem to have been designed for each other." It is so easy to see how the reason he associated with Protestantism seemed his only hope against the phantasmagoria that occurs in the interior of the chapel, a metaphor perhaps for his own consciousness. We see particularly in this story how susceptible he regards the human mind to depressing suggestion and bullying. No sooner has he talked himself down from hysteria through reason, than he is reporting that his surroundings "had a most appalling effect upon my spirits."[38] Here, however, he is referring to the open, murky, and silent spaces outside the chapel, the countryside surrounding the house that the Captain intends to burn, taking its inhabitants with it. Carleton's portrayal of a mind unable to assent to the power of reason is one that cannot stand up to the menacing voice within that warns, as the Captain does, "if you don't join us, remember that we can revenge."[39]

The absolute power of the group over the individual is depicted most elegantly in the story by means of the Captain's device to cross the inundated land that surrounds the targeted house. He orders certain of his men to form a human bridge that will enable others to walk over the shoulders of their cohorts. The conceit figures not just human collectivity but, less benignly, the destiny of the individual to be used for the passage of the juggernaut of history. This affront to the individual appalls Carleton. Again, it is possible, of course, that all this demonization of his own people springs from a self-hatred in Carleton so great that he was willing to consign his own people to hell in order to gain the heaven of public recognition, but the evidence in the stories of anguish and terror is too intense and immediate to suggest such cynicism. When the actual violence begins in this story, Carleton's sincerity and abiding fear become most incontrovertible. It is here, too, that Carleton makes the Irish landscape resemble the hell of which Saint Patrick's Purgatory was the official symbolic representation. The house, when it is set on fire, becomes reflected in the floodwaters around it, and the picture produced is of the molten lake of Milton's Hell ("darkness visible"). Time collapses, the present folding into the eternal, as the historical narrator relapses into a still-traumatized authorial consciousness. The motif of the boy at Lough Derg, so flooded with hellish fantasies that he jumps to his death, is repeated and modified here by the similar arabesque of the owner of the house being impaled on a pike and then thrust by the devil himself, the Captain, into the inferno. That these two sacrificial objects clearly possess both personal and historical identifications points to the impossibility of executing any facile split between the public and private in Carleton. That the final division we are left with is an image of all this horror reflected in the mirror of those smooth floodwaters points to an ineradicable doubleness.

It is precisely this infinitely proliferating and receding ambiguity that finds ideal accommodation in the reflecting pool of the blank page. Representation per se, the paradox of its innate doubleness and singularity, accommodates all these productive levels of division in Carleton. This hell of all that was imprinted by his early experience is mitigated only when it is replaced by the indicting of his own corrective image in print. That fateful night, we are told, was most appalling for its silence, a silence broken by the Irish words the fiend himself speaks: "gutso nish, ovohelhee—come hither now, boys."[40] The mere anglicizing of the Irish for the English reader bespeaks the flooded, molten lake within the author's head, the hell of forsaking one's own people as the devil himself. Being molten, this condition assumes a protean power, transmuting into diverse, often apparently discordant narrative strategies and postures. "Wildgoose Lodge" contains a vision of the legendary hell medieval penitents found in the Lough Derg cave. This is also an image of the hell of human perversion and violence bequeathed by Ireland's consuming, incendiary history of colonization and its aftermath. It is also, however, a private hell:

> Just then the flames rose majestically to a surprising height. Our eyes followed their direction; and we perceived, for the first time, that the dark clouds above, together with the intermediate air, appeared to reflect back, or rather to have caught the red hue of the fire. The hills and country about us appeared with an alarming distinctness; but the most picturesque part of it was the effect of reflection of the blaze on the floods that spread over the surrounding plains. These, in fact, appeared to be one broad mass of liquid copper, for the motion of the breaking waters caught from

the blaze of the high waving column, as reflected in them, a glaring light, which eddied, and rose, and fluctuated, as if the flood itself had been a lake of molten fire.[41]

This highly reflexive description above all conveys the flooding of reason that consciousness effects when it is saturated with a sense of pure evil. That the reflection is worse than the actual, religiously perverted pillar of fire is both a demonstration of the curse of consciousness and of the power of representation itself to amplify and affirm feeling beyond the boundaries of reason. Reason, after all, is warped and fragmented by its own reflection in rationalizations, such as those that sustain an empire, and by acts of revenge.

Carleton ends his horrific account with the addendum that he later saw the Captain and his cohorts "withering in the wind, where they hung gibbeted, near the scene of their nefarious villainy."[42] Carleton, true to the most inner dialectical workings of his imagination, registers both gratitude that he barely escaped such a fate and satisfaction that justice was done. It is ironic that he finds even somber satisfaction in the perpetration of revenge, a response that shows how truly implicated he is. That he recognizes the depth of his involvement comes out when he emphasizes "his narrow and almost undeserved escape."[43] Closing his story with a biblical quote, "Whoso sheddeth man's blood, by man shall his blood be shed,"[44] he manages, because of the insistent dialectics of the narration, to sound both self-righteously Protestant and genuinely petrified.

3

Denis Florence MacCarthy

A True Irish Poet?

WHO WAS DENIS FLORENCE MacCARTHY? The name, so unforgettable for its sheer sonority, has nonetheless been largely forgotten by history. It is not that Mac-Carthy failed to enjoy his share of achievements, but his biography is uneven, full of stops and starts, lurches, plus surprising, frequently unpopular choices. In addition, as we shall see, history seems to have almost willfully conspired to deny Mac-Carthy recognition for his modest but real accomplishments. Born in May 1817 in a house on Sackville, later O'Connell, Street in Dublin, where Clerys now stands, he was educated at Trinity College and Maynooth, decided against the priesthood, and was called to the bar in 1846; but an aversion to public life, some said an in-grained laziness, made him practice law only sporadically and to no great effect. In 1855 he was appointed by Cardinal Newman as the first professor of English litera-ture at the new Catholic University. Six months later he gave up the chair because of ill health and a predilection for privacy and repose. (Interestingly, because it re-veals a similarity of class and mind, Denis Devlin would lecture in the same uni-versity and department and similarly give up the position.) The arc of MacCarthy's career, starting with his association with Young Ireland, illustrates David Lloyd's insight about the isolated condition of this cadre of intellectual urbanites, increas-ingly dedicated to a spiritual liberation for Ireland.

After the death of Thomas Davis, the failure of Young Ireland, and the Famine, MacCarthy retreated resolutely into the career of the nineteenth-century literary man, contributing poems to *The Nation* under the pseudonym "Desmond" and eventually producing two collections, *Under Glimpses* and *The Bell-Founder*. He would go on to edit two anthologies, *The Poets and Dramatists of Ireland* and his *Book of Irish Ballads,* both including long, discriminating, and benighted prefaces by the editor. In addition, he would write *Shelley's Early Life,* a biographical sketch that fo-cuses on the Romantic poet's messianic visit to Dublin in 1812. The literary effort, however, of which he appears to have been proudest, since his son somewhat de-fensively highlights it in the biographical preface to his father's posthumously published *Collected Poems,* is MacCarthy's translation of fifteen plays by Calderón. This achievement brought MacCarthy recognition to a reading public beyond Ireland but also filled his countrymen, Catholic-Nationalist and Protestant-Unionist alike, with worry about this both quirky and conventional man's priorities. That he could stir anxieties at both political poles illustrates the unresolved contradictions in the image MacCarthy presented to the world, perhaps to himself. It also locates the compelling interest his singular character and career generate.

Despite this diversity of literary efforts and contradictory image, an anonymous contributor to the *Irish Ecclesiastical Review* of July 1882 in a memorial essay dedicated to MacCarthy, who had died that April, identified the deceased with a large question and a succinct, platitudinous answer: "What was his work? He was simply a true Irish poet. On the occasion of the Moore centenary, he was hailed as the Poet Laureate of Ireland."[1] The passive aggression behind such assertions of racial authenticity seems directly caused by the weight of contradictory evidence, such as the fact that MacCarthy, the laureate, left his home in Dalkey in 1864 and lived on the Continent and in England for nearly twenty years. His own delicate health and that of his family was his professed reason for leaving Ireland. He did not, however, present a figure of total misery and loss, as he haunted continental and British libraries, supported by a civil list pension of a hundred pounds a year conferred by Gladstone for this Irish scholar's efforts. He returned to Dublin, however, in late 1881, tracing a full circle in order to die. This consummate gesture may be read equally as a purely personal need, to die in the arms of his daughter, and as an eleventh-hour patriotic aspiration, to realize at last the total communion of the individual life with that of the nation.

The innocent author of this obituary, one of the many effusive, obviously forced eulogies published in 1882, could use the term "true Irish poet" without a twinge of conscience about reducing his subject's complexity or that of a period. Indeed, such terms of praise, identifying the pure and genuine and celebrating it, are the common coinage of critical discourse at the time. If such a creature ever existed, a "true Irish poet," or if MacCarthy were it, that would not be the reason for being interested in him. What compels is that, although he may be less than illustrious as a poet and a patriot, somehow his value exceeds the sum of these failures, is even contingent on them. Still, when even the scant details about his life are laid out, in lieu of a full biography, which does not yet exist, the skeptical listener might justifiably ask, why MacCarthy? Why bother? If mere curiosity or the desire to redress an injustice were the reason for looking deeper into the life and writings of this obscure nineteenth-century figure, that would not be enough. The surface facts of his life are noteworthy but not magnetic. Also, in the wake of David Lloyd's *Nationalism and Minor Literature,* anybody attempting to view the phenomenon of Young Ireland, and the Dublin intelligentsia generally in the middle of the nineteenth century, should be cautious before selecting another window that looks out from and into the house of cultural history. To read Lloyd is to come away with the impression that the poet James Clarence Mangan is the perfect aperture. The premise on which Lloyd's entire book is predicated, however, refuses to enforce this essential-ism. Lloyd's conviction is that one man does not epitomize a movement or a nation, that he is irreducibly one man, a product of culture but also an individual caught in a complicated, often conflict-ridden relationship with family and society. This view justifies the exploration of another individual from the period whose intersection with events and attitudes creates another pattern of personality and utterance, in its own way complex and elusive, challenging our understanding of an age.

Lloyd is intent on delivering what in Mangan was the "ineradicable residue of a self-conscious and alienated selfhood, which cannot be assimilated to the 'spirit of the nation,' "[2] in the words of James Gavan Duffy. I believe there exists such an unseen core to MacCarthy, which eludes not only assimilation but also even knowl-edge, perhaps even self-knowledge, as I have suggested. Thinking about this hid-den MacCarthy and the potential excitement of discovery reminds me of MacCarthy's feelings on making a substantial literary discovery. In the course of doing the research for his Shelley biography, he discovered a poem by the Roman-tic poet that had been furtively published but was still unknown over half a century later. MacCarthy compares his feelings on coming upon this signal fact to those of Keats in "On First Looking into Chapman's Homer": "Then felt I like some watcher of the skies, / When a new planet swims into his ken." MacCarthy has to add the caveat that by knowing of the poem's existence but never seeing it, he had "discov-ered the surrounding light that indicates the presence of the star," but had "not yet detected its nucleus."[3] That may be the view of MacCarthy to which we are limited, so effectively did he achieve his own seclusion. In an appreciative essay about Mac-Carthy, Reverend Matthew Russell writes that he, MacCarthy, Gavan Duffy, and John O'Hagan "travelled around Ireland in the summer" of 1846, including a "ram-ble through Donegal."[4] Russell records that MacCarthy kept a diary of those trips. Knowing of the existence of that diary without being able to read it is like seeing the light around the star but not its nucleus. That we may never penetrate these secrets, however, may be more salutary for the study of what we do possess than a fuller knowledge, which might encourage a spurious certainty. MacCarthy's shrouded center is a constant reminder of the ultimate elusiveness of all individuality, not just that it may resist assimilation into prevailing ideologies but that it may even resist conscious understanding, let alone unity of being. Therefore the attempts, the pub-lished probes at understanding to which we do have access, must be read for the cryptic center they only imply. Before trying to approach these penetralia, let me turn to Lloyd for help in sketching the public climate in which these privacies are hoarded.

Lloyd convincingly traces an evolution from a nationalism based on Enlighten-ment principles of reason and inclusion under Tone and Emmet to a pragmatic, quite secular sectarianism under O'Connell and on to, as a reaction against such a use of religion, the Romantic nationalism of Young Ireland under Mitchel, Duffy, and Davis. Lloyd makes the point that Young Ireland is the dream child of a "culturally deracinated urban Catholic intelligentsia," the dream being in direct proportion to the reality of alienation:

> Marginalized doubly, both in relation to a predominantly rural economy and in relation to the loci of government and economic power, this displaced and largely urban intelligentsia was driven to seek an alternative political center. It was in this context that the theory of the spiritual nation, transcending actual social and economic difference and offering a ground for unity that would integrate disparate interests into a coherent political force, gains its crucial importance for the first time in Ireland.[5]

Lloyd also draws attention to the intended correspondence between the processes of cultural recovery championed by Young Ireland and the accepted teleology of how a nation develops. The two processes were meant to be parallel and eventually to dovetail. Lloyd includes a third process in his reading of this period: the evolution of the individual into his own autonomous selfhood as a reflection of the nation's. Lloyd, bringing his own values to bear on this mythology, sees all three processes as flawed not just by this romanticization and fictitious convergence, but by a subjugation of the individual to essentially the hegemonic design of imperialism, which requires such simultaneous but skewed acts of faith. Therefore, the spirit of the nation is supposed not only to bestow a miraculous unity among disparate groups, but also to confer a mirroring interior unity. It is easy to see how this synthesis might be disrupted by other spiritual dictates, of, say, a believing Christian, Protestant, or Catholic.

I contend, somewhat differing with Lloyd, that the values bolstering the "spirit of the nation," being borrowed from religious discourse, may in fact be retained as exclusively religious values and compete with their illicit use. For example, Carleton's conversion to Protestantism, which I do not reduce just to early evidence of the clout of British culture but attribute also to his authentic love-hate relationship with Catholicism, was undertaken to protect an inchoate, volatile self from the erosion of collectivity. In addition, Carleton genuinely abhorred as a Christian the deadly acts of violence that he saw going hand-in-hand with nationalism. "Wildgoose Lodge," as we have seen, demonizes Catholic Ribbonmen, a stance that must owe some of its virulence to Protestant diatribes against Lough Derg, but also to Carleton's sincere, ethical convictions. From the Catholic perspective, MacCarthy eventually transgresses the dogmas of Romantic nationalism by his fidelity to a religion that has its own cultural reservoir, including literature that undermines the pastoral and innocent essence of an artificial Irishness. In other words, autonomy does not always have the negative implication of colluding with imperialism. In addition, Catholicism, while frequently underpinning nationalism, can, if embraced for its globalism, an innate internationalism, also oppose the nation, when an absolute clash of values occurs. From our postmodernist perch we may be skeptical of the romance of autonomy per se, the integration of the individual within a larger social unit, which this consummate and constructed identity is meant to signal. That does not mean, however, that we cannot appreciate how an identity constructed under the laws of the Church can deviate from one cleaving to the values of the nation. Take the sacred status of martyrdom, for example, purloined from religion by nationalist fanaticism. Lloyd, referring to Emmet's request that his epitaph remain unwritten until Ireland "takes her place among the nations of the earth," locates the premise of this wish in Romanticism: "It is exactly in becoming—in the strictly Coleridgean sense of the term—a symbol . . . that the martyr is transformed simultaneously into a 'confessor': by his absolute identity with the fullness of meaning that the spiritual nation embodies, he invokes the realisation of that identity by the members of the nation that is yet to be."[6] Beyond an antipathy to "sacrificing the real in the name of the ideal,"[7] or of losing one's actual identity, not to mention one's life, through such an extreme gesture, there is the consideration for some of the impact of the willed act of suicide, which martyrdom might represent to a Catholic.

MacCarthy was a man of such skepticism and conflict. For example, when Shelley visited Dublin in 1812, he addressed a meeting, along with O'Connell, at Fishamble Street. MacCarthy, in his introduction to his biography of the poet, takes pains to set the record straight, emphasizing not the rapturous, but the furious, response of the crowd to Shelley, whose visit represented a messianic appeal to free the Irish people also from the self-limiting shackles of Catholicism. In his report of that meeting in the preface to his book, MacCarthy jettisons class and nationalistic biases and priorities for his overriding defense of a Catholicism quite distinct in his mind from both. MacCarthy's otherworldly innocence, however, is betrayed by his conviction that Daniel O'Connell would obey the same hierarchy of internal injunctions:

> At the meeting in question there were several Protestant gentlemen, one a noble lord, of higher position than Shelley; but whatever his rank, I believe that O'Connell would have repudiated his political support until he had withdrawn the atrocious calumnies on the religion of the people of Ireland which Shelley had so innocently put forward in both of his Irish pamphlets.[8]

The driving force of MacCarthy's book is the inexhaustible conflict created by his attraction to Romanticism, as one would expect of a Young Irelander, and his commitment to Catholicism. His mission seems not just to explain the freedom and transcendence that can reside in religious submission but to bring this paradox to fuller fruition in himself. MacCarthy's biography of Shelley is a work of pure opposition and self-affirmation both. Not only does it cut in two directions, to the heart both of imperial and nationalist cultures, rendered as mirror images by British hegemony, but at the same time it defends a set of personal beliefs. It also attempts to recover Catholicism from the separate declensions it suffered by means of its appropriation into O'Connellite utilitarianism and nationalist Romanticism.

From the snatches of biographical information we have about MacCarthy, we piece together a man who kept himself at some level clearly separate from the movement he officially espoused. The author of an article in the *Irish Monthly* in 1908 tells us that, in the context of Young Ireland, MacCarthy "was an outsider and sympathiser with his friends in a poetical way."[9] I construe "poetical way" as meaning not by way of frontal agreement with certain principles and policy. In the same publication Reverend Russell, who had access to MacCarthy's letters, cites MacCarthy's writing to John O'Hagan about a Sunday morning get-together of cronies: "So you have heard of our Sunday prayers and peripatetics—here is a change with a vengeance! Getting pious and constitutional at the one moment."[10] The fusion here of religion and politics, and one could add maybe poetry, what "peripatetics" might mean to certain ambulatory Romantics, appears to catch Mac-Carthy off-guard, but his somewhat disingenuous surprise also registers his skepticism. Charles Gavan Duffy, in his *Young Ireland: A Fragment of Irish History 1840–1850,* encapsulates MacCarthy's character by means of a few hand-picked, affectionate, but distinctly critical words: "McCarthy [*sic*], like Charles Lamb when he was the associate of Hazlitt and Hunt, loved the men more than he shared their political passions. He was a law student soon to be called to the bar, but he was essentially a poet and man of letters, happy in his study, charming in society, where his spontaneous humour was the delight of his associates, but never thoroughly at home in the council room or on the platform."[11] The unease MacCarthy clearly felt in company and which his gentle nature converted to self-protective humor is registered in the anxious tone of Gavan Duffy's encomium. MacCarthy seems to have had the innate sense not to risk assimilation, to question by instinct, in Lloyd's words, "the narrative . . . in which the individual subject is achieved through his integration with the nation itself." In relation to Mangan's "Dream of Connaught in the Thirteenth Century," Lloyd observes, explaining how the poem's Germanic and Oriental elements make it unreadable as simple allegory about the Famine, that Mangan embraces a "willed estrangement"[12] not just from his putative subject but from the representation of it as well, the poem itself. MacCarthy, while not this subtle or capable of constructing a poetry with such recesses in which to hide, nonetheless exhibits another form of willed estrangement, which amounts to a cognate act of resistance. The theme of "not being at home," announcing a posture not unlike that in Mangan's "Nameless One," recurs in writing by and about Mac-Carthy. Yet this is the poet, who in self-elected exile, wrote the humorous but existentially bleak poem "Not Known," about receiving a forwarded letter from Ireland addressed to his old home, "Summerfield," which the author for ironic distance translates as "Campo de Estio." This is a man with distinctly ambivalent feelings about home. MacCarthy sought the domain of literature, especially translation, as a safe habitation, sealed off from such conflict.

Yet literature, be it translation or his own poetry, only replicated and prolifer-ated the unresolved. Indeed, the pattern of his activities is dominated by duality. The aesthetic fails MacCarthy or he fails within it. Of course, Lloyd is quite right to make us appreciate any aesthetic as to some degree an internalization of the politi-cal principles that prop a culture. Given MacCarthy's doubts about thoroughly be-longing, he was bound to find the available aesthetic coming up short. Lacking the talent to achieve subversion through true originality, MacCarthy the poet writes with an uninspired obedience to certain formal demands while working out his op-position in oblique ways. By Gavan Duffy's assessment and that of history, Mac-Carthy was less than successful as a poet. Gavan Duffy states authoritatively, "The man most essentially a poet among the writers of *The Nation* was Clarence Man-gan."[13] Just as the phrase "true Irish poet" leads nowhere in particular, the distinc-tion between someone "essentially a poet" and another "most essentially a poet" is equally unhelpful. The premises of these assertions and discriminations are vague; but I suspect the author's meaning is simply that MacCarthy had a poetic tempera-ment but that Mangan wrote poems. Largely by working as a translator, an editor, and a scholar MacCarthy will express the conflict, which Mangan was able to put into poems, many of which are "after the Irish." As a translator of Calderón specif-ically, MacCarthy will present the phenomenon, as Mangan does, of someone whose cultural identity has been traduced by an imperial power, rediscovering and asserting authenticity by means of translation. MacCarthy's entire canon displays the accommodations and strategies adopted by a "Christian gentleman,"[14] as he was called, to untangle the class and religious implications of this tag. In addition, he was attempting to align himself, as much as honesty would allow, with the na-tionalist values summed up in this dubious compliment.

In a memorial essay by a friend, this revealing disclosure occurs, shedding light on MacCarthy's wasting of certain career opportunities but more deeply on this searching for personal autonomy: "In truth he disliked any task save such as he had chosen for himself."[15] Lloyd adheres to the idea that the concept of autonomy is deeply implicated in the advancement of the values of hegemonic culture; hence for him personal integration hinges on the integration of the nation. MacCarthy, however, displays the elusive stubbornness necessary for an effort akin to the "willed estrangement" Lloyd ascribes to Mangan, an assertion of independence not necessarily predicated on the possession of unity of being. Unlike Mangan, however, MacCarthy never achieved the individuality of voice in his poems that would have distinguished him from the group with which he is automatically identified, the poets of *The Nation*. An axiom seems to be lurking in his example: to the degree that a writer seeks to symbolize the individuality of the nation, he may fail to represent himself as an individual. Yet MacCarthy, choosing ultimately indi-rect means, difficult to pinpoint and therefore to censure, persisted in choosing for himself, persisted in covertly protecting Denis Florence MacCarthy from the avatar of the nation. His chief tactic, beyond embedding half-spoken iconoclastic impulses in the predictable rhythm and language of his own poems, was essentially Mangan's: translation. MacCarthy's strategies as a translator, however, differ from Mangan's, as do the personal motivations behind the activity, and obviously the quality of the eventual product. MacCarthy remains torn between a desire to conform, to find peace in the bosom of racial and individual harmony and the need to strike out, act out the aggressive imperatives of his veiled but rebellious personality. Fate offered him the ideal vehicle for enacting this tension when Calderón's canon yielded up a play about Lough Derg, *Saint Patrick's Purgatory* (the title according to MacCarthy's translation). It was especially apt, given the conflict at the heart of every opportunity MacCarthy embraced, that his introduction to Calderón was through Shelley. Mary Shelley wrote a life of Calderón, and Shelley himself was drawn to the playwright's rendering of magical transformations. However split MacCarthy's life and writing remained, there is a perfect logic in donning the mask of this foreign artist. Calderón constituted a borrowed identity sought as an escape, which actually brought MacCarthy straight back to the conflicts he had with Ireland.

Yeats, in his essay "The Celtic Element in Literature," uses the European involvement with Lough Derg as an argument not for the enrichment of Ireland through Europe but for the reverse. He writes, projecting his own politics onto the infinitely obliging fantasy of the Celtic: "It has again and again brought 'the vivifying spirit of excess' into the arts of Europe. Ernest Renan wrote about how the visions of Purgatory seen by Pilgrims to Lough Derg . . . gave European thought new symbols of a more abundant penitence."[16] MacCarthy is evidently impressed by this European subtext. In nine pages of endnotes to his translation of *Saint Patrick's Purgatory*, he goes to pains to explain the closing sixteen lines of the play, an epilogue that constitutes a litany of Lough Derg writers, mainly Europeans: "For with this the history closes, / As it is to us presented by . . ." and the list unwinds from Dionysius the Carthusian, to "Bede, Jacobus, and Solinus / Messingham, and to express it / In a word, the Christian faith / And true piety that defend it."[17] By translating Calderón, MacCarthy, who elsewhere in his career expended great energy excavating an exclusively Irish past, recovers Ireland's connection to the rest of Europe. His extensive documentation of the play's sources, presented as endnotes, exhibits his pride in his own scholarship and in Catholic Ireland. Both find a focus in the life of Saint Patrick; MacCarthy, with the excavating fervor Shane Leslie will demonstrate, is able not just to cite at length from another seventeenth-century text, Montalvan's *Vida y Purgatorio de San Patricio*, the immediate source of Calderón's play, but also to pinpoint where the two deviate, and the sources for the Montalvan. Listen to MacCarthy discussing the scholarly problem of where Saint Patrick was born: "Considerable controversy has arisen as to the exact location of the place. See *The Life of Saint Patrick*, by Lynch, Dublin 1828; *Saint Patrick Apostle of Ireland*, by J. H. Todd, D. D. (1864); and *The Life of Saint Patrick*, by M. F. Cusack, Kenmare, Co. Kerry (1869), a most elaborate and beautiful work."[18] All MacCarthy's intellectual, religious, and literary life had been leading up to this propitious moment: an opportunity to link by iron, demonstrable fact Catholic Ireland with Catholic Europe. MacCarthy's mission, to connect Europe reciprocally with Ireland, suffuses every small, scholarly detail, such as his explaining point by point Moltalvan's reliance on "Messingham, Messingham's chief authority being the Life of Saint Patrick by Jocelin."[19] There is no major, modern Irish Lough Derg text that does not allude, with either pride or suspicion, to Europe and the liberation or threat it might carry. Heaney in "Station Island" locates a rare oasis of sensuousness and true spirituality during his pilgrimage in section 11, when he translates Saint John of the Cross. The act of performing the translation is a penance prescribed by a priest just returned from Spain "to our chapped wilderness and intended as balm for the poet's raw soul. MacCarthy, according to his son, learned his Spanish, a providential acquisition, in his youth from a priest who had spent much time in Spain."[20] For Heaney and MacCarthy, actively translating rights (writes) the wrong of a culture translated into something other than itself.

The poets of *The Nation,* however, display a different diversity, being both Protestant and Catholic. MacCarthy, a failed seminarian but devout Catholic, as a poet of *The Nation,* rubbed shoulders with prominent Protestant writers. The submerged reality of Young Ireland is that, while it purported to underwrite the unity of Ireland, it embodied divisions. Its unifying force, however, which ironically set it off from the country as a whole, was class. In the introduction to *Ballad Poetry of Ireland*, the rival anthology by Gavan Duffy, that author in his preface says that these "Anglo-Irish ballads" are "the production of educated men, with English tongues but Irish hearts."[21] Yet it is these poems that will "give voice and form to sentiments and aspirations which are common property of the entire people."[22] The contradiction is blatant. MacCarthy, however, freely embraced, even courted, these ecumenical situations. He wrote for the *Dublin University Magazine* as well as *The Nation* and dedicated his *Book of Irish Ballads* to that spokesman for cultural unionism, Samuel Ferguson, whose principles of transparency in translation MacCarthy emulated with slight reservations, while falling short of embracing the latitude Mangan as a translator afforded his individual genius. MacCarthy, an intellectual and devout Catholic, felt bound to affirm the doctrinal asperities of Catholicism and to insist in the face of Irish Protestant bigotry on the artistic richness to be found in a broader, truly Catholic culture. At the same time, MacCarthy must have been frustrated by the nationalist injunction to produce pan-Irish sentiment, the common aim of Protestant and Catholic literati. By translating Calderón, MacCarthy joined both a narrower and a wider circle of Catholic, European artists, an elite. By translating *Saint Patrick's Purgatory,* he joined a third group, which he could not have foreseen, of modern Irish Lough Derg writers. Even within this tradition, however, he is the dark horse.

MacCarthy's individual artistic identity never fully emerged from the camouflage provided by these group endeavors or self-effacing translations. Indeed, he suffered certain indignities because of this propensity only to half-show his face on any given literary occasion, be it as editor, biographer, or "Desmond" of *The Nation,* or most obviously as a translator. Perhaps the most famous slight was when the much-anthologized poem, "Waiting for the May," was ascribed to Mangan, not to MacCarthy, its true author. Furthermore, his monumental service to Calderón was not even given a footnote by Oxford hispanologist Sir Francis Doyle in his book on Calderón, which uses MacCarthy's translations without a flutter of indebtedness. There is evidence littered all over MacCarthy memorabilia of such wounding oversights. In an *Irish Monthly* from 1908 largely devoted to MacCarthy, there is a little piece entitled "An Amiable Grumble," which registers mild chagrin because one Father Bearne quotes MacCarthy in a poem called "Baranaby Bright" but doesn't appear to know, let alone acknowledge, the source of this "rare translation of a lyric."[23] In a 1904 number of the same magazine a letter from MacCarthy himself is quoted. There he groups with the Doyle misappropriation a lapse on the part of Longfellow, who failed to include MacCarthy's poem "Alice and Una" in the anthology *Poems of Places—Ireland.* Longfellow, an acquaintance of MacCarthy's from his days on the Continent, cites four poems about Glengariff, the very place featured in MacCarthy's poem: "What bad taste not to have quoted 'Alice and Una.' This is nearly as bad as that stubborn old donkey, Sir Frances Doyle. . . . He [Longfellow] seems to have taken his specimens chiefly from books printed and reprinted in America."[24] It is telling to see this "Christian gentleman" seething, a still not uncommon sight in literary Dublin, over such setbacks in his quest for recognition. That MacCarthy was wounded by these slights is recorded in numerous letters and prefaces bristling with a resentment not abated by years of recognition for other achievements. Even the conclusion to the preface of his *Book of Irish Ballads* reveals how powerful the lure of fame was for MacCarthy. After painstakingly laying out a teleology of the ballad that will culminate in the recovery of Ireland's tradition in that genre, MacCarthy clinches his argument with almost a salesman's pitch: not only will poems "racy of the soil" be true to the "spirit of the nation," they will sell. The very novelty will attract attention and ensure success.[25] Demonstrably, an ambition and ferocity burned behind the modest, scholarly facade and both poles of his pursuits, with Irish and European literature, were intended to indicate the central axis of an integrated, powerful personality.

The prevailing ethos of conflating the self with the nation appears to create no small obstacle to such self-realization. The overriding theme of MacCarthy's preface to his collection of ballads is how that populist form will heal a rift within the national psyche. His essay, however, deepens that chasm by defining the genre in polarized terms borrowed from imperial discourse. Expounding on the contrast between song and the ballad, MacCarthy implicitly makes the former Celtic, the latter Teutonic: song is lyrical and transcendent, the ballad narrative and ordinary. Indeed, song is said to pour forth "in that Pythian moment when the mind is in its state of utmost activity, and the dominancy of passion is supreme."[26] While song

58 ❧ WRITING LOUGH DERG

appears to have its own self-synthesizing powers, it awaits the ballad as its higher calling, as the Celt awaited the Saxon for ultimate self-realization: "The ballad, on the contrary, requires not the same degree of excitement—narrative, which is almost an essential portion of it, being incompatible with that mental and sensuous excitement which gives birth to the song, and which is but momentary in its abiding."[27] The ballad is more durable, less ephemeral, less like the volatile, doomed Celt.

MacCarthy, whose essay traces the destined development of the ballad throughout Europe, thereby dedicates his anthology toward restoring Ireland's place among nations. While the Scots and Irish have their share of ballads, the Spanish have an even richer tradition, made possible by the invasion of the Goths, a fortunate cross-fertilization implicitly paralleled by that of the Saxon on the Celt. Of course, the richest tradition of all is in the German language. Generally, the recovery from the decadence of the excessively lyrical, Latinate Mediterranean was to be found by looking northward toward the Germanic, a racial perspective Leslie will recommend. "A new order of things was maturing amid the mountains and forests of northern and western Europe," proclaims MacCarthy,[28] marking the emergence of the German ballad as a milestone in a literary history of unrelenting progress. By restoring Ireland's ballad tradition, MacCarthy aims to play his part in restoring the health and fortitude of the nation. He will strive to make it, in short, more like Germany, since as a consequence of being rich in ballads "the German intellect is honoured and respected . . . the German land is strengthened and enriched." This reinvigoration will result largely from the reinstatement of historical accuracy. MacCarthy points to the power of ballad with its cultural transparency to provide a window on the past, therefore to correct the falsifications of history perpetrated by the imperial gaze. The problem is that the recovered history he projects occludes in another way, by idealizing, blurring history. The ballad, MacCarthy muses, will deliver the Irish to themselves.

Nevertheless, MacCarthy presents the maddening but typical contradictions of an intellect held in the vice of colonization: resisting and complying at once. On the one hand, witness the way he addresses the blatant contradiction of rendering a Gaelic past in the English language, seeing this linguistic marriage of convenience as a perfect union. Essentially reinforcing the unionist doctrine that true self-realization will come only through the marriage of Celt and Saxon, MacCarthy claims, imposing the further binarism of a mind/body split, that the spirit of the nation will be revealed in poems written in English but which will "endeavour to be racy of their native soil, use their native idiom, illustrate the character of their country, treasure her legends, eternalise her traditions, people her scenery, and ennoble her superstitions."[29] This claim is yet another example of MacCarthy, as he separates style and content in translation, winnowing the culture to preserve the version of continuity and reconciliation he seeks. That final phrase alone, "ennoble her superstitions," nearly divides from within, given the contradictions it glosses over. From the evidence alone of Protestant harangues against superstition, we can see how difficult this act of assimilation will be, the verb "ennoble" on its own exposing a shame on MacCarthy's part not that far removed from Carleton's complicated feelings.

On the other hand, MacCarthy can display an admirable resistance to cant and false solutions. These prefaces could have been the occasions for irresponsible hyperbole, extolling the glory of Ireland. They are not. MacCarthy reserves his most energetic assertions, however, to temper nationalist, not imperialist, claims. We witness him in these essays, in fact, vacillating, trying to do his patriotic duty and at the same time to deploy detachment. For example, with acuity and prescience he surveys the pitfalls attendant on resurrecting and validating a culture. In his introductory remarks to *Poets and Dramatists of Ireland,* he sums up the ongoing and increasingly urgent project of evaluating the legacy of literature in Irish by regarding it as a process "in which the fondest enthusiasm, or the coldest analysation, the most unhesitating credulity, or the most stubborn scepticism, has each born its part."[30] Both prefaces are searching rather than polemical in tone, unfolding contradictions that are never satisfactorily identified, let alone ironed out. In this preface to *Poets and Dramatists* the surprise for anyone unprepared for the joint stranglehold of London and Rome is not MacCarthy's ambivalence toward England but toward Ireland's pre-Christian past, where its presumed cultural treasures are buried. In relation to England and its colonial presence, he lodges the standard lament for the cultural routing that predated the Act of Union: "Long before that period the principles of imperialism had been applied to our literature."[31] His answer to the problem begins with an antisectarian bias characteristic of Young Ireland, claiming that all writers born in Ireland, regardless of racial origin, are Irish; MacCarthy arrives at a pluralist insight about English literature—"What a composite thing, after all, is this so-called English Literature."[32] This declaration is as prophetic as it is purblind.

Cultural nationalism appears to be far more threatening than colonialism. MacCarthy reviles the glorification of a Celtic past for its misplacing of piety on the pagan. It is in his attitude toward an imperial church that MacCarthy truly displays the involuntary need of the colonized to self-replicate forms of oppression. He regards the pagan period with suspicion, constructing a fragile alliance with it through a pedantic fixation on Old Irish prosody, an antiseptic obsession with technique severed from passionate thought and belief. This undue attention to technique accounts for the besetting sin of his verse: an almost too polished style. One reviewer commented on "Alice and Una," perhaps providing in advance an excuse for Longfellow's later betrayal: "Take it all and all, this is a very fine legendary poem; yet it is not without its faults. There is almost too much melody about it . . . the rhythm is too round . . . the rhymes too frequent, so that while we are surprised by the great mastery of language, we are yet somehow fatigued by it."[33] Language becomes a way to simplify and prettify rather than to deliver a fully complex meaning. Similarly, in relation to history, MacCarthy extrapolates what suits his argument and leaves the conflicting remainder in the occluded past. He is insistent, for example, on the central, triumphant role of Saint Patrick in Irish culture, another providential marker on the path that will lead to translating *Saint Patrick's Purgatory.* The irony in this attribution of a unifying function to Saint Patrick, however, is that the thesis is constructed by thoroughly severing the pagan past from the present. Throughout the essay, MacCarthy remains skeptical about the actual wealth to be found in this shadowy, unregenerate past. Adopting the cool tone of the scholar, he contends that one should mine this resource for "information,"[34] not, mark, edification. The reason for not abandoning the past is that truth forbids such rashness. It is forked statements like this one that locate MacCarthy's own complicated mind. On the one hand, it reveals the pursuit of a historical continuity typical of Young Ireland, a pursuit resting on an irony in the fervent MacCarthy's case of blithely severing the Christian from the pagan. On the other hand, his cautionary intervention argues for a genuinely detached examination of the past, a view not averse to discovering rupture. This intellectually self-possessed side to MacCarthy is always capable of catching his reader off guard. For example, he corrects his enemy Sir Francis Doyle, who opines in a preface that no one can truly understand Calderón who is not Catholic. MacCarthy, demonstrating a detachment from even his beloved religion, roundly chastises the don for such a relinquishment of rigor, responding that no one can understand Calderón without a knowledge of Catholicism. The final irony with regard to MacCarthy is that Catholicism is responsible both for disinheriting him from his Irish past and for bequeathing the means to free him from the tyrannies of nationalism.[35]

There is a hidden moment on the first page of the introduction to *The Book of Irish Ballads* that hints at the healthy maverick in MacCarthy. He refers to the silent, eviscerated spectacle presented by history without the human voice. He speaks of the inevitability of human expression, saying, "A people of passionate impulses, of throbbing affections, of dauntless heroism, will invariably not only have done things worthy of being recorded, but will also have recorded them. Myriads of human beings cannot be moved about noiselessly, like an army of shadows."[36] That army of silent or muted shadows summons up an entire tragic history of oppression culminating in famine. It also hints at the conceit of an underworld, perhaps a hell of consciousness, which forms the basis for all Lough Derg literature. Lough Derg offers MacCarthy a way of speaking about and putting on record dark truths he could not approach any other way but through Calderón, behind the veil of translation. Translating will, in fact, concretize the doubleness of self-image that sums up the colonized condition and always eludes self-reporting. The tactic of translating Calderón appears to have solved a number of problems simultaneously. First, the compromise of translating Irish culture into the English language is obviated. Two wrongs somehow make a right. Start with the premise that translation skews the original and, if you begin at two removes from it, admitting at the offset the inevitable falsity, greater authenticity may result. What is more, the vitiation of the Irish spirit resulting from commingling with the body of the English language is avoided if the spirit meeting English is the old imperial power of Spain, venerable English foe and friend to the Irish.

The relationship between body and soul is used by MacCarthy himself as an analogy for that between the dramatic genres of *auto* (a short medieval play on a sacred subject) and full-length play: "As spirit is to matter or the soul to the body."[37] Speaking of translation theory in mid-nineteenth-century Ireland, Lloyd refers to "the relation of the language to the nation, the former becoming the spirit, the latter the body." Within the safe space of translation from Spanish into English, Mac-Carthy was able to oppose the despotism of that presiding language and even to reverse his conditioned preference for the ballad over song. The airborne *auto* is song; the grounded play a ballad. No wonder with Calderón's interest in pure conversion, epitomized by the sacramental *auto*, that MacCarthy found his best means to express the spirit of the nation and his faith. From a purely political perspective as well, the act of translating becomes even less a crooking of the knee when an Irishman, displaying his mastery of an adopted tongue, chooses to enrich English by assimilating this venerated example of another national and Catholic culture. It is a matter of power. Future instances of assimilation of Irish cultural products will be less traumatic and demeaning; Ireland will drop its degrading, colonized status by being on equal footing with other non-English but imperial cultures whose art has been translated. The displaced patriotism behind the gesture is perhaps most manifest in the transfer of pedantic obsession with the fine points of prosody from poetry in Irish to that in Spanish. MacCarthy replicates Calderón's assonantal rhyme with fiendish fidelity. Drawing on a separate authority, MacCarthy explains, " 'the asonante,' says the late Lord Holland, 'is a word which resembles another in the vowel on which the last accent falls, as well as the vowel, or vowels, that follow it; but every consonant after the accented vowel must be different from that in the corresponding syllable.' "[38]

MacCarthy's zeal with this exacting form predicts Austin Clarke's procrustean efforts to replicate Irish prosody in English. There is no mistaking the politics of MacCarthy's supererogatory devotion to the Spanish original. And yet, despite espousing a transparency advocated by Ferguson, MacCarthy, in his introduction to the plays, deviates somewhat from this strictness, leaving room for perhaps the personal identification behind this work, the poet in himself, to peep through. He regards the question of preserving every foreign trace of an original as "a matter of taste."[39] Although not being doctrinaire, his preference as a translator is nonetheless to preserve "the peculiarities of the original, not sacrificing them for the sake of familiarity or fluency," further "to retain every peculiarity of the original . . . with the greater care, the more foreign it may happen to be, whether it be a matter of taste, of intellect or of morals."[40] This fidelity begins with assonantal rhyme which is "opposed to anything that bears the semblance of rhyme in English." This project is nothing less that a quiet, veiled assault on English, a concerted attempt to force it, not its foreign guest, to make accommodations.

The aggressiveness of the strategy did not go unperceived. One review of the Calderón translations in the *Dublin University Magazine* seethes with indignation at such an unwelcome invasion of the English language. This reviewer's argument against assonantal rhyme is simply that the English ear cannot hear it. It is a "delicacy which the Castilian ear has practised itself to but to which our duller organs are quite insensible," because they are programmed to receive good, straightforward sense, not these intricacies of the devil. Assonantal rhyme, the papacy, and imperial Spain are on the same continuum of corruption: "No other country in the world could have produced this perverted genius,"[41] this author avers, referring to Calderón. The reviewer then suggests as a retaliatory, self-protective measure that someone translate *Pilgrim's Progress* into Spanish to check the noxious influence of MacCarthy's translation of Calderón into English. This is precisely the response MacCarthy covertly seeks. He is much more subversive and radical in his translations of Spanish than in his critical prefaces to collections of works "from the Irish." One of the primary benefits of translating Calderón is the affirmation of his identification with a Catholic, European elite, thus countering colonial aspersions on Irish Catholicism. The motive is not unrelated to that involved in writing his biography of Shelley, thus identifying himself with the great Romantic poet who is already, through his anarchic ideology, separate from imperial Britain. What is more, Shelley stayed, when he was in Dublin, in a hotel on Sackville Street near what would become MacCarthy's birthplace a few years later. Being propelled by such identification might suggest a superficiality on MacCarthy's part; but nothing could be further from the truth either with regard to Shelley or to Calderón. Rather, MacCarthy engaged with projects that drew on his entire being. Through Calderón, for example, MacCarthy sounded the deepest recesses of his complicated and intense faith, a territory unavailable to him through direct expression in poetry. One test of his success as a translator is precisely the vehemence with which his Calderón was received.

One particular flailing and bemused attack centers on the whole point of MacCarthy's attraction, the magic in sacramental transformation. Sounding like a latter-day Caesar Otway, this reviewer in the *Dublin University Magazine* criticizes one of Calderón's plays from nothing less than the perspective of the entire Reformation:

> In the "Devotion of the Cross," he represents character as playing fast and loose with right and wrong, and yet getting off in the end through the magical effect of some superstitious amulet. Can a man hold a fire in his hand and not be burned? Yet, Calderón exhibits characters who escape the deadly consequence of their conduct by touching the lignum vitae. They play with evil with impunity, as serpent-charmers with serpents, or as wizards drink off deadly potions to the astonishment of the wondering crowd. This doctrine of indulgence in sin not only debases those who witness it, but it turns the drama off from its legitimate use as a moral instructor to be what it has become, a spectacle to amuse the senses or surprise the fancy, not a school to elevate the feelings and instruct the conscience.[42]

For this reviewer, who pits "feelings" and "conscience" against "the senses" and "fancy," the material world is pitted against the spiritual, and a prejudice lodged against transcendence from one to the other. This argument is the same one lodged against a visionary Lough Derg. Spiritual lessons are ethical lessons learned in this world and productive of an elevation of character, not of a transformation of the soul. The premises of this reviewer are of the kind that lay the foundation for a poetic. What sort of reality, real or ideal, do we inhabit? Can transformations of this essential nature occur in our mortal lives? Is sacrament, essentially transubstantiation, possible? While it is easy to see how subscribing to Calderón's poetic of transformation may be a short step away from envisaging such radical change for a nation, especially one after the Famine, every bit as besieged as a person bowed by sin, indeed even construed as unregenerate on a racial scale, it is also possible to view MacCarthy as being simultaneously anxious for his own salvation, looking for a private solution to sin and mortality.

Writings about MacCarthy after his death stress his religious rectitude, how central to his character it remained. That same eulogist who claimed of MacCarthy, "that during his chequered career no word escaped his pen that could wound the most sensitive modesty," sums up this very complex man as "a gentleman, respectful of modesty." This euphemism is, of course, shorthand for sexual propriety. This familiar tone about MacCarthy echoes Ferguson's on the subject of female sexuality: "Female purity is ever the concomitant, the crown and halo of true love and the sentiment of legitimate desire."[43] That Ferguson is implying the blameless marriage of the Anglo imperial culture over the vulnerable but pure Irish does not prevent this from being a motif for nationalist and unionist alike. Irish gentlemen, Protestant and Catholic, commonly subscribed to this ideal. No wonder MacCarthy feared promiscuity as he looked on the beauty of Dublin Bay and fantasized about a rival. Translating Calderón, who possesses the "consecration of genius,"[44] an appreciation of human complexity, along with a pure Spanish, Catholic pedigree, is intended to quell all such doubts in the Irish poet's soul and all public accusation.

The irony could not be more florid. Even a glance at *Saint Patrick's Purgatory* would have confirmed that hispanophobic reviewer in the *Dublin University Magazine* in his opinion that Calderón is perverted. The play is a fabulous conversion story. Montalvan and Calderón together, however, provide much more of the "before" that makes the "after" a miracle. That is the key, I believe, to MacCarthy's deepest attraction. Calderón, in contrast to the prevailing, idealizing ethos of MacCarthy's time, does not shirk from a full inventory of disruptive human and historical truths. The key to Calderón is a belief in the freeing and cleansing effect of the sacraments, penance being a crucial one. Luis Enius, the Knight Owen figure, arrives at the Lough Derg cave, the site where he will receive penance, only at the tail end of the play, after, that is, a long history of violent crime and lurid sin. Most of the drama consists of a spectacular exposure of the sins that necessitated a penance as dramatic and dangerous, physically and spiritually, as a land and sea excursion to Lough Derg, then descent into hell. Luis Enius recounts in graphic detail or commits before our eyes all his outlandish sins, for instance the murder of a "young maiden's father" and the murder in turn of that man's wife's lover. Fleeing this complicated carnage, he enrolls as a mercenary in the French army under King Stephen, where in the war with England his adeptness at killing wins him honors, an advantage soon eliminated by his double murder of two officers in a brawl. Seeking asylum in a convent, he recognizes a nun as his cousin, violates her under cover of night, abducts her from the convent, and tries to turn her into a prostitute to provide money to support his other pleasures, but she escapes back to the convent and dies. Afraid, as MacCarthy might have been just for translating such abominable doings, that the "very land might reject him," the florid sinner Luis nonetheless returns to his motherland, Ireland, for refuge. On the way, however, he is captured by pirates, who in turn are shipwrecked. Surviving, he ends up at the court of the King of Ireland, where the previous recitation of his crimes is given, but not before his fellow survivor, Saint Patrick, tells his own story, the moral opposite of Luis's narration.

Saint Patrick's story is one of chastity, temperance, and forbearance. His parents are so holy that after Saint Patrick is born they both, as we have seen, retire to "two separate convents." The orphan Saint Patrick leads a life centered on sacred scholarship and the reluctant performance of miracles, until he is captured by the same pirates who have snared Luis. The two are allegorical twins representing Christian goodness and pagan evil. The king handily has two daughters; one, Lesbia, is attracted to Saint Patrick's purity, the other, Polonia, to Luis's abandon. The play's subtext is about moral and psychological conflict. Egerius, King of Ireland, who dreams of such moral opposites, wakes in the first scene prophetically to observe that "I myself upon myself make war." These seem the most personal lines MacCarthy ever wrote. All the doubles in the play are projections of an essential inner conflict. Even the peasant Lucy of the subplot, who torments her phlegmatic husband, Paul, with her adulteries, is there to illustrate the corruption of the flesh. The sins recorded in this play all involve a link between sexuality and violence. Conversion, which occurs instantly, through revelation, involves a magic that makes short work of psychological integration. In the final scene Luis emerges from the cave, where he has witnessed every form of hideous torture, imploring, "Bless me, heaven! In pity bless!" By contrast, in his first appearance, after he and Patrick have both been shipwrecked and survived, he not only asks the devil rather than God to save him, but renounces Patrick's bid for pity from the king and his daughters. Luis boasts, referring to such succor: "I disdain it / From God or man I never hope to gain it." In the conclusion, Luis is suddenly and truly a changed man, transformed from the arrogant soldier who boasted to Polonia earlier, "I dare / Be what now I am, nor care / More to be what I have been."[45] Then he assumed a miracle has happened, but he was still a man of will, not humility. The contrast between the unrepentant and penitent Luis is as stark and absolute as that between hell and heaven, the devil and God, conflict and peace. However much Mac-

Carthy's investment in a form so dependent on a dualistic grid may have made him even more prone to the binarisms of the colonized mind, it also offered a liberation from within, a hope. Listen to him describing the heart of Calderón's religious vision: "Namely, the power of Man to resist, or at least, to triumph over temptation, if he will only listen to the voice of his own soul, and the silent whisperings of repentance and grace."[46] By venturing out, far beyond his national but not his religious culture, for the two were not synonymous, MacCarthy ventured inward, and, I believe, heard the voice of his own soul through the medium of another.

MacCarthy's unique genius led him to Calderón. The integrity of the Catholic Church was his defense against a ravenous nationalism; but that defense left him exposed to another enemy with overweening, conformist designs on the individual: the *Irish* Catholic Church. As Carleton gravitates toward the vertigo he most fears, so MacCarthy is led toward the sanctuary where his real demons live. Calderón's sacramental poetic, building complete spiritual transformation not just into content but form, becomes MacCarthy's opportunity to subvert an already dominant devotionalism. While Calderón's absurdly virtuous Saint Patrick may appear to epitomize the dutiful Irish Catholic, his indispensable alter ego is anything but. The personal transformation achieved according to Calderón is as total as that evoked solemnly by Rilke with the injunction, "You must change your life." Seamus Heaney quotes this at the end of his essay "The Placeless Heaven," written around the time of "Station Island," a poem in which such fundamental psychic and spiritual change is earnestly sought, with unsure results. Heaney's Catholic background does not translate in adulthood into *deus ex machina* angels and devils who perform moral miracles. Still, it is telling that the conflicts that weigh down that poem closely resemble those in the MacCarthy-Calderón. Again, sex and violence are close to the surface. Examination of all the Lough Derg works yields similar comparisons. The very ritual of Lough Derg perennially involves this attempt to reconcile obedience to law, be it religious or social, with obedience to the anarchic impulses integral to the artist, prominently an erotic energy. Personal guilt is perceived as racial guilt. Saint Patrick laments the unregeneracy of his country: "Woe to thee sin stained Ireland."[47] The Irish people themselves are represented as the shadows who wander in hell. Place beside this perception of a people transmogrified by sin, the equally vivid image of the Lough Derg cave as female genitals:

> An open mouth the horrid cavern shapes! Wherewith the melancholy mountain gapes
> This then by mournful cypress trees surrounded between the lips of rocks at either side
> Reveals a monstrous neck of length unbounded,
> Whose tangled hair is scantily supplied
> By the wild herbs that there the wind hath grounded.[48]

Hell itself is referred to in the play as "that dread mother." Place this explicitness beside the coyness of MacCarthy's adulterous guilt about Killiney Bay and you have a measure of the self-discovery accomplished by immersing himself in Calderón, as medieval pilgrims immured themselves in the Lough Derg cave. The purification the cave promised operated on the deepest and most mysterious psychological levels. The sacred ritual, as we have seen, could be described in psychological terms as a male initiation rite, a rebirthing ritual aimed at achieving psychic separation from an Oedipal identification with a voracious, pagan mother. A "Christian gentleman" is the hoped-for result of the rebirth.

Denis Florence MacCarthy died on Good Friday in 1882. Several of the obituaries mention that his mother also died on Good Friday, and that he fervently wished for the repetition. How much he achieved separation from either his mother or from his motherland, indeed how much the two were conflated, we will never know. A crucial moment in the morphology of a Lough Derg underworld experience is the utterance of the all-powerful name of Jesus. The word spoken by a believer banishes demons. In psychological terms, it is as though the father, perceived as integrated, is internalized in the final phase of the Oedipal crisis, thus giving the son a lawful sense of owning his surname. This achievement would represent a redressing of the personal and familial depredations attendant on colonialism. In this resolution, the integrated self triumphs and the psychological demons depart in defeat. I would contend that in translating Calderón, MacCarthy was trying to locate this ideal double who would make personal integration possible. Moreover, translating *Saint Patrick's Purgatory* provided him with an Irish framework, an allegory in which all the human complication he repressed when writing in English for an Irish readership was found in a foreign tongue. MacCarthy, whose translation of Calderón's *Purgatorio* is his uncanny means of entering the unquiet souls of Ireland's dead, achieves his own self-realization through an act of empathy with the dark recesses of human nature, a bold identification that could take place only in secrecy, behind the blinds of translation. That MacCarthy was forced to adopt this indirect route home becomes undeniable from the obituaries. He was caught in a vice of competing but ultimately complicitous expectations, to write in English, to imitate English culture, and to express the pure Irish spirit. In a retrospective essay from an 1831 *Irish Monthly*, we are assured, "With MacCarthy there was no sowing of wild oats. He never wrote a line that might not be read aloud around the family fireside even on a Sunday evening." [49] Clearly, the essayist never read MacCarthy's translations of Calderón. However, even if he did and stumbled on some salacious scenes of murdering, pimping, or adulterous sex, he could take refuge in the knowledge that these inventions were the vile imaginings of a foreigner, not of a true Irish poet.

4

O'Connor, Leslie, Curtayne, and O'Faoláin

Perfect Ease in Home Surroundings

THERE IS NO MAJOR LITERARY Lough Derg work occupying the space between 1880 and 1930. It may be that the pilgrimage, with its penitential core and chthonic aura, speaks more in times of cultural darkness and despair—the Penal Laws, the Great Famine, failed revolutions—than during times of promise and incipient revolution. The glow of cultural nationalism and the literary renaissance did not seek the sepulchral corrective of Lough Derg. The 1930s, however, far from presenting the picture of a sunny resolution to a tragic past, was a period of new darkness. In the aftermath of a bitter civil war that bestowed a legacy of continued division on society, the newly independent state sought a semblance of unity through the invention and imposition of an idea of unsullied Irishness. This ersatz racial purity ironically enjoyed a historical imprimatur. A nation that had suffered repeated traumatic ruptures sought an image of unbroken continuity. This image, bolstered by law, demanded sexual repression, an agricultural base, economic self-sufficiency, a wholesale cultural xenophobia; in short, the steely maintenance of an ultraconservative, ever-devotional Catholicism.

This theocratic culture, which suppressed all hints of heterodoxy, marked the eerie fulfillment of British hegemony. For the poet, an anti-Catholic, Joycean posture might have seemed the only healthy response, but matters were not that simple. The legacy of the literary renaissance via Yeats and Synge involved an anti-Catholic bias supported by a pagan fetishization. This legacy, too, had to be cast off. The problem for the native poet, caught in this vise, became how to assert independence against the double tyrannies of a Catholic state and an anti-Catholic literary paradigm. The thirties heralded the resumption of the project MacCarthy was forced to pursue covertly. After independence, however, it became possible to initiate a realistic and open exploration of Catholicism as a spiritual and aesthetic resource, beyond and distinct from the despotism exercised by the Church as represented by the hierarchy and clergy. Reassessing and refurbishing this link with Catholicism, often by regarding it less as an unassailable monolith and more as an evolving entity with good and bad aspects, became part of the recovery of self-definition, even of connection with the rest of Europe. As we shall see, European Catholicism, with its philosophical predisposition, offered a way for the Irish poet to expand even into modernism, with its internationalist poetic.

On the other hand, there is no doubt that the rabid assertion by the new state of a Catholic identity determined and distorted ordinary life in Ireland in the thirties. There is no need here to go over again the well-charted ground of the actual legislation and cultural projects that shaped this reactionary Catholic state. Terence Brown's *Ireland: A Social and Cultural History, 1922 to the Present* is exhaustive, itemizing various repressive pieces of legislation, such as the Censorship of Films Act of 1923 and the Censorship of Publications Act of 1925, plus the prohibition on divorce in 1925, and successive draconian measures designed to Gaelicize the nation, especially education, through a promotion of the language by punitive means. Brown quotes a joint pastoral letter issued by the Irish bishops in 1927 that laments the susceptibility of the Irish to the moral dangers of modern culture: "The evil one is ever setting his snares for unwary feet. At the moment, his traps for the innocent are chiefly the dance hall, the bad book, the indecent paper, the motion picture, the immodest fashion in female dress—all of which tend to destroy the virtues characteristic of our race."[1] What is, of course, most disturbing about this proclamation is not the litany of lurking snares but the predication of every word on a racial premise, an ironic internalization of Renan and Arnold, of imperialist caricature. All this, the assertion of superhuman purity, the existence of a race apart, is reflected in prose narratives of Lough Derg's history from the period.

Joseph Timoney, for example, an avid, regular pilgrim, wrote a pamphlet on the station for the *Fermanagh Herald* in 1926. Timoney gives us a vivid, detailed picture of the physical place and order of exercises as they were coming up to the thirties, providing a specific context, therefore, for the key modern Lough Derg poems by Kavanagh and Devlin. What is most valuable about the Timoney piece, however, is its tone, an indication of the extravagant piety of the time, and more, of a piety braided tightly into patriotism. This is the new twist added to the Lough Derg legacy. This stance, foreshadowed by D. Canon O'Connor in his book *Lough Derg*, first published in 1879, is brought to lush fulfillment in loyal pilgrims and citizens like Timoney, who claims of Station Island, although he might have been speaking of Ireland, so locked in place is the synecdoche by this point: "It is a Holy Isle, where sin and sorrow never dwelt; a haven of peace, where nothing evil ever entered, another world, where souls find final rest, because they rest in God, secluded from the tumults of the world—a sanctuary of peace, prayer and penance."[2] This is the voice of political isolationism filtered through fervor. Another aspect to all these writings is the sudden, unquestioned acceptance of the historical veracity of Saint Patrick's initiation of the actual pilgrimage. Timoney, modulating certainty with slight approximation, informs his reader that the national apostle founded it "in about the year 445."[3] What is most important, again echoing the efforts of O'Connor, Curtayne, and Leslie, but more immediately reflecting the cultural industry intensified by independence to forge a unified past, is that Timoney puts together a montage of all the texts that add up to a rich, unbroken tradition. He proceeds to construct a legacy composed of everything from the Fenian renditions of the lake's origins to the various accounts left by waves of European pilgrims. What is most remarkable in his assemblage is the way it manages thoroughly to bowdlerize the literature and sanitize the past.

Brown, however, indicates another strand of Catholic influence on culture, not necessarily countering this narrow devotionalism, but providing another dimension, another route for exploration. He points to the international character of Catholicism that also had its place in the mind-set of the period:

> If then the Irishman was faithful to his church because it secured for him a sense of national identity, gave spiritual sanction to his hold on the land, and provided for his sons and daughters respected positions in society without the need for developed intellectual or cultural endowments, it is important to recognize that there was a further altogether more remarkable element in that attachment, which accounts for an important strand in Irish cultural history. For many Irishmen and women the church was an international institution which allowed their small country a significant role on a world stage.[4]

Brown is indicating a profound paradox: an internationalism within the most intractable, narrow nationalism. Lough Derg, given its history, exhibits this convergence and inspires its exploration by a range of authors, not just poets and fiction writers, but a group of writers of popular history. It is no coincidence that, with the establishment of the new state and the process of constructing an identity, Lough Derg comes to the forefront again. It emerges as the quintessential symbol of an Ireland essentially defined as home to an undiluted Catholic race. The vicissitudes suffered by Lough Derg, its various suppressions and revivals, become an extended conceit for the trails and triumphs of the nation itself. At a deeper level, however, the way various writers handle the crosscurrents of Irish and European influences at Lough Derg indicates the interesting variety of positions at this time that chip away at a granite isolationism and devotionalism.

Prior to examining the poems of Kavanagh and Devlin, I would like to look at three monumental efforts, the first ever to provide a comprehensive history for Lough Derg, efforts that parallel the creation of an unbroken lineage for the nation. The first effort displays cultural nationalism at full tilt. It is the pioneering history that brings together MacCarthy's discoveries and much, much more, but all with the kink, ironically, of smoothing over discrepancies and controversies to present a clean line from Saint Patrick forward. This work is Reverend D. Canon O'Connor's *Lough Derg,* first published in 1879, revised in 1903, and reprinted into the 1930s. The second effort is that conducted by Shane Leslie, culminating in his encyclopedic anthology of Lough Derg writings, *Saint Patrick's Purgatory,* published in 1932.

Finally, Alice Curtayne published her *Lough Derg* in 1944, a revision of the history produced by O'Connor. All three works, by exhibiting everything from the rural devotionalism perpetuated by Lough Derg to an increasing awareness, often wariness, of its European ramifications, create a context for Kavanagh's and Devlin's poems, both produced in 1942. O'Connor leans more toward a rural perspective, Curtayne toward the cosmopolitan, but both also defy this pigeonholing. More than anything, they provide telling backgrounds against which to place Kavanagh and Devlin, who as poets will further complicate these two poles from which Lough Derg, implicitly Ireland, is viewed. Fiction writer and cultural critic Seán O'Faoláin, whose "Lovers of the Lake" provides a conclusion to this chapter, occupies a particular niche looking simultaneously in both directions, toward the city and the countryside. Shane Leslie, the convert to Catholicism, whose father mounted the final challenge to the Church's total ownership of "Station Island," exhibits a worrying reflection of the racial essentialism championed by the new state, which in turn mimics the racial undertones of an earlier, Yeatsian idealization of the peasant and the racial rumblings of MacCarthy.

In the second edition of his Lough Derg book, O'Connor also grasped the opportunity to feature at the front of his later edition accolades earned by his earlier one. Along with a string of critical endorsements, the publisher included testimonials from several bishops and an archbishop, thereby imparting the imprimatur of the Church alongside that of the press, a sign of the times. Also, the magazines and newspapers cited not only originate throughout Ireland but range beyond it, tracing in their datelines part of the map of Irish emigration: London, Liverpool, Glasgow, Melbourne. There is even a letter from John Joseph Lynch, archbishop of Toronto. He in fact conveys news of "The Apostolic benediction of Our Holy Father, Pope Leo XIII." He writes from Rome on 25 September 1879, "My Dear Father O'Connor, —This morning the Holy Father favored us with a most agreeable audience." During this conversation, in which the Pope inquired about "everything connected with the state of religion in Toronto," Bishop Lynch, most likely an emigrant to Canada, was able to slip in a plug for Lough Derg: "I then briefly described the great pilgrimage of Saint Patrick's Purgatory, telling of the numbers that frequent it, and the penitential exercises there practiced. The Holy Father said he had already heard of this pilgrimage; and he expressed a great satisfaction at the penance and good works of the pilgrims."[5] The bishop then relates an anecdote that implies all the differences between the penitential asceticism of that remote site on the edge of Europe and the more sumptuous style ensconced at the Vatican. The bishop offers "the Sovereign Pontiff a specimen of the oaten bread and lake water used daily by the pilgrims at their solitary meal. Hereupon he shook his head, as if he considered the dietary scale a very low one."[6] A similar fate befell another souvenir, a shamrock plant brought from Ireland by this bishop, who appears to be representing Canada *faute de mieux*. He reports that the plant "through confinement in my desk, had sickened and lost its leaves, though repeatedly aired by me."[7] The languishing plant, ailing for air, seems a prophetic emblem for the self-enclosed Ireland that will emerge almost as a culmination of this revival in piety after the Famine. Yet another printing of O'Connor's book, a fifth edition, appeared in 1931, including this compendium of praise and encouragement from an earlier time. Because this is the Lough Derg history that sets the tone for reception of the shrine, it is the edition to which I will defer, at the same time indicating crucial, illuminating revisions between the earlier and later versions.

For all the provincialism displayed by the homogeneity of such endorsements, all emanating from Irish Catholic presses, the international reach of these publications indicates the role emigration increasingly played after the Famine in puncturing Ireland's insularity. Not surprisingly, many of these accolades from beyond Ireland play into the self-sufficiency of the insular nation, its singular, spotlighted role as the epitome of Catholic piety. From the *Glasgow Observer* we hear that "every Catholic should read" O'Connor's book "if only for the object of realizing more forcibly that it is not necessary to go to the Continent in order to visit sacred shrines, where spiritual favors are bestowed in a special manner on the children of the Church."[8] What we hear is the retrospective hagiography of Ireland itself by the emigrant. What is more, these snippets of letters and reviews also indicate the major cultural perspectives of the time. A reviewer from Melbourne, for example, picks up on one of O'Connor's key points about Lough Derg, a political more than a religious perspective, that the history of Lough Derg encapsulates the essence of the history of the Catholic Church in Ireland. The reviewer observes, "The fortunes of this little islet bear a curious resemblance in miniature to the history of the Catholic Church in Ireland at large."[9] The speaker is really referring, as is O'Connor, to the history of Ireland, which to them is synonymous with that of the Church. A letter from Charles Gavan Duffy dated 17 October 1895 makes a similar point, but includes a suggestion of the way in which Lough Derg also stimulates a personal and unforced ancestral connection. Says Duffy, "When I was about ten years of age—about 1826 I think—I visited the island with my mother and made a station there. Whenever Ireland shall possess a perfect history, the author will owe you valuable suggestions on the customs and manners of a pious race intensely conservative of old habits and traditions."[10] The phrase, "a perfect history," to denote the redress of a tragic history is telling for the way such restoration of the nation is equated with a total elimination of imperfection. Duffy also suggests the means by which this will be achieved, namely through the emulation of a piety and conservatism modeled by a Catholic past epitomized by Lough Derg. This is nationalism with a penitential cast. More positively, this nationalism is rooted not just in an abstract idea of the purity of individual, purged souls and a purged nation, but in the recovery and validation of an oral culture, a chain of memory particularly generated by women, who are always associated stereotypically with the obedient observance of Lough Derg. The pilgrimage itself becomes like the thread attached to Carleton's blister. It draws one back to vital memory, though for the purifying nationalist it is memory cleansed of pain. This period, a hundred years after Carleton's birth, is a time for reviling the Tyrone author for his treacherous misrepresentation of Lough Derg. Bishop John K. O'Doherty writes from the "Bishop's House, Derry, September 5th, 1895" and reflects sentiments of relief but vigilance after Catholic Emancipation:

> It is worthy of admiration to see so many writers of late years preserving for posterity the glorious history of our ancient shrines and sanctuaries. That history, it is true, lived in the traditions of our people through the long, dark night of persecution, but with the light of freedom there was danger of its being forgotten were not some faithful chronicler found to inscribe it in our annals. This task you have nobly done for the sanctuary of Lough Derg; and when the foul calumnies of Richardson are forgotten, and the sneers of Carleton have gone down to the grave of oblivion, your history will remain as a text book and an authority on all that pertains to the hallowed Purgatory of Saint Patrick.[11]

Such pseudo-historiographical speculation, that negative representations of Lough Derg will disappear and this glowing view prevail, bespeaks the same alchemical effort Gavan Duffy alludes to, of achieving a "perfect history."

O'Connor himself sets the gold standard for such revisionism. What is more, such an effort intensifies with the actual revisions he made in the second edition, where he excises the following melancholy description of the ruins remaining at Lough Derg because any suggestion of bleakness and forlornness might inadvertently support Carleton. This passage, from the first edition, *Lough Derg*, does not appear in the introductory words to subsequent printings: "the monumental ivy itself, which is swathed round their walls, as if to preserve them from the mouldering influence of time, waves mournfully in the sobbing wind over the ruins, seeming still to reach the solemn strains of the pious inmates who used to chaunt within those hallowed precincts."[12] Later and with only minor revisions in the second edition, O'Connor roundly chastises Carleton for his many betrayals, not least for being a protégé of the bigoted Caesar Otway. Carleton is dismissed as opportunistic and vindictive:

> William Carleton himself had been in his early days an aspirant to the priesthood. Being foiled in this, and failing to obtain from Bishop Murphy an appointment to one of the diocesan burses in College, he placed himself under the patronage of Caesar Otway, and thenceforth devoted his versatile talents to ridicule not only the foibles and peculiarities of an untutored peasantry, but even the religious customs and practices of Irish Catholics. Born in the town land of Kilnahussoge, parish of Clogher, in 1795, he came as a pilgrim to Lough Derg in 1820 [sic]. Of that journey he wrote a very ludicrous account in which he himself figures as the Lough Derg Pilgrim. Caesar Otway, it is averred, retouched the tale, supplied not only its colouring, but much new matter, and had it published at his own expense.[13]

According to this narration, Carleton, though wily, is practically denied authorship, certainly the key role in publishing such heresy. Like Adam tempted by Eve, Carleton, however corrupt, is the Catholic victim of the ultra-Protestant Otway's proselytizing and scheming.

This revisionist mission is evident throughout O'Connor's nonetheless impressively researched tome. For example, he can both boast of the medieval fame of the pilgrimage and deny the central place of the vision literature attached to this strand of the tradition. Such contradictions are sprinkled throughout the original version of the book. On an opening page O'Connor proudly claims of the pilgrimage, "so celebrated was it that during the Middle Ages it enjoyed a continental fame."[14] He quotes Rev. Sylvester Malone's earlier claim: "There was a time when a pilgrimage to Lough Derg was scarcely less famous than that to the shrine of the Apostle to St. James at Compostella in Spain."[15] Although the later edition tones down this dubious visionary link to the Continent, the cited reviews of O'Connor's first edition gloat about this medieval distinction, especially the effect of Lough Derg on classical literature. The critic for the *New Ireland Review* applauds O'Connor's "knowledge of his subject in all its developments," going on to single out this example of influence in the Middle Ages: "The medieval chronicles and visions connected with the penitentiary have left their impress on portions of Europe's greatest literature. The vision of Enius or Owen suggested and helped to mould the immortal *Commedia* of Dante; while kindred stories inspired one of Calderón's dramas."[16] Another reviewer in regard to O'Connor's treatment of this European legacy strikes a negative note, a rare inclusion in this garnering of overwhelming approbation. Commenting on O'Connor's coverage of the Dante intersection, this critic chides, "our author might have made more, since numerous and competent Dantesque authorities maintain that the great Italian poet derived much of the general idea of the *Divine Comedy* from the widely bruited western lake."[17] This critic, writing for the *Journal of the Waterford Archaeological Society,* errs in the one direction, exaggerating the medieval influence, especially that on Dante, of Lough Derg, but O'Connor is guilty of the opposite, downplaying this effect, even in the first edition. In his opening words to the second edition, in dramatic contrast to those reviewers who trumpet this medieval fame, O'Connor expressly warns, "During the Middle Ages poetic imagination and romance had invented a very erroneous and misleading picture of Saint Patrick's Purgatory."[18] O'Connor is reacting specifically to all claims of the fantastical and supernatural associated with the site. In a footnote he mentions as an instance of such error the unhinged hyperbole of twelfth-century writer Gautier de Metz, who revealed: "In Ireland there is a place from which day and night issues fire; it is called Saint Patrick's Purgatory, and, if any persons enter it without having repented, they are immediately carried off, and no one can tell what has become of them."[19] O'Connor will eventually come straight out and discredit the Knight Owen story, the basis of the very works of great literature hitherto enlisted to bolster Lough Derg. He says of that seminal text:

This narrative regarding the Knight Owen is to be received with the proverbial "grain of salt"; for it is written at a time when the love of the marvellous held great sway over the minds of men. Highly sensational and chivalrous accounts of the Christian Knights, of the exploits in the Crusades, together with the passion for romance, kept alive by the Trouveres and Troubedours, pervade the literature of the period and obscure passing events under the colouring of fiction. Hence, we may regard the different accounts of the Knight's Vision, and of the poems founded thereon by Dante, Ariosto and Calderon, as containing much that is largely imaginary and poetic.[20]

Tellingly, O'Connor's language firms up from the original to the second edition. Originally he tells us that "this narrative is to be received with great limitation."[21] "Great limitation" becomes "the proverbial 'grain of salt'." O'Connor's judgment, half-grounded in scholarship and half in obedience to his betters, is exerted to protect the Irish Church against any vitiation in the mechanical and perfect exercise of works.

The most emphatic evidence of the tenor of O'Connor's narrative is his preference for a penitential rather than a legendary, purgatorial Lough Derg. Grappling with the origin of the name, "Saint Patrick's Purgatory," O'Connor provides two textual foundations for the purgatorial association: one is from "a Louvain treatise of the 17th century, called the 'Mirror of Penance' "; the second is attributed to "Matthew of Paris, whose opinion is followed by Denis the Carthusian and St. Antoninus."[22] According to the first, Saint Patrick entered the cave "that the pains of Purgatory might be revealed to him."[23] Having been granted his request, he "ordered that henceforth the island should be made a terrestrial purgatory."[24] (Notice O'Connor's care not to make the island the real, extraterrestrial purgatory.) According to the second version, the saint, frustrated by the unrepentant and skeptical Irish, prayed to gain the power to reveal to his flock "those pains and pleasures of the future life of which he preached."[25] Granted this power, he struck the earth with his staff and a huge pit opened up "into which those who might enter truly repentant and remain there one whole day and night would be cleansed of the offenses of their whole life."[26] Citing the textual foundation for the "very erroneous and misleading picture of Saint Patrick's Purgatory,"[27] O'Connor, as though having ceded ground to the enemy, immediately acts to reclaim an orthodoxy based in works, not fireworks. This turn in his argument foreshadows the particular use of Saint Patrick that we will see in these early, expository twentieth-century Lough Derg writings: Saint Patrick becomes the exemplar of a plodding, sober piety. O'Connor is careful to ascribe no more to Saint Patrick than works the ordinary Catholic can emulate. The preceding paragraph relating the story of the earth opening under the National Apostle's staff discourages such albeit textually based belief in the origin of the name, "Saint Patrick's Purgatory," for an explanation born merely of common sense: "The origin of the name, however, is sufficiently accounted for by the fact that Saint Patrick selected this island for the performance of those works of penance, for which he was so remarkable, and that so many saints and pious pilgrims alike imitated his example."[28] "Saints and pious pilgrims alike" can be put on the same footing because both perform exemplary "works of penance." Furthermore, O'Connor accounts for the gap in historical records of the shrine in the early Christian centuries of Ireland by seeing the site as "a place of private devotion and penance."[29] This, too, is a prophetic turn in the argument, which predicts the tenor of later, postindependence arguments that locate the true Lough Derg as this devotional, penitential, above all Irish site, a penitentiary, not the purgatory of spurious European visions.

O'Connor's overriding purpose is to use Lough Derg to trace an unbroken tradition in Irish history that compensates for and ultimately denies the pain of rupture. He also uses the continuity of Roman Catholicism as a means of redressing disruption suffered by Irish Catholicism. Turning his attention to the destruction of the Augustinian priory and the routing of the monks themselves by Cromwellians in the seventeenth century, he latches onto the aftermath of this attempted erasure as evidence not just of endurance but of immortality. The source of unflagging life is the people themselves, the Church in its broadest and most essential sense. The survival of Lough Derg, however, takes place in tandem with the survival of Ireland. This ringing declaration appears in both editions:

> But mid weal and woe the Irish heart had entwined round the holy island of Lough Derg. Though the Augustinian Canons were not destined to return to Saints' Island, a place of residence for the officiating priests was erected on Station Island; the ruined Church and crosses and oratories were again put in some sort of repair by loving hands; and the pilgrimage rose again, phoenix-like from its ashes.[30]

The most compelling aspect of O'Connor's narrative, however, is the way it displays an assimilation of Reformation criticism of Lough Derg. His disapproval of the visionary claims attached to Saint Patrick's Purgatory is a direct mirroring of Reformationist objections. It is ironic that he dismisses the "so-called Reformation," then replicates one of its postures. He sees "poetic imagination" as the culprit. It "conducted those who visited the island . . . first to the regions of Purgatory, and afterwards to the abodes of the blessed or of the damned."[31] Then follows evidence of his collusion with the site's seventeenth-century detractors: "At the outbreak of the so-called Reformation, Protestant writers seized on these legends and tales, as if they were matters of fact, and made use of them in order to cast ridicule on the pious practices of the Catholic Church."[32] It is clear that "poetic imagination" will be quashed to preserve "pious practices." Furthermore, the Vatican is credited with steering the course of orthodoxy, of carefully avoiding the excesses of fancy on which the Church might founder. So much does the hierarchy subsume the pilgrimage for O'Connor that, despite the irony of crediting the people with its preservation under Cromwell, its closure by the Vatican at the end of the fifteenth century is adduced as evidence of a continuity based in a preservation of doctrinal correctness. In the wake of the infamous Dutch monk's disclosure of simony and fraud, Pope Alexander VI ordered the pilgrimage to cease, an act, according to O'Connor, that shows how "the Church guards her holy places against even the least infringement of the established and authorised disciple."[33] No obstacle to a myth of continuity fails to be dissolved by rationalization. In sum, all the attacks over the centuries on the pilgrimage are homogenized into proof of its undeniable sanctity.

Again, the synecdoche of Lough Derg as Ireland is implicit. Nothing can be such a consistent object of doubters and detractors, he asserts, that is not holy and unique: "It is a mark of the sanctity of a place to be made the constant object of attack by heretical and infidel writers."[34] So absolutely intent is O'Connor on preserving an inviolate and uninterrupted tradition of sanctity that, when the attacker is the Vatican and the object is precisely one of the "pious practices" associated with the pilgrimage, still the verdict is that its purity has been preserved. In 1805 the Holy See, in response to a fifteen-year renewal for the "usual faculties and indulgences vouchsafed to this pilgrimage"[35] denied the application. Yet another disruption is touted as continuity. O'Connor interprets that action as a sign by which to understand "with what vigilance the authorities in Rome had watched over this sanctuary."[36] The reason for the assurance is that Rome had checked yet another excess, the performance of the circling of the beds, the *turas,* on hands and knees. Although O'Connor is quick to point out (in parentheses) that the reports of such overly zealous, self-mortifying practices were "(perhaps groundless and gratuitous),"[37] he is still encouraged in arguing for the pilgrimage's impeccable and continuous history. That he is implicitly agreeing with Carleton and his Protestant cohorts, who were repelled by such mindless self-mortification, is an irony that O'Connor does not register.

To be finally ratified, this seamless tradition must enjoy a pristine, incontrovertible, sacred origin. In fact nothing will do but to locate a beginning in the life of the National Apostle himself. In a work displaying an impressive amount of historical research, O'Connor's *Lough Derg* is open about predicating this patrician origin finally on folk tradition:

> In the absence of positive historical records, there are grounds of presumption so strong as to bring with them conviction. In the first place, there exists a vivid and continuous tradition, that he visited it for deeds of penance, for retreat and silent prayer; and, seeing that the Irish race have always regarded their patron saint with the most affectionate veneration, and have carefully treasured up, and handed down from generation to generation, the minutest particulars regarding his life and labours, we should attach great importance to this tradition.[38]

While O'Connor may be found guilty of rationalizing and succumbing to the pressure to affirm legend, such is the paradoxical heart of most advances in postcolonial recovery that he may also be seen as giving a new credence to oral culture. Nationalism dictates the specious reasoning of the myth of origin; nationalism also gives the voice of the disenfranchised, for so long an Irish rather than English tongue, legitimacy. As the twentieth century progressed, resulting, for example, in the establishment of an Irish Folklore Commission in 1935, stories that had been handed down through the generations became an increasingly important resource. With regard to Lough Derg, even material culture will prove a significant addition to a rounded history of the site, since not just stories but objects can be passed down, especially souvenirs from a place to which people travel.

For example, on the last page of the 1843 edition of "The Lough Derg Pilgrim," there is an illustration meant to accompany the story's conclusion. The center of the etching rests on a depiction of amulets from Lough Derg. Carleton's text mentions only "Lough Derg pebbles, taken from the lake, brought home and distributed to loved ones, and flouted as proof of one's piety."[39] The accompanying illustration, however, is of two women, one dipping into a deep pocket, presumably fishing up the money to pay some huckster for a crude crucifix. The disjunction set up by the text and the illustration asks a question. Were there special crucifixes that served the same memorial purpose as the retrieved pebbles? In 1958 a landmark archaeological argument appeared in a pamphlet by A. T. Lucas entitled "Penal Crucifixes."[40] Lucas essays and proves that a number of carved wooden crucifixes found in a variety of locations in Ireland share a common provenance in Lough Derg, either manufactured for a pilgrimage or purchased at one. The crosses, found in places that cleave to a demographic map of where Lough Derg pilgrims in the early nineteenth century came from, locate a verifiable custom. I include this digression as a way of underlining how O'Connor's appeals to popular culture may be as prescient as they are wrongheaded.

That O'Connor's primary aim as an author is racial edification resting on a nationalist platform rings out as he emotes in his conclusion:

> Seeing the peculiar efficacy of the exercises of this pilgrimage towards renewing and increasing the spiritual life, the sanctity of the place, and the graces and indulgences there received, what wonder is it that the eye of the pilgrim is charmed, his heart elevated, his faith enlivened, nay, even his love for holy Ireland increased when first the island of Lough Derg meets his view?[41]

O'Connor casts this imperative as a rhetorical question (One will be so edified!). Even attaching the qualifier "Nay even" to a final injunction, that a "love for holy Ireland" be produced on a first sighting of Lough Derg, does nothing to blunt the social pressure carried by such rhetoric. The clear message is that such feelings are part of an orthodoxy as Irish as it is Catholic. That such a gush of piety defies the grim experience of the Irish bards is another irony lost on O'Connor, who serves both a historically determined and a subjective idea of the nation. O'Connor is ensnared in the dialectics of postcoloniality. His is the ultimate correction of the unfortunate swerve in heterodoxy and independence achieved by Carleton. Deviation from a prescribed response is prohibited. Yet the transport O'Connor envisages is meant to be instantaneous, an outrageous irony, a lapse into favoring lurid vision over penitential process. O'Connor not only unwittingly endorses such magic but sees it even more miraculously as occurring by anticipation alone. O'Connor sets the watermark for the knee-jerk and illogical nationalistic piety of the century that lay ahead.

Shane Leslie—landlord, scholar, racial theorist, and nationalist—offers such a mixture of attitudes in relation to the native population, from glints of sensitivity to glaring snobbery, that it is almost impossible to distinguish and separate positive and negative qualities. These are so completely melded that they, too, bespeak the paradoxes of postcoloniality from the Anglo-Irish perspective. Leslie's Celticism and conversion are both signs of a proprietary pride and a genuine appreciation culminating in emulation. His apotheosizing of the peasant is as Yeatsian as it is de Valerian. Both those romanticizing strands are, in fact, twisted and turned upon each other and more than twice as strong because of this collusion. To speculate sympathetically about Leslie's life is to sketch a sensitive personality atoning for the rapacity of his landlord ancestors by becoming more Irish than the Irish. It is also tenable to adduce, however, a personality warped by petulance, an Englishman, an Etonian, who did not quite succeed in these imperial terms and retreated into the quite comical superiority of being a Celt manqué. To the student of Lough Derg, Leslie is best known for his compendious anthology of Lough Derg writings. There, Leslie lays out the European heritage of the site in its impressive variety and breadth. An earlier and a later book, however, provide hints as to the motives for this scholarly Lough Derg project. Leslie wrote two memoirs, one prematurely, *The End of a Chapter,* penned when he was just over twenty years old and recuperating from a wound incurred at the front in World War I. To this young man of promise and pedigree, that juncture in history seemed indeed like the far end of an era. Much of the material in that early work about his youth is reworked in the first sections of his late memoir of 1966, *Long Shadows.* In 1917, the year of the publication of *The End of a Chapter,* Leslie also brought out a crazed treatise on race, an unfortunate product of the times, a pseudohistory called *The Celt and the World.*

In *Long Shadows* Leslie writes innocently enough, "During the First World War, when all our family were absent, an enormous pike was netted in our Donegal lake, Lough Derg."[42] Today's guileless reader registers a shock to realize that this legendary site, which seems by now owned by history, actually belonged in the early part of the twentieth century to a particular family. This proprietary fact radiates out from this quite comprehensive anthology of Lough Derg writing complied by Leslie. While Shane Leslie (born John Randolph Leslie, but changing his name "in an outburst of Celtic fervour"[43]) will see the dispersal of almost all Leslie lands after Irish independence, the lake is so surrounded by family myth for him that it may as well still be "our lake." To appreciate how selectively Leslie discloses the details of the intricate relationship of the Leslies to Ireland, especially Lough Derg, which in his time is Ireland, it is necessary to begin with another, no less biased version of this tangled matter. Indeed, to place these two skewed narratives side by side is to receive an elegant lesson in the paradoxes of postcoloniality. The two accounts mirror each other, both replicating and opposing the other's perspective.

As Curtayne will relate in 1944, the Leslie family for over 250 years, from 1661

to 1917, was at the center of a dispute over Station Island. According to her, repeated generations of Leslies opposed in British courts the claim of the Catholic
Church to ownership of the island. As Lough Derg achieved the status of an emblem for Ireland, so this alleged usurpation by the Leslies looms as an emblem, for
Curtayne, of British colonialism as a whole. A story of seemingly endless litigious
ploys and ruses, in short it is about efforts by the Leslies to prove their ownership
implicitly by securing rents from families retaining huts on the islands where pilgrims slept. Curtayne registers no irony when she relates how an indignant Church
responded in kind. A certain Catholic Bishop of Clogher interceded boldly in the
early nineteenth century by essentially evicting tenants in order to prove de facto
Church ownership. Curtayne, however, avoids the verb "evict." She refers to the
Bishop "ejecting" the cabin keepers, who were then "reinstated."[44] The Church
thereby demonstrated its power and proprietary right by this maneuver that mim-
icked landlord tactics. The very Catholic Curtayne's verdict is: "Great honour indeed is due the Clogher diocese for the determination with which they held on to
their rights on Station Island."[45] In contrast, while elsewhere singling out the convert, Shane Leslie, as an invaluable scholar, she, by her own lights, paints his ancestors as devious, grasping and petty to a man. For example, she explains the legal
saga of how an attempt in 1880 to build a hostel to house pilgrims resulted in Sir
John Leslie, Shane Leslie's grandfather, objecting to the encroachment of the building out onto the lake, specifically onto a ledge of rock usually covered with water.
As undisputed owner of the lake, he directly challenged the right of the Church to
erect this building and indirectly challenged once again ownership of Station Island. In 1916 Shane Leslie's father, also Sir John, tried legally to appropriate a cottage on Station Island lived in for generations by a family called Muldoon, who had
bequeathed the house to the Catholic Bishop of Clogher. Both these cases were finally settled out of court with the Leslie family coming to some accommodation
with the Catholic Church. In a no doubt conciliatory gesture, perhaps prompted by
his son, Sir John in 1929 donated a Murillo Madonna to the diocese to decorate the
new Basilica on Lough Derg. As Curtayne tartly puts it: "to the owner's disappointment, the painting was not hung in the church. Both Sir John Lavery, whose
opinion was sought, and the architect were firm in their opinion that no picture
should be hung there, as it would conflict with the design and planned simplicity of
that interior. The painting was, therefore, hung in the outer sacristy,"[46] a gesture of
retaliatory marginalization, as conveyed by Curtayne's lethal understatement. Not
incidentally, cosmopolitan Catholic sensibility is also shown as possessing a restraint and taste unavailable to Sir John, whose lavish, guilty generosity is two centuries too late.

Curtayne narrates a tale of certain doom at Lough Derg. She positions the site
as destined to suffer repeated Protestant interference from the Leslies. Shane Leslie,
in contrast, portrays his gallant family as Catholic sympathizers to their own cost.
Curtayne locates the seed of loss of Catholic autonomy in the treacherous machina-
tions of what she dubs the "apostate McGraths,"[47] the lake's original owners. Ac-

cording to Curtayne, "The cloud of disputed ownership first settled on Lough Derg in 1596, when Donough Magrath made that historic surrender to Queen Elizabeth of all the lands around the lake (known as 'termon Magrath') 'for the purpose of reducing the lands to English tenure.' "[48] Curtayne sees Magrath as a dupe succumbing to the "surrender and re-grant fiction."[49] Magrath naïvely believed, in other words, that ceding his lands to England would result, as promised by the English, in an immediate return of them to him as a "gift."[50] He saw such a maneuver, an act of cooperation with the Crown, as providing greater security of inheritance for his male heirs. Curtayne reads cooperation as collusion, a pattern repeated when a later McGrath turned over his lease of *termon* Magrath to an heir and successor of the notorious Protestant Bishop Spottiswoode, despoiler of Saints Island. From then on Lough Derg was part of extensive Protestant See lands in the area, and all this devolved onto Bishop John Leslie, "when he was installed in the See of Clogher in 1661."[51] Curtayne implies that by nefarious means Bishop Leslie bequeathed church land privately to his son and in so doing established Leslie ownership of Lough Derg. Shane Leslie, the eventual recipient of this legacy, portrays his family as having staunch Catholic connections from the beginning. This impeccable line starts with the original "Fighting Bishop,"[52] John Leslie, so named because, as his descendant puts it in *The End of a Chapter,* he "kept his diocese of the Isles creditably clear of Cromwellians during the Civil War. In Ireland, as Bishop of Raphoe, he built a fort instead of a palace. . . . Before battle he used to invoke divine neutrality on the plea that "though we are sinners, the enemy are not saints."[53] This is the even-handed neutrality we shall eventually see Shane Leslie arrogate to himself.

If isolated, prominent threads of this ancestral tapestry are picked out from the opening lines of the later *Long Shadows,* we observe the following as the religious and political coloration of the Leslies. Leslie roundly declares: "The Glaslough Leslies came to Ireland from Scotland thanks to the Stuarts whom they served to the end. They were Jacobites, stood by Jacobus (King James) and refused as Non-Jurors to swear to King William the Usurper."[54] The Fighting Bishop's son Charles, exiled by Williamites and living in France, "acted as a liaison between Stuart 'pretenders' and the English Church."[55] Shane Leslie rounds out this history by saying, "In spite of being on the losing side of the Boyne, the Leslies were allowed to take a seat in the Irish, and later the English, House of Commons."[56] Illustrating a closeness with the native population, he boasts, "Old Irish Clansman made up the mob with which the Leslies fought the Westenras (Lords Rossmore) on election days."[57] This putative bond with the natives is reinforced, according to the author, when he exhumes from an O'Callaghan grave and reerects on a pedestal the fourteenth-century sacred monument, the McKenna Stone and Cross. The ownership of this icon was as bitterly disputed over the centuries as that of Station Island. Leslie's authoritative retrieval is greeted, according to him, with "the satisfaction of Protestant and Catholic alike."[58] The controversial stone was, according to Leslie, restored to its proper place in "the old cemetery, which Bishop Leslie abandoned, although it was consecrated by Saint Patrick himself." Routed by Williamites, the old Fighting Bishop, and therefore the Leslies, in other words, enjoyed the imprimatur of Saint Patrick. Here, in short we have a counternarrative of impeccable origin and a similar fixation with demonstrating an unbroken lineage.

On a parallel course, Leslie is intent on installing his family, with their Jacobite tenacity, as paragons of English aristocracy, if not in fact closer to a true monarchy than the racially compromised Hanoverians. Speaking of the common Teutonic domination of England and Germany, he opined in 1917, "The thrones of Hanover and England composed a single, joint-stock monarchy."[59] Much of *The End of a Chapter* and *Long Shadows* both are devoted to establishing a pedigree for Leslie that not only rivals that of the reigning monarch but bests it. Winston Churchill was Leslie's cousin; his mother is the more subdued sister of the beguiling and flamboyant Jennie Jerome, Churchill's mother. The family story that links Leslie directly by blood with the monarchy implies that he belongs to a truer line than that of the enthroned. The story, a reprise of the Jacobite struggle, concerns a Mrs. Fitzherbert. According to Leslie, Mrs. Fitzherbert is the first and only valid wife of George IV and the mother of the woman Leslie's grandfather married. Again the cause both of the purity of this line and its marginalization is its staunch Catholicism. Mrs. Fitzherbert was a Catholic who was married, by whom we are not told, to George IV "in the presence of her brother and uncle when Prince of Wales."[60] Further, "even after he slighted her and married an official queen, she was willing to return to him with the permission of the Pope, in whose eyes her marriage remained legal and binding."[61]

The choices with regard to Ireland and England, Protestantism and Catholicism, that Shane Leslie makes suggest that he locates the ideal, Arnoldian balance of the opposite but interdependent qualities of Saxon and Celt in himself. Leslie found Eton an essentially secular institution where sport and decency were inculcated as the upper-class British religion: "The religion taught at the great schools amounts practically to a light coat of moral disinfectant with a sentimental affection for the school chapel thrown in."[62] Speaking more generally of Anglicanism, he observes, "The Ideal of the English Church has been to provide a resident gentleman for every parish in the kingdom and there have been worse ideals."[63] Leslie, a Cambridge graduate, converted to Rome while serving as a volunteer in London's docklands with a Christian-communist organization manned by Oxford, Newmanesque converts. Although the chapter in *Long Shadows* on this postgraduate period of his life, which also involved a stint in 1907 in Russia, contains its own unprobed shadows (his attempt to translate Plato's "Symposium"—an act which may have "paved the way for a serener view of those sexual entanglements which still disturb the British conscience"[64]—and his zealous effort at reforming, indeed his excessive curiosity about, prostitutes),[65] Leslie would like his reader to see his conversion to Catholicism as effecting a resolution of both personal and historical complexity.

Leslie's conversion, clearly a complicated process entailing the otherwise clashing demands of class and spiritual issues, produced in him a religious bearing in the world that for sheer dread of the body rivaled any born member of "Clan Jansen," as Devlin would call the Irish. Leslie, for example, confesses with pride: "My wife remembered that on our wedding night I drew out a bottle of holy water which I scattered upon her bosom to the slow chant of the Asperges."[66] The staged, self-conscious theatricality of this mime is perhaps explained by a master script encoded elsewhere, which divulges feelings and prejudices toward Ireland that make an embracing of that country's dominant religion a very complicated act. That Leslie equates Ireland, specifically the abstract, racial concept of Celticism, with Catholicism is the key to his decision. Unlike the native writers on Lough Derg, such as MacCarthy, intent on erecting a barrier between pagan and Christian Ireland, Leslie sees Catholicism as refining and consummating all that is Celtic. His derivative but fanatical racial theories hinge on a conviction that the Celt is the last and finest representative of an Aryan race; similarly that Catholicism exists at this apex: "Saint Patrick and his order came to fulfil rather than destroy what lay behind the Celtic mind."[67] The Great War is cast as a battle between Celt and Teuton: "All the minglement of blood shed on European battlefields cannot conceal the fact that at heart the great War is a Teuton family split."[68] The battle over the legitimacy of Mrs. Fitzherbert's line is a miniature illustration of this larger battle, centered finally in Britain and over its throne. As he puts it, "Medieval Europe was built on faith, but modern Europe on force."[69] Originating in Asia, the Aryan moved west coming to rest in its last stronghold on the western coast of Ireland:

> The Celt of western Europe was the foam on the crest of the Aryan wave, and his descendants in Ireland as the most insulated of the Celts should be the purest and strongest in blood. If the Aryans left descendants, the Irish are among them. In Europe the Aryan formed his true inheritance, for the Aryan instinct moves west and ever west.[70]

To read these words, "west and ever west," is also to hear Gabriel Conroy's somnolent resolve to make his journey west, into death, into an absolutism he has feared, given the fetishizing of the west in the literary renaissance in response to the direction pursued in Old Irish journey myths. Leslie's imposition of an Aryan gloss on this romanticization adds a menacing layer to it, more generally to the literature of Lough Derg and Ireland at this time.

It is this besieged Aryanism, pushed farther and farther west and into extinction, that adds a controversial twist to Leslie's portrait of Ireland. He describes it as "a Celtic nation stranded in a Teuton world,"[71] as a "martyr nation," that "seemed to suffer a perennial Purgatory for the sins of others."[72] This posture, of a country offering itself up for the sins of others, will be reprised in Denis Devlin's "Lough Derg." For his part, Leslie telescopes the bloodshed of 1916 into a more universal apocalypse, therefore exponentially intensifying the fusion of religion and patriotism: "Patriots went out to die for Ireland and found themselves martyred for religion."[73] This climax meets with his approbation, being the opposite of English and German secularism: "When Germany and England abandoned Catholicism they sought other gods."[74] The salvation and freedom of Ireland become synonymous with the spiritual preservation and liberation of Europe. Lying in a hospital bed, composing *The End of a Chapter* and *The Celt and the World*, Leslie is arriving at what he perceives to be the deeper issues of the Great War, that "Teuton family split"; this fallout comes to rest not just in Ireland, but virtually in his back yard, at Lough Derg, seat of that medieval Catholicism that Teuton greed destroyed. Leslie outdoes O'Connor in his denunciation of the Reformation, but from another point of departure avers: "The Reformation proved a dividing and scattering force among Aryans."[75]

Nothing less than the complete reparation of Europe and ensured dominance of the white, Christian race rests on the preservation of Irish culture. The linked symmetry of nativism and Nazism is scarily to the fore of Leslie's theories. On the other hand, the irony of loathing Germany and espousing Aryanism is not noted. Ireland becomes the supreme, God-given, Aryan nation. Leslie views it as not only a western refuge but also as a northern one. Indicating the direction in which salvation lies, he tells his reader, "Irish legend says that Christ looked northward from the cross."[76] Christ was clearly overlooking the southern, non-Caucasian latitudes. If the Great War created monumental doubt about the values of Western civilization, their restoration lay for Leslie in a reaffirmation of white supremacy: "If hope in the future is clouded and clarity excluded in the present, the baffled optimist must renew his faith in the destiny of the white man out of the past."[77] The warning note the war has sounded is not for him in the extinction of a set of values but of a race to which he attaches these values. The consequence of the pure, white Celt being overcome by the racially compromised Teuton, the enemy within England, is that "the supremacy of the European and the priority of the white man may be threatened."[78] The abrogation of certain basic principles of human behavior is nothing compared to the breaching of racial and national barriers that a world war has caused, further creating an apocalyptic flooding and commingling of different kinds of blood: "The law of race is the primary Aryan law. For the Aryan to mingle with the non-Aryan—the dark, Negroid yellow Mongoloid—is fatal."[79] In sum, "Nature approves the blending of similar race stock, but abhors the mongrel and mestizo."[80] Ireland presents the potential for being a paragon of racial homogeneity, the very myth constructed by means of cultural nationalism, then ratified by independence.

How does Shane Leslie, an Anglo-Irishman, fit himself seamlessly into this constructed identity? First, his retrieval of the threatened Celt in his English soul appears to be an act of faith. It aids an evolution that could go another way, but now has a chance of a positive outcome: "It is perfectly scientific to include Englishmen under the wide term Teutonic, though efforts have been made recently to show that English blood is more Celtic than German."[81] Just as an argument for the existence of God can be made from the fact that some external force inspires belief, so Leslie seems to assume that his very election of the Celt in himself and demonstration of a martyred, besieged condition, plus an innate aversion to the Teuton, are sufficient proof of his racial superiority: "Wherever Celtic blood survives today, it has asserted itself in intractability to the Teuton."[82] And yet the actual Irish seem to baffle and defy him, creating cracks in his racial conceptualization and categorization that threaten his project. He is particularly perturbed by the alliance between Ireland and Germany that developed before 1916 in an effort to secure arms: "The Irish have no racial or historic right (whatever the pressure of ephemeral politics) to be pro-German."[83] That use of the word "ephemeral" alerts us to Leslie's distance from the pressing, actual reasons for Irish independence, his focus being more on the massive and slow, seismic shifts in the contours of race. Ireland's battle should not be with the English but with Teutonic philistinism and racial impurity. Leslie has no doubt on which side God is fighting: " 'To war against France is to war against God,' cried Joan of Arc, like a Celtic prophetess inspired."[84] As abhorrent as this thinking is to the post-Holocaust reader, Leslie, unaware of this consequence of racial theorizing, regards his vision as favoring religious over materialist values, for "great as the Teuton may be, greater must be the God who made him, but the Teuton has never quite forgiven the Celt for thinking so."[85] For Leslie, the presence of Lough Derg in Ireland illustrates, as it does in a complex way for Denis Devlin, how such values have always resided in this far-flung place, particularly a clemency, available, of course, exclusively to Christians. Lough Derg's contribution to the development of the idea of purgatory exhibits the moral supremacy of the Celt: "Their first idea of Hell was of a cold, wintry place. Later the comfortable doctrine of Purgatory, while inherent in the Church, was especially developed by the Celts, to whom pity and forgiveness were second nature."[86] How Leslie responds to the actual Irish, as distinct from the abstract Celts, however, is a separate matter.

Leslie, a representative of the colonizing class, nurtured this racialist theory that, rather than more typically casting the colonized as nonwhite, defined them as ultrawhite. Luke Gibbons recently has exposed the racial premises behind, as he titles it, the *Gaelic Gothic*, "a literary genre with a distinctively popular or sensational appeal."[87] Gibbons identifies this appeal as the product of a Cromwellian racializing of Catholics "as immersed in superstition, savagery, and the general credulousness associated with primitive cultures or 'doomed races.' "[88] Leslie may be seen as inverting this demonization, particularly by his own conversion, but also as supporting its racial premise. What is more, the inversion still results in distanced, superior responses on Leslie's part. His references to individual Irish people betray an entrenched bigotry. Moreover, his comments on the various nonwhite peoples subdued by Empire betray not just a prejudice against the nonwhite but also toward all non-English. As for the Irish, one of Leslie's more revealing comments occurs in relation to the successful emigrant Irish he encountered in America in 1911, when he went there "to raise interest in the Gaelic movement and send home funds to endow Irish scholarship."[89] Meetings with "Irishmen of the top grade" made Leslie think that "the Irish could one day run finances and industries of their own."[90] Despite mythologizing Michael Collins[91] and regarding O'Connell as "Celtic to excess,"[92] Leslie offers that "Only in time of war are the Irish of serious account."[93] There is the tired feel of Arnoldian cliché off his stereotyping, a threadbare sheen off his ahistorical universalizing, especially in relation to marriage practices, sexuality in general, facets of social conduct very much determined by the economic repercussions of the Famine: "Their affections are barely earthly, for they leave marriage to be fixed by the priest. The passionate go to America or take to drink, for their women have beauty but not fire."[94] Or more pithily, "Ireland is a paradox. The sages say there are three paradoxes which shall never be understood—the Trinity, Woman and Ireland, but the greatest paradox is Ireland."[95] In one neat locution not only are Ireland and Catholicism, especially the Patrician legacy of it, conflated, but the feminine as well, all objects of Leslie's simultaneous adoration and denigration. He says, speaking of the Indians he encountered at Cambridge, that their admission reflects a dubious policy. This idealizing and inevitable denigrating is contained in such off-the-cuff remarks as: "Government stupidity sends Indians to English universities to forget their inferiority at the price of that in which they are superior."[96] What is more, "a few more sentimental mistakes and Oxford and Cambridge will pass like old English boxing and London society into the shadowy well of cosmopolitanism."[97] Celticism, as the last vestige of Aryanism, is projected as propping up certain worthy institutions: "old English boxing" and "London society," precisely and ironically the causes espoused by his benighted Eton.

For Leslie, the Aryan law of east and west as well as north and south, white and nonwhite remaining absolutely segregated, is absolute: "It is forbidden the east to meet with the west."[98] Such pronouncements can scale risible, dizzying heights: "Antony's escapade with Cleopatra became a symbol of Aryan treason and decadence."[99] No doubt projecting his own self-described neutrality and fairness onto the Celt, he proclaims, "The Celt has never persecuted the Jew."[100] On the other hand, Leslie can offer this sage but reluctant advice: "Anti-Semitic feeling is as degrading and out of date as the pillory, but social discrimination can be an ethical necessity."[101]

Shane Leslie is not a spokesman for an age, class, or ethnic group. There is nothing typical in his attitudes on race. As a Lough Derg writer, however, his racial discourse acts as a shadow both thrown on and by the ethnic purity celebrated by Irish nationalism. If we look at the work of Alice Curtayne, we see the exquisite intellectual and spiritual lengths to which this purifying zeal can extend. Her book *Lough Derg* covers the same ground as D. Canon O'Connor's, but views it from the perch not only of fifty further years of scholarship but of triumphant nationalism as well. Her tone is as urbane as it is pious, her unspoken assurance is that the Irish have achieved an ideal balance of self-realization and cosmopolitan presence. The degree to which this formed identity rests, however, on a rigid, still very Jansenist

Catholicism is most revealed in another of her many, many books, *A Recall to Dante,* published in 1932, more than ten years before her Lough Derg history. Given the connection between Dante and Lough Derg, the earlier book predicts the cultural and spiritual direction of the later effort. Both icons, Dante and the pilgrimage, will be seen through the same lens that concentrates and resolves complexity into a burning purity.

Curtayne's reading of Dante is openly revisionist. It aims, by correcting secular readings of Dante, to promote the restoration of a spiritually and intellectually refined European, Catholic culture in Ireland. From another perspective, her prose exudes a pride about Ireland as once more bringing an exemplary Christian energy to Europe. She will challenge especially two readings, which she regards as heretical: one associated with Yeats, that Dante writes of purity from the paradoxical standpoint of one corrupt; the other associated by Curtayne with a variety of predatory, English critics, that Dante was an enemy of the Vatican. Later we shall see that Heaney's reading of Dante, particularly as received through the Russian poet Osip Mandelstam, celebrates Dante as being so wedded to the innate, sublime order of creation that he pays homage to it in his own devotion to form. Reading Curtayne, with her emphatic presentation of Dante as a Catholic poet concerned first and foremost with the tenets of the faith, is to derive some feeling for the subtle subjugation after independence, especially and ironically among the intelligentsia, of aesthetic concerns to a putatively higher truth. Curtayne's *Recall to Dante* also reveals, the more dramatically because her subject is not explicitly Ireland, how the nation infiltrates all her thinking. Nationalism saturates her Catholicism; her religious fervor is also her patriotic staunchness. A discernible anti-English bias is part of her revisionism, and she reads Dante essentially as resembling an austere, medieval, Irish poet, a universal model of that chaste, Irish spirituality that is the steady concern of her Lough Derg history. She sees Dante also as doctrinally correct in all matters, as a venerator of Our Lady and early proponent of Mariolotry. Dante, in short, as an indisputably great European poet, the Catholic answer to Shakespeare, whom Shane Leslie called the "greatest of Teuton mystics,"[102] provides an imprimatur for Irish confidence in a cultural superiority crowned by a high Catholic piety. Ironically, given her nationalism, Curtayne's Dante is not far removed from that of the Anglocentric T. S. Eliot, who regards Dante as a model of Catholic rectitude. Further, the identity she bestows on Ireland is not that far from the cosmopolitan, Catholic fastidiousness that animates Devlin's work.

One of the questions Curtayne must broach is how the hypothetical Irish Catholic reader of Dante, whom she is encouraging and guiding, should cope with the hoard of Dante scholarship. Her answer is quite direct and is the consequence of her perception of Dante as essentially a Catholic writer. The reader's first responsibility, therefore, is to read this fellow believer as a Catholic would, to be true to his or her own faith. Taking her own advice, Curtayne relies on her religious barometer to read the moral weather in Dante, in particular allegations of Dante's "sins of the flesh":

> Thus the Catholic who reads the *Commedia* finds within his own mind a corrective to a great many of the false theories about Dante. He may, for instance, find it stated in one of the innumerable books on Dante that the poet was a victim to sins of the flesh, and he will know immediately, by intuition, that that is not true, even before he approaches any of the erudite essays to prove that is not true.[103]

Theories may come and theories may go, but "The Faith is the only immutable thing in the poem."[104] So while scholars can adduce evidence for and against presenting Dante as a flawed being capable of lust, informed Catholic intuition has the power to surmount such secular and relativist arguments to arrive at the absolute truth. Curtayne labels this use of intuition "The Catholic short cut to the truth,"[105] which, she adds, "proceeds somewhat like this: Dante is indicted mainly on his own general and vague confession. When the Catholic reader has accompanied Dante through the Three Kingdoms, he knows his man."[106] Putting words in the ideal Catholic mouth and conscience, Curtayne sums up, "Dante was simply not on the plane of men who are ready victims to 'sins of the flesh.' "[107] Earlier she put forward as irrefutable evidence of Dante's innocence his "extraordinarily sensitive and ardent soul, whose standard of moral conduct was not ours."[108] This means, therefore, that, because Dante suffers so exquisitely for even phantom sins, he cannot possibly have committed real ones. The resulting portrait is of a labyrinthine, almost morbidly introspective, consciousness. In other passages she expands on this sensitivity, revealing rather a finely tuned scrupulosity of conscience, a rarefied power of self-examination, quite at odds with the practical, robust Christianity that others, notably Dorothy L. Sayers, Heaney's early Dante mentor,[109] ascribe to the worldly Florentine. One sees in Curtayne's tracing of Dante's spiritual and moral cogitations the aspiration to provide a template for the elegant, early Christian Irish mind that she constructs and idealizes, but she endows it with such an attenuated sense of sin that she betrays this chaste simplicity. It is a short step from Curtayne's filigreed replication of Dante's mind to the elaborate, more baroque than medieval, meditations of Devlin's poetry.

Curtayne invests a great deal of space in speculating about Dante and allegations that he was licentious and loose of faith. Having rejected the factual basis of the accusations, she acknowledges textual evidence in Dante of some ineffable falling off in moral and spiritual perfection. One can glimpse the scholastic, almost casuistic, skills of the intellectual Catholic at play in her conclusion: "Dante's wandering from the path of righteousness was not a definite betrayal of either principle involved in the two extreme theories, but was rather a confusing of values, a general disordering of life."[110] Her most sophisticated ploy is to see Dante's scrupulosity itself as irrefutable proof of his near spiritual perfection. Besides, the chief perpetrator of rumors of Dante's sins of the flesh was Boccaccio, and "What reader who knows the *Commedia* and the *Decameron* would dream of appraising Dante from the muddy depths of Boccaccio's mind?"[111] Curtayne's assertions set a significant precedent: that the moral value of a man may be read and measured from the work of his imagination. It is not a large step from this stance to censorship. Hence we get from Curtayne the expurgated version of the life of Dante: "When Beatrice died, Dante took refuge in books. . . . But philosophy did not prove a sufficient substitute for what had been lost, and some brief part of this transitional period from youth to manhood Dante apparently squandered. . . . The lapse was not serious; in a figure not exalted it could not even be called a lapse."[112] "The short cut to the truth" leaves us with a man so exalted, so dedicated to the straight path of purity, that this slight downward swerve is all that associates him with the earth. This is the bar Curtayne sets for the Christian, more specifically the Irish Catholic, life.

This accomplished hagiographer resists presenting Dante to us as a saint, because he had this slight, fortunate, human lapse. This lapse makes him all the more useful as a lesson. His minimally flawed manhood makes him a natural exhibitor of the role intercession can play in any spiritual progress, prominently aided by the Virgin Mary: "The *Divina Commedia* is really the story of Dante's rescue by Our Lady."[113] Curtayne, again anticipating Devlin's preoccupations, views Dante's Beatrician vision as an early endorsement of Mariolatry, proof of the Virgin's autonomous power to intercede. That is how Curtayne arrives at this anachronistic playing out of a relatively modern Catholic doctrine in Dante:

> Dante is alone, in darkness, struggling but not prevailing against odds that are too powerful. But compassionate eyes have discerned his plight. Mary in Heaven makes a gesture to save him. She sends Saint Lucy to Beatrice, who is Dante's only intimate friend among the Blessed, and Beatrice in turn seeks out Virgil, who immediately hastens to the dark wood in which Dante is astray, and leads him out of it. Mary is therefore the mainspring that sets in motion the whole action of the poem. The high importance of her intervention is this: that she rose up to deliver from danger a man who had invoked her. Dante opens his great work with a statement of Our Lady's universal mediation.[114]

Curtayne's contributions to female hagiography, book-length studies of Saint Catherine of Sienna and Saint Brigid, in addition to her learned engagement with Mariology, constitute an early, quite radical feminist intervention in a period when roles for women in Ireland were severely confined. Her interest, particularly, in the intellectual attainments and daring of female saints such as Catherine of Sienna, anticipate the quietly subversive poetry of Eiléan Ní Chuilleanáin, who also has an imaginative investment in female saints and Mary. Ní Chuilleanáin's oeuvre includes "St. Mary Magdalen Preaching at Marseilles," "St. Margaret of Cortona," and most notably, "Fireman's Lift," a poem that explicitly connects the intercessory power of the Virgin with the strength of ordinary mothers and women who assist in transforming daily life. Whereas Ní Chuilleanáin, a generation removed from Curtayne, imbues her saints with a sublimated erotic energy and earthed vitality,

Curtayne's eye is always on a purity achieved in the crucible of intellectual and spiritual intensity. Nonetheless, as an early example of a woman writing about women but making them cleave to an impossible standard of noncorporeality, Curtayne retrospectively spares her male contemporaries, such as Devlin, the full brunt of feminist censure today. Reading her helps to position Devlin's tightly woven poetry not just within its compressed verbal and mental constructions but within a broader, neo-Scholastic culture. Curtayne, with no audible blushing at the double entendres the less pure of mind might read into her prose, provides a glimpse of the cultural expectations of a religious passion cleansed of lust toward the inviolate, exemplary female. Speaking in Dante's words, Curtayne invokes the ideal of the Beatrician vision: "Her image that was always with me . . . was yet so perfect a quality that it never allowed me to be overruled by love without the faithful council of reason." [115] Curtayne adds, without a hint of irony, "He discovered a luxury in solitude, and he formed the habit of rushing to the loneliness of his own room as a place of immeasurable relief and repose." [116]

Curtayne's own subversive energies are always subsumed, as reflected in her view of Dante, by a stern discipline and obedience to the faith; therefore, she has no qualms whatsoever about assigning the explication of Catholic doctrine as the reason for the existence of Dante's masterpiece. She assures us that Dante was "an expert theologian," who "loved to debate the most abstruse points in theology," [117] and further that the final purpose of the poetry is polemical, to promote Catholic teaching. For example, referring to seven incidents in the *Inferno* that have drawn the attention of most readers, Curtayne asserts that "the five or six points which sum up all Catholic belief on the subject of Hell could be drawn from every incident, so that each of the seven incidents would form an outline for meditation." [118] On the *Paradiso* she says, "His Heaven is the Heaven of the Catholic Creed," adding, "Dante's Heaven is the Heaven of the intellect." [119] These two statements together add up to the telling premise, resonant of de Valerian Ireland, that a refined intellect will automatically embrace orthodox belief.

Curtayne's central conviction is that the *Commedia* is not simply religious in spirit but doctrinally sound in the letter of the law. This premise leads her to resent and revise Reformationist hijackings of Dante that serve as vehicles for anti-Catholic, anti-papist argument. She sees these Protestant and secular readings as diminishing not just Dante's legacy but that of Catholic, European culture generally. Her anti-English bias is patent, her means of attack a formidable, countervailing scholarship deployed to defend the Church. Curtayne sums up this misuse of Dante simply by saying, "For centuries every enemy of Rome has delighted to misquote him." [120] The most notorious example of such an enemy is "Bishop John Jewel, great light of the Reformation," who, according to Curtayne's research, in his *Defense of the Apology of the Church of England,* dedicated to Queen Elizabeth I, contends: "Dantes [*sic*], an Italian poet, by express words calleth Rome the whore of Babylon." [121] Curtayne goes on painstakingly to prove that "Dante never made that statement 'by express words' in reference to either the Church or the Pope." [122] Curtayne swings so far in the direction of defending the faith that she dehistoricizes Dante and underplays the political complications of his very public life, especially in relation to the Vatican, an institution for Dante quite separate from religion. Curtayne, however, also inserts the caveat that "the intention here is not the silly impertinence of trying to minimize the value of English Dante research."[123] Rather, she sees herself as compensating for a lack: "The fault is Catholic poetical interpretations do not exist."[124] Closer to home and much more involved with nationalism, her rescuing of Dante, much as Our Lady rescued him, is meant to participate in an intellectual, spiritual liberation of the nation on the heels of political independence. She sees her work in short as a correction to English, cultural hegemony: "Since the emancipation of the Church in these islands, Dante has been practically excluded. . . . He is still wandering outside the bourne, banished without a hearing, perpetually outcast."[125]

Read at its deepest, most covert level, Curtayne's *Recall to Dante* is a recall of a Catholic, medieval splendor, which she regards as animating the early Christian Irish Church, revivifying and lending moral invincibility to modern Ireland. It can seem that the purpose of her lifelong scholarship and publishing about Catholic letters and lives is ironically to emulate that same spirit of deliberateness, even artificiality, that was applied under cultural nationalism to pagan myth and folklore. Her object is to nurture a Catholic intelligentsia, a new ruling class, cosmopolitan and learned but emulative of the strictest, most rarefied spirituality of the early Irish saints. I believe that in her hyperbole applied to Dante one hears an echo of "In Memory of Major Robert Gregory," Yeats's paean to the ideal of the Anglo-Irish gentleman: "Soldier, scholar, horeseman, he, / as 'twere all life's epitome." Curtayne cautions about Dante,

> Let it be remembered about him that he served his country not only with his compelling and eloquent tongue, with his diplomatic skill as ambassador, with theories which he elaborated in comprehensive and detailed treatises, but with his skill as horseman and lancer, too, with long hours of fatigue in the saddle, with sweat and wounds under the banner of Florence in the front line of battle.[126]

He is not "our Sydney and our perfect man"; he is our Dante and our perfect man, a non-English and European Catholic paragon for the Irish gentleman, the new aristocracy of the Irish Republic, to emulate. So strong is the Irish nationalist undercurrent of Curtayne's 1932 book on Dante that she even places Dante's conception of heaven in an idealized Irish domestic setting. Heaven for her evokes feelings of homecoming, the attainment of safety, ease, and quiet self-possession, the same feelings that sum up for her the essential *gestalt* of political independence. The lyrical lengths to which she goes, particularly her gradual elision into a future tense, may betray, however, more hope than reality. Reflecting ostensibly on Dante's use of homely, familiar, readily accessible imagery even at his most climactic, sublime moments, Curtayne explains:

Of all ideas, the most alien to the Catholic belief in Heaven would be one of strain, ill-ease, or even effort. The thought of rest, of perfect ease in home surroundings must predominate. Possibly that sense of repose can be conveyed only in familiar, even crude, imagery. There is an expansive feeling of comfort, which can be described only by saying it is like a man sitting in an armchair at his own fireside, with his feet on the mantelshelf. That is immediately comprehensible, and a more elegant picture could not render the idea in the same flash. When the children of the household are gathered home, there will be an ending to sitting uneasy, sullen guests at a patron's table; an end to exile; an end to alien company. We shall all be where we belong.[127]

No longer "sullen guests" at the feast of English culture, Irishmen now are at home and free to partake of their rightful portion of Catholic riches. The quiet centeredness of this projected feeling of being home is as much the presumed gift of political independence as of confirmed faith. While a rediscovery and active reassessment of European literature poised Irish culture then for participation in modernism, for which Dante, for example, is a key figure, the brand of Catholicism espoused ruled out the relativism and fragmenting doubt also central to that experiment. Curtayne herself addresses the problem of modernity, envisaging an approach that is defiantly antimodernist, maintaining "Dante never 'thinks' or 'supposes' or 'ventures.' Where the present day mood is fluctuating and uncertain, Dante is positive."[128] She further adds that, "where the modern is perpetually toying with the disconnected parts of his theory of life, Dante's is all securely welded in beauty and harmony."[129]

It is this animating, elegant spirit of medievalism that Curtayne sees still circulating at Lough Derg. The quiddity of the pilgrimage for her is that austere form of Irish spirituality epitomized by the Gaelic bardic poetry that centers on the site. The titles of certain chapters alone in the first half of the book announce Curtayne's nationalist thesis. Chapters 3 and 4 are "Medieval Fame" and "Caves and Fantasies"; chapter 5 is "The Irish Way." Her purpose, in keeping with O'Connor's, is to discredit the European fabulist legacy and legitimize the penitential Irish response as the true one. Curtayne, however, conducts this xenophobic campaign armed with a daunting scholarship. She traces the evolution of the Knight Owen story through history and its many embellishments, culminating in the baroque rendering in 1627 by Juan Perez de Montalvan, the immediate inspiration, as we have seen, for Calderón. Her dismissal of this Spanish extravagance is as withering as any of the Anglocentric attacks on Calderón's poetry as translated by MacCarthy. Curtayne's revision of Lough Derg history, reflecting a greater confidence than O'Connor's, who can still expose a giddy, provincial pleasure with the European fame of the remote Donegal site, is aimed at renouncing as misguided and doctrinally unsound, emphatically not Irish, this intoxication with the fantastical. Preserving the austere, reasoned, nontranscendent core of her Catholicism, she is even prepared to dispel the myth of Dante being influenced by Lough Derg. As we have seen, her attachment to Dante is to a pristine embodiment of an elegant faith, and this remains her priority, since it is her priority, too, for Lough Derg:

> No serious literary comparison is possible between Dante's Comedy and the Saltrey writing. . . . One work is a discussion of the whole Christian scheme of re-demption, the other is just a colourful description of a vision. . . . Dante, as most readers know, described in his Comedy the states of Purgatory, Hell, a kind of ter-restrial Paradise (ante-chamber of Heaven) and Paradise itself. . . . The Saltrey manuscript, on the other hand, describes a state of punishment which is both Pur-gatory and Hell, and a terrestrial Eden. . . . There is no resemblance, then, between the Purgatory described in the Saltrey manuscript and that detailed by Dante. Dante includes all the souls in Purgatory in the Communion of Saints and invests them in an atmosphere of love, patience and hope.[130]

Curtayne will not consider the possibility that the graphic and sensory imagin-ing of the Knight Owen story arrested Dante's attention. Nor can she entertain even historically the Saltrey text as an early contribution to a mapping of the doctrine of purgatory. Its lack of doctrinal articulation of clear and distinct domains of hell, purgatory, and heaven rules it out as an influence on an orthodox Dante. Similarly, she turns to her primary female model, Catherine of Sienna, and reveals the saint as a powerful voice rejecting the Lough Derg of spurious, even spiritually dangerous, medieval fame and endorsing its truer, less glamorous, penitential discipline. Cur-tayne refers specifically to a letter Catherine of Sienna wrote: "to Don John, a Carthusian Monk in Rome, who was tried by temptation, and who wanted to go to Saint Patrick's Purgatory, when permission was not granted him, became sorely af-flicted in his mind."[131] Curtayne gives us the background to Catherine's "nearly two thousand word letter," written in 1372 when she was twenty-five, but already "had a grasp of moral theology that was purely intuitive."[132] The Carthusian monk in question, on being denied his pilgrimage, entered a fit alternating between de-spair and rebellion, thereby upsetting his entire monastic order. Catherine of Si-enna sets out to put matters straight; she "goes to the root of the matter and reminds him of his obedience."[133] Curtayne's paraphrasing of Catherine's advice is essentially a homily to the Irish people:

> The obedient man, she said, never trusts to his own judgement, which he suspects is faulty. . . . The man who is obedient does not obey in one place, or time, but he obeys in everything, everywhere and always. He is never scandalised no matter what he is told to do. . . . Catherine tells the Carthusian that, in reality, his chief af-fliction is his own stubborn will. Therefore he will never find peace until he gets the better of himself, and casts out obsession with what she calls "holy hatred". . . . She insists that Don John's idea is nothing more than a delusion of the devil. She con-cludes by saying: "Bow your head to obedience and stay in your cell. Guard against doing your own will as you prize the life of your soul."[134]

Visions are linked to egoism and diabolism. The restraint of the individual will is the only path to salvation. So much does Curtayne believe this that her concluding words to this chapter ironically echo Protestant diatribes against the site: "It is a tribute to Lough Derg and evidence of its pre-eminence in Europe that, in the Italy of the later fourteenth century, the devil could use its renown to trouble even the souls of the elect."[135] Curtayne manages to assimilate Carleton's anti-Catholic complaints and convert them to Catholic doctrine. The entire tradition of Lough Derg as a site of transcendent experience is relegated to the devil's work, offering the temptation of "an antiseptic for any known suppuration of the soul."[136] The only cure for maladies of the soul is the hard regimen of the Irish saints, self-abnegation and a stony bed, the Lough Derg of unremitting penitence and, above all, of obedience. This is the regime recommended for the new Irish Republic.

The touchstone associated with Lough Derg, which Curtayne presents for the edification of her reader at this juncture in Irish history, is the example of the bardic poets who did the pilgrimage and were resolutely not transported. Their writings, as we have seen, bemoan the recalcitrance of the flesh, the elusiveness of the soul. In order to establish the preeminence of these poems, which date from the thirteenth to seventeenth centuries, Curtayne is pressed to affirm the continuance of the pilgrimage as an Irish exercise during this period. She attributes a corrective influence to the Irish, who during this period resisted the exaggerated claims for the exercise: "Irish pilgrims, however, still held to the original concept of the place as one which gave man a chance to do penance. The foreign idea of the sanctuary was exciting and fantastic, the native one wholly spiritual."[137] In making this distinction, she can assume a xenophobic tone: "The Irish people were always level-headed in their view of the place. According to them, one went to Lough Derg to do penance and hope for grace—nothing more. It was a foreign pilgrim who first spread the tale of having seen visions there and it was chiefly foreigners who believed him."[138]

The iconic poem in this group is, for Curtayne, predictably, Ó Dálaigh's "Vain My Visit to Lough Derg." Curtayne, who ascribes deliberate resistance on the part of Irish pilgrims to the hyperbole and error surrounding the site, stresses that Ó Dálaigh, who died in 1244, "could have known people" who had known Knight Owen firsthand, providing "he were an historical personage."[139] She stresses, too, the synchronicity of the writing of this first Irish Lough Derg poem with the beginnings of the site's European fame: "This poet flourished just as the vision-cycle was beginning its meteoric course."[140] Positing these oppositional forms of religion, ecstatic and reasonable, as engaged in a still-unsettled contest for Christian souls, Curtayne adds the weight of her argument to the side of sober, ascetic, Irish spirituality. She portrays the Irish bard/pilgrim as positively expecting punishment, chastisement as an integral part of penance. Turning to Ó Dálaigh's famous poem about an abortive spiritual experience, she asks, "Did he see the afterlife? What was he to say about it? Nothing whatever that is in the least sensational. Absolutely nothing."[141] This minimalism, approaching stoicism, of retaining the faith when all the signs are discouraging, is her theme. Speaking of the disciplined position held by the Irish bards, but imposing her own proselytizing motives onto her interpretation of their legacy, she urges:

One would really imagine that the Irish bards had never even heard of the fantasies! Yet they must have known about them. It is quite impossible to imagine that no echo from the large corpus of European literature had ever reached their ears; or that they had never even heard of those foreign notabilities travelling through Ireland with their retinues. The Irish bards must have known about the fantasies, but the fact is that they did not think the matter worth a single half-line of poetry, or even the most cursory allusion. The hunger for visions and the facility in inventing them arose from a kind of spirituality with which the bardic poets had absolutely nothing in common: to them it smelt of morbidity and disease; their form of religion was so clean and hard by comparison, they could entertain for the miracle-mongers no sentiments save wonder, distaste, perhaps resentment. Both the Irish poets and their less cultured brethren went to the island in the mood of athletes prepared to endure, with no hope of any reward, not even sensible consolation. Even if contrition were denied to them, their belief in the rite remained unshaken. The native appraisement of the devotion was the original idea; it is that which has endured. The other is like the crests of foam spouted to the surface by the lake when it boils up in a sudden storm—that afterwards vanish without a trace.[142]

The isolationism described here is considered and deliberate, an assertion of superiority, not deprivation, or indeed even actual isolation. What is more, it is a stance adopted in order to guarantee continuance of an "original idea" that would be lost sight of by swervings in foreign directions. It is this Spartan ideal, evoked by words like "hard" and "clean," that bear a "northern" ring not entirely removed from Leslie's Aryanism, that Curtayne is establishing as the bright star toward which modern Ireland should turn for direction. What an irony this aspiration is, considering Carleton's crusade for moral and spiritual freedom as the stamp of manliness.

Curtayne's book received in fact the official imprimatur of the Church. Furthermore, the Bishop of Monaghan wrote a foreward and attached his official seal to his name. Curtayne argues throughout her book that the purity of the devotion has been safeguarded by the scrupulous attention to it and interventions performed by the hierarchy. Like O'Connor, she reads instances such as the Dutch monk's denial of entry as evidence of self-protection on the part of a vigilant Church against miracle mongering. Overall, Curtayne concurs with the Bishop of Monaghan, who in the book's forward describes the rite as benefiting from the "fostering care of successive popes."[143] Like O'Connor too, Curtayne must anchor this argument for origin and continuance of an inviolate, Catholic idea in the apostleship of Saint Patrick. While current scholarship, for example that of Peter Harbison, categorically rules out the possibility of Saint Patrick's founding the pilgrimage, Curtayne, following O'Connor, must keep this foundation stone in place. Harbison comes to this conclusion: "One fact which some modern commentators have had to admit with a certain degree of regret is that, although we know Saint Patrick passed through County Donegal, there is no source earlier than Henry of Saltrey to connect him with Lough Derg."[144] Although Harbison supports the view that Irish participation in the pilgrimage might well predate the Saltrey text, thus concurring with Curtayne, she insists that Saint Patrick set foot on Station Island and initiated the tradition. As a Patrician scholar, she has all the facts, particularly about the routes of his ambulatory mission, but ardor forces her reasoning and rhetoric to fabricate a certainty that is not there:

> Think of him located somewhere near Templecarne for several months and thus surrounded. The lake would certainly invite him with its promise of refuge and sanctuary. It was inevitable that he should escape to it. The island on which Saint Patrick's Purgatory is now located happens to be the island farthest away from the mainland no matter from what point of the shore it is approached. This is the very island he would naturally choose. . . . He had to make sure that he was absolutely alone. The tradition that he visited this island is continuous since this time, universal in the Irish Church, and peculiarly circumstantial.[145]

The rhetoric makes it clear that "it was inevitable" Saint Patrick would visit Station Island because "the tradition that he visited is continuous since this time, universal in the Irish Church." This continuity and apparent cultural consensus makes circumstantiality a positive rather than a negative attribute. Indeed, the foreword contributed by the Church's representative, Bishop O'Callaghan, stresses not just the unbroken continuity of Lough Derg, but also the reflection of this fact in Curtayne's narrative: "Many books have been written on Saint Patrick's Purgatory, viewed from different aspects, but there was still room for a consecutive record of the Pilgrimage from its foundation by our National Apostle fifteen hundred years ago down to the present day."[146] The bishop further validates a means of arriving at historical truth beyond the establishment of fact: "Tradition, when jealously guarded and carefully handed down, is a reliable source of information."[147] Such an assertion may be regarded as a part of an overall sanction of native authority, especially rectifying the status of oral culture. It is also indicative of an authoritarian clergy that can appoint itself as the arbiter of culture. Curtayne's own claims to Saint Patrick's founding of the pilgrimage rest ultimately on her need to endow the site with the spiritual resonance she attaches to the National Apostle. The key to this sentiment is in her naked projection onto Saint Patrick of a need for solitude, to be "absolutely alone." This is a revival of the spiritual requirements ascribed to Dante, and to the bards. It is also the resource the author herself appears to possess, to lodge in the ideal of Lough Derg, and to prescribe for Ireland: a sense of solitude found in a collective response, a paradox explored by most Lough Derg writers but not always rescued from pure contradiction. That Curtayne's subjective experience suffuses and determines her historical narrative is most apparent from the penultimate paragraph to her chapter "The Coming of Saint Patrick." In essence, she asks that impressionistic evidence be admitted as proof of Saint Patrick's original and continuing presence:

> In that red-eyed combat with sleep in which pilgrims must engage, in their three-day struggle with the "noontide-devil" of hunger, in their burden of fatigue, in the discomfort of walking barefoot over sharp stones, in the inescapable weariness of

long prayer, they come face to face with Saint Patrick. His authentic voice becomes audible. Strong and ineluctable, he is there.[148]

Tellingly, such a sighting from the distant past is not one produced by a "piercing of the veil of the unknown,"[149] one of those visions Curtayne has condemned. This certainty comes from a heightened sense of connection produced by imitating the spirit of penitence Saint Patrick had laid down. It is his penitential, solitary discipline that Lough Derg fosters; therefore, Saint Patrick must have founded it. These are Curtayne's concluding words to this critical chapter on the problem of locating the place of Lough Derg in the reconstruction of Ireland: "His Confession finds a living illustration today in the island practice and nowhere else in the Irish Church. The 'way' that he taught and practiced is perpetuated there in a manner that, without him, defies rational explanation. He who submits to that discipline discovers that he is touching the live chord of community with Celtic Christianity."[150] As Curtayne highlights Saint Patrick for banishing the "dethroned devils" of the Druids, so Lough Derg is endowed with the power to lead Ireland both backward and forward to its true spiritual glory. Not only does it represent Ireland; it is the only place on the island that embodies the real, continuous Ireland.

It is no wonder that from the 1940s on, Lough Derg is a frequent subject for poetry that not just assesses Ireland culturally but more obliquely assesses the place of the individual artist in this construct. To estimate the influence Curtayne had on creating the climate in which Devlin and Kavanagh confront Lough Derg, it is important finally to identify the class issues raised by her study. That her view represents a later, mirror version of the fetishizing of the West performed by the Irish Renaissance surfaces most on the few occasions when she alludes in a glancing fashion not just to other, more ordinary pilgrims, but to the people who actually live near the site in County Donegal. Take, for example, this reference to traveling in the vicinity of the lake bent on a project of recovery, an indulgence only the urban elite of the new state could afford. She is describing how to find the archaeological remains referred to as Dabheoc's Chair: "It is a narrow road, very steep in places, and so stony throughout its length that it is a trial to the most willing motor car and an ordeal to any driver. On the first mile, one disturbs the privacy of several cottages, being forced to skim close to their gable ends and stone wall crofts, with the risk of upsetting their cooking utensils, usually left standing outside the doors."[151] One cannot help but think of Kavanagh's groundbreaking shunting of perspective achieved in section 13 of "The Great Hunger," where for the first time in Irish literature written in English he tells us what the cottagers thought of being so distorted by the condescending and romanticizing gaze of the urbane visitor, Protestant and Catholic alike: "The travellers stop their cars to gape over the green bank into his fields:— / There is the source from which all cultures rise, / And all religions."[152] Kavanagh takes us up close to the hypocritical, venal and confused pilgrims stripped of Curtayne's idealizing. One thinks, too, of Carleton, seeing the pilgrimage with such myopic intensity that he has to flee its vaunted spell, but not without leaving an indelible and realistic description of the event and place.

Predictably, Curtayne also does her part to reverse the blight of Carleton's withering description of the desolate place that is Saint Patrick's Purgatory. She, typically, foregrounds its remoteness and bleakness, seeing it as the ideal setting for the solitary trial enacted there. Her description of the landscape encodes her prizing of solitude above all: "In all that rolling expanse of barren hill and moorland, in which this water is set, only a couple of houses are visible. These dwellings look like white dots in the hills."[153] That Curtayne herself is isolated in this rural context is the sociological, as distinct from spiritual, truth conveyed. Her Lough Derg is a receptacle for all the superior taste and spiritual refinement that ironically rips this brand of nationalism apart from the people who make up the nation. One hears her fears of inevitable violation and declension in a closing chapter to the book, "The Basilica," which focuses on the example set by a pared-down, restrained architecture:

> It has been difficult and will always be difficult to preserve that austerity so deeply satisfying. One can but pray that the successive Priors of the pilgrimage will be always strong-minded. The donors of shrines, those ubiquitous monied persons with devotion and no judgement, will be busy here too: they will seek to intrude in this church as everywhere else, longing to spoil the fresh miracle of its interior with their wearisome disorder of pious fripperies.[154]

Those ostracized by Curtayne's aesthetic are not just the opprobrious Leslies but the Catholic merchant class also disdained by Yeats. Like Yeats, she has conceived an aesthetic and translated it into a spiritual stance. She further parlays her intuitive understanding, her "short cut to the truth," of theology to the soul of a peasantry, which in its unsullied simplicity and suffering enjoys a direct link with Saint Patrick.

Before turning to Devlin and Kavanagh in the immediately following chapters, I would like briefly to consider two other responses to Lough Derg from this period, one by the already mentioned rural versifier Joseph Timoney, the other by the celebrated short story writer Seán O'Faoláin. Superficially the two are stark opposites: one a model of devotionalism and, as it happens, low art; the other of cosmopolitan secularism and artistic accomplishment. These clear oppositions, however, become muddied on closer inspection, a predictor of the way a close comparison of Kavanagh and Devlin reveals them to be less diametrical than their reputations suggest. This is a complication also true in relation to O'Connor and Curtayne: he a detached scholar for all his fervor, she a doctrinaire Catholic for all her intellectualism. So, most of these apparent Janus faces eventually break out of the stone of stereotype and turn toward each other. This is an important observation to lodge in approaching Devlin and Kavanagh, Heaney's immediate precursors and, therefore, his double handle on the diverse, often contradictory, inheritance out of which he will try to wrest integration on all levels, from the cultural to the psychological, to the metaphysical, to the moral, thus enabling maturation and independence.

At the time when Joseph Timoney, an avid, regular, ordinary pilgrim, published his "Impressions" of Lough Derg, Kavanagh and Devlin both were in their early twenties. Timoney's pamphlet is germane for my purposes for several reasons, not least because it describes the physical place and order of exercises exactly as they were then, providing, therefore, a context in which to place the two great Lough Derg poems from the 1940s. More, he wears the halo of a rapturous, unquestioning piety, already associated with patriotism, that encompassed the shrine in the public imagination. We have seen O'Connor's aggressively chauvinistic and anti-Protestant work. Mild-mannered, poetical Mr. Timoney, in contrast, merely claims that "It is a Holy Isle where sin and sorrow never dwelt; a haven of peace, where nothing evil ever entered, another world, where souls find final rest, because they rest in God, secluded from the tumults of the world—a sanctuary of peace, prayer and penance."[155] He then goes on to reconstruct the lake as the sum of texts, from the Fenian rendition of its origin to the various accounts left by European pilgrims. Borne aloft on this pious afflatus, Timoney produces a past that is remarkably pure and sanitized. His Fenian story, for example, contains no reference to the misogynistic mutilation scene it usually contains; and his European pilgrims are distinguished aristocrats rather than egregious sinners. Timoney appears to have a positively ahistorical mania that rescues Lough Derg from all conflict and vicissitudes.

Much of the fuel for such lift-off from historical fact is gained from the transcendent power he attaches to all literature, good or bad, and especially to poetry about Lough Derg. Timoney also attempts to repair the irreparable fractures of time by appealing to space, the international fame of nationalistic Lough Derg. Indeed, Timoney's pamphlet anticipates Heaney's masterful poem in this single characteristic: the way it proceeds by means of intertextuality, from one Lough Derg touchstone to another. Timoney's lack of discernment, however, betrays itself not just in a leveling of difference in the realm of history, but also of aesthetics. Resorting to literature as the ultimate proof of the site's power to move, he includes one of his own verses in praise of it, which opens with these lines:

> My limbs were sore on its barren shore
> My eyes were closing too;
> I left the pew—the vigil o'er,
> The sweet, fresh air to woo,

rising to a triumphant "O God, O God, I love this spot / Lough Derg in Donegal." The arresting point for the reader of the Lough Derg canon is the way Timoney's "O God, O God" echoes the ending Devlin finds to his Lough Derg poem, which as an aesthetic artifact stands at the antipodes to Timoney's doggerel. While Devlin possesses perfect rhythmic pitch, notably in long lines, as distinct from the thumping predictability of Timoney's beat, unaided by equally unsurprising rhyme, Devlin ends his poem with ostensibly borrowed speech from a pilgrim beside him, who says simply, in contrast to the compressed and convoluted language that comes out of Devlin's mouth, "My God, My God." With his inclusion of poems possessing every degree of value, works from Thomas D'Arcy Mcgee to Margaret Gibbons, Timoney inadvertently signals the way in which Lough Derg forces even the first rank of artists to embrace at some level the most common aspects of their ethnic identity. Likewise in this pamphlet, which peddles Lough Derg's sublimity, pedestrian devotionalism is omnipresent, as, for instance, when Timoney delves into certain legalities about the shrine: spiritual matters that boil down to parsing the differences between plenary and partial indulgences, outlining the practicalities of what exercises one must do and in what quantity—the number of prayers to be said at each station, the exact number of stations to be completed in a day, the number of days and nights required by the pilgrimage. With this blend of shrewd, mercenary devotionalism and genuine spirituality, Timoney might be any one of the midland-burgher pilgrims encountered by Devlin or Kavanagh. Even for Timoney, however, the pilgrimage brings out the artist or artist manqué in him, a need to be not just the object of mechanical, mind-numbing exercises but a rapt center of consciousness.

Seán O'Faoláin would be widely perceived as residing culturally at the opposite pole from Joseph Timoney. In his fiction and nonfiction, including a biography of Daniel O'Connell, whom he rescues from charges of easy accommodationism by lauding the consummate politician for his hardheaded practicality, O'Faoláin presented himself publicly as someone wedded to a forward-looking, unsentimental cultural program for Ireland. This pragmatism was the theme consistently advanced in the landmark periodical *The Bell,* which he founded and edited in the early 1940s. Terence Brown, referring to the magazine's repeated sabotaging of the idealized Gaelic Ireland invented by Daniel Corkery, O'Faoláin's former mentor in Cork, says that "O'Faoláin launched attack after attack on these romantic conceptions in the name of a pragmatic realism. The Gaelic revival had become mere jobbery, the enthusiasts for the language 'vivisectionists' who had actually 'done irreparable harm to the language.' The vision of the heroic virtue of the west was mere escapism."[156] O'Faoláin's view of Irish culture, however, is not without its own complications, even contradictions, its own yearning for a cultural purity that had to be countered by summoning a willed realism. Brown, implicitly recognizing the resonance of this piece, also quotes O'Faoláin writing as late as 1941 about his discovery of the Aran Islands:

> It was like taking off one's clothes for a swim naked in some mountain-pool. Nobody who has not had this sensation of suddenly "belonging" somewhere—of finding the lap of the lost mother—can understand what a release the discovery of Gaelic Ireland meant to modern Ireland. I know that not for years and years did I get free of this Heavenly bond of an ancient, lyrical, permanent, continuous immemorial self, symbolised by the lonely mountains, the virginal lakes, the traditional language, the simple, certain, uncomplex modes of life, that world of the lost childhood of my race where I, too, became for a while eternally young.[157]

This retrospective description of how essentialism creates a hobbling nostalgia relies on a Carltonesque irony of exposing the past by means of the present. We must believe, however, that the author is truly free of this "heavenly bond." The slightly risqué allusion to skinny-dipping in a pool of racial purity, the need to shock, suggests perhaps unresolved attachment. There is a later John Montague story that, focusing on a clash between European and Irish sexual mores, has the stamp of O'Faoláin on it. "An Occasion of Sin" is about a French woman living in Dublin and outraging the local population not just by disrobing on a beach in order to change into a bathing costume, but also by chatting freely with clerical students. That this beach is a stone's throw from the "Forty-Foot,"[158] the gentlemen's nude bathing place adjacent to the Martello Tower, which serves as a site for the opening of *Ulysses,* only twists the knife of hypocrisy further in Montague's theme of Irish prudery and sexism. Men undressing is one thing, women quite another.

Montague's exploration of a cultural anxiety about the body, centered on the link between nudity and sexually charged swimming, recalls the nineteenth-century revision of the nude bathing practice at Lough Derg. Montague's protagonist, Francoise O'Meara, "a chubby, open-faced girl, at ease with herself and the world,"[159] cannot understand what the fuss is about. She seems immune to the rarefied and prurient vision of the female body that results from an Irish Catholic indoctrination, though she overhears one young student pronounce, "Pius always had a great cult of the virgin. They say he saw her in the Vatican gardens."[160] O'Faoláin, too, in his powerful evocation of the innocence of Aran, invokes the idea of the mother, indeed of Mother Ireland—"finding the lap of the lost mother"—and positions himself in that lap, a child again, the very image of the baby Jesus held by the virgin. What is more, in a supremely essentialist rhetorical move, he collapses the childhood of the nation into his own youth, conflating the two identities, the very ideological error that results in a range of repressive policies aimed at creating an pure race.

Perhaps the piece that most economically exposes these crosscurrents in O'Faoláin is a sketch entitled "The Sugawn Chair." The four-page sketch takes as its point of view a young boy observing his urban, middle-class parents in a moment that reveals their atavistic, unresolved relationship toward their rural, idealized pasts. Although ostensibly about a small family, a trinity of figures isolated from the extended families each parent left behind in the country, the portrait, given the correspondence O'Faoláin embeds between the individual and the culture, is implicitly one of the new, deracinated nation. The feelings of loss and nostalgia experienced by the mother and father are hypostatized, tellingly, in separate objects deriving from their two original homes. For her, this totem is a burlap sack of spuds and apples received annually from Limerick relations on the farm where she grew up; for him, it is a rustic sugawn chair, a relic and reminder of his origins. The father's fixation on the chair, preferring it after a hard day's work to one of their "plush-bottomed chairs, with their turned legs and their stiff backs," furniture "for show, not for comfort,"[161] indicates more widely a discomfort with the new urbanized, middle-class Ireland. The comfort he feels in the old chair, in which he "could tilt and squeak and rock to his heart's content,"[162] is reminiscent of the contentedness we have seen Curtayne evoke as a way of describing what it feels like to be in heaven. This complete sense of peace is predicated on the self-possession she implicitly connects with the achievement of political independence for Ireland. To repeat only a part of this previously quoted passage, Curtayne advises: "The thought of rest, of perfect ease in home surroundings must predominate. Possibly that sense of repose can be conveyed only in familiar, even crude, imagery. There is an expansive feeling of comfort, which can be described only by saying it is like a man sitting in an armchair at his own fireside, with his feet on the mantelshelf."

The point of O'Faoláin's story, at least half of its final point, is that such an ideal state is irrecoverable in modernity. In the story the father eventually falls through the worn seat of the chair, a not subtle metaphor for the old, romantic view of Ireland being no longer serviceable. To repair the chair according to traditional methods, the father enlists the services of some dissolute, inept locals, again émigrés from the countryside to the city. Not only do they make a botch of the eventually aborted job, they also set upon each other in argument and, in the mayhem, husband and wife turn as well on one another, arguing the superiority of their separate childhood homes. The contest for superiority is a domestic civil war. The chaos climaxes in the mother, like a keener orchestrating a lament, expressing in her sobs, her head buried in a fistful of hay, the grief for an entire, permanently lost, mythical way of life. While such ironies might point to the story's steady purpose to undermine nostalgia, the closing remarks of the child, representing the consciousness of the next generation, now two removes from the countryside, register the continuation of the dream of rural bliss. Recalling his sad duty many years later of dispensing of his dead parents' effects, he mentions this adult encounter with the permanently broken chair of no monetary worth. Its inestimable value, however, is as a mnemonic, recovering a powerful memory: "As I looked at it I smelled apples, and the musk of Limerick's dust, and the turf-tang from its cottages, and the mallows among the limestone ruins, and I saw my mother and my father again as they were that morning—standing over the autumn sack, their arms about one another, laughing foolishly, and madly in love again."[163] Finding a way to recover this innocence and passion by means of a reasoned, grown-up pragmatism demanded by actual circumstances becomes one of O'Faoláin's abiding themes.

Perhaps the substitute to which O'Faoláin's deracinated urbanites most regularly resort is a European Catholicism that enables both a recovered faith and a sensuality associated with that smell of apples and turf. Yet such an exchange often fails to resolve conflict, in fact makes it more intense, winds it up to an uncomfortable pitch. This is what happens in O'Faoláin's Lough Derg work, the short story "Lovers of the Lake." What better place to situate the clash between the atavistic dream of rural innocence and urban experience than a site associated as much with Tridentine devotionalism as with European high art and extravagant sin? In another story, "The Faithless Wife," where he similarly explores the European influence on bourgeois, urban Irish sexual mores, O'Faoláin depicts an affair between a French diplomat posted to Dublin and the restless wife of a dull merchant originally from rural Ireland. The story enacts the essential criss-cross, ironic movement at the heart of "Lovers of the Lake": the worldly, morally relativist male ends with an awed appreciation for strict, Catholic morality; the apparently chaste Catholic wife proves herself a tigress in bed who is also able, with surpassing sophistication, somehow to balance her appetites with religious doctrines held as sacred as middle-class decorum. In "Lovers of the Lake," the initial blasé, bachelor sophisticate is an Irish surgeon, Bobby; his adulterous, married lover is Jenny. The story opens with some casual banter between them that has a serious undertone, this counterpoint being indicative of the conflict that surfaces in the story between ancestral, ascetic religion and the new, cosmopolitan hedonism:

> "They might wear whites," she had said, as she stood sipping her tea and looking down at the suburban tennis players in the square. And then, turning her head in that swift movement that always reminded him of a jackdaw: "By the way, Bobby, will you drive me up to Lough Derg next week?"
>   He replied amiably from the lazy depths of her armchair.
>   "Certainly! What part? Killaloe? But is there a good hotel there?"
>   "I mean the other Lough Derg. I want to do the pilgrimage."
>   For a second he looked at her in surprise and then burst into laughter; then he looked at her peeringly.
>   "Jenny! Are you serious?"
>   "Of course."
>   "Do you mean that place with the island where they go around on their bare feet on sharp stones, and starve for days, and sit up all night ologroaning and ologoaning?" He got out of his chair, went over to the cigarette box on the bookshelves, and, with his back to her, said coldly, "Are you going religious on me?" [164]

In the same way as there is a verbal confusion over which Lough Derg Jenny means, the inhospitable Donegal bog lake or the large lake in the West to which avid European anglers make a pilgrimage, the title also contains a crucial verbal ambiguity. Are we to witness lovers at the lake, Lough Derg, or lovers who love the lake, because this ancient shrine alerts them to the possibilities of divine love? From these opening lines, we know that a conflict between pleasure and pain, purity and impurity, is in the offing, and that the representatives of opposing points of view initially are Bobby, speaking from cosseted depths and a nicotine fog, and elevated Jenny, looking down in distress on an upstart class that fails to wear whites for tennis. Bobby, preoccupied with comfort rather than correctness, worries that there might not be a good hotel at Lough Derg. This too is ironic, since the opposite of sumptuous accommodation awaits Jenny at "the other Lough Derg," where the most famous "beds," *turas,* circles of striated stones set in the ground, are hardly comfortable platforms for adultery. Folklore depicts certain saints—Brigid, Saint Patrick, Columcille, Brendan, Davoec, Molaise and, anomolously but critically, European Catherine—laying their chaste bones down on these jagged mattresses, as unyielding as their flinty souls. That Jenny in O'Faoláin's story seeks such purification is signaled by her fit of fastidiousness about a minor sartorial law. She is really worried, it turns out, about a greater infraction, of not playing the game of Irish marriage by the Church and society's rules. A personal, moral, social blemish obsesses her.

The irony of the story is that Bobby, who tags along on the pilgrimage, is more converted by it, to the point perhaps of following the rules of abstaining from food that apply to pilgrims up to the midnight after they leave the island. Although the narrative leaves his decision undisclosed, the extended implications of such abstinence are clear, that it may also mean an eschewal of adulterous sex. What is more, the entire tenor of the story propels us toward the irony of this reversal. In the beginning, when Bobby objects to the way Jenny proposes to subject herself and their relationship to this ordeal, she defends herself by countering that he has not objected to her doing her Easter duty and going to mass on Christmas. She is essentially defending herself by means of logic, accusing him of inconsistency. He retorts with unwitting and revealing irony, in relation to these rote observances, "Because all that was just routine. Like the French or the Italians. Lord God, I'm not bigoted. There's no harm in going to church now and again, I do it myself on state occasions or if I'm staying in some house where they'd be upset if I didn't. But this sort of lunacy isn't routine."[165]

Routine social Catholicism, an equivalent of good manners, which involves discreetly turning a blind eye to infidelity, is equated with reason, sanity, manhood. Bobby's possible conversion at the end presents the further possibility that the legendary, magical spell of the site has acted on this male cynic, but even this reading of the ending cuts two ways. It gestures both in the direction of a specifically Irish Catholic piety and its opposite. After all, O'Connor and Curtayne, patriotic Catholics in their separate ways, make it nearly seditious to endorse this European myth of magic at Lough Derg.

5

Denis Devlin

Clan Jansen

PERHAPS BECAUSE we are neurologically wired to construct unities, we search for the threads with which to weave a continuous narrative out of the knotted language and nonsequentiality of Denis Devlin's long Dantesque poem, "The Heavenly Foreigner." The intriguing result of these efforts, to go against the bias of modernism, is that the threads picked out from Devlin's poem suggest the material of an O'Faoláin story: a sophisticated Irishman abroad, most likely a civil servant, has an affair with a married European woman, who is much more at ease with her body and her God than he is. To say that about Devlin is to be guilty of gross reductionism, of course, but it is also a useful response to register, since the poem includes this level of erratic, sociological engagement. In "The Heavenly Foreigner," Devlin also weaves in passages that employ the point of view of an émigré to Dublin from the country. It is as though Patrick Maguire, the farmer at the center of Kavanagh's epic, "The Great Hunger," had left Monaghan and become a civil servant.

In a long poem organized by means of sections with titles largely taken from the map of Europe—"St. Malo," "Chartres," "Schwabing," "Ile-St-Louis," "Notre Dame de Paris"—two subtitles in "The Heavenly Foreigner" return home, not just to "Dublin" but to "Galway," the west, the epicenter of Romantic Ireland. The poem centers on a conflict between worldly experience and nostalgia. Within "Isle-St.-Louis," the narrator, who begins the section with an allusion to "the virgin she crowns / This moment with the diadem of her time"[1] or a romanticized woman, then appears to experience the opposite of the ideal love invoked. He refers to sex either procured or simply casual: "Love's earnest gift being frivolously given."[2] The section ends with a recovered memory of bourgeois, neutered, seedy Dublin, hardly an idealistic contrast to the worldly continent. Devlin offers us this thumbnail sketch of a frustrated, pretentious civil servant, a countryman uprooted to the city but terrified of the mud still on his shoes:

> In all these one-room flats, while the street-lamps, unseasonably awake all night long,
> Mutter their proverbs—that it's not worth it, it makes no difference—

How many white-collar clerks sit alone over a thin drink
    Singing ballads out of anthologies,
Reading, in a spurt and laze, the provincial eyebrow raised,
The Essays of Sorel, the novels of Maxim Gorky! and brush their teeth,
    Take two aspirins and fall between the soiled sheets,
    Thinking of the good brother and sister who have stayed at home
    In the country where the trucks are loading now
    With greens and tuberose and cackle;
    And fall asleep and resume the dream
    Of the fern and roses altar in childhood,
    Of the campaigns of childhood
    Against the fortress of the Snow Princess.[3]

Placing this beside "The Great Hunger," one wonders if the lonely, onanistic waste of individual life is essentially any different between the "soiled sheets" in Dublin or in Monaghan? Both Devlin and Kavanagh present riven identities through their narrative strategies. In both cases an urbane voice speaks of, almost to, a benighted other from the country, a tactic reminiscent of Carleton, where a not sufficiently distant past ghosts the present. Both Devlin and Kavanagh also are capable of viewing this past through the lens of a modernism acquired as much in a second-hand fashion as sentimental nationalism. Devlin's civil servant gleans his patriotism from undistinguished books, from "ballads" fished out of diluted "anthologies." The temptation in Paris takes place in the vicinity of "Ile-St.-Louis," the island connected to Ile de la Cité, where the cathedral of Notre Dame stands as a monument to the Virgin Mary. Furthermore, the crisis occurs on a bridge, a liminal space between two others: the hell of carnal existence and the heaven of faith. This is the same basic fissure occupied by the civil servant with his nightmarish daylight existence and dream world in the dark.

Although the purveyed image of Ireland is pastoral, the modernism gleaned from books accurately depicts the officially denied, jangling modernity of thirties Ireland. The grim one-room flat of the solitary bachelor and the "thin" faux intimacy of the pub belong as much to the Dublin of that transitional time as to Prufrock's London. In "The Waste Land," the bridge that leads to Notre Dame retraces the arc of London Bridge, which, not coincidentally, leads to the church of apparently obsolete Saint Mary Woolnoth. Like Eliot, Devlin is intent on presenting an "unreal city," made inert by no true, animating belief or human connection but made doubly "unreal" by the insistent, nationalist mythologies of both. With Devlin, therefore, the mimesis swings in two directions, toward Eliot's aesthetics and toward the Ireland he knew firsthand, a society itself swinging between modernity and a rural myth of what Antoinette Quinn calls a "primitive Eden."[4] So in "The Great Hunger" Kavanagh employs free verse and desultory diction to deliver Maguire to us as "sitting on a wooden gate, / sitting on a wooden gate, / sitting on a wooden gate,"[5] caught in a dead-end daydream that merely swings back and forth, going nowhere. Both Devlin and Kavangah reach out to modernism when they find themselves arrested in atheistic doubt: there may be no God, only a mean-ingless diurnality and carnality. Both, however, part company with modernism when an insistent, unstoppable need for belief reasserts itself and puts a pressure for unity and transcendence on both style and vision, a pressure manifested by dif-ferent strategies for each: Devlin more inclined toward cerebral symbol, Kavanagh toward the radiantly tangible.

In the same way, however, that O'Faoláin can be glimpsed at the bottom of the well of Devlin, so, too, can the early Kavanagh with his urgent realism. Obversely, Devlin with his symbolism, his ineradicable yearning toward a "dream of / the fern and roses altar in childhood," is distinctly visible in the early Kavanagh with his immersion in a numinous natural world. It is worth mentioning, too, that glimpses of the halo Heaney places around the homely simplicity of remembered objects from a rural kitchen redolent of maternal love are also to be found in Devlin. Only here they carry in their wake the most terrifying lessons attached to the Patri-archal God with whom Mary interceded:

> Since the time in childhood
> When dishes gleamed on the dresser,
> And the tall, blue benignant
> And black, malignant ghosts
> Meant what they said,
> Blue for heaven's haven,
> Black for the fear of hell.[6]

In this fluent movement from a memory of loved things to that of evanescent, persistent ghosts, Devlin demonstrates the play on the spectrum from concrete image to symbol that characterizes his style. Although, therefore, it is Kavanagh who is usually credited with a documentary dissection of Irish society between the wars, notably in both "The Great Hunger" and "Lough Derg," Kavanagh's early poetry, too, is charged with a religious and symbolist energy, a precursor to the mystical leanings of the later poet. This push in Kavanagh for transcendence, how-ever tutored by readings of the Romantics, which run parallel to Devlin's readings of the Symbolists, is grounded in a Catholic past. Also, Devlin, with his European profile and content, is associated with a bohemianism that separated him not just from the prevailing ethos of provincial Ireland, but from the people as well. Ka-vanagh, on the other hand, the "ploughman poet," is typecast as of the soil and of the people. Yet in both of the long poems we've been examining Kavanagh not only makes reference to Europe, but above all displays a self-conscious identity as "the poet," who speaks for the people from the standpoint of painful separation, if not ostracization.

Both men, precursors of Heaney, are engaged in passionate attempts at an inte-gration, which triumphant nationalism was equally adept at thwarting. Both poets attempt to reconcile, at least on the level of their art, a range of dichotomies, not least nation and self, the numinous and the material. Adopting different but not opposing strategies, both struggle with the still-unsolved puzzle of Lough Derg. All the pieces of that historical puzzle are visible in both poems, indeed, both oeuvres. For the sake of economy, I will consider both poets from the standpoint of their respective "Lough Derg" poems, and, as implied, other closely related works by each: Devlin's "The Heavenly Foreigner," written long after his "Lough Derg," and Kavanagh's "The Great Hunger," written just before his. I will also introduce Kavanagh's "Lough Derg" by means of the directly seminal "Why Sorrow," and "Father Mat," which was derived from the latter. This evidence of rewriting in itself indicates anxiety surrounding the subject at hand, primarily of the intersection of sexuality and the Church.

First, in relation to Devlin, because the patterns of highly colored agreement and disagreement formed by certain critical judgments and observations about him crudely map his complexity, I would like to set out some of these responses. The basic problem in locating Devlin is how to reconcile his affinity with modernism and its skepticisms with his Catholicism. J. C. C. Mays sees Devlin initiating a second generation of modernism, essentially following the example of Joyce, not just by exile, but also by departing from realism. Devlin did not choose to subvert the idealizing example of Yeats by a recording of the deflating facts, as Kavanagh did.[7] This explanation, however, does not fully accommodate Devlin's engagement with his faith, the point where he departs from Joyce. Tim Armstrong, summarizing Mays, asserts that Irish writers in the thirties faced a choice between "international experimentalism and a conservative, representative aesthetic associated with 'true Irishness.' "[8] The problem with this assertion is that the experimentalism fostered predominately in the generation following Yeats and exemplified by Beckett relies, in its metaphysical underpinnings, on a stern and—this is crucial—sustained and unrelenting interrogation of a belief in God.

It can be argued that Devlin's poetry is ultimately intent not on exploring subjectivity, though it does this too, but on approaching the divine through language. Seamus Deane regards Devlin on all levels as a poet struggling to produce synthesis. Deane sees Devlin in his faith as possessing a "fascination with the European Catholic tradition and its devotional Irish counterpart" and in his poetic as "representing a rare instance of a metaphysical poetry in a symbolist mode."[9] Because "fascination" is not belief, the problem remains to account for how the poetry negotiates the contradictions between the two terms proposed in each of Deane's formulations. Devotionalism with its mechanical oversimplifications can seem more a travesty than a "counterpart" of a more experiential, expansive Catholicism. Furthermore, cracks in Devlin's belief system make the relationship between metaphysical and symbolist poetry display as many dissonances as harmonies, suggesting modernism as a mode.

Using a cognate contradiction as a starting point, Tim Armstrong refers to a statement made by Arthur Cleary in 1918: "To speak of a Catholic Revolution is practically an oxymoron. Yet Pearse's movement inevitably claims that."[10] To speak of Catholic modernism may equally at first seem an oxymoron. Armstrong, however, finally proposes that a dialectical, oppositional process underlies most Irish modernist experiments, tacking between historical givens and poetic ambitions. Speaking of Devlin, Brian Coffey, and Thomas MacGreevey, Armstrong maintains that "All three poets produce their best poetry when most challenged by the force of experience and history, at those points where they are not merely relying on an established morphology outside the poem to create a sense of ambient meaning."[11] To adopt this useful perspective, and to group modernism, Catholicism, and nationalism equally among the various received morphologies challenged by specific circumstances, is to pay heed as well to Mays's key observation, that the history of modernism in Ireland is as particular as the country's political history. For one, Mays, in keeping with John Wilson Foster, who earlier revealed the Irish Renaissance for its modernist bent, sees modernism as having become part of Irish literary culture at an earlier date than in America or England.[12] He also sees Ireland's early-twentieth-century history as inflecting the second wave of modernism: "Popular revolution had already proved itself to be bourgeois, and freedom as a nation had produced other, severely felt constraints." To the degree that Devlin registers, not only through his escape into Europe but through direct confrontation with Irish society, his ambivalence toward the very bourgeoisie and government he represents, he also reveals an immersion in and political critique of Ireland. Lough Derg offered itself as a natural vehicle for this complicated project. Indeed, Devlin gravitated, like a moth to a flame, toward subjects that symbolically intensified, to a painful degree, all the contradictions and ironies in the nation and the self that both thwart transcendence and promise its validity, to the extent that to ignore them is to engage in falsehood.

No aspect of Devlin's work offers itself more readily for an examination of this fraught tangle of provincial and cosmopolitan attitudes, social conditioning and aesthetic strategy, religious aspiration and doubt, than his intense focusing on the Virgin Mary. Dillon Johnston characterizes this dense confluence of concerns and influences, featuring particularly an involvement with Mary, as eclecticism:

> To the living tradition of an Irish poetry Devlin can contribute an eclectic receptivity toward literature and philosophy, an Irish-Catholic sensitivity toward the flesh, a modernized Mariolatry in which women offer access to the divine, and a poetic reticence which soon became integral with his subject but which also may have reflected Devlin's uncertainty about a primary audience.[13]

While identifying the rich mixture of elements in Devlin, Johnston also begs certain questions. For instance, with Devlin's "Irish-Catholic sensitivity toward the flesh" and his, granted, "modernized Mariolatry," why does he nonetheless arrive at the audible alienation finally heard by Johnston? I believe it is because Devlin is earnestly attempting to synthesize in his work elements that outside it belong to radically divergent and totalizing belief systems, which, because each demands all-or-nothing assent, shatter when one tries to fuse them. Only a suprarational force such as the Mother of God (regarded as an intermediary between man and the divine), offers a hope of resolution; however, the very recognition of Mary's status as that of intermediary makes prayer to her contingent. In addition to this ontological conflict, Devlin embraces, through the symbol of the Virgin, a series of other unresolved conflicts. For example, his indigenous Irishness and acquired Europeanness come to a finely honed and infinitely split point. In relation to Ireland alone, Mary is both the rural focus of the nightly rosary and a middle-class intellectual fixation, as exemplified by Alice Curtayne in her reading of Dante. Mary is equally, however, a recurrent motif in European literature, from Dante through the troubadours. (Another echo produced by Seán O'Faoláin's title "Lovers of the Lake" is that of Arthurian romance, echoed, too, by the content of an adulterous affair and Bobby's possible conversion in the end, which would ratify the romantic tradition of an idealized woman being the route to faith.)

In directing "The Heavenly Foreigner" toward a contemplation of the Virgin, Devlin not only evokes this rarefied Mariolatry but also its cruder rural version. Both, however, entail the tortured attitude toward the female body that John Montague's "An Occasion of Sin" depicts, a mind-body miasma skimmed over by Curtayne's doctrinal certainty. Likewise, in appealing to Dante and the whole Renaissance tradition of depicting Mary, Devlin treads that thin but glimmering line between aesthetics and belief inherent in all these works that explore romantic love of a woman as a means to salvation. He also implicitly asks where such aesthetic practices may part company with ingrained Irish religious scruples. Furthermore, he both joins the ranks of modernists with their renewed interest in Dante and the Renaissance, and he diverges from them by means of his Irish Catholicism, which demands more than an artistic use of Mary. In the same way, therefore, that Lough Derg offers the perfect vehicle for exploring all the potential forces that fail to make integration possible but also promise it, if a way can only be found to resolve them, so the image of Mary offers a similar split focus. She is a means for him to be true to the provincial and the cosmopolitan in himself, the believer and the skeptic, the man worried for his soul and the artist intent on transformation through language.

To look closely at Devlin's moments of engagement with the idea of the Virgin is also to see more minutely how he both emulates modernism and separates his style and vision from it. Such an examination is also a valuable precursor to examining his "Lough Derg" for at least two reasons. First, like Mary with her role as intermediary, Lough Derg in its incarnation as Saint Patrick's Purgatory is a place endowed with a similar mediating identity. Second, with its longstanding association with Dante, Lough Derg offers a strong link with modernism, especially with Eliot, and therefore attaches itself to the abiding question of the relationship between metaphysics and aesthetics. Eliot's Prufrock, over the repressions and reticences of the tea table, fantasizes about the consequences of raising the startling reality of miracle. "I am Lazarus, come from the dead / Come back to tell you all, I shall tell you all," only to imagine his languid, self-centered interlocutor replying, "That is not what I mean at all. / That is not it, at all."[14] This unnamed female voice, which is completely authoritative, shatters a momentary religious impulse, leaving belief in bits, as unredeemable as the souls in hell who, by means of an epigraph from the *Inferno,* usher in the urban nightmare of "The Love Song of J. Alfred Prufrock." With Devlin, subversions are performed by interior consciousness alone, and so much is the body of the female other in the poem molded by the lover's mind, she has been read as evidence of solipsism by some and of vision by others. The language itself, depending on how you hold it up to the light, can display the corrugated, broken surface of modernism or the smooth unity of symbol. In a single, yet also always double, slice of perception, the female is both the mother of God, generated herself by an immaculate conception, and a sexual being generated by the "lust of the eye," to borrow Carleton's phrase.

Dipping into "The Heavenly Foreigner" at almost any point yields such oscillation. Even in the opening section, where the loved one is recalled, the memory is divided like two opposing tragic and comic masks between implications of hell and heaven. This opposition is delivered particularly through color:

> In the night-bar, black and red;
> And the gold on the hair of a girl entering brings back
> The noon, all that placid light-veiling shadow . . .
> While I weep somewhere in the distance. . . . [15]

The contrapuntal pattern of night opposed to noon, black and red opposed to gold, comes to a compressed climax in "that placid light veiling shadow." The paradox conveys a rich darkness, both benign and malign, necessary for the obscuring and revealing of light. This movement from contradiction to culminating paradox is typical of the poem. It also reveals its own aesthetic existence as partaking of the shadow that both delivers and hampers the revelation of light: "How she stood, hypothetical-eyed and metaphor-breasted, / Weaving my vision out of my sight."[16] Notice, too, how regarding hypothesis and metaphor as equal impediments, reason and imagination both being inadequate compared to faith, also enables the transformation of mere sight, all this limitation, into vision.

Yet this frantic dialectical movement yields no absolute, and throughout the poem the loved one, female, is distinguished from God, male: "Our absolute Lord had not been me, not me or you, / But an instant preconising eternity / Borne between our open eyes."[17] This use of "preconising" in the complex, temporal meaning it carries comes close to the use of "proleptic" in Devlin's lines from "Est Prodest": "And he will move breathing / Through us wing-linked / Proleptic of what Eden."[18] "The Heavenly Foreigner" is organized by means of space, with all those place names punctuating its different movements, but its theme, announced by the memory that initiates the reverie, relates to time. The poem explores how love can liberate us, through a glimpse of eternity, from the constraints of the mortal body tied to place:

And there were two, always in soft sunlight drawn close
Together, so by the sensuality of all the particles and particulars of nature
In such an embrace of space that the thrust of sunlight in the
    failing wind and the lapse back of the little winds upon the
    sunmotes took place at the same time and the same place.[19]

What with the "thrust of sunlight" and the "lapse back of the little winds," the erotic content of the experience is patent. So too, though, is the spiritual sensation of subject and object, self and other, "particles and particulars," being almost joined into "the same time and the same place," however much stubborn dualisms, embedded in the language, inhere. Note the repetition of the word "same," a sameness doubly delivered, a tactic that we will see in his "Lough Derg," particularly in its conclusion, where repetition per se signals continuing ambiguity.

One central paradox animates "The Heavenly Foreigner" and propels its spiritual odyssey. This hope is that love of another's body might enable not just the divesting of the lover's body, but of a stubbornly implicated intellect that mediates sensory information:

what pleasure
To strip off my flesh-bound intellection
That shard which does protect, yet
Rots the heart.[20]

The loved one is depicted and reported as constantly coaxing her lover to take this step into faith, unreason. The power of rationality is recognized as a dubious gift: "How I might make my soul / In a freedom that might destroy it?"[21] Yet reason insists on trying to discern whether the woman is the Virgin or a temptress in league with the forces of darkness. Describing unregenerate lust, Devlin, anticipating Heaney with a similarly repressive Catholic upbringing at his back, draws on the image of a phallic rat:

Rodents in the corn like the black gas in the heart of the sun.
The chase and the loving under the damp ditch;
Her blond laughter now indecent, her sexual
Ascetic face with the bones loosened.[22]

Only a Jansenist could portray a woman's face as both "sexual" and "ascetic." For all of Mary's intercessionary powers, for all the erotic transport of the poem, it ends with a confrontation with a stern and elusive God:

I know there is one thing, which is You, it is the unique
Which also in part is she,
You, not seen by her,
You, not to be reduced by my eyes' famine of her.[23]

Finally, in this historically and racially resonant use of the word "famine" in the context of spiritual despair, the mortal body is compromised but not discounted as a route toward transcendence. Rather, a trinity of pronouns—I, You, She—are left forever ricocheting in outer space, bouncing relativist signals off each other, and yet somehow managing to be proleptic of the Trinity.

Parallel to the way in which Devlin's own skepticism dismantles this feminine ideal, modern readers, particularly from deconstructionist and feminist viewpoints, have leveled at Devlin allegations of solipsism and manipulation of a distinct reality other than his own. Alex Davis states the case succinctly: "The subject's existence in the here and now is an echo chamber of the past, and this prompts an epistemological problem: the knowledge of the Heavenly Foreigner granted by the woman he recalls is, perhaps, knowledge of nothing more than his own mental images of that love-object."[24] Davis adds for further emphasis, "language becomes a Nietzschean prison-house, in which a personal style chatters away to itself, speaking of nothing but its own private concerns."[25] The problem with this otherwise incisive criticism is that it overlooks both Devlin's own admission of such tragic limitation and the oppositional effect of Devlin's language to transcend it, that is, the "light veiling shadow" he makes of style. Devlin must include this modernist despair for the faith toward which he reaches also to be grounded in modern, everyday reality. Anne Fogarty, cutting to the feminist chase but essentially aligning the charge of solipsism to expose a failure on Devlin's part to recognize female subjectivity, avers:

> Problematically . . . for a feminist reading, Devlin's discovery of the non-identity at the core of identity does not alter the fixed repertoire of tropes which he utilizes in order to depict either femininity or the female beloved and muse. This struggle to act upon the world and to reconcile being-in-itself, or mere existence, with being-for-itself, or consciousness, is mediated by images of a reified feminine other who alternately mirrors or opposes the male subject.[26]

Fogarty's intervention is useful as an indicator of the gradual emergence of gender sensitivity in not just Irish poetry but Irish culture generally, a painfully slow evolution apparent in Lough Derg writing. Devlin's poetry, however, presents a special problem for such secular readings, simply because "consciousness," "being-for-itself," is not his goal. Again, he himself presents the inert dilemma created by the intransigence of an alternately mirroring or opposing "other." He seeks a third transcendent term beyond these two. His arid dialectics are aimed at releasing a fountain of faith by means of a religious morphology, "a fixed repertoire of tropes," which has been dominated for centuries by a projection of purity onto the essence of woman.

What is more, contemporary Irish female writers, notably the poet, Medbh McGuckian, frequently use a male muse to achieve a cognate transport. McGuckian characteristically begins with the premise of perceiving a mortal man as God, then ascends into her own religious-erotic ecstasy. In her most successful adoptions of this stance, the deified object is her father. In "The Partner's Desk," for example,

McGuckian enters the mind of her dying father, who has already entered a different, freer realm, which yields a new order of perception for her:

> Saying, "The finest summer I can ever remember
> Produced you," and I remember a second,
> Gentler dream, of my wedding year,
> Where we took a walk across loose stones,
> And he took my hands and stretched them out
> As if I were on a cross, but not being punished,
> You know the renewed rousing of your fingers
> In a dream, your hand glides through air.[27]

McGuckian is Carleton inside out, having no fear of the loss of ego boundaries attendant on transcendent experience. Her similarity to Devlin on this score is striking. Her initial Lough Derg-like reference above to "a walk across loose stones" actually paves the way for a vaulting of the spatial, temporal, and corporeal ironically by means of the sexual, a feat that depends, as it does in Devlin, both on symbolism and Catholicism. McGuckian, Heaney's former student and devoted reader, is equipped by means of a spiritual lexicon derived from Catholicism to explore and name extreme experience. Carleton, given his struggle within the vise created by the hegemonies of the official Church and the Enlightenment, cannot make free use of this spiritual legacy. Certainly by McGuckian's time, with Heaney at her back resisting the fusion of Catholicism and nationalism, we see the signs of dramatic change. What is more, McGuckian can employ Catholicism for all the paradoxes it enables. For her, an unapologetic self-apotheosis hinges on its apparent opposite: the empathetic entering into her father's inner conversation just before death. This fantastic leap on McGuckian's part signifies a radical transformation of the legacy of patriarchy in its familial and imperial manifestations. More than a transformation of a woman's body, well nigh a reverse transubstantiation occurs when the erotic "rousing of your fingers" climaxes into "your hand gliding through air." Furthermore, McGuckian's manipulations with gender, be it the apotheosis of her father or a lover, demonstrate the persistence of the use of the opposite sex in poetry, even by the female, as a means of spiritual transport.

Perhaps the closest approximation to an explanation both of Devlin's complex engagement as a poet with the feminine and of his limitation in this regard is an inadvertently self-revelatory essay by Joseph Brodsky, another male poet invested in an idealization of the female. Brodsky, in this particular essay, is concerned with the generative, interdependent relationship he perceives between poems by Marina Tsvetaeva and Boris Pasternak on the theme of Mary Magdalene. (It seems more than coincidental that Tsvetaeva is one of McGuckian's icons.) The Magdalene might be seen as the alternate figure lurking behind the radiant image of the Virgin Mary in the "Heavenly Foreigner," given that poem's allusions to prostitution and lust. The two Marys might be imagined as the two faces of the female produced by

Devlin's rapidly alternating current of adoration and disgust. Brodsky produces an arresting thesis in relation to an affinity he sees between the treatment of Magdalene by a female "equal in stature"[28] to a male poet. Notwithstanding either his patronizing tone or likely error in judgment about Tsvetaeva's status as a poet compared to Pasternak, Brodsky manages to earn the attention of even the feminist reader who also is a serious reader of poetry.

Brodsky argues, by means of his Russian example of cross-fertilization between a male and female imagination, that poetry, especially religious poetry, can be a stronger force than the conditioning of gender. At the same time, Brodsky is nuanced enough still to regard gender as playing a mysterious role in the dialectic of arriving at faith. The stimulus for this essay appears in part to have been an indignation of a quality and intensity usually isolated to the feminist reader. As Brodsky explains, Pasternak includes two poems on the Magdalene theme in the final section of *Doctor Zhivago*. There, as the fiction would have it, the reader is seeing some of Yuri's poems about Lara, works intended to "add another dimension"[29] to his heroine. These poems, later collected by Pasternak's son in his father's *Selected Works,* are annotated with a reference to Magdalene poems by both Rilke and Tsvetaeva, works that, according to the editor, Pasternak knew. Speaking of the Tsvetaeva poem, and these are the offending words, Pasternak's son, the presumed editor, asserts that his father's poem "frees it [Tsevtaeva's] from erotic overtones."[30] It is this typical patriarchal parceling up of the material-corporeal realm to the female and the metaphysical to the male, the dichotomy his detractors attribute to Devlin, that elicits Brodsky's contempt and ire. The full measure of what Brodsky initially calls "moral and metaphysical misinformation"[31] only appears midway in the essay where he explains:

> For all the distance she maintained from the church, Tsvetaeva was a Christian, and for her the degree of sensuality present was always a reflection of the degree of love—a profoundly Christian sentiment. It is quite possible that Christianity's prime merit is that it instilled this sentiment with a metaphysical dimension. In that light, the commentators' remark that Pasternak freed the Gospel theme from eroticism betrays their Paganism, to put it mildly.[32]

It is this anti-Jansenist brand of Christianity, which takes its posture toward the physical world from the mystery of the Incarnation, that animates the speech of Devlin's woman in "The Heavenly Foreigner" and constitutes the promise she extends.

Once embraced, Brodsky demonstrates, such a paradox extends to the interdependence of male and female elements in the individual poetic imagination. This is a working belief that Heaney shares. Brodsky, however, takes his thesis to such a length that he ends by asserting that Pasternak's Magdalene poem is not just a response to Tsvetaeva's, or even half of a duet. Rather, they are essentially one poem, an imaginative, metaphysical unity that bridges the chasm of mere time that separated the compositions of these two halves—Pasternak writing his part in 1949,

Tsvetaeva in 1923. The psychological and creative process by which Brodsky sees this collaboration occurring (and it hardly matters if this is literally true of Pasternak, because it clearly reveals a truth about Brodsky) is extraordinarily complicated and involves subtle interchanges and exchanges between female and male imaginative strategies, also between art and life. The crux of Brodsky's faith in the poetic imagination is to see it as endowed with the capacity to enter the inner life of the other and to see that, when it fails to do this, it also fails to produce poetry.

In relation to Pasternak's two Magdalene poems, Brodsky regards the first as stillborn and the second as living, the former being influenced by Rilke's poem, the latter created by Tsvetaeva's. The Rilke response is doomed because it operates primarily on a level of technique, what Heaney calls "craft." As a result, for Brodsky the resulting poem is "more words than voice." Concentrating in this first effort primarily on the fine points of meter and rhyme, Pasternak, as re-created by Brodsky, who presumes to narrate from the older poet's consciousness, finds himself in a self-limiting trap. This is a bind created by the rational character of technical judgment: "Our very ability to do this job is itself an obstacle to faith, for our ability to set and fulfil a task—-our goal and our means—are essentially rational . . . faith is always an overcoming of limits." Then Brodsky performs the leap of genius that enables his own wildly speculative essay to create a radically new perspective on gender in religious literature. Reflecting on Pasternak's emulating and revising of another male poet's work, Brodsky, again speaking from inside Pasternak, muses: "Could it be that our failure is explained by our professional male timbre, while Magdalene was, after all, a woman?"[33] To the feminist reader's ears the assumption behind this conjecture can sound like a particularly infuriating, because extra refined, reprise of the very sexism that accompanied the implicit assigning by Pasternak's son of quite separate imaginative tasks and abilities to male and female, but as Brodsky's tortuous argument, delivered with a breathless urgency at every turn, unwinds, the picture is much more complicated and fluid.

On the one hand, obeying rigid traditional stereotypes, we hear Brodsky making retrograde value judgments regarding the personal and impersonal in poetry. He aligns, typically, women with the former, men with the latter. For example, again either hubristically or empathetically inside Pasternak's (the Male) head, Brodsky imagines the older poet's response to the receipt of Tsvetaeva's *After Russia*, where the Magdalene poem not just appears but where "not less than one-third of it was imbued with Pasternak's presence."[34] Brodsky calls the book "an act of love" to which Pasternak had a "physical inability to respond adequately . . . (like someone dropping a hot, burning dish)."[35] So, on the other hand, we have an evolved Brodsky imputing a brand of imaginative impotence to another male writer who fears female sexuality. Somehow, Brodsky implies, the learned, detached male stance fails the occasion, even though a collusive Brodsky inadvertently registers approval of it. Brodsky clearly identifies with Pasternak in his "professional male" way having been "most interested in the poems that were not directly related to his person."[36] Brodsky leaves room, however, for another, more liberated and risky response: that Pasternak may equally have regarded this book "as more than a literary fact."[37] Whichever, Brodsky concludes, Pasternak, "by 1949 . . . found himself, to a certain extent, dependent on several poems from *After Russia*. And one of them came to his rescue at a difficult moment."[38] This poem, Tsvetaeva's "Magdalene," rescues him precisely because it upsets this disabling, static categorization of the personal as female and impersonal as male, allowing Pasternak personal, dynamic access to the human grief at the heart of the Magdalene story. This immediacy makes the saint's prophecy of salvation affecting, a matter for poetry, rather than doctrinal, a matter for theology.

Brodsky sees Tsvetaeva herself in a male-manqué posture, using the biblical figure in two of the three sections of her "Magdalene" as a mere mask for herself. Magdalene is "metaphoric material, not much different from Phaedra, Ariadne, or Lilith. Here the issue is not so much one of faith but of female archetypes and their sensual potential, that is self-projection."[39] It is Tsvetaeva, in other words, acting like a "professional."[40] Then in a reflexive moment Brodsky immediately adds, changing our view of Tsvetaeva and pinpointing a change in her strategy: "Self-projection, hardly. Rather a projection of Christ onto oneself."[41] As he goes on more fully to characterize Tsvetaeva's transition from the first two sections of her poem to the third, which embraces Christ's consciousness as he speaks to Magdalene, Brodsky attributes to Tsvetaeva the crucial act of pure imagination, which makes Pasternak's leap of faith at the end of his poem possible. Describing Tsvetaeva's achievement in the third section, Brodsky explains:

> What is remarkable about it . . . is the fact that the author speaks in a man's voice. That is, relinquishing her own self and looking at herself from the outside, the heroine hears a voice which sounds like a postscript to her own and her addressee's existence. The meaning of the third poem, both evangelically and personally for Tsvetaeva, consists precisely in acquiring a tone for which it's worth giving up one's own tone. In other words: there is someone out there, and I will try to speak in his/her/that voice . . . here we have a woman performing a man's part, that she is looking at herself through His eyes, from the outside. We are dealing here with an extremely radical relinquishment, with a shift into a different quality, into the other gender. This is no longer a literary conceit; this is not love poetry, but spiritual poetry and it was precisely what Pasternak needed at that moment.[42]

Despite an entrenched sexism on Brodsky's part, manifest in everything from allowing Pasternak to identify with Magdalene's Jesus as himself ("The voice addressing Magdalene was male, and therefore, logically his own"[43]) to seeing a woman as more equipped to register the grief of Christ's death because women experience in life the loss of men, Brodsky manages in the end to present a pattern of an exchange of identities and genders that defies the usual distribution of roles to the male and female imaginations. For example, Pasternak, speaking as the Magdalene, opens his poem on a "plane of regard,"[44] to use Brodsky's useful phrase, that takes in the physical, the domestic, and the lowly. His poem begins with Magdalene, whom Brodsky in full misogynist flight sees as a portrait of Tsvetaeva, down on her hands and knees scrubbing a floor. Regardless, the breakthrough into faith, beyond the ego, into a "tone for which it's worth giving up one's own tone," the discovery that "there is someone out there," is all hers. It is this kind of breakthrough that Devlin is struggling, albeit without full success, to locate through the use of a female persona in "The Heavenly Foreigner." That his love object remains an inert archetype seems less the result of misogyny than of an inability to accept the link between sensuality and divine love. That was the saving core of Tsvetaeva's vision, a benign, forgiving Christianity little in evidence in 1930s Ireland.

In Devlin's "Lough Derg" the feminine represents the less than alienating, even inviting, edge of a vast land mass of anonymous pilgrims mostly referred to as "them." The problem in "The Heavenly Foreigner," of whether the speaker can make a leap into the identity and faith of the female beloved, symbolic of the intercessionary power of Mary, is rehearsed and revised in "Lough Derg." Here the problem is whether the speaker can empathize with the plain people around him. This exercise of charity, humility, and compassion is linked to every religious breakthrough Devlin makes and fails to make in the poem. He finds tiny openings in the various walls that divide and connect a range of antinomies associated with religion: reason and faith, pleasure and pain, faith and works, a personal and cold God, good and evil. These in turn are connected with the dualisms of self and culture, Europe and Ireland. In the end, I argue, Devlin maintains an ironic tone that preserves a layer of doubleness; however, his headlong rhythms and rhetorical legerdemain, his dialectical velocity and cascading figuration, create a sensation of transcendence disputed by the meanings on the level of reason set up by the poem. This dualistic dynamism can all add up to Devlin either staying on the fence about all these questions or, given the rhythmic and argumentative and metaphorical momentum, fluidly partaking of opposites without having to choose between them. As with "The Heavenly Foreigner," which ends its fugue of I and She with the insertion of He, "Lough Derg" may be read for the pattern of pronouns it creates, ultimately aspiring to a triumphant, replete, trinitarian shape. To trace simply the zigzag and telling path of Devlin's use of first and third person pronouns in the poem illustrates how ambiguity is cultivated and sustained, but also how the yearning toward transcendence, a breaking out of this unrelenting doubleness, is never relinquished.

The poem dialectically features pronouns that denote Them and Us, with a single reference to a synthesizing, divine Thou: "O Lord! The Temple trumpets / Cascaded down Thy sunny pavilions of air."[45] A direct, experiential I/Thou relationship between God and man is both hobbled and enabled by the narrow space between Them and Us, subject and object, through which one must pass. The poem shows Devlin tacking between these two poles, locating an "I" in safe isolation and a "they" in threatening collectivity. Occasionally a blending occurs and the pronoun "ours" appears. Let us see when the postures of separation and fusion are typically struck. The ending of the poem is usually read as a singular climactic moment of empathy with the once-distant masses, mouthing the exact words of prayer that come out of a pilgrim's mouth, "My God, My God."[46] This conclusion may equally be an ironic moment. Interpretation depends entirely on the many options for syllabic stress and tone available for the speaking of these four key monosyllables. While "God" is the word that at first arrests attention, "my" is no less significant and may indicate a false perception of connection, even presumptive possession. The two phrases double the chance to make the same choice between options. What is also significant, and less visible than a glimpse of the divine, is the fact that the overheard, adjacent speaker is female: "This woman beside me murmuring My God! My God!"

The poem also begins by affording a prominence to the feminine, first by its opening reference to the rosary with its repeated Aves: "The poor in spirit on their rosary rounds."[47] Prominent among the "poor in spirit" are variously repellent males—"the jobbers with their whiskey-angered eyes / The pink bank clerks, the tip-hat papal counts"—who stand in contrast to the inoffensive "drab, kind women."[48] The final, percussive word of the very next stanza will be "kind," the noun denoting a species or group, but resonating in context as a pun including the adjective, meaning to be kind. This second appearance of the homonym occurs in a question, "were they this kind?" referring to the "thief and the saint," an image of the symmetrical but opposing crucified figures who flanked Jesus on Calvary.[49] The interrogative mode of the line not only questions the true moral makeup of Devlin's fellow pilgrims but also the means by which salvation is found. Like the two thieves, one of whom confirms his soul through his appearance, while the other belies it, Devlin's fellow pilgrims cannot be judged by outward signs. Devlin is invoking a Jansenist, near-Calvinist God, who in absolute, almost playful, even scornful autonomy and arbitrariness balances the final scales of justice: "God's chance who yet laughed in his mind / And balanced thief and saint. Were they this kind?"[50] The memory of the adjective in the first stanza surfaces as we hear Devlin ask, not just whether a God who chooses one sinner over another is kind or indifferently cruel, but also what the moral disposition of his fellow pilgrims truly is. Devlin seems to be epitomizing and diagramming his endless dialectics in the shorthand of the ideogram of the three crosses on Calvary. There, the central, synthesizing crucifixion of Jesus, itself an image of contradiction resolved by means of paradox, is framed by two opposing, but mirror images. This is a difference remarked on only by Luke, who has one of the thieves both rebuke the other for his mockery of the so-called "King of the Jews" and beg for salvation.

"Mockery," incidentally, is a word Devlin associates with the Catholic hierarchy as it arrogantly apes a holiness and humility associated with a touted monasticism. The poet refers caustically to their "tonsured mockery."[51] As reported by Luke, the "good thief," the "saint" of Devlin's "Lough Derg," said, "Jesus, remember me when you come into your kingdom." And he said to him, "truly I say today you will be with me in Paradise." When Devlin asks of the people around him, "were they this kind?" he is directly posing the Jansenist question of whether works or faith will save. This is a probing question in the context of institutional Lough Derg, which suggests for Devlin the declension of the Irish Church from a pristine monasticism into an excessive dependence on works and a hierarchy to dispense and control the sacraments, including penance. The way in which this complicated meditation takes place, through ellipsis and figure, reveals the method of the poem, how it preserves ambiguity and complexity, even downright confusion. In this case, while stringently questioning the devotionalism of the Lough Derg exercise, Devlin also embraces the humility of not judging these people. He suspects that the saved, good thief, may be counted, given the statistics, among half of them. Most of all, Devlin's own superior knowledge of theology and church history guarantees him nothing.

Perhaps because of this humbling recognition of the inscrutable ways of divine judgment, Devlin can use the self-inclusive, possessive pronoun "ours" in the next stanza. Referring back to a comparison between "mullioned Europe" and "this rude-sainted isle" in the previous stanza, where Devlin seems poised between the two locations, sympathetic with and distanced from both, he goes on to sketch the place of Irish Catholicism in the history of European religious thought. He is especially and personally drawn to the autochthonous God of the Renaissance, summed up in the previous passage with the line: "Europe that humanized the sacred bane."[52] Now, in the third stanza, switching to the barren Lough Derg landscape—"Low rocks, a few weasels, lake / Like a field of burnt gorse; the rooks caw"[53]—he goes on to observe more metaphysically, "Ours, passive, for man's gradual wisdom take / Firefly instinct dreamed out into law."[54] The Irish sensibility, in which he participates and against which he rebels, seems to eschew process, temporality in the discovery of truth, favoring rather instant flashes of insight, based on images. The concrete, the sensual, however, immediately attenuates, rarefies, then suddenly reifies into law, the opposite of playful, ephemeral firefly instinct. Yet to follow the span of the spark ignited between "firefly instinct" and the lake at sunset, "a field of burnt gorse,"[55] a "red lake" suggestive of Dante's lake of blood in the *Inferno* (canto XXV), is to suspect that these seminal instincts can lead to visions. This is crucial to note given the allusive reliance of the poem on Revelation, announced in the fifth stanza by "Temple trumpets." "Firefly instinct" also may be an acknowledgment of a gnosticism at the heart of this faith. The Gnostic overtone also fits in with Devlin's own search for images that unfold vision, for a distrust of materiality and for his risky flirtation with knowledge over simple faith.

The historically informed, theological mind behind this poem is acutely aware of the eventual assimilation of heresy into doctrine, or at least into the practical experience of faith. A further example of this kind of irony occurs later in the poem with a reference to a specific victim of the Inquisition: "No better nor worse than I who, in my books, / have angered at the stake with Bruno."[56] Bruno, burned for his pantheistic beliefs, preached immanence not unlike that which radiates from

Devlin's poetry occasionally, when the balm of the natural world is admitted. The straitjacket within which Devlin squirms is not just Irish Catholicism but Catholicism generally, especially as it conflicts with a symbolical poetry, dependent particularly on immanence. His argument with the Irish way of being a Catholic ranges from, on the one hand, ruing a sclerotic practice that hobbles faith, to, on the other hand, rejoicing in an involuntary mysticism. In the next stanza as well, Devlin will refer to the Irish as "Clan Jansen,"[57] an ejaculation quite rightly identified by Robert Welch as indicating a criticism of the Irish as diminishing Jansenism, corrupting it with the cronyism and anti-intellectualism of the Church.[58] The phrase, however, particularly put beside the previous "Ours passive," also recognizes the preservation of Jansenism, much as the Celtic monasteries rebelled with their tonsures against Rome. Ireland, epitomized by this "rude-sainted isle," preserves the passivity that lies at the heart of Jansenism, which nullifies the significance of works as a means to salvation. It seems, therefore, that the indirections and connections of the poem underscore an unresolvable, intricate debate in Devlin about both his Irish and European heritage and his place in both. The final irony in this third stanza, more indicative of this deep conflict, surfaces when Devlin in the last two lines observes that "the prophets' jewelled kingdom down at heel / Fires no Augustine here. Inert they kneel."[59] A second Augustine, the theologian most drawn on to support Jansenism, will not be produced by mere intermittent, "firefly instinct," and yet this very fitfulness, this minute display of light, is precisely what the Jansenist contends lays the seed of faith. In other words, those very "inert," supplicant pilgrims, ignorant of Augustine, may be the most scrupulous adherents of Jansenism, simply waiting for the "firefly instinct" to ignite and save them. In the end, it is the abased, patient posture of the Lough Derg pilgrims that the discerning, learned poet has no choice but to adopt.

The stasis of "Inert, they kneel" imposes a cessation of motion also on the argument. This poem, with its lapidary six-line stanzas, rhymed *ababcc*, counterpoints its own chiseled lines and stanzas with fluid enjambment working between both. The syntax that links and separates stanzas is an especially powerful structuring tool, slowing down or speeding up, demarcating or blurring sections of the poem, the intricate argument and meditation. The line that opens the stanza after this temporary cessation begins, announcing an aesthetic and ontological concern, "All is simple and symbol in their world."[60] With this statement of an equation between simple faith and symbolism the most modernist section of the poem is launched and elaborated through three sentences spread over five stanzas. In this space, by surveying the ironies and contradictions in the spiritual history of western civilization, Devlin asks how justified simple faith and symbol both are. For example, by placing the "scroll-tongued priests," another reference to Revelation, next to "galvanic strumpets," caustically rhyming with "Temples trumpets," Devlin asks whether any vision can be trusted.

In Revelation (10:8) the speaker, John, reports being commanded by the voice of God to take from an angel's hand a scroll and eat it, literally ingesting the gift of prophecy. The closing of the Devlin stanza, which presents an insidious, secular power harking back to the "tip-hat papal counts," ratifies his doubt about the holiness of "scroll-tongued priests." This corrupt clergy is so insidiously and thoroughly implicated in religion as to be indistinguishable from it: "The Pharisees, the exalted boy their power / Sensually psalmed in Thee, their coming hour."[61] The inseparability of body and soul, corruption and purity, summed up in "sensually psalmed" recurs as a theme in the next stanza's reference to the "orphic egg."[62] Devlin is alluding to the essential belief of Orphism, that the soul is imprisoned in the body. The Manichaeanism implied by the earlier reference to Augustine, credited with disproving the Manichaean heresy, rears its head throughout a poem riddled with unresolved dualisms, where darkness appears to be given the same valency as light. Manichaeanism is the heresy that comes to mind with Devlin's deliberately shocking image of "Christ the Centaur."[63] Although the image, from a modernist perspective, which refutes the simple equation of faith and symbol, makes sense as an integration and assimilation through time of the Classical and Judeo-Christian traditions, the gross sensuality of the centaur, part animal, part man, harking back to "stone dreams and animal sleeps and man / Is awake,"[64] is also ironically found overly intellectual by simple faith.

The next stanza begins "Water withers from the oars,"[65] an image of the Lough Derg boats filled with pilgrims plying toward the island. As in "The Heavenly Foreigner," movement from European to Irish locations is part of the meditative movement of the poem; these returns to Ireland also involve a return to a yearning for faith. The Lough Derg boat will be iterated with approbation soon in a reference to the "coracles," rhyming with "oracles,"[66] of the Irish monks. They, retracing in reverse this movement between Europe and Ireland, poles of secular complexity and simple faith, take their "belled and fragrant,"[67] pure, uncomplicated message to the Continent:

> their oracles
> Bespoke the grace to give without demand,
> Martyrs Heaven winged nor tempted with reward.
> And not ours, doughed in dogma, who have never dared.[68]

This prominent "ours" is noticeable all the more in this eleventh stanza for being the only such self-inclusive moment since "Ours passive." (The seventh stanza contains the lines, "sleep with its drama on us bred / Animal articulate,"[69] but this is an observation of the human, not specifically Irish, condition.) As "water withers from the oars," it is as though all the erudition of the preceding stanzas also drops away as so much intellectual vanity. Still, the poet keeps his distance from this severely pared down, anti-aesthetic stance. Having earlier referred to "these pilgrims," he now refers to "their sin," which they are here to "masticate."[70] This jibe constitutes a derisive, defensive dismissal. Part of the need to keep the pilgrimage at arm's length relates to the preceding impressive encapsulating of complex history. The poet is embarrassed that present-day Lough Derg represents a falling off from the site celebrated by Dante: "Where Dante smelled among the stones and bracken / The door to Hell (O harder Hell where pain / Is earthed, a casuist sanctuary of guilt!)"[71] It is with this epitomizing phrase that Devlin's own honesty enters, identifying both his powers of ratiocination and feelings of isolation. When he therefore idealizes a chaste, monastic past, one similarly exalted by Curtayne, as we have seen, he also includes himself in the falling off from pure, truly "simple faith" into uninspired devotionalism. It marks a radical departure from Curtayne, the apologist, that Devlin, the poet, includes himself in "this race": "ours, doughed in dogma, who never have dared."[72]

Like and unlike Prufrock, who asks himself if he dares to eat a peach or wear his trousers rolled, Devlin here asks himself if he dares the apparently simple but highly consequential act of empathy with his neighbors. The point in the poem where Devlin succeeds in finding a distinctly Irish opening within modernism occurs in the fourteenth stanza where, having returned to his meditation on the consequences of the synthesis of Classicism and Christianity in the Renaissance in the previous stanza, he suddenly, in the light of the chaos produced by two world wars, declares, "O earthly paradise / Hell is to know our natural empire used / Wrong, by mind's moulting, brute divinities."[73] From this point on at some level, beneath recurring conflicts and paradoxes, Lough Derg assumes a new role in the post-apocalyptic, post-world wars present. It is the site for the severe penance due after such evil. While the exclusivity of this Hiberno intervention into European postwar culture echoes Shane Leslie's exceptionalism, the deeply anguished, penitential tone of Devlin rules out any hubris in the stance. Nonetheless, the Irish become representative of flawed humanity, including himself: "Say it was pride that did it, or virtue's brief: / To them that suffer it is no relief."[74] The simple observation of common suffering releases a conditioned but distinct empathy in the poem.

The concluding four stanzas, two full sentences, include three uses of the word "we," the final one typically undercutting the potential for transcendence in such a trinity: "What John the Blind / From Patmos saw works and we speak it";[75] "Courage kills its practitioners and we live, / Nothing forgotten, nothing to forgive";[76] and finally "We pray to ourself."[77] The ambiguity, the swinging between community and isolation in "We pray to ourself," capturing perfectly the sense of being alone and with others true to every pilgrim on Lough Derg, is prepared for by the second use of "we." The penultimate stanza records a plunge inward not unlike the perilous yielding at the end of "The Lough Derg Pilgrim." As Devlin puts it, "Then to see less, look little, let hearts' hunger / feed on waters and berries."[78] No less addicted to the "lust of the eye" than Carleton, Devlin takes his penitential leap into sensory, cultural, poetic deprivation, a temporary vow of poverty that finds expression in paraphrasing a banal hymn and according it half-belief: "The pilgrims sing: / Life will fare well from elder to younger."[79] Distancing himself by means of the irony ensured by objectifying "the pilgrims," but also counting himself among them, Devlin comes to the moment of realizing simply the mystery of his own life: "Though courage fail in a world-end, rosary ring. / Courage kills its practitioners and we live, / Nothing forgotten, Nothing to forgive."[80] These two nihilistic "noth-ings," like the two thieves, will balance in conclusive irony the two "My Gods" of the absolute conclusion, itself a balancing act. As that final ejaculation of simple faith, "Nothing forgotten, nothing to forgive"[81] also registers a moment of pure penance, a contradictory sensation of being shriven, because sin has been acknowl-edged, so a momentary truce between reason and faith may be struck.

There is a pressure felt stylistically, emotionally, and intellectually in Devlin's "Lough Derg" to push against and expand the boundaries of conventional reli-gious culture, as distinct from religion, in Ireland. In addition to his pointing to-ward the irony of yesterday's heresy becoming tomorrow's doctrine, Devlin, through his serial allusions to heresy, is also lodging his own rebellious instinct, summed up in the reference to Watt Tyler, the martyr-leader of the Peasants Rebel-lion in England in the fourteenth century. In coupling this secular martyr with Bruno, a martyr of the Church, Devlin is also exposing the collusion of middle-class respectability and Catholic piety in the newly independent Ireland. This attack is not unrelated to that launched by Yeats a generation earlier in "September 1913" on the occasion of the anti-labor Dublin Lockout. Although Devlin reveals his class stripes, striking a range of postures resembling those of Curtayne and even Leslie, unlike them, and demonstrating the subversive role poetry can play, he also attacks his own collusion with a pat, unquestioning faith. Nonetheless, he ends "Lough Derg" with an image that splices itself onto the discourse of racial purity we have seen in both Curtayne and Leslie. With the lines, "Whitethorn lightens, delicate and blind, / The negro mountain" preceding the final zooming in on the woman mur-muring, "My God! My God!"[82] Devlin appears to be sketching the redeeming effect of Catholic-Christian belief on an otherwise savage, pagan landscape. The closest approximation to the spiritual essence of whitethorn in this elliptical, final stanza is "prayer without content," the rote ejaculations surviving a Catholic childhood.

The opposite, more rebellious side of this concentration on the colonizing, mis-sionary zeal of the Irish is, however, the sustained invocation of Ireland's monastic tradition throughout the poem. References to the stubborn adherence to the ton-sure in the face of pressure from Rome, of the salvation of Europe achieved by Irish monks and now effected by the plain people doing penance for the evil of war, are all part of an anger on Devlin's part with the declension of faith that has come with so-called independence. An arch-conservatism, outrunning the hierarchy by miles in its orthodoxy, is the ironic backlash of Devlin's critique of the purblind Irish Church. Although one side of him, as Deane suggests, is indeed fascinated with European Catholicism and its Irish counterpart, another side of him is disgusted by both for the reduction of faith they complicitly enforce.

We have seen Curtayne provide for Lough Derg a more sophisticated version of the narrative of continuity created by O'Connor. For her, the hierarchy of the Catholic Church, notably the Papacy itself, saw to the management of an unbroken tradition of religious rectitude at Lough Derg. For O'Connor this unbrokenness is the same sacred, essential truth, but for him the people primarily maintained the tradition. This is a division within the narrating consciousness of Devlin's "Lough Derg," where some attempt is made to explore the fallacies and verities of both. While Curtayne elevates Lough Derg in its pre-European, pristine phase, Devlin on the level of content embodies this monastic, prayerful perspective. "Vain My Visit to Lough Derg" is reprised to a modernist tune but with the same recalcitrant content, for there is a way in which style and content diverge in Devlin, creating his poetry's most ingrained doubleness. Dillon Johnston remains the most meticulous describer of the minutiae of Devlin's style. Time and again, Johnston's close inspections lead him to the overall observation of verbal dynamism:

> Difficulties in Devlin's verse are usually fluidities; where we cannot grasp meaning, we must trace it in a motion that has a definable course. . . . Meaning in Devlin's poetry is dynamic rather than static. He breaks stasis not only through the volleying between alternative meanings of a word but also through active paradoxes. . . . Devlin will also disrupt stasis and set meaning in motion through the various forms of internal reference, frequently to some antecedent in a remote line of the poem. Finally, perhaps, Devlin's most characteristic device is the use of internal references, what Joyce calls, "ipso-relative" allusions, which sometimes occur in a sequence: one term will refer to another which refers to a third, setting in motion a relay or short circuit of reasoning.[83]

If you obey the rhythmic imperative of the style, this fast-flowing stream creates the sensation of oneness, ecstasy, faith confirmed. If you allow the contradictions set up by such volleying to slow you down for a split second, you drop to the bottom of all this and the stream dries up, fragments like caked mud. What is more, given this split between an aspiration lodged in style and a doubt in content, a reversal begins to occur: when the style stalls, doubt predominates. Yet the fast-moving dialectic of thought in itself sets up a flow. The result of this added reversal is an implied intertwining of thought and sensation, so very close, so nearly fused as to approach a still fugitive unity.

This near and continuous splicing of thought and feeling, both wrought to the uttermost, may be seen as the condition of prayer. Just as "Vain My Visit to Lough Derg" finally communicates a frustrated but incandescent piety, suggesting more authenticity than a vaunting ecstasy, so Devlin's meditations convince for their inclusion of every possible impediment to faith. As we examine, in relation to Heaney, Milosz's struggles with the relationship between belief and poetry, it will be clearer how central Devlin is to a European as well as an Irish tradition of a scrupulously honest religious poetry. Not only does he set a standard for gender engagement through his deconstruction and restoration of a Beatrician ideal, an exploration perhaps not yet equaled for its ardor in Irish poetry, but he also sets the bar for prayer in poetry.

Nonetheless, a barrier is felt by Devlin and his reader that is never breached, no matter how fast and furious linguistic and intellectual energies surge. Because the faith he seeks is all-inclusive, so too this barrier extends along a broad front. It is not just between faith and reason, Ireland and Europe, but between Ireland and Ireland, an urban myth of a rural Eden and separate but continuous hells on both sides of this hypocrisy. Devlin resorts to a "prayer without content" at the end of Lough Derg because the words of prayer are uttered by a person, a woman he hears and sees but cannot dare, through true empathy, touch. In the same way, he shuns himself as mere flesh. It is with such a miraculous breakthrough into the skin of another, even another gender, that Tsvetaeva, according to Brodsky, discovers that "there is someone out there," a discovery for which it is worth "giving up one's own tone." For all that he achieves in scrupulous self-examination, this does not happen for Devlin, the leap that would have permitted change. That leap persists for him as essentially the same self-annihilating act Carleton witnessed at Lough Derg, when the deranged boy hurled himself from the gallery. Devlin imbues his style from "Lough Derg" to "The Heavenly Foreigner" with an increasingly Baroque and filigreed language, quite unmedieval in its excess, but a substantial barrier against dangerous and untenable transport. For all the dynamism of this style, the experience contained in Devlin's poetry remains static—blessedly so, perhaps.

6

Patrick Kavanagh

Compassion's Ecstasy

EVERY ACCOUNT of the genesis of Kavanagh's "Lough Derg" mentions the by-now infamous comment the poet made about his subject, "The moment you think of Lough Derg your mind goes blank, your mind atrophies."[1] Antoinette Quinn, in her recent biography of the poet, emphasizes how rebarbative this penitential material was to Kavanagh, who visited the shrine twice, in 1940 and in 1942. He performed both pilgrimages ostensibly for the sacrilegious reason of doing journalistic research for two separate articles, the earlier for the *Irish Independent*, the later for the *Standard*. Quinn informs us that the first attempt was meant to add to a series he had already written about various Irish pilgrimages, and that from this sampling he had concluded that "the less austere the pilgrimage, the better he liked it." He especially favored those where sociability was to the fore: "Good-humoured crowds dressed in their Sunday best; tea and sandwiches in the open air; hawkers and stallholders plying their wares: such easy commerce between the secular and the sacred, piety and gaiety, met with his approval."[2] Lough Derg with its loneliness, its siege in "prison," and its fasting, couldn't be further from an excuse for a day out. Yet, the fact that journalism was the prod that got Kavanagh going with this central poem is telling. Lough Derg was at the time a supremely populist destination, and Kavanagh's almost helpless focus on people, including aggravated fits of misogyny, provides the fulcrum for him that shifts the inert mass of Lough Derg as material for poetry.

By now it is a commonplace to observe that a corrosive internalization of inferiority, foisted on a native population by imperial acts and judgment, is one of the most persistent consequences of colonization. It is equally common to add that this conditioned response is contagious, replicating a rash of analogous forms of oppression, particularly and ironically those invoked in the name of freedom. Further, this slavishness is linked, reflecting the sway of a conquering patriarchy, to a concomitant feminization. Lough Derg, as we have seen, can be experienced as the site where these self-perceptions are most acute: a self-abasing obedience to

Church authority and a herd instinct stripping the self of all autonomy and, for the male pilgrim, manhood. Marjorie Howes in *Yeats's Nations* provides a succinct and trenchant summary of the incremental buildup of this eventually internalized projection onto the native Irish, particularly via the racial theories of Matthew Arnold. She indicates how feminization enabled the metaphor of an imperial marriage: "Femininity marked the Celt's difference from the Saxon, but also placed her in a relationship of natural complimentarity to him. Like man and woman, they were meant for each other, and should acquiesce in the dictates of nature and history, combining to make a more perfect whole."[3] This projection of union on an interpersonal level made it possible to interpret the "Act of Union" as a contract between equals, a way of accommodating the anomaly of a white, colonized people both similar and dissimilar to their English rulers. To borrow Howes's language, a "neo-imperialist nativism" is what we are seeing in Shane Leslie, an essential Irishness Leslie regards as rising to a pinnacle at Lough Derg. Notwithstanding Declan Kiberd's *Inventing Ireland*, much less noted and analyzed, however, than this onslaught on confidence, is the process by which recovery takes place, especially from the self-imposed, indigenous but imitative nativism of the newly independent nation.

We have seen all the Lough Derg writers under scrutiny here so far in their separate ways managing conflict on countless levels in their writing. Carleton, reacting in part to an imposed imperial view of the peasantry from which he springs, both colludes with this verdict and uses it as a way of escaping an already conformist native culture. MacCarthy, living and working in the more essentialist climate of the 1840s, compared to the earlier years of the century, is largely at odds with the definition of Irishness within which he was expected to operate. Carleton in his "Lough Derg Pilgrim" displaces part of his own inner conflict onto an altogether separate voice in his text, that of Caesar Otway. This inclusion anticipates Carleton's later use of a range of voices, a heteroglossia lodged consistently and covertly throughout his narratives. MacCarthy chooses translation, the alterity of an entire other language, as a way to explore forbidden areas of identity beyond those politically sanctioned by the ethos of his time, the racial superiority and purism, say, of Charles Gavan Duffy. Devlin, who builds doublessness into style and content at every level in his poetry, tries to find room to maneuver in the crack created within the hypocrisy of an urban elite, which imposes a fiction of idyllic simplicity, only notionally inclusive, on a rural and urban population alike. Patrick Kavanagh, who like Carleton was actually born into that doubly objectified peasantry, is also born, given the time and place of his start in life, into the ideal position to speak an individual, spiritual truth. For him this finally means the dismantling of a more and more petrifying and degrading idealization, which has been transferred from imperialist to nationalist discourse.

The place to begin such reparation is by constructing a rounded subjectivity that displaces that former flat, obsolete objectification. This is one of the achievements of "The Great Hunger." Antoinette Quinn, in her comprehensive and authoritative critical survey of Kavavagh, *Born-Again Romantic,* has dubbed his most successful long poem with its truth-telling, revisionary mission as a "rural sequel to *Dubliners.*"[4] Although Yeats and Synge, and even native Irish Padraic Colum, who was swept up in the Irish Renaissance, construct a peasantry devoid of a deep and pervasive Catholic consciousness, Kavanagh corrects this lack. He endows his central character, Maguire, with a rich inner life animated not just by the teachings of the Church but also by an instinctively heterodox spirituality. Maguire's consciousness puts pressure on the constraints of an Irish Catholicism that is as over-determining as the nationalism with which it is fused. Quinn understandably calls Maguire an "Irish rural Everyman."[5] The overall aim of the poem, however, is to negate such essentialism on every level. While Maguire is indeed representative of the rural, Irish male after independence, the particularity bestowed on him by Kavanagh in his rich, detailed, interior portrait rescues Maguire from being an emblem. As well, the spiritual questioning and philosophical openness of the poem defy the certainties of allegory. Quinn is astute in pointing to the cinematic qualities of the poem's method, which add to its subversive realism, providing an inbuilt resistance to any agenda of transcendence: "the camera, which converts everything into image, gives a metonymic dimension to his metaphoric readings."[6] This coexistence of metonym and metaphor with their separate, ontological implications of materialism and idealism, the poem's "documentary and visionary dimensions,"[7] in Quinn's words, predicts the forked, unresolved ending of the poem, which embraces the eschatological poles of absolute finitude and infinity, death and an afterlife, atheism and faith.

The further question of whether Maguire is an author surrogate or not has been debated. Quinn takes the commonsense stance that so many external differences exist between the biographies of Maguire and Kavanagh that the farmer-protagonist is obviously not the actual poet, that the two are separate entities, Maguire being a crafted persona.[8] Although the poem is not literal autobiography, Maguire has the soul of the sort of poet Kavanagh was becoming; further, Kavanagh deliberately deploys the persona of Maguire to help birth his nascent poetic. As Yeats uses serial masks and Heaney, as observed by Helen Vendler, empathetically enters various, alternative identities in "Station Island" to explore personal recesses beneath the surface of everyday conduct and consciousness, so Kavanagh uses the alterity of Maguire. As a poet, Kavanagh sets himself such a strict standard of truthfulness that his poetic will seem to him unproven and invalid if it does not confront the harshest life circumstances he has known. The same perverse principle will apply to Lough Derg. In "Pilgrims," an earlier (1940) short poem, one of two precursors to the long poem, Kavanagh satirizes specifically the Lough Derg pilgrims he observed in his season of pilgrimages:

> I saw them lying on the burning stones—
> It was vision, vision, vision they desired:

Vision that is forecasting a mare's hour of foaling,
Vision that is catching the idler newly hired.[9]

Kavanagh demonstrates the shrinking of a medieval visionary religion in the grip of a mercenary devotionalism. In "The Great Hunger" Kavanagh deliberately foregrounds the contingencies of money, labor, and sex in order to test whatever religious vision survives such vitiation. Although Quinn is right in pointing out that Maguire at the opening of the poem is the age Kavanagh was when he left Monaghan for Dublin, it is precisely this fact that gives the poem its there-but-for-the-grace-of-God humility, which roots the author's current spiritual and aesthetic questions in his past. It tests faith in an exacting context, as the Book of Job does. Kavanagh's poetic will become indivisible from his unorthodox private faith, and yet both derive ultimately from the terra firma of his rural beginning with its conventional Catholicism.

In this poem, through a fluid and often indiscernible blending and separating of authorial and protagonist voices, a searching meditation occurs, an interrogation of rural Catholicism that breaks down what previously has been a diamond unity. With a deceptive ease, Kavanagh, through Maguire, separates that faith into its ecclesiastical, doctrinal, mystical and vestigially pagan elements. More than anything, he asks how imagination negotiates these various areas of belief, teaching, and tradition. Beyond constructing this rich subjectivity, however, Kavanagh intervenes by means of apostrophe to enlist the reader's healing sympathy, as distinct from Joyce, who with his inviolate detachment simply leaves his creations to wither in the light of reader inspection. However one divides Kavanagh from Maguire, the end result is to witness Kavanagh weighing in unequivocally on the side of a justice too long deferred. As Quinn resoundingly concludes:

> In "The Great Hunger" the people's need has created a voice. Its narrative gives utterance to inarticulate peasant Ireland, as if the very stones were crying out, speaking the unspoken and unspeakable, defying the taboo that keeps desperation quiet, unsaying the pastoral platitudes, gainsaying the literary myths of the noble savage and the prelapsarian peasant. The "speechless muse" has found a language.[10]

As though testifying to the success of such compassionate, redemptive poetry, Heaney later registers the pleasurable shock of self-recognition and affirmation provided by Kavanagh. Heaney will assert that "if 'The Great Hunger' did not exist, a greater hunger would, the hunger of a culture for its own image and expression."[11] What is more, Kavanagh's taking up of the scales of justice performs the kind of redress Heaney later comes to advocate, not as an overtly political act but as a metaphysical undertaking that places human existence in a context more capacious and ultimately more forgiving than narrow, harsh circumstance. Whereas Heaney at this point in his career is urging, with reference to Simone Weil in *Gravity and Grace,* the value "of counterweighting, of balancing out the forces, of redress—tilting the scales of reality towards some transcendent equilibrium,"[12] Kavanagh at the early stage of a career with a similar trajectory to Heaney's, from a broadly physical to metaphysical emphasis, is eliciting a cruder, more full-blooded response to injustice. He prompts this human attention by an accurate presentation of distressing facts.

In "The Great Hunger" even the satirizing of ecclesiastical religion is mitigated by a recognition of the communal value of the Church. Kavanagh's trenchant critique of Irish Catholicism never descends into simple anticlericalism. Further, not only is a certain sympathy built up for Maguire, even when he is at his most slavish to the institution and the hierarchy, but the author seems as invested in the earnest reflections of his protagonist as in the sardonic overlays of the narrator. Two major sequences take place in the physical structure of the Church, one centering on Maguire as a young, somewhat casual worshiper, spitting beside a pillar, the other as an older, metaphorical pillar of the Church. While the reader is predisposed to be suspicious of the Church as a key player in the conspiracy not only to neuter the sexuality of the masses but also to numb their capacity for spiritual vitality, a more truly catholic viewpoint pervades the poem. This more generous view refuses to rule out as a source of comfort and even revelation any religious activity, especially one that brings people together. So, while Maguire's greedy and sly mother stirs reader suspicions with her manipulative injunction, "Now go to Mass and pray and confess your sins / and you'll have all the luck,"[13] space is created for a more positive view, at least of the clergy, with Maguire's independent assessment "that the priest was one of the people too— / A farmer's son—and surely he knew / The needs of a brother and sister."[14] Although irony might be picked up off this objectively dubious, perhaps naïve expectation, the rest of the passage, with its Kavanaghesque tone of both soul-searching and speech-making, suggests an author earnestly thinking aloud:

> Religion could not be a counter-irritant like a blister,
> But the certain standard measured and known
> By which man might re-make his soul though all walls were down
> And all earth's pedestalled gods thrown.[15]

The complexity of this apparently straightforward, discursive passage is considerable, not least for the probably unwitting evocation of Carleton through that image of the blister. Moving swiftly from the corporeality of that irritant, implying a Church that fails to serve the soul, to an apocalypse destroying the world as we know it, including all our gods, Kavanagh registers a need for an absolute faith that will absolutely save.

His portrayal of the ecclesiastical Church both questions and affirms its efficacy. The narration proceeds by means of irony and approbation. The young Maguire at mass, who, safely obscured, "knelt beside a pillar where he could spit / Without being seen," wanders freely in his attention, musing, for instance, "should I cross-plough that turnip ground." He also, however, ends by ceding his individuality as "the congregation lifted its head / As one man and coughed in unison."[16] All these details, not to mention the final gesture of coughing "the prayer phlegm up"[17] in an amen, all weigh in as negatives. Within this flawed and compromised spirituality, however, there is room for split seconds of transcendence:

> Five hundred hearts were hungry for life—
> Who lives in Christ shall never die the death.
> And the candle-lit Altar and the flowers
> And the pregnant Tabernacle lifted a moment to Prophecy
> Out of the clayey hours.[18]

This brief levitation, however, appears to be fueled by collective human passion, the masses, rather than the mass. Even when the venality of both the Church and its members is seen to taint Maguire, who becomes ostentatiously pious in late middle age, the reader still does not begrudge him his envied, respectable status in the congregation because this seems one of his few rewards in life. Also, he is no credulous fool. As he leaves the church, he regards heaven "angle-wise,"[19] with skepticism. At the very least, the Church provides a communal cohesion, but this hardly compensates for the routing of sexual intimacy it more definitively achieves.

Just as he sees Catholicism interpenetrating every part of his protagonist's being, from the sexual to the social, so Kavanagh also regards the Church as an elaborate, living organism within which all its constituent parts, like the Trinity itself, are interdependent and fluid. A compromised ecclesiastical infrastructure, therefore, is not separable from a more compelling, though still controversial, doctrinal core, and finally, from mystical experience, an analogue of poetry. Having said this, it is also apparent that for Kavanagh there are ascending rungs of spiritual experience. Tellingly, personal epiphanies most often take place not just outdoors, but in down-to-earth circumstances: sudden stabs of redemption in the middle of mindless rural labor. Since such flights occur when one is most grounded, even ground down, the phrase "Heaven dazzled death,"[20] is to be found in the midst of a rote, soporific litany. Of course, the phrase also trails a whiff of irony, like cloying incense from a thurible. Nonetheless, Kavanagh sees true transformations as so inclusive that they must embrace their opposite; hence, the most quotidian moments also include the potential for ecstasy.

It is in his "Lough Derg" that Kavanagh explores the way spiritual blood can be got from the unyielding stone of a hard religion. This labor is prepared for, however, by "The Great Hunger," which, in the appeal its title makes to the specter of the Great Famine, also implies the life-denying Tridentine devotionalism that emerged stronger than ever from that nineteenth-century cataclysm. As Kavanagh delves particularly into doctrinal Catholicism, he also gains a purchase on the more transcendental aspects of doctrine that devotionalism nearly trapped in legalisms: blind practice rather than informed faith. Moreover, the Lough Derg pilgrimage performs a shadow play behind the screen of "The Great Hunger," not just in references to purgatory ("And Patrick Maguire / From his Purgatory fire";[21] "the purgatory of middle-aged virginity"[22]) but more specifically in symbolic evocations of the physical structure of the Church as a prison: "the chapel pressing its low ceiling over them."[23] Also, a purgatorial, permanent in-betweenness, the living death of Kavanagh's Maguire, is conveyed through images of and references to incarceration: "the enclosed nun of his thought,"[24] a further reference to the feminizing that results from the Church's colonization of the individual. If Kavanagh's too believing, mother-dominated ploughman fails, unlike his once sexually active mother and shrewder mates, to understand how "religion's walls expand to the push of nature,"[25] this denizen of a "metaphysical land,"[26] for all its aridity and his barrenness, has the ability to push the walls of doctrine wider than a cramped devotionalism.

Although Kavanagh is not the Church historian or theologian Devlin is, "The Great Hunger" nonetheless conducts a refined and incisive inventory and investigation of doctrine, saving kernels of faith from the husk of rules. For example, through the lines, "A door closes on an evicted dog / Where prayer begins in Barney Meegan's kitchen,"[27] the culturally regulated, nightly rosary gets sardonic exposure by being seen as ostracizing all things animal. (It is as though all the beasts were expunged from the manger.) The worship of the Virgin is not invalidated, however, despite the paramount role of Mariolatry in repressing carnal desire between real men and women. While loving "the light and the queen / Too long virgin"[28] can lead to secreting desire in the dark pockets where "the twisting sod rolls over on her back" and the fantasized "virgin screams before the irresistible sock,"[29] such perverting idealism also has its noble aspect. The narrator, in a section where he is unequivocally distant, asks bitterly, speaking at a steely, anxious remove from "the poor peasant" in himself, why he should submit to a doctrine that insistently converts matter to spirit. Why place your faith in "a soul / That is only the mark of a hoof in guttery gaps?"[30]

Furthermore, this reflex conversion of messy life into pristine but empty idea is never more exercised than in relation to sex, particularly the idea of the female. Living in a world "where flesh was a thought more spiritual than music," Maguire sees in his relatively lusty youth "a girl carrying a basket," and promptly "rushed beyond the thing / To the unreal. And he saw Sin / Written in letters larger than John Bunyan dreamt of."[31] For all the harm that this contorting of natural impulse wreaks not just on the psyche but on the species, such absolutism also fosters everything that is anti-opportunistic and idealistic in human character. Kavanagh makes us see, by the way his religiously speculative narrator blends seamlessly into both the wondrous and slavish piety of Maguire, how being bowed by the Church can translate into a consistently spiritual, brave, upright posture. This paradoxical relationship between a tyrannical and truly spiritual absolutism is most revealed in section 6, where in the same way that he sped from sexual attraction to "sin," Maguire fantasizes about a spiritual fulfillment unavailable to mere mortals. Tutored in such

all-or-nothing expectation by the promise inherent in the synecdoche of transubstantiation itself—"In a crumb of bread the whole mystery is"—habitually,

> He read the symbol too sharply and turned
> From the five simple doors of sense
> To the door whose combination lock has puzzled
> Philosopher and priest and common dunce.[32]

While far from solving the relationship of matter to spirit, Maguire is at least an
aspirant in the struggle to understand. Because his religious background predis-
poses him to the large inquiries, which lie within the poets' as well as the philosophers' ambits, the line between narrator and farmer-protagonist consistently and
deliberately blurs. Kavanagh, after all, as the ultimate correction to the muting effected by colonization, is revealing the proto-poet in the most oppressed victim of
the empire, the Vatican, and the nation. So it is that in section 6, where a literal point
of view is set up in Maguire's head, through the lines, "As he sat on the railway
slope and watched the children of the place / Picking up a primrose here and daisy
there—"[33] the dash at the end may indicate equally the direction in which
Maguire's thoughts might lead or the transition into the voice of the narrator. It is
the narrator who makes of this bucolic image the philosophical, heretical sense that
these innocents, unwarped yet by Catholic absolutism, "were picking up life's
truth singly."[34] While it sounds like the narrator's angry, retrospective irony that
denounces his double's "all or nothing" propensity, averring, "And it was nothing,"[35] a sense of certainty does not result from this denunciation:

> All or nothing. And it was nothing. For God is not all
> In one place, complete and labelled like a case in a railway store
> Till hope comes in and takes us on his shoulder—
> O Christ, that is what you have done for us:
> In a crumb of bread the whole mystery is.[36]

The end-stop with "God is not all" suggests that unreined idealism falsifies,
that there is no "absolute, envased bouquet,"[37] that God, as the next line tells us, is
to be found scattered and in fragments. Yet when the eventuality of hope tapping
one on the shoulder is broached, the speculation swings in two directions, both
backward to reinforce the idea that only by accepting reality can a positive outlook
be preserved, and forward to underscore the way belief redeems reality's fragments into God. Kavanagh himself, by means of a fusion of narrator and character,
seems to exclaim "in the crumb of bread the whole mystery is."[38] While even these
excited words emerge out of a shell of irony and anger, the resulting spectacle, on
balance, is of awe.

The specific doctrines that most stimulate Kavanagh's imagination are those
that constellate around the Incarnation. Beliefs associated with events in Christ's
life—the Crucifixion, the Resurrection—are natural magnets for a poet meditating

on the place of human suffering in circumstances either providential or without redeeming design. Less obviously, Kavanagh's persistent appeals to the Holy Ghost spring from a belief that the Incarnation is consistent with a pagan animism. Sporadic, uncontrolled apprehensions of the divine in nature support Christian doctrine:

> These men know God the Father in a Tree
> The Holy Spirit is the rising sap
> And Christ will be the green leaves that will come
> At Easter from the sealed and guarded tomb.[39]

These final four lines of a jewel-like sonnet, dropped nonchalantly like a stone in water into the midst of this overall loosely constructed poem, anticipate, in the way they convey vision as a random gift, Kavanagh's much later canal bank sonnets. There, nature offers a similar earthed transport. By exchanging a shamrock for a tree, Kavanagh folds this quiet ecstasy into the fabled paradigm of Saint Patrick's teaching of the Trinity. Kavanagh thereby enforces the role of traditional Irish Catholicism in his eventual discovery of a self-liberating relinquishing of the ego by means of yielding to the flux of the creation. Similarly, the narrator in "The Great Hunger" halts his flow toward the beginning of the poem, which entertains at the offset the possibility of atheism, and asks, "Is there some light of imagination in these wet clods?"[40] The imagination at this stage is identified with the Holy Ghost, which is considered to possess similar life-giving properties. It quickens the natural world as the Holy Ghost did Mary's womb.

A large part of what makes Maguire's life appear possibly to be without redeeming meaning is the economic fact that he has little time for regarding nature as amenable to the animating and plastic powers of imagination. The earth remains inert to the exhausted ploughman who sees the return of the seasons less as a miracle than as a monotonous recurring cycle, like a workhorse circling a field. This, however, is precisely the challenge posed by Maguire as an alter-ego: both imagination and religion, to be valid, must survive physical exhaustion, penury, and a lack of leisure. They must, in fact, transcend a dependence on beauty, on matter and flesh. All of the going indoors—"Come with me, Imagination, into this iron house"[41]—are preparations for the Lough Derg vigil in prison. A further, necessary preparation is a confrontation with one's common humanity, stripped of an assuaging humanism. A philosophy that starts with the beauty inherent in nature, then ascends and ascribes this exquisiteness to the soul, is seen as a form of civilized vanity that must be purged.

The event in the life of Christ, therefore, that most arrests the author's attention, most serves his attempts to find redemption in Maguire's life and his own, is the Crucifixion. Maguire's sacrificing of his life's blood for the good of his fields is both ironically and movingly likened to the sacrifice of Christ's life on the cross. When this farmer's eyes do not rest in rare moments of spiritual remission on the natural world as evidence of transcendence, they rest on earthly evidence of the opposite: human suffering. Again, it is important that the following passage contains an apostrophe and an imperative to the reader, giving us no choice but to

> Watch him, watch him, that man on a hill whose spirit
> Is a wet sack flapping about the knees of time.
> He lives that his little fields may stay fertile when his own body
> Is spread in the bottom of a ditch under two coulters crossed in Christ's Name.[42]

Like Arthur Miller through the voice of Willy Loman's wife, Linda, calling for the witnessing audience to pay attention to the tragedy of an otherwise invisible man, Kavanagh is insisting that we see Maguire's Christlike suffering. Maguire is enduring in daily life the crucifixion he projects onto "two coulters crossed in Christ's Name"; and it is even possible, given the blurring of narrator and character, that Maguire foresees his own dead body making the sign of the cross as a gesture of futility, or faith, or both.

The poem's most affecting sections question, through the example of Christ's sacrifice, the role of human suffering in a plan of redemption. In section 1 the narrator delivers an apostrophe about a possible meaning of Maguire's brutal life. He urges himself, as much as his reader, toward compassion first and foremost as a route to such understanding:

> Let us be kind, let us be kind and sympathetic:
> Maybe life is not for joking or finding happiness in—
> This tiny light in Oriental Darkness
> Looking out chance windows of poetry or prayer.[43]

The fact that relief from the darkness is figured as random glimpses through the structuring frame of "poetry or prayer" makes both activities redemptive. While both locate minute signs of faith, both also are initiated by a force beyond human consciousness and control. This moment in Kavanagh also locates his revision of comedy, not as humor or conventional good fortune, but as a faith in faith, and in the way things simply are. When Maguire is depicted suddenly, while waking up from sleep, as making the entire journey from grief to acceptance—"And he cried for his own loss one late night late on the pillow / And yet thanked the God who had arranged these things"[44]—Kavanagh is in miniature tracing the arc of his entire career. It is precisely this gratitude for the way things are that quickens his late poetry. In "Canal Bank Walk" the divinely orchestrated arrangement of things—"The bright stick trapped, the breeze adding a third / party to the couple kissing on an old seat"[45]—provides not just the "nest for the Word"[46] but the nest for the poet's jaded soul. The concept of the "nest for the Word" rings a change at the far end of the poet's career from the idea of the Logos both invoked and subverted at the beginning of "The Great Hunger": "Clay is the word and Clay is the Flesh."[47] "The Great Hunger," up to its forked ending, never relents in its balancing of faith and skepticism. Its opening entertains the atheistic position that no soul at all informs the echoing imprint of a horse hoof in mud, that the idea of God being synonymous with the word, with creation itself, is blatantly false. In the last phase of Kavanagh's career, the absolute inherence of the divine in language and language in matter, the radical idea that initiates the Gospel of John, is transfigured into a less absolutist but more consoling, benignly maternal trope of containment and protection. The word and man are held in the nest of the perceivable world.

Such holding and cherishing is what Kavanagh is already asking of his reader, and much more importantly of himself, in "The Great Hunger" with regard to Maguire, to himself. In section 3, much discussed from a postcolonial point of view, Kavanagh is demanding that he rid himself of mental postures and projections imitative of neoimperialism and a parroting nativism. He asks that we switch the focus of our irony from Maguire—"let us salute him without irony"[48]—to those who idealize the peasant as someone "with no worries," who "ploughs and sows" and "eats fresh food" and "loves fresh women."[49] More trenchantly, however, he asks us to fling aside the veil of spiritual idealization that impedes the true, much more difficult and mediated spirituality of any fully realized humanity. The "peasant" perceived as a "child of Prophecy"[50] with a direct line to God unhindered by the static of civilization is a debilitating fiction created by others. It is also a fiction that robs the likes of Maguire of the difficult faith that enables the complexity of poetry. By submitting to and passively assuming his place in a cosmic schema devised by others, the peasant also enables others' poetry. He plays an obliging simplicity to their complexity. In "The Great Hunger," however, even in its unbridled and sustained anger, a precursor to the ennobling grief Maguire rises to at the end of his life, Kavanagh is preparing the way for the spiritual breakthrough to come in his own life as a poet. For example, when he implores us and himself to abandon the superiority of irony in relation to Maguire, Kavanagh reaches down into that very darkness that his irony has glossed over, speaking bitterly of "the peasant ploughman who is half vegetable."[51] This bitterness even boomerangs back on him at the end of this stanza, where the narrator in collusion with the peasant's idealizing detractors, hazards that the peasant "is not always blind: sometimes the cataract yields / To sudden stone-falling or the desire to breed."[52] Even here, however, Kavanagh is slowly, tortuously performing his own and his people's liberation through the expression of a self-destructive anger that is also the productive source of recovery.

Maguire's late, reposeful acceptance of the divine arrangement of things, which will eventually be Kavanagh's, is won after a wrestling that contorts him with rage and remorse. The poem repeats the word "twisted." Trying in section 11 to reach an acceptance that includes seeing a place for "grief and defeat"[53] in God's design, the narrator muses, "The twisted thread is stronger than the wind-swept fleece."[54] Earlier he advises:

> And Saint Patrick Maguire
> From his Purgatory fire

Called the gods of the Christian to prove
That this twisted skein
Was the necessary pain
And not the rope that was strangling true love.[55]

Anticipating "Lough Derg" and its legendary suffering derived from being caught between a heaven of occasional moments of faith and a hell of daily living, Maguire is asking that this painfully twisted, unrelieved ambiguity, a state of mind close to Devlin's in the end, not be without meaning. The crucial difference between Devlin and Kavanagh is that Kavanagh makes the bold leap into a compassion toward himself and others, the only remedy for a torture resistant to metaphysical intervention. It is as though the suicidal leap of the poor boy in "The Lough Derg Pilgrim" were waiting for this transformation.

Kavanagh's religious conditioning and specific engagement with the doctrine of the Incarnation lead him to implore the reader, in relation to Maguire, to "kneel where he kneels," literally to put ourselves through imagination and empathy into the body of this poor farmer. Instead of digging deeper and deeper into an endless grave of reasoning, Kavanagh goes in the other direction toward feeling, even occasionally too far into faux simplicity, even levity, rhyming, for instance, the word "grass" initially with "arse"[56] and only later, more subtly and aptly, with "Mass" and "bless."[57] Although not always true to the gravity of this insight, Kavanagh comes to locate solidly man's holiness in the same physicality that brings pain and doubt. This continuous twisting of faith and doubt leads to a tortured poetry authored by an animist natural world: "Nobody will ever know how much tortured poetry the pulled weeds on the ridge wrote / before they withered in the July sun."[58] The implication is that we cannot ever know the unexpressed poetry, which a "twisted skein" like Maguire's might have produced. History no doubt inters hieroglyphic tomes of confused emotions below the level of language. For Kavanagh, the ordering of inchoate and powerful, competing feelings in poetry is equivalent to a redemption of the entire context of rural life from a projected ideal at odds with the richly diverse reality arranged by God. All this order, however, rests on the acceptance of the placement of one man in that design. We must, for the sake of an entire culture, "kneel where he kneels."

The choices Kavanagh makes in the creation of "The Great Hunger" have had a profound, determining effect on contemporary Irish poetry. The healing properties of that historical poem have been difficult not to emulate. Devlin's inability to locate compassion consign him to the purgatory of modernism. The fragmentation that is the hallmark of that style can be seen as the result of a collision of belief and cynicism that occurs with resounding, lasting effect when Prufrock's interlocutor devastates him with her reply: "That is not what I meant at all." The philosophical idealism of the Logos lies as a memory behind the shatters of modernism. "The tortured poetry" of Kavanagh's Maguire, minus the blessing of human understanding and connection, also aptly describes the work of Devlin. Modernism may be regarded as the result of "reading the symbol too sharply," as Maguire did the Eucharist, insisting that its transforming truth radiate out and suffuse all reality. The consequence of this failure of cosmic transubstantiation can be a permanently shattered faith. Freed emotion, anger and love, especially self-love, provide the necessary resilience to make things whole again, to weave the wreath that will hold the word, to present images one by one, like the flowers picked by a child, and to trust that the resulting arrangement is replete. Kavanagh's eventual ability to perceive things in their place, as well as in a divine scheme of things, comes above all from his struggle in "The Great Hunger" to accept Maguire as a man, the final lesson of the Incarnation. This achievement, ultimately of self-acceptance and of the self's Christ-likeness, is the central, essential component in Kavanagh's later spiritual repose, which depends not on imposing immanence on outside objects, but on allowing the self to assume its place in a God-given, natural arrangement.

If we put two phrases from "The Great Hunger" together—"the priest was one of the people too" and "chance windows of poetry or prayer"—we get the threshold over which Kavanagh's "Lough Derg" is entered. Devlin reasons like a theologian, and he even was, like MacCarthy, a seminarian for a while; Carleton's sartorial ruse in "The Lough Derg Pilgrim" reflects his adolescent ambition to become a priest; and one of Heaney's alter egos in "Station Island" is that of a young man from home in Mossbawn who became a priest. For Kavanagh, too, entering the persona of the priest is a key step in finding his way as a poet. For the rural Catholic mind Kavanagh is entering, the priesthood edges close to the mystery of the Incarnation: the paradox of God as man. It is precisely this apotheosized manhood that Kavanagh will hubristically bestow on his poet-persona in "Lough Derg" and must revise, in the radical and unrelieved direction of simple manhood: Christ on the cross rather than risen from the tomb. Quinn informs us that the fragment "Why Sorrow" was a precursor to "Lough Derg." In that quite lengthy snippet, "Why Sorrow," the central character who replaces Maguire and might be considered a priest-ploughman as well as a poet-ploughman, is a country cleric, the eponymous Father Mat, the title of a poem that is a fragment of the also partial "Why Sorrow." "Father Mat" was published in the erroneously titled, earlier *Collected* as distinct from the later *Complete Poems* by Kavanagh. The major excisions applied to "Father Mat," censored for reasons of Catholic sensitivity, account for the most powerful content in "Why Sorrow."

Father Mat, whose common humanity is the attribute most valued by his congregation, is first seen in the poem of that name on "Confession Saturday, the first / Saturday in May,"[59] a day of preparation for the May Devotions to our Lady. In the more complete "Why Sorrow," Father Mat's forgiving, easygoing nature in the confessional informs a major dramatic section of the poem, but it is the priest's own confession, excised from the abridged version, in addition to crucial cuts in the confessional narratives of others, that provides the spiritual pivot of the original. In this version Father Mat from the beginning, for all his appearance as a natural priest, a "part of the place, as natural as / The stones in grazing fields that are not seen / By those whole walk the ridges,"[60] has something in him that he, for one, secretly considers unnatural. Indeed, the opening of the poem is an accident that happens when his mind is venturing to heretical, sacrilegious heights, where he knows a priest should not venture. He trips over a stone, a fall from grace that precipitates the crisis of the poem.

As part of exercising empathy with the priest, Kavanagh investigates Mat's background. Kavanagh is also showing the reader the way in which the impoverished rural Irish family, especially its mother, may see the transformation of an only son into a priest as the greatest possible moral vindication. Mat has come from such a poor family and is the product of a mother's and a sister's designs, but, even as a boy, he is aware of a demon within him ready to defile the potential priest, also latent. Kavanagh shows us how such imagined lapses from purity at an early stage are the stuff of normality, psychic health, before such apparently contrary urges are truly twisted. Mat, the young man, headed for the single, all-sacrificing destination of the priesthood—"he had only to grow / The flower was in the seed"[61]—senses a shadow presence in himself, the potential of "twin flowers."[62] Already a young Manichaean, his world is split between the pious and impious, which largely consists of pagan, classically inspired fantasies about the "Garden of the Golden Apples."[63] Crucially, this fantasy world is one where the malleability of poetic imagination reigns supreme and anything can be molded to desire: "old boots were flying sandals,"[64] recalling Mercury and the velocity and magic of unchecked imagination. His good, or priestly, self cleaves strictly to untransformed, suffering reality.

Tellingly in this poem, Kavanagh bursts into formal poetry, typically four-line stanzas of iambic pentameter, when exhilarating heresy is being entertained. This is a perverted inversion of his practice in "The Great Hunger," where he bursts into ad hoc sonnets at accidental moments of transcendence. In "Why Sorrow," Mat's childhood memory of a patch of garden "between a railway and a road,"[65] an otherwise unremarkable plot transformed into the "Garden of the Golden Apples," is encased in such a seven-stanza sequence. Then again, recalling the legendary domicile of gleeful sinners in the parish, a "house of pleasure," where sex and dancing prevail and "lilacs grew before that door and roses / More prosperous than roses anywhere,"[66] a re-creation of his proverbial, lush secret garden, the narrator ascends into nearly formal poetry: five taut quatrains and two stanzas of five lines each. This spontaneous formalism ends with a sudden scene of collective remorse, an entire family penitential: "Four generations wept in a squalid corner / For tomorrows that would tell the shame in them."[67] This reckoning with a judgment beyond themselves is triggered by the entrance of the "old priest" into the shadowed interior of their house. Once this fall from innocent hedonism occurs, the style, too, takes on a more modernist look: unrhymed lines of irregular length, enjambment balanced by fragmentary exhalations, all beginning with the question "Why should this be?"[68]

The young Father Mat asks himself this same question, the question that haunts "The Great Hunger" about the meaning of human suffering. In his youth the image that appeared to heal the rift within Father Mat, exacerbated by the onset of sexuality, was that of the Virgin Mary:

> And when years brought loving on
> He was deep in love with one—
> Mary Queen of Heaven.
> She was every girl he knew,
> Nimble-footed, daring too.[69]

From this first, albeit partial finessing of desire ("daring too") Father Mat sets his life's course of denying the flesh. Hearing the laughter of people passing by on the road, the old priest muses:

> I might
> Have eaten like these
> Life's leavened bread that has mysteries
> Marvellous as the wafer consecrated.[70]

The persistent doubleness of his nature, mirrored in the distinction between a communion wafer and "leavened bread," provides the moral conflict for a lifetime, a struggle centered on cracking an obdurate pride at his center: "His pride lay between the hammer and the thing / That he was striking at."[71] What is more, his pride stays connected with an appreciation of and escape into beauty. Snobbishly, Father Mat holds himself above his curate, Father Ned, a man who "never reads in brook or book."[72] Father Ned, mindlessly obedient to the authority of the Church— "a man who was never late / For train or chapel. He had the sins / Of men card-indexed"[73]—is also someone incapable of the foolish extravagance of true spirituality. Nonetheless, Father Mat is afraid of Father Ned, precisely because he lacks the imagination to sin. Father Mat's accident at the beginning of the poem is precipitated by an aestheticism and hedonism so unrestrained he conjures "the unspeakable beauty of Hell."[74] Not unlike Maguire, Father Mat, by twisting his need for pleasure around the unyielding law of his celibacy, has forced his desire into unnatural shapes, taking root in taboo places. The priest, who is loved because he is like the people, learns in the course of the unexpurgated "Why Sorrow" that he is like the most unregenerate, vile sinner in his parish. In his moments of most intense suffering and sensual deprivation, he reminds himself that "His people needed him. / His people needed Him."[75] These may as well have been the words Kavanagh said to himself as a poet, anticipating the need for cultural affirmation that would be felt by poets of Heaney's generation. It turns out that Father Mat most fulfills the people's need by admitting to himself how much like them he truly is, more like than they ever could imagine.

In the confessional he hears everything, the gamut of human sin. The particular confession Kavanagh chooses to include at length is that of a young sexually abused girl who, obeying the self-loathing of the Church's indoctrination, especially in regard to sins of the flesh, reads her abuse as a sign of her unique, solitary sinfulness. She describes a scene where in the midst of a piano lesson, a standard tableau of adult authority over the young, the male teacher molests her: "He said her fingers on the keys were the hopping feet of hungry birds. / He told her of a strange world. / And then? He gave her loneliness forever."[76] Echoing the molester's fine phrasing, Father Mat's words of consolation have the dubious ring of the poet: "My daughter, you are the mystery in the piano's tune."[77] Not only is this section left out of the recycled "Father Mat," but a much more scandalous and cryptic narrative is cut altogether. "Cryptic" may be a generous word for confused and unrealized. It may also recognize deliberate or unconscious obfuscation. In any case, the following passage demonstrates how some of Kavanagh's least successful transformations of the raw material of life into art also mark, paradoxically, the most fertile psychological moments in his work, sites of potential growth rather than assured language. Full of ellipses and unanswered questions, the following passage relates a reverie presumably but not definitively emerging from Father Mat's past:

> Mumble of prayer
> To the Queen of May,
> The Virgin Mary with her school-girl air.
> The priest was seeing her, a girl
> Of fifteen. She sits and listens to
> The wandering poet who has come (indeed!)
> To talk with her mother of times they both knew.
> He sits one side of the fire dandling the tongs
> The mother the other side, Mary by the dresser.
> The tea is made and as they drink the mother
> Marvels at the scholar,
> His indifference to girls and dancing and the world's bother.
> The mother goes out to milk the cows. Says he:
> "How many miles to Babylon? With me
> Beside you it is just to dream. . ."
>> The childhood of the priest cried out: "Beware
>> Of the evil spell in all poetry."[78]

The furtive ejaculation, as it were, contained in parentheses, "(indeed!)," calls attention to the sophomoric pun in "come," which reveals by half hiding its shameful content. This puerile device of the parenthetical comment is also used in the midst of someone confessing to Father Mat: "I vexed my father until he swore / And beat my mother till she screamed (for more)."[79] The very slyness of the pun, a narrative touch, indicates the twisting of the priest and author. In the extended passage above, the story has the tone of undigested autobiography, a reminiscence of a visit paid by Kavanagh to a friend and her daughter. Given that tantalizing impression, it is important not to lose sight of Quinn's strict separation of poet and persona. In her biography of Kavanagh, however, Quinn discloses unequivocally that his first sexual encounter was with a fifteen-year-old convent schoolgirl, "her plump young body tantalising in a gym dress." What is more, "the girl confessed to him that she had already been sexually violated by a priest."[80] Quinn, when discussing "Lough Derg," which contains another such reference to molestation, asks why, "when clerical pedophilia was an unmentionable and unmentioned topic in Ireland" at the time, did Kavanagh so explicitly engage with it? She concludes that it is only when these sexual details of his, the poet's, biography are known "that it becomes evident he is unburdening himself of a guilty secret."[81] In the context of "Why Sorrow," however, the identification Kavanagh makes between Father Mat and the molesting piano teacher, someone closer to art than religion in his daily work, shows Kavanagh's overriding purpose in this poem: to make the priest connect with his most unvarnished identity as a fellow sinner. It is part of annihilating his pride. We have heard Maguire speak of pedophilia:

> He had an idea. Schoolgirls of thirteen
> Would see no political intrigue in an old man's friendship.
> Love the heifer waiting to be nosed by the old bull.
> The notion passed too—there was danger of talk
> And jails are narrower than the five-sod ridge
> And colder than the black hills facing Armagh in February.[82]

The relief and guilt he finds through masturbation, a recurrent motif in "The Great Hunger," is another means of exploring the essential crime of pedophilia: a self-centeredness that can rout another's innocence. Nonetheless, Kavanagh is deliberately making Maguire and Father Mat face especially vile evidence of their own sinfulness, the most cogent evidence to counter false pride. What is more, considering the legacy of Dante's Beatrician vision in relation to Lough Derg, Kavanagh's wrestling with pedophilia, especially in reference to a female child, is a critical item on his generally demythologizing agenda. Resurrecting such memories is part of a programmatic debasement of the self, such as that effected on Station Island. Indeed, within "Why Sorrow" Father Mat reaches a nadir associated with the Lough Derg ordeal, where the priest cries to himself "O despair! O despair! O despair."[83] Following on the cryptic passage about the perverted poet and the evil of poetry, the despair is with his own spiritual fraudulence, that he is a counterfeit of piety. The people need him as their "final surety," while he is "signing with a lie / Their checks of holy constancy."[84]

Deliberately couching this expression of self-loathing in the language of usury, at this point Father Mat is as far from God as possible. His return to faith, however, is accomplished through a return to the sacraments that does not occur in "The Great Hunger." While speaking to oneself of one's sins is a step toward penitence, confessing them to a priest is the only doctrinally correct route toward absolution. Father Mat, abasing himself, relinquishing pride, confesses his sins to Father Ned. Although the confession remains unrecorded by Kavanagh, the reader assumes its lurid content. The result is less exultation in a newfound purity than renewed recognition of flawed humanity:

> Now he was with his people, one of them.
> What they saw he saw too
> And nothing more: what they looked at
> And what to them was true was true
> For him. He was in the crowd
> A nobody who had been proud.[85]

The reward for the relinquishment of pride is not just empathy but a renewed faith. Father Mat not only sees what "they saw," but by accepting their truth discovers that "what was true was true / For him." The link between empathy and faith is affirmed; the end stop registers the return of belief. In "Why Sorrow" this recovery of faith does not survive a recurrence of doubt in the final section of the poem, when Father Mat goes to Lough Derg to further extend his penance. The poem ends on a note of doubt and distance from the people even greater than Devlin's "Lough Derg": " 'O God is good,' the listeners said. / The Cynic whispered to Father Mat."[86] The Cynic is the irrepressible, demonized voice inside him that inserts distancing, wicked, parenthetical asides into others' confessional narratives.

It will take the full-length exploration of the pilgrimage in "Lough Derg" to bring Kavanagh's humility the final distance from this personal discovery of oneness with the people to a seminal oneness with himself. There is no early poem of Kavanagh's that so uncannily predicts both the triumphs and failures of his final work. Kavanagh's last poems will swing wildly between bitter satire bespeaking an inordinate vulnerability and mystical lyricism bespeaking what Heaney will call a rare permeability. A culminating paradox, of going inward in order truly to see the outside world in its pristine, given glory, is Kavanagh's resolution of a conflict expressed throughout the early poetry. There a contest is waged between the impulse of retreating into the self and emerging to take in the splendor of nature. A dialectic is set up and neither stance provides repose. At Lough Derg, where even the order of exercises encodes a movement from the outdoor activity of doing the beds to the vigil in the basilica or "prison," this conflict is stripped for Kavanagh, the pilgrim, to the bare bones. Each position is starkly defined for him, revealing particularly the dynamic of unfolding toward the world as also a merging with community, a ceding of individuality. Because the poem is composed under such pressure, a certain chafing and champing at the bit, the opposite of the "wise passiveness" of the later poetry, where repose is key, "Lough Derg" has few moments of radiance, or even full artistic possession. When these occur, however, they are so startlingly sublime that their genesis within the poem is worth noting for its prophetic value.

Toward the end, there is a series of apparently spontaneous sonnets that break with the predominantly unrhymed free verse of the poem as a whole. That the sonnets are also prayers is significant, but more that they are the imagined prayers of others. It does not lessen the transforming empathy displayed here to discover in Quinn's biography that his prayer-poems are based on actual pilgrim petitions left at the altar in the basilica. Kavanagh read these highly personal documents because, in Quinn's words, he "was anxious to achieve more than mere cinematic reportage . . . he wanted to penetrate the minds and hearts of his pilgrims."[87] It is precisely this motivation that enables Kavanagh to make an extraordinary breakthrough in "Lough Derg": he manages to protect his own individuality while yielding to that of others. He does that by directing his imagination, prompted by his subjects' own words, to render the full individuality of others. The collaborative aspect of this endeavor only underscores the reduction of egotism it effects. As though drawing on the persona of Father Mat, Kavanagh here implicitly becomes the priest, God's surrogate, who hears and captures the spiritual essence of each penitent. Kavanagh as priest and spiritual midwife delivers into speech and form the poetry trapped inside each sinner: "Prose prayers become / Odes and sonnets."[88] This resolution largely by means of selflessness makes peace with the vanity of the poet, which religious scruple worries over. Later he is able to expose his own exceedingly private and self-contained epiphanies while knowing that to the degree that he is true to the particulars of his own experience, he is true to that of others. This later stance is predicated on the egalitarian belief that the reader, too, has such an inner life, such capacity for wonder. Those crucial sonnets in "Lough Derg," each inside the head of a separate penitent, mirror the later sonnets where Kavanagh writes about his own discovery of acceptance beside the banks of the Grand Canal in Dublin.

The "Lough Derg" sonnets make this apparent indulgence in self possible because the poet has already made his peace with the felt burden of redressing a racial injustice, of finding a way to be politically, poetically, and spiritually responsible at once. Kavanagh in these reported prayers revives the Catholic inferiority that the Irish Renaissance attempted to erase. Having said this, I believe Quinn is surely right in assessing the poem as less than an artistic success. She identifies as the source of this relative failure a "narrative uncertainty"[89] caused by the poet coming at his subject "with mixed feelings, as skeptic and believer, outsider and insider."[90] As a result, according to her, "the text wavers between that of observer and poet-pilgrim," the narrator's engagement between "alienation and empathy."[91] If we judge the poem, however, less for what it discretely achieves than for what it enables later in Kavanagh, it is an extraordinary accomplishment, the more remarkable for the amount of conflict it gathers to a point and partially resolves. As we have seen repeatedly, and as we will see in Heaney, in an individual oeuvre Lough Derg works are usually necessary stations on a larger pilgrimage, but a visit that must be observed, a penance that must be exacted of the self and paid.

Indeed, much of the poem alternates between excoriating observations of the venality of the herd and defensive inner reflections on God and beauty. The extremity of both these postures is accounted for by the way Lough Derg, with that bleakness of scenery Carleton makes doubly indelible, offers little to excite the "lustful eye" or even to console the chaste one. To look beyond the self is to see those anonymous others with whom one is supposed to merge in an act of humility, thereby tampering with the mainspring of the poetic imagination. As the narrator puts it bluntly, "Lough Derg overwhelmed the individual imagination / And the personal tragedy."[92] Kavanagh, like Heaney, is deliberately placing himself in a situation that is potentially death to the poet in him in order to be reborn. He needs to find a poetic that reconciles a range of disparate, apparently mutually exclusive needs and responsibilities. Overtly linking this fatal threat to poetry with that to the individual, Kavanagh observes of the three characters he has sketched on Lough Derg—a country schoolteacher, an ex-monk and a shopgirl—"Now they were not three egotists / But part of the flood of humanity / Anonymous, never to write or be written."[93] Here a presumed good, a loss of egotism, is balanced against and placed in conflict with another loss, that of poetry. Finding a way to hinge writing on a loss of egotism is the project of his later, sublime poetry. Kavanagh for much of the distance of "Lough Derg" displays flagrant, flailing conflict. In the first line, the poet announces a more overt, self-conscious attempt at the representation of an Irish Everyman than anything we have seen. Robert Welch calls "Lough Derg" the "diastole" to the "systole" of "The Great Hunger," the former embracing a crowd, the latter centering on an individual.[94] Seen as such, "Lough Derg," a relative failure, is also a bolder encounter with the self-annihilation that eliminates an earlier poetic and creates the ash from which the phoenix of the later work arises.

Kavanagh opens "Lough Derg" with a line that surveys Ireland's most lackluster, Lough Derg-ish counties, "From Cavan and from Leitrim and Mayo."[95] And yet such distance from the particulars of individual lives and townlands leads Kavanagh to a gross generalizing that allows for an undisciplined venting of molten, racially colored anger, alarmingly free flowing in his peremptory listing of the pilgrims around him as

> Solicitors praying for cushy jobs
> To be County Registrar or Coroner,
> Shopkeepers threatened with sharper rivals
> Than any hook-nosed foreigner;
> Mothers whose daughters who are Final medicals,
> Too heavy-hipped for thinking.[96]

An inner opposing life is here and there feebly gestured toward in these opening lines, but largely in negative, even anti-Semitic, references to what all these philistines cannot appreciate: "Love-sunlit is an enchanter in June's hours / And flowers and light. These to shopkeepers and small lawyers / Are heresies up beauty's sleeves."[97] Allusions to nature are but distant personal memories, sights not even within the purview of those who are congenitally blind to beauty. The poet himself is almost overwhelmed by the weight of this obscure, oppressive notseeing. The crucial twist in this poem, however—what incarceration on Lough

Derg forces—is that Kavanagh turns his own power of vision toward the people, looking more carefully than that initial disdainful glimpse.

Kavanagh, like Heaney, is a poet who is most at home, most fluent and assuaged, most alive even to good and evil, when seeing into nature. Yet both poets produce Lough Derg poems that, by focusing largely on other people, redeem individual conscience, make them face themselves simply as men. In this same caustic beginning, therefore, Kavanagh ameliorates his stance, observing "half-pilgrims" who are "the true / Spirit of Ireland."[98] It is vital for an understanding of Kavanagh's remarkable spiritual and poetic growth to see that the gift he attributes to these ordinary people is that which will enable his finest work. They "joke through the Death-mask."[99] In other words, they innately possess the comic vision, which he will not just earn, but in a sense recover from within himself, as one of the people. Kavanagh turns toward that very barrenness that repels Carleton and makes his precursor take refuge in a defensive superiority. Indeed, Quinn informs us that this was precisely Kavanagh's response at the onset of his first pilgrimage in 1940. As though compulsively repeating and imitating Carleton's high dudgeon, Kavanagh took umbrage at the slight of being chastised by self-appointed authorities before he even arrived on Station Island. As Quinn describes the incident:

> On his arrival at the shore of Lough Derg, he had attempted to distinguish himself from the group of pilgrims waiting for the ferry, signalling his special status as a mystical poet by standing apart in meditative pose, gazing intently at the island. This "bogus trance" (he acknowledged it was an act) aroused the suspicions of two ferrymen, who took him for a nutter and accosted him insultingly, while his fellow pilgrims looked on appreciatively.[100]

That Kavanagh's adopted, not altogether feigned, protective stance was that of the artist, further reinscribes the image of Carleton.

Kavanagh, however, uses his second visit as an opportunity to confront both his vanity and the stoniness of his own heart. By this process he can join in the hereditary, collective effort of "Trying to encave in the rubble / Of these rocks the Real / The part that can feel."[101] This association of bare rock and the beginnings of feeling lodged somewhere deep in this numbness is further connected with the Famine later in the poem. With this additional leap in connection, one can see the fullness of the historic recovery Kavanagh is attempting: "The middle of the island looked like the memory / Of some village evicted by the Famine."[102] Typically, as Kavanagh imagines himself walking through such a hypothetical, deserted village (the remains of old dwellings on Lough Derg), he recites the names of fictional former inhabitants of the ghostly place: "O that was the place where Mickey Fehan lived / And the Reilly's before they went to America in the Fifties."[103] As he says in one of his later luminous sonnets, "The Hospital": "Naming these things is the love-act and its pledge."[104] The inclusion of the word "pledge" is crucial, suggesting the act of pledging one's troth. With this naming, Kavanagh is joining himself with his people, identifying with a need larger than his own: "So much alike is our historical / And spiritual pattern, a heap / Of stones anywhere is consecrated / By love's terrible need."[105] Here Kavanagh is adding colonization to the leveling force of Catholicism and, laying his finger on the way too aggressive a fight for individuality, the wrong kind of egotistical energy, can also represent a fleeing from a common sorrow absolutely integral to the self, therefore crucial to the imagination.

It is this embracing of pain, available in abundance on Lough Derg, that enables a terrible need to surface early on in the poem preparatory to a culminating series of sonnet-prayers, an eerie, revisionist parallel to the "terrible" sonnets of Gerard Manley Hopkins, loved by Heaney and Devlin. Although Quinn is eager to pinpoint Kavanagh's argument at this time with the Church, calling his response to it "at best ambivalent,"[106] Tom Stack, in his recent work on Kavanagh's religious poems, detects more orthodoxy. Although this bias in his reading of the poet overall leads Stack to ascribe less individualistic, iconoclastic energy to Kavanagh's later poetry, Stack's perception of a particular doctrinal correctness in "Lough Derg" aids in securing the pivotal place of that poem in Kavanagh's oeuvre. Stack's point revolves precisely around Kavanagh's investment in human pain. Where the poet shows a "theological sureness of touch"[107] is in appreciating that pain in the Christian scheme of things finds its only literally redeeming value in the context of love. Kavanagh, more in line with Quinn's perception of him at this point, may not equate love as much with Christ on the cross as with suffering humanity, both dispensing love and embodying its need. This need transforms the venal, anonymous, openly loathed pilgrims into human beings capable by means of inner resources and by the intervention of divine grace to become essentially poets:

> The Castleblaney grocer trapped in the moment's need
> Puts out a hand and writes what he cannot read,
> A wisdom astonished at every turn
> By some angel that writes in the oddest words.
> When he will walk again in Muckno street
> He'll hear from the kitchens of fair-day eating houses
> In the after-bargain carouses
> News from a country beyond the range of birds.[108]

Kavanagh here is describing the poet he will become, one who cultivates a "wisdom astonished at every turn." This deeply spiritual and private consciousness, however, accomplishes the full circle of achieving political redress. Note how Yeats's automatic writing is written over by this patently religious, visionary experience that makes man an amanuensis to "some angel." Note, too, how this vision is almost inextricable from the sights and sounds, the ripe smells of a cattle-fair in a small provincial town. The fertile bustle of the actual Ireland, not an idea of it, spawns this redemption.

A later poem, "Prelude," is similarly brought down by discursive bitterness and made airborne by vision. In that poem Kavanagh, who makes his mistakes and corrects them in full sight of the reader, a candor more affecting that any lapidary perfection, lodges a by-now famous imperative to himself about how to get back on track. In a poem that begins with the flat-footed anger of "Give us another poem, he said / Or they will think your muse is dead,"[109] Kavanagh arrives in the middle of an increasingly freeing meditation at this soaring wisdom:

> But satire is unfruitful prayer,
> Only wild shoots of pity there,
> And you must go inland and be
> Lost in compassion's ecstasy,
> Where suffering soars in summer air—
> The millstone has become a star.[110]

This defiance of gravity, which begins with not defying the way things are, starts at Lough Derg, where, though one is on an island, one goes "inland," to the heart of midlands anonymity, to the heart of the Famine, to the inwardness imposed by the vigil in prison. Nonetheless, just a few lines earlier in "Prelude," still mired in satire, Kavanagh urges himself to "link your laughter out of doors / In sunlight past the sick-faced whores."[111] Turning outward, where the sun may be seen to bless, also means seeing people, but more, seeing a flawed humanity reflected back on the self, the muck of unresolved personal problems, like sexual frustration here displaced onto demonized women. The true route outward is by means of a paradoxical inwardness. "Compassion's ecstasy" is found in the human heart. It is this radiating forgiveness that informs the apparently paradoxical ending of the "Lough Derg," the last lines of which are, "And three sad people had found the key to the lock / Of God's delight in disillusionment."[112] Despite the rhetorical balancing of opposites in the final line, this conclusion is qualitatively different from that of "Why Sorrow": " 'O God is good,' the listener said. / The Cynic whispered to Father Mat." In "Lough Derg," Kavanagh himself finds the key to "delight in disillusionment," and this discovery is announced in his lodging of a final wisdom in the unholy trinity of three different but commonly flawed people. Compassion is the key to delight, to a comic vision.

"Lough Derg" in its unfolding releases as a gradually gathering force this forgiveness toward others and the self. The way in which resisting painful self-examination can lead to an alienation from the self that makes one a stranger with others is evident at many moments in the poem. This is never truer than when Kavanagh sounds as though he is paraphrasing, versifying a guidebook, and the poem sounds programmatic, like something he had to write, because the Lough Derg pilgrimage is so central to the culture explored from the inside in "The Great Hunger." The tinny sound of secondhand speech, of unintegrated detail can be heard off such a superfluity as:

> Beside St Brigids Cross—an ancient relic
> A fragment of the Middle Ages set
> Into the modern masonry of the conventional Basilica
> Where everything is ordered and correct.[113]

He can even sound as though he is straining to describe the site to a foreigner, referring to the "concrete stilts of the Basilica / That spread like a bulldog's hind paws."[114] The reader is aware, however, that Lough Derg has been an effectively blank space in Irish literature since Carleton. MacCarthy's translation does not count because it would not have been widely read. Yeats's "The Pilgrim" resides at a great distance from the actual place. Devlin's poem will not be read by Kavanagh until 1946, four years after the composition of his own "Lough Derg," and then with disappointment. Kavanagh, therefore, is breaking a silence so long and thick that he almost has to start anew. His reportage, therefore, possesses an immediacy and urgency of tone that anticipates the transparency of ego in the later poems. When Kavanagh testifies at the end of the poem that this "all happened on Lough Derg as it is written / In June nineteen-forty-two,"[115] that phrase, "as it is written," harking back to the uncomprehended writing of angels in a grocer's soul and suggesting biblical authority, cuts both in the direction of immediacy and of eternity. Kavanagh is revising history by being true to one day, rather than three unified days, on Lough Derg.

Similarly, Kavanagh's attempt to solve the problem of social inclusiveness, an embrace of otherness, without depicting merely a crowd scene, results in his bestowing a formulaic individuality on three characters. This strategy is also a compromise between self-disclosure and empathy toward others. All three characters in some way uncover shrouded psychological problems in Kavanagh himself. Robert Fitzsimons, the teacher, like poor, precipitate Saint Patrick Maguire, overwhelms love with ponderous moral reflection. He is also a pedant, largely an autodidact. One cannot help thinking of Kavanagh at his most stentorian. And the ex-monk is surrounded by more double-talk about child molestation. The young woman, Aggie Meehan, hugs a guilty sin referred to almost melodramatically as "Birth, bastardy and murder."[116] Although the reference to infanticide is prescient in terms of Irish history, considering the Kerry Babies' Case of the 1970s, Aggie, along with the two typified male sinners in this corporeal trinity, is not fully human. The character sketches are too perfunctory and stock to resemble life.

It is once again in the process of confession, as inward as one can go on Lough Derg, that life blossoms, fills out the contours of an actual person. To look at just one of these plainspoken sonnets, found almost like wildflowers in a field, is to see how much raw life, personal and interpersonal, Kavanagh compresses into fourteen lines, the explosive energy expected of a sonnet. The poem is presumably spoken after confession:

Saint Anne, I am a young girl from Castleblaney,
One of a farmer's six grown daughters.
Our little farm, when the season's rainy,
Is putty spread on stones. The surface waters
    Soak all the fields of this north-looking townland.
Last year we lost our acre of potatoes
And my mother with unmarried daughters round her

Is soaked like our soil in savage natures.
She tries to be as kind as any mother
But what can a mother be in such a house
With arguments going on and such a bother
About the half-boiled pots and unmilked cows.
O Patron of the pure woman who lacks a man
Let me be free I beg you, St. Anne.[117]

Venturing so far into the interior of a figure, anonymous but for this intimate insight, almost redeems the previously satirized venality of the people. Here a marginal economic existence is seen to dictate life without access to higher spiritual levels. Most notable about this and the other sonnets, however, is their language, its transparency. This moment in Kavanagh is reminiscent of that which Eliot spots in Yeats's "In the Seven Woods." Eliot describes Yeats, thanks to his experimentation with drama, coming there to a plain language that could be spoken. Regarding as a sign of maturity Yeats's eschewal, for the most part, of rhetorical, especially figurative, effect, Eliot points to Shakespeare's simple, limpidly trochaic pentameter from Lear, the line, "Never, never, never, never, never," as epitomizing this courageous speech.[118] Robert Welch, who credits Kavanagh with writing in the form of Shakespearean sonnets, praises him for a generous bestowal of empathy in "Lough Derg." Welch also ascribes a Wordsworthian influence to what he sees as Kavanagh's use, given this empathy, of the "real language of men."[119] Welch further claims: "Thus the poetry becomes an invocation of 'the spirit of life' (another, lesser known phrase, from the Preface) that is in the poet, in the reader and in the Universe itself."[120] Although this argument identifies the thrust provided by these early epiphanies, the Wordsworthian example fails to do justice to the ethnically specific mixture of the hieratic and humble tone of the poet in "Lough Derg." Nor does it explain the documentary and transformative energies in the poetry, paradoxes rooted more in the corporeal incarnation than in Romanticism.

In revealing the interior life of strangers, Kavanagh is also being true to a very specific history. Resisting complete transcendence, these sonnets constitute a pivotal, penitential moment for the poet. It is as though he is giving identities to the faceless lost of the Famine. Sitting uncomfortably between history and poetry, circumstance and form, he also anticipates the eclecticism of the poetic that marks Irish poetry to this day. The more modernist, free-verse sections of "Lough Derg" are as important to its overall truth as the sonnets. This formal variation reflects Kavanagh's later philosophy of waiting through diurnal aridity for freshets of eternity. So, too, his personifying of the poet ranges from a god to another faceless person in the crowd. Somehow Kavanagh has to find the poetic to accommodate these apparently contradictory extremes. He begins in a paranoid mood of self-exceptionalism, equating the poet with God, lashing out at mediocrity, noting "the envy / Of the inarticulate when dealing with the artist."[121] By the end of the poem, this very inarticulacy is an invitation to empathic, compassionate imagining of speech. The essentialism that might be attributed to the sonnet form, that truths can

be rendered down to such potent, homeopathic doses, is countered by the rough-
ness and length of the stony Lough Derg path by which these moments are reached.
Kavanagh permits himself the self-aggrandizement of the priest-persona, burdened with, as well as buoyed by, the secret lives of others. The cultural specificity
and veracity of the role mitigate any pride, particularly by the way Kavanagh, slip-
ping behind the masks of others, is honest about the sins he shares with his fellow
pilgrims. He is much more honest by this indirect means than he is in his slyly con-
fidential, subjective mode, where he invents obvious surrogates whose sins are
proudly inflated by this furtive, authorial denial. It is as though by truly penetrat-
ing the soul of another, Kavanagh finds a release from himself that permits a more
realistic and compassionate reentry into the ego.

Two lines identify the guiding star of all this searching: "Only God thinks of the
dying sparrow / In a war."[122] Immediately following, Kavanagh makes an equation between the poet and God that nonetheless discounts and justifies the rebarbative arrogance that opens the poem:

> The ex-monk, farmer and the girl
> Melted in the crowd
> Where only God, the poet
> Followed with interest till he found
> Their secret, and constructed from
> The chaos of its fire
> A reasonable document.[123]

The ferreting voyeurism that finds a home on the priest's side of the confessional as well as the vesting of the unredeemed self in priestly garb all are vindicated by the moral use to which secrets and power are put: to achieve justice, to
recognize and name not just the anonymous but their unspoken lives. Within the
text two images appear of what the poem itself looks like: a baggy monster and an
elegant object. At one point, he likens Station Island to an iceberg, "But the iceberg
filled a glass of water / And poured it to the sun."[124] These are the sonnets: discrete,
transparent containers of individual lives synecdochic of a broader culture but
sparkling with individual identity. At the other end of the aesthetic spectrum he declares, exhorting a caution against a too-controlling formalism: "Let beauty bag or
burst / The sharp points of truth may not be versed / Too smoothly, but the truth
must go in as it occurred / A bulb of light in the shadows of Lough Derg."[125] Truth
goes in but then radiates out, in Welch's words, "systole" and "diastole," almost
Whitmanesque in its adherence to a process. Those spikes and the radiant center
must be given equal valency. So it is that those final sonnets can occur like islands
less on an ocean than in a swamp of satire. When Kavanagh ends by sitting by the
Grand Canal observing himself from the outside, because he has dared to venture
inward, he has the self-possession Curtayne summoned in her image of a man leaning against his own mantelpiece.

The restoration of repose and confidence Kavanagh achieves, however, does not bestow on him a permanent and general amnesty from the usual range of imperialisms. The same arduous pilgrimage, involving repeated but ever-invented steps, will have to be conducted over and over. The time for reinscription of Kavanagh's footsteps, directly over Carleton's, will never be more urgent that when the North erupts in the 1970s and the conformist demands of Church and nation once again threaten the poetic imagination. Besides, the whole point of Kavanagh's spiritual journey from simplicity into complexity and back again is that it is a personal and lonely feat. It may well advance the culture, but more by indicating the ordeal to be faced by each individual in every age.

7

⤳

Seamus Heaney and the Politics of Poetics

Strumming a Harp of Unforgiving Iron

SEAMUS HEANEY'S LONG POEM "Station Island," the most recent major addition to this tradition of Irish literature about Lough Derg, is also the most self-referential and intertextual. Given the density of its introspective and retrospective content, Heaney's Lough Derg can be viewed as larger than the other contributions. The sphere of its consciousness encompasses them, its own abundant life being predicated either explicitly or implicitly on their previous existence. "Station Island" itself resembles a rich stretch and slab of bog. The poem's various epiphanies and unresolved questions, the pointed allusions and images embedded in it, are contained and preserved as a legacy for the future. The shards of references to other works and cross-references within his own oeuvre, which Heaney includes in this account of his pilgrimage, are intended collectively to synthesize past interpretations of Lough Derg and to further complicate and advance the accumulated literary response. Ultimately, he will dissolve the celebrated tribal certainties about nationalism and Catholicism, separately and together, only to unearth certain solid imponderables about the self and the idea of God.

This progress includes a reassessment of the poetics previous writers have adopted, not just Lough Derg writers but all those attempting, as Kiberd puts it, to "invent Ireland." By poetics, I have in mind the kind of metaphysical shift that led Kavanagh to forsake, in favor of the mystical bent of his later work, the realism of "The Great Hunger." This transition has caught Heaney's attention, particularly since it graphs a movement away from an exclusive fidelity to the quotidian life of an actual place toward including the symbolic configurations of the mind as it contemplates the possibility of God. Heaney, directly through his prose and indirectly through his poetry, has carefully weighed all the possible positions one can maintain toward Ireland, poetry, and belief. He has also tried to decide to what degree the answers to these separate but linked questions must fall into line with each other. Must they assume the shape of a logical chain or may they strike out in separate, apparently anarchic, independent directions? The position of the Irish artist after "Station Island" involves both more freedom and more consequential choices. Heaney assigns political repercussions to metaphysical and moral positions, a reversal of the conventional causality, where politics typically enjoys such agency.

The poem, published in 1984, reads as urgent cultural, personal, and poetic work that needed to be done when it was done, just as some troubled believers feel they must do the Station to make sense of a difficult time, to figure out a way forward. "Station Island" is written both during the thick of the Troubles and at a time when Heaney had gained a never greater physical distance from them. Purgatory is the ideal site in which to locate this backward look that leads forward. Having moved to the South, to Wicklow, in 1972, then on to Dublin in 1976, Heaney culminated this transition with the acceptance in 1981 of an academic position at Harvard University, which entailed spending one semester there every year. "Station Island," published shortly after this new beginning, and therefore written in the midst of the transition, is a poem about a number of purgatorial passages that feature images of earthly hell. It is telling that two great events in recent Northern history coincide with these framing life events for Heaney: his initial departure from Belfast and his later departure for Cambridge. "Bloody Sunday," the day British paratroopers killed thirteen unarmed civil rights marchers in Derry, occurred in January 1972. In 1980 and 1981 ten Republican prisoners died in the hunger strikes. As vitally informative as these framing political events are, however, they do not indicate the full range of experiences as a man and a poet that contributed to Heaney's two major decisions. My reason for stressing this intermeshing of personal and political events is that the poem itself is ultimately aimed at an integration of these spheres, the fulfillment of a need that Heaney's movements and decisions on the relative surface of life might appear to belie. This is also a point in his career as a poet when both radical change and profound reconciliation are in order. At the time of writing "Station Island," he had behind him as a poet both *North* and *Field Work,* collections employing dramatically different poetics, *North* wed to the artifice inherent in elaborate conceit, *Field Work* more pervious to an unmediated natural world.

On the far side of the personal and public juncture demarcated by "Station Island" lay both an incremental, not unretracing approach to peace in the North and devastating but also transforming losses in Heaney's personal life. The deaths of his parents will reconfigure his poetic from the ground up, aiming it toward the sky. "Station Island" finds Heaney anticipating, trying to prepare for, these not altogether unpredictable changes by reevaluating the past, but also by being arrested in a nearly despairing position, reflecting a mood, both public and private, of a specific, confused, and confusing time. "Station Island," as a contribution to culture, especially Irish poetry, grapples with a number of nearly intractable problems. It considers the place and role of poetry in relation to public, as distinct from private, suffering. It ponders as well the responsibility of the poet to the human being in himself, if appropriate to his soul. The liberating quality of Heaney's long poem is the way it offers a responsible and autonomous means of entering the future without sacrificing complexity to facility. Indeed, if anything, matters are more various and turbid at the far end of the poem, but also, miraculously, more manageable and lucid.

As we have seen, Lough Derg works tend to emerge, like eruptions on the body, at times of intense cultural and personal pressure, hence at crucial intersections in the lives and careers of the relevant artists, and of the body politic. Just as the pilgrimage itself is essentially about a passage between one world and the next, so writing about it takes place on a number of crucial borders indicating geographical, political, moral, metaphysical, and aesthetic divisions. These conflicts and crises are often experienced as both internal and external. Further, these historical circumstances and the personal and creative problems bound up with them demand rigorous examination on several fronts. Let me encapsulate the evidence so far of this gradual cultural work in preparation for appreciating Heaney's handling of his bequest. As we have seen, Carleton wrote the "Lough Derg Pilgrim" in 1829, on the cusp of the 1830s, overall a period of land agitation, sporadic famine, and incipient insurrection, but equally a time of great personal change. Not only had he moved from rural Tyrone to Dublin, but as a believer he switched from Catholicism to Protestantism, and as a writer from obscurity to recognition. In relation to Carleton's cultural and political involvement, Barbara Hayley tells us, "He was closely associated with the great non-sectarian revival of Irish Literature in the 1830s and later with the more political writers of the *Nation* newspaper."[1] These are the same activities enlisting the energies of the slightly younger, Dublin-born Denis Florence MacCarthy. He, however, eventually faced the failure of Young Ireland, the death of Thomas Davis, and the resultant further narrowing of the definition of Irishness. This was the disappointing result of a spate of scholarly activity—translating, reviewing, and pamphleteering—on the part of his generation in the name of an idealized Ireland. His own contribution to this movement climaxed in the publication of his two anthologies of Irish poetry. Enduring, therefore, the exhausting combination of intensive work and poignant loss in the name of Ireland, MacCarthy chose exile in Italy. Devlin, the cosmopolite, and Kavanagh, the rustic, wrote their "Lough Derg" poems in the 1940s, sending up their quite separate but similarly alienated cries from the dark heart of the new nation's Catholic isolationism. Devlin, having spent considerable time in the company of Brian Coffey and Thomas McGreevy in Paris as a postgraduate, had already absorbed a hybrid European poetic, both symbolist and modernist. Kavanagh had moved to Dublin but was determined to undermine the Yeatsian idealization of rural Ireland by starkly exposing its stifling claustrophobia, a central theme in "The Great Hunger." Kavanagh abandoned the countryside forever in 1939, the year he came to Dublin and, as Heaney himself has pointed out the on many occasions, the year his Derry scion was born.

"Station Island" faces squarely but also from a number of angles the most trau-matic phase of the Northern Troubles, climaxing in the hunger strikes of 1980. The poem equally faces the personal and creative repercussions, especially guilt for a newfound mobility, that only began with Heaney's leaving an incestuous, violent North in 1976. By accepting the professorship at Harvard, Heaney found relief from the tight bind of living primarily between Dublin and Belfast, the axis that had defined his life for more than five years. Yearly substantial contact with Amer-ica would expand Heaney's poetic frame of reference, in fact, far beyond the United States, because his attachment to and admiration for certain American poets, such as Robert Lowell and Elizabeth Bishop, had already been formed. Heaney was to gain now, however, further exposure to a variety of émigré poets, such as the Pole, Czeslaw Milosz, whom he had first encountered in Berkeley in 1971, when Heaney taught there. By teaching at Harvard, he would also enjoy a geographical proxim-ity to the Russian Joseph Brodsky, who was at Mount Holyoke in western Massa-chusetts during the eighties, in addition to fellow postcolonial Derek Walcott from Saint Lucia at Boston University. The examples of these fellow international poets would offer strategies for coping with varieties of Irish cultural problems, from confronting the ongoing repercussions of colonization, to, given the example of Polish poetry especially, prizing the artistic conscience free of the hinged jaws of patriotism and Catholicism.

In "Station Island," however, Heaney works from the ground up, from where he started to where he wants to go, just as Dante proceeds under the guidance of Virgil to climb his way painfully up through purgatory. In the end, Heaney bestows the most encompassing identity yet, a true overview, on Lough Derg. He sees it equally as the epitome of everything associated by means of Kavanagh with rural Ireland—provincial, philistine, and fitfully mystical—and as the site of cosmopoli-tan resonance found in Devlin. Heaney's poem registers as a given the fame of me-dieval Lough Derg, as portrayed in that fresco in that little church in Umbria. This urbanity also echoes more broadly in the involvement with translation that the poem displays. This engagement with alterity, bearing more than a glancing remi-niscence of MacCarthy, entails not just literal translation from one language to an-other but from one consciousness to another, a concatenation of diverse voices recalling Carleton. Heaney, however, for all this sophistication, begins at the begin-ning in this grueling moral, spiritual, and creative pilgrimage: an actual bog lake in Donegal, after all, the ancient province of Ulster, where Heaney's life began. It is telling that he makes no overt reference to those urban-identified, previous Lough Derg writers, Devlin and MacCarthy. We are reminded of Heaney's concentration on his actual beginnings by his sketching of the Lough Derg literary tradition in "Station Island" from Carleton to Kavanagh, Tyrone to Monaghan; Heaney clearly regards the pilgrimage as an especially Northern, rural practice, another memory from childhood to be excavated, inspected as a grown-up.

Who better to respond to the liminal connotations of the Lough Derg pilgrim-age, with the middle ground of purgatory as its spiritual terrain, than a poet from a place dominated by a border, someone who has lived, as it were, on both sides of an arbitrary line and who has given one of his most socially astute early poems the title "The Other Side." "Station Island," however, avoids being solely, even primarily, about politics, deliberately undercutting a climate of tribal blame and counterblame for an attitude of personal accountability. Heaney's poem is the first piece of Lough Derg literature, since the flowering of great bardic poetry that culminates in "Vain My Visit to Lough Derg," to focus on the condition of the individual soul. This fact alone is a measure of the recovery accomplished by Heaney. The poem offers a mature moral angle on sectarian strife precisely by winning through to a range of honest, tough insights about the self. These hard-won perceptions will lead the way forward for Heaney. Although the deaths of both his parents radically alter his poetic, the very foundation on which poems are erected, politics remain an influence, a black, iron pressure. The purely religious concerns, however, which begin to illuminate corners of "Station Island," anticipating the revolution in his poetic to come, provide Heaney not just with another strenuous challenge but with an opportunity. From there on in, he increasingly conducts his art on a new light-filled and intangible plane. He never, however, fully abandons the terra firma of his youth. Rather, Heaney strikes a continuous balance between these two domains. The title of his late collection, *The Spirit Level* (1996), evokes this equipoise by nodding toward both the metaphysical and the physical: spiritual experience that is also on the level.

Although grounded in the Northern situation, the anguished late 1970s and early 80s, "Station Island" also transcends politics, pushing in directions that anticipate the gradual ascent undertaken by Heaney's more and more metaphysically informed, radiant later poetry. "Station Island," resting on the solid narrative paradigms structuring Virgil's *Aeneid* and Dante's *Inferno* and *Purgatorio,* is the beginning of a long trudge upward for Heaney, which never peaks in certainty but comes closer and closer to a spiritual affirmation. Significantly, he uses not just the *Purgatorio* but also the *Inferno* as double points of reference spiritually to render Lough Derg, which, with its legendary cave, rests in the imagination more as an underworld than the mountain Dante chose as his location for purgatory. In keeping with this merging of two templates, two extremes of topographical visualization, Heaney's purgatory includes as inhabitants everyone from alleged murderers to good, imperceptibly flawed men. Take, for example, "big-limbed, decent, open-faced"[2] William Strathearn, "the perfect, clean, unthinkable victim,"[3] who in section vii of "Station Island" is just that, a victim. He is portrayed as a shopkeeper who responds to shouts in the middle of the night to provide medicine for a sick child and who is assassinated apparently for his humanity. What could his sin possibly be other than the slight shortness of temper he shows toward his wife moments before his almost certain death? What we do know is that this essentially good man defines purgatory as a way station prior to a transfer to heaven. On the other hand, compare him to IRA man Francis Hughes, "a hit man on the brink," who has watched with surreal detachment, "the bomb flash / come before the sound."[4] The moral poles represented by the extremes of ghosts Heaney consigns to his purgatory bring together the two Lough Dergs of the mind identified by O'Connor and Curtayne, one domain with approval, the other not. First there is the Irish Lough Derg where ordinary country people receive a penance only a little more arduous (just many, many more *paters* and *aves*) than that performed after Saturday confession. Then there is the Lough Derg of the European medieval past, where the most egregious of malefactors, resembling Luis Enius of Calderón's play, came to save their souls by risking death in order to see visions. The more immediate political point for Heaney, however, is that a stringent moral inventory is regarded as equally critical for the ordinary peaceful individual as for the conspicuous sinner directly implicated in public horror.

The moral problem such wide divergence creates for Heaney is: where does he stand? This is the internal challenge he poses himself as a deflection from the usual external focus of politics. The foul self-loathing to which he confesses in the midst of his own seemingly eternal, nightmare vigil, when he drifts "down a swirl of mucky, glittering flood,"[5] would suggest heinousness. That, of course, is denied by the evidence of the poem, which amounts more to excessive scrupulosity than to anything else. The point is less the degree of sinfulness than the acknowledgment of personal culpability per se. Heaney's subsequent works attest to the cleansing, tonic effect of this transitional poem of tough self-reckoning. The journey begun with "Station Island" continues into the 1990s, approaching a more hopeful destination. More than fifteen years after "Station Island," Heaney will translate and insert a portion of the last canto of the *Paradiso* into a poem of his own, "A Dream of Solstice," which contains, in its original version, these lines: "Who dares say 'love' / At this cold coming? Who would not dare say it?"[6] Here, where the word "love" is unavoidable, both in affirming and rejecting an idea of God, the line between belief and skepticism is as thin as the hair from the devil onto which Dante and Virgil cling, gaining that first life-or-death purchase for their climb out of hell toward heaven.

It can be instructive to observe precisely where in Heaney's canon "Station Island" lies. Consider, for example, the two superb sonnet sequences that flank the volume *Station Island:* the "Glanmore Sonnets" from *Field Work* (1979) and "Clearances" from *The Haw Lantern* (1987). The first sequence, though perhaps the most grounded of his poetry, still allows for sudden, lightening illuminations, which anticipate later moments. In *Seeing Things,* the volume following *The Haw Lantern,* there is a four-part sequence of poems called "Squarings," which are—significantly—not sonnets, so far do they depart in content from what Heaney calls "diamond absolutes."[7] These poems alert us to the metaphysical complication as well as to the illumination that identify his later poetry. In the first section of "Squarings," subtitled "Lightenings" these lines occur in section xii:

> And lightening? One meaning of that
> Beyond the usual sense of alleviation,
> Illumination, and so on, is this:

A phenomenal instant when the spirit flares

With pure exhilaration before death—
The good thief in us harking to the promise![8]

"Squarings" is Heaney's most modernist, most metaphysically searching and deliberately destabilizing effort to date. It therefore seems appropriate that, with or without intention, Heaney's allusion to the "good thief" sets off an intertextual echo with Devlin. The reverberation also extends to archmodernist Beckett, whose Vladimir and Estragon in *Waiting for Godot* also ponder the problem, which Luke's account of the Crucifixion raises, of how to explain the ways of grace. In contrast to Devlin, the inveterate outsider, whose reference to the "good thief," as we've seen, prompts a humility about judging others, Heaney's use of the allusion rests on his own identification with the fortunate criminal, with the mercy he received. The apparent randomness of such salvation, a mirror image of the death meted out by terrorism, however, perplexes as much as it assuages. "The Glanmore Sonnets," prior to "Station Island," are more about a human fallibility lightened, paradoxically, by the gravity of simply being on this earth, a visceral, vital sensation translated into language: "Vowels ploughed into other, opened ground, / Each verse returning like the plough turned round."[9] Jumping ahead to "Clearances," which follows "Station Island," these poems, though imbued with the balance of strict truthfulness, their fair share of the physical and diurnal—peeling potatoes, folding sheets—are nonetheless much more centered on the metaphysical. The sequence concludes with nothing less than an attempt to come to terms with the awe felt at witnessing death: "And we all knew one thing by being there. / The space we stood around had been emptied / Into us to keep."[10] Although the "one thing" known is deliberately not named, perhaps to prevent its reduction to a literalism, the unsaid nonetheless vibrates like a divining rod. One or the other absolute, "nothing" or "everything," both fathomless, both ineffable and incomprehensible, is the possible word in reply. Both poles of possible meaning prompted by belief and doubt are equally entertained. The critical fact, however, is that the poet's consciousness is completely inundated by mystery, flooded by an emptiness, and perhaps some private intuition, which in not yielding to language preserves its oceanic fluency and the poet's privacy.

Readers, given the evidence of this later numinous poetry, argue the exact placement of Heaney's personal belief. Not even the closest of close readings, however, necessarily can detect this, as poetry may not be the location where such disclosures are lodged. They may not even fit, being both too fluent and fixed, into words, though words with their paradoxical fluency and fixity may also deliver a close approximation. And today Heaney is still writing, growing as a poet and a man. It is, of course, impossible for oneself, let alone another, to pinpoint the position of one's soul, but there have been a number of attempts to locate the bearing of belief or its lack on Heaney's poetry. Take Helen Vendler's sure, clear reading: "The invisible, in Heaney's upbringing, was the prerogative of either nationalist politics or the Catholic religion. Heaney takes on, in *The Haw Lantern*, the job of exploring the use, to a secular mind, of metaphysical, ethical and spiritual categories of reference."[11] This assessment depends on two premises. The first is that Heaney is stalled in a posture of defying either or both "nationalist politics" and "the Catholic religion." I, however, read "Station Island," a necessary precursor to the radiant *Haw Lantern*, as a rigorous poem about psychic separation, about taking the consequences for one's own actions and giving oneself the responsibility of choice. The second premise surrounds the word "use," which implies that Heaney's explorations of religion are utilitarian, conducted to yield poems. It is certainly true that most poems are to some degree opportunistic, seizing an occasion, seizing language, seizing the reader's attention, gaining recognition. Poems may be occasioned by mystical experiences, but they are not, as even Kavanagh's late poems show, the experiences themselves and can seem, compared to a saint's ecstasies, like applied science to pure. Adrian Frazier has tried to tease out this paradox of how the religious both eludes and inheres in Heaney's poetry. Picking his words as carefully as stepping from stone to slippery stone in a stream, Frazier comes to the assessment that Heaney is "prayerful but weak of faith," further, that his "visionary experience also stands between the mystical and the metaphorical, rather than straightforwardly purporting to be supernatural as in the case of Yeats."[12] Such careful discernment is welcome, both the shying away from blunt dismissal in "weak of faith" and the gesturing toward Heaney's sincere, spiritual engagement in "prayerful." Frazier, however, moves perceptibly in a more secular, aesthetic direction when he places, a little incongruously, Heaney's "visionary experience," a phrase suggesting the immediate and authentic, somewhere between art and religion. Heaney, however, will question the legitimacy of even this limit on poetry.

Heaney's own quite recent reading of Yeats, for the transformative energy his supernatural leanings lend poetry, ultimately tests Frazier's contrast of Heaney with Yeats. In the essay "Joy or Night," a crucial text for all such queries about belief and poetry, Heaney compares Philip Larkin and Yeats precisely on the question of the finality of death; and in an only apparently casual, rhetorical remark Heaney nonetheless allies himself, and us, to a limited extent with Yeats. "He was, moreover, as complicated as the rest of us when it came to his beliefs in a supernatural machinery,"[13] says Heaney, who is pointedly among "the rest of us." Although protecting here the privacy of both doubt and belief, the tenor of the rest of Frazier's essay supports an argument for a substantial alliance between the later Heaney and Yeats on matters of the spirit. Also, a passage from the introduction to *A Vision* that Heaney quotes and with which he clearly identifies—where Yeats refers to his "circuits of sun and moon" as "stylistic arrangements,"[14]—reinforces Frazier's wisdom in retaining the metaphorical as a critical factor in Heaney's spiritual equation. Yet when Heaney questions the poetic behind Philip Larkin's "Aubade" on eschatological grounds, by means of a comparison with Yeats's "The Cold

Heaven," he imposes a split between aesthetic and metaphysical considerations. We hear such discernment in these remarks:

> When language does more than enough, as it does in all achieved poetry, it opts for the condition of overlife and rebels at limit. In this fundamentally artistic way, then, Larkin's "Aubade" does not go over to the side of the adversary. But its argument does add weight to the negative side of the scale and tips the balance definitely in favour of chemical law and mortal decline. The poem does not hold the lyre up in the face of the gods of the underworld; it does not make the Orphic effort to haul life back up the slope against all the odds. For all its heartbreaking truths and beauties, "Aubade" reneges on what Yeats called the "spiritual intellect's great work."[15]

Heaney's rhetoric is complicated and deceptive for its surface conviction and underlying contradiction. On the one hand, he makes a clear distinction between aesthetic treatment and deep-down belief. On the other hand, the terms in which he couches belief are in themselves aesthetic, appealing to the myth of Orpheus. Furthermore, mention of "the gods of the underworld" does not approach or test Heaney's own belief in one God or an afterlife, the nub of any eschatological musings, given his monotheistic Christian past.

Sins of omission, evasion generally as a moral failing, are a persistent note struck in "Station Island." In that poem the most damning accusation against the poet, ironically spoken by the poet himself through words of his own creation, is leveled by the ghost of his cousin, Colum McCartney, a victim of sectarian assassination. McCartney who, like all the ghosts in the poem, significantly remains nameless (or at least without a surname), a departure from Dante, accuses Heaney in section viii of not only failing to attend his funeral, but also spending the day selfishly. Heaney indulged himself in an outing with other poets to Jerpoint Abbey, an aesthetic ruin, not the corpse of a close relation. What is even harder, Heaney retrospectively flagellates himself for exploiting this terrorist incident and moment of personal loss for mileage both in conversation and poetry, furthermore a poem embellished with a learned allusion to Dante. Says McCartney's ghost, "You whitewashed ugliness and drew / the lovely blinds of the *Purgatorio,* / and saccharined my death with morning dew."[16] In an exceedingly reflexive, rhetorical moment Heaney uses McCartney to accuse himself, Heaney, of not using direct accusation in his elegy to McCartney, "The Strand at Lough Beg" several years earlier in *Field Work.* Heaney's reassessment in "Station Island" of that surpassingly poignant, delicate poem is: "You confused evasion with artistic tact."[17] These are the supposed words of McCartney, who goes on to add, "the Protestant who shot me through the head / I accuse directly, but indirectly, you."[18] Yet, very importantly, Heaney, either guilty of recidivism or determined to follow his better artistic judgment, remakes this same decision in another place in "Station Island." In section vii, the sectarian identification of William Strathearn's killers is deliberately finessed. "Station Island," therefore, although determined to take the low road as far as artifice is concerned, and deliberately in terms of style juxtaposing the demotic with the poetic, is also fighting for the values of poetry itself. The primary value is that it must appeal to, approach a truth not only beyond the local and the political, but beyond even the material. The entire point of this transcendent poetic, however, is a moral accountability in the here and now, gained through an experience of being judged *sub species aeternitatis*. Arriving at this inner revelation requires self-scrutiny rather than finger pointing.

This need for a larger truth brings Heaney to regard Yeats as far less bizarre than others have found him for his embracing of supernatural realities. It is the need, too, that gives Heaney the independence to find an affinity with a poet with whom he parted company in the early essay "The Makings of a Music," where Yeats's magisterial posture is associated with colonial entitlement. In "Joy or Night" there are many passages that let Heaney's affinity with Yeats's spirituality shine through. We feel the weight of Heaney's by this point considerable metaphysical authority in such passages. Permit me to list a few, since their sheer accumulation over the course of the essay adds up to a powerful preference on Heaney's part. Also bear in mind that "Joy or Night" is to be found in Heaney's third essay collection *The Redress of Poetry*, published in 1995, roughly a decade after "Station Island." I have isolated some telling sentences, especially for their tone of enthusiastic approbation where Yeats's poetic is discussed:

> "The Cold Heaven" is a poem which suggests that there is an overall purpose to life; and it does so by the intrinsically poetic actions of its rhymes, its rhythms, and its exultant intonation. These create an energy and an order which promote the idea that there exists a much greater, circumambient energy and order within which we have our being.[19]

Heaney's judicious words make it clear that belief does not have to be located on one end or the other of a spectrum between the binaries of metaphor and metaphysics; these two can be continuous, mutually reinforcing, both true. As he continues on the subject of Yeats's spiritual investigations, however, Heaney makes it seem that a poetry without belief, or the pressure of striving for belief, suffers a fatal lack. He says with ringing admiration, "Yeats was always passionately beating on the wall of the physical world in order to provoke an answer from the other side."[20] Later, comparing Yeats to Hardy, Heaney by means of speaking for Hardy (therefore to some extent still at a remove from himself), comes as close as possible in his tone to an apologia for poetry. Speaking first of Yeats, Heaney says, "Towards the middle of the twentieth century, he continued to hold the tune which 'the darkling thrush' announced to Thomas Hardy at its very beginning. The thrush's song proclaimed the basis of song itself was irrational, that its prerogative was to indulge impulse in spite of evidence."[21] Far from ascribing to Yeats, and I believe by inference to himself, a blind dismissal of rational demurrals, Heaney sees poetry as the place where language can include both skepticism and affirmation: that "in spite of the evidence" there is "a circumambient energy and order within which we have our being." The strict believer might sniff at this deftly handled, minimally secular locution, sensing more than anything a circumlocution, but, in fact, this is quite straight talk for Heaney, for any poet, whose interest is not doctrine but religious impulse.

Heaney's most self-revelatory moment in "Joy or Night" comes when, in a spirit of detached investigation, he quotes the words of Dorothy Wellesley, who confessed to coming to a dead halt in a conversation with Yeats when she questioned him aggressively about his exact beliefs. That frustrating exchange climaxed in Wellesley's trying to jolt Yeats into a disclosure by telling him he sounded just like a Roman Catholic. Yeats's only response, she lamented, was a laugh. It is Heaney's gloss on that reverberating laugh that is revealing: "The laugh was not really evasive. The laugh, in fact, established a conversational space where the question could move again."[22] The prayerfulness Frazier rightly identifies is less a posture than a process, further a profound, all-inclusive process that incorporates both the playfulness of poetry and the seriousness of doubt.

Also, Heaney has found a spiritual mentor more congenial than Yeats in Czeslaw Milosz and other guiding examples from eastern Europe, such as another Polish poet, Zbigniew Herbert, and the Czech Miroslav Holub, whose poem "The Dead" launches Heaney's argument with modernism in "Joy or Night." Such revisionism of modernism, a persistent project in the later work, occurs as much by embracing as rejecting that poetic. Milosz, with his perpetual yoking of moral and metaphysical opposites, has given Heaney an entry into an intellectual Catholicism far broader and more amenable to poetry than the hidebound pieties of Irish Catholicism. Furthermore, in his later poetry and in his prose, notably in his Nobel Prize acceptance speech, Heaney has increasingly weighed in with Milosz, using regularly, emphatically, for instance, the word "transformative," one of Milosz's favorites, to describe the effect of poetry. Speaking in his own voice toward the end of "Joy or Night," Heaney asserts simply: "In order that human beings bring about the most radiant conditions for themselves to inhabit, it is essential that the vision of reality which poetry offers should be transformative, more than just a print out of the given circumstances of its time and place."[23] In the context of the eschatological argument being conducted in his essay, Heaney seems to be arguing for poetry to adhere to a belief in a life beyond the physical, something which defies the finitude of death. His indebtedness to Milosz in this stance comes out in a previous juncture in the argument, where he openly recruits the Polish Nobel laureate:

> As Czeslaw Milosz has observed, no intelligent contemporary is spared the pressure exerted in our world by the void, the absurd, the anti-meaning, all of which are part of the intellectual atmosphere we subsist in; and yet Milosz notices this negative pressure only to protest against a whole strain of modern literature which has conceded victory to it. Poetry, Milosz pleads, must not make this concession but maintain instead its centuries-old hostility to reason, science and science-inspired philosophy.[24]

Milosz and Heaney share a range of cultural and historical similarities, not least the felt presence of a paganism not far below the cultural surface. Milosz's idyllic and magical autobiographical novel, *The Issa Valley,* records the early influence of a pre-Christian ethos on his work, as an Irish equivalent works on Heaney's. The difference between these two poets and cultures, however, as earlier remarked, is also substantial and plants the question as to how far Milosz's example can help Heaney. Milosz is responding not just to death and violence but to atrocity on a scale, as I have said, not approached by the Northern Troubles. Milosz's historical burden is not just the Nazi and Stalinist occupations of Poland, but the Holocaust itself. It is that nightmare vision of evil that stokes his persistent Manichaeanism.

All that Milosz has written positions Poland at the center of a millennial nightmare suffered in Eastern Europe with an intensity not quite grasped in Western Europe. Ireland, of course, being neutral in the war, is both further peripheral to that nightmare but also in a limited sense less complicit in it. As well, Ireland has sustained its own massive horror in previous centuries. One reason for Milosz's great importance as a voice in contemporary poetry is his articulation of a history that does not tally with the history that birthed modernism, in itself a response to World War, but not necessarily experienced at its darkest center. The particular history Milosz witnessed is not adequately matched by the metaphysical underpinnings of modernism. For Milosz to stand up as a poet to the absolute, engulfing evil he witnessed, he requires an equally potent, if not superior, faith. For very separate historical and psychological reasons, which may eventually give rise to a divergence between Milosz and Heaney, the Irish poet appears to see in the older, Polish poet a model for dealing with his own spiritual inheritance and historical circumstances. The example of Milosz may help to explain the less-than-perfect fit of modernism's paradigm onto Ireland's both postcolonial and traditionally religious culture. During the eighties and nineties the common aim of Heaney and Milosz was to imbue poetry with a questioned but also felt religious impulse quite at odds with the metaphysics of modernism and postmodernism, ranging from agnosticism to atheism. For Heaney, this cultural side step into Milosz also represents an independent assessment of, and partial break with, Joyce. In addition, both Milosz and Heaney by means of their respective poetics break with Romanticism and its basis in the ego. Anglocentric literary criticism, with its own genealogy threading through Romanticism and modernism, offers resistance to the resistance of Milosz and Heaney. "Station Island" is the place where the "good thief" in Heaney begins to hearken to "the promise."

"Station Island," however, gives no indication of sliding over into the doctrinal or sure. Nothing in it relents for one moment from a spirit of intense interrogation and earnest self-scrutiny. Opposition is maintained as a salient part of this tough reckoning. There is no jettisoning of stubborn moral and political difficulties for the sake of artistic resolution or personal salvation. Rather, instances of nonresolution are fixed with more unblinking honesty than we have seen in him before.

Heaney in "Station Island" rehearses the raw frankness of, say, "Mycenae Look-out." In contrast to the "bog poems" from *North,* where the importing of a conceit from another culture, a series of sacrificial burials in Jutland, results in allegorical abstractness, in the later poem the conceit of the Trojan War is used to strip bare rather than "redress," be it cloak or rectify, the violence and hypocrisy of home. "Mycenae Lookout" revisits the Troubles by means of a conceit but keeps verbal facility, the lure of artifice, sufficiently in check to stay true to certain brutal facts, reflected in a newly stripped, for Heaney, sometimes quite startlingly coarse language, as in "Cassandra":

> No such thing
> as innocent
> bystanding.
>
> Her soiled vest,
> her little breasts,
> her clipped, devas-
>
> ated, scabbed
> punk head,
> the char-eyed
>
> famine gawk—
> she looked
> camp-fucked.[25]

This is where the pilgrimage of "Station Island" brought Heaney. The penitential bed around which that poem continuously circles is the moral observation that there is "no such thing / as innocent / bystanding." This change in Heaney with regard to bearing witness, as illustrated by "Cassandra," flows from the religious crisis explored by "Station Island." Subsequent to writing it, as Dante sought Virgil, Heaney would seek Milosz as a spiritual guide. Ironically, Milosz, some ten years before the publication of "Station Island," had chosen Thomas Merton to fulfill this role for him. The phrase "innocent bystander," in fact, is a resonant one within the correspondence between the spiritually tortured Polish Catholic and the restive Trappist monk. That phrase is the title of an essay Merton submitted to Milosz for European publication, but the subject of that work, the responsibility of bearing difficult witness, is the theme of their early letters generally. There Milosz, for his part, tries to explain the moral pain of living in Paris, near but not in besieged Communist Poland. Heaney's contact with Milosz may be telegraphed by that phrase, but more surely and diffusely by the sea change in his moral perspective. Compare the passage above from "Cassandra" to its clear predecessor, "Bog Queen," and observe how much more indulgent Heaney is with himself in the earlier poem, beautifying, eroticizing horror, even putting these poetic words in the once punished girl's mouth:

> My body was braille
> for the creeping influences:

dawn suns groped over my head
and cooled at my feet.[26]

"Station Island" is the poetic moment when Heaney takes himself to task for poeticizing violence and pain.

Being true, therefore, to raw facts and rigid differences, beginning with those that dominate Northern politics, and speaking openly of repeated, failed attempts on his part to create a poetry that does not betray its art, yet is adequate to such grimness, "Station Island" exposes a series of conflicts, choices, and dilemmas. Many of these have already been exposed or hinted at by previous Lough Derg writings. Because this is a poem about purgatory, about stasis, the near hopelessness of being almost but not quite overwhelmed by confusion and despair, the reader must be careful not to underestimate the ponderous tug of the words, the murky moral confusion unrelieved for most of the poem. Only through the poem's own narrative movement does a very gradual emergence into the sunlight of self-knowledge take place, and always, in keeping with Dante's example, accompanied by a paradoxical sensation of ever-increasing obscurity, of being drawn back down from where we have come. Even at the end of Heaney's poem, we earn along with him never more than partial illumination, our most palpable reward being nothing more than the key to everything: the right questions.

One of the most persistent questions asked by "Station Island," asked in an endless number of ways and guises, is whether Catholicism can ever be separated from nationalism in Ireland. More specifically, is it possible that changes in the apprehension of one can translate into changes in the other, better still, whether the relationship with each can advance along separate tracks? So completely interconnected are these two massive areas of involuntary belief and niggling doubt, a starting point of mimetic accuracy for a Catholic Northerner, especially at this juncture in history, that it is difficult to find a seam by which to crack open this dangerous, then too-often-unexamined unity. The tribal taboo at that time on such independent analysis is precisely one of "Station Island"'s primary themes. Yet, miraculously, by the end the poem manages to dismantle this received truth and voice a number of important questions. If I list a few of them here, it is with a full awareness of betraying for a brief moment the artistry of the poem, which allows these matters to come into focus with the greatest psychologically and spiritually faithful slowness. Nonetheless, an impressive array of incisive, life- and culture-changing questions, which have no simple answers, emerge from the self-inquisition conducted in the poem.

The first question, concerning this problem of separating religious Lough Derg from its iconic, political status, is whether the shrine can ever be rescued from its role, its most recent reification in history, as the standard bearer of the extremely conservative Catholicism essential to de Valera's vision of Ireland? The Tridentine, devotional-based, exercise-driven, mechanical version of the faith, which actually overtakes Ireland in the early nineteenth century and comes to eclipse the more ecstatic, experiential, and to some, superstitious character of the pilgrimage in earlier centuries, is one of the major cultural givens Heaney implicitly challenges. He also questions the degree to which this legalistic version of religion is implicated in a similarly obedient, knee-crooking form of nationalism. Both forms of piety are intensified and rigidified by the besieged position of Catholics in the North during the eighties. So, can faith and the nation be considered as separate, both to rescue Catholicism from a reductive and rule-bound manifestation and nationalism from a pinched bigotry? Further still, can spirituality be embraced, the religious impulse affirmed, apart from the over-defining structure of the Church? More precisely, can the experience of faith, indeed even the liberating sensation of transcendence, be freed from the self-mortifying penitential exercises of Lough Derg, Carleton's great question? How much room is there in embracing Lough Derg to espouse a more relaxed, sensuous, European way of being a Catholic, a posture gesturing back to medieval Lough Derg? Could such an expansion and loosening of the shrine's legacy allow the Irish artist to practice his or her craft well beyond the imaginative construction of Lough Derg with less constraint, a sense of more elbow room within the parallel construction of Ireland? One thinks of Heaney's poem "Triptych," the first movement, "After a Killing," and the lines: "I see a stone house by a pier / Elbow room. Broad window light."[27] Typically for Heaney, he places a frame around the rich privacies of domestic life to provide a space for poetry. Furthermore, is there a way in which Lough Derg with its fortuitous European pedigree might facilitate a finessing of the by this stage jejune dualism set up by colonialism, which chronically pits Irish culture against English? Can Europe intervene as a third term just as Cambridge, Massachusetts, inserted itself between Dublin and Belfast for Heaney? Slightly altering the metaphor of Lough Derg writings as periodic eruptions on the body, I see "Station Island" as a fine incision made by Heaney, who cuts through layers of personal and cultural questions, both exposing and widening divisions at first, only to stitch them back up. The conscientious, modest poet does not produce a miraculous cure, nor is this his aim, but he certainly improves the overall health of the composite patient: Ireland, Irish poetry, poetry as a whole.

It is not that Heaney is presenting himself here as a scholar or theologian or polemicist or cultural diagnostician. "Station Island" is, of course, first and foremost poetry, a work so true to the somatic of doing the Station, the woozy, out-of-body, dreamlike feelings induced by the hunger, cold, sleep deprivation, the hypnotic effect of prayer and herd instinct even today, that its language induces the slippage of reason, acute sensory awareness, and distortion of time, which makes the Station so threatening to self-esteem, even sanity. What I am suggesting is that everything from childhood memory, received legend, study at school, and a certain amount of selective, discerning reading as an adult about the pilgrimage, particularly a joyful, transforming discovery of Dante, lies behind the gestation and composition of the poem. As in amber, all these facts and insights and impressions float like fragments fixed in the medium of the poem. "Station Island," too, represents a new form of excavation for Heaney, digging far beyond the familial and personal, as in *North*, beyond Ireland and yet paradoxically never deeper within it. "Station Island," more detached and scientific, less essentialist than *North* as a whole, may as well be a reliable core sample of Ireland, from its pagan prehistory to the present, illustrating the distance covered from the largely agrarian self-identity of the forties to the urban, urbane European Ireland of today, which was being born in the eighties. Heaney knew firsthand through his rural Derry childhood the conservative, pious, sexually repressed yet perversely sensuous life Kavanagh indelibly limned. Heaney registers this recognition in two essays, one early and the other late, "From Monaghan to the Grand Canal" and "The Placeless Heaven."

In addition, Heaney's own prior immersion both in Scandinavian and Celtic, pagan Ireland through the writing of *North,* and immediately before "Station Island," through the translating of the Irish myth "Buile Suibhne" as "Sweeney Astray," prepares him for his excavation of Lough Derg. In "Station Island," Heaney avoids all fetishizing preciousness with regard to his subject, applying his spade now to ordinary ground. This no-nonsense approach could not be a greater departure from O'Connor, Curtayne and Leslie, who approach Lough Derg, each in their different ways, as an undifferentiated epitome of Irish Culture: this gem mined from a rough history. It is as though Heaney is confronting cultural essentialism per se, breaking it down, freeing it, precisely by exposing its fault lines: lines of historical indebtedness that overlap and crisscross, amounting both to continuity and inconsistency, permitting both pattern building and free association, conveying what it means to inhabit time and form history simultaneously. "Station Island" makes it a point to expose discontinuity and disruption and to show how these fractures create spaces for fresh invention, choice, a new range of heterogeneous, heterodox feelings and impulses.

Everything from reverence to iconoclasm is allowed by the poem's eclectic method, which takes its cue from the physical and cognitive effects of doing the Station, thereby grounding the poem in autobiographical reality and specificity: the great distance covered from Derry to Belfast to Dublin to Cambridge. Part of the penance Heaney inflicts on himself is a ban on venturing too far from where he began. Yet, once this grounding is sure, he spreads his wings with equal determination. The genius behind "Station Island" is that of Heaney's persona, Sweeney, the bird man, the pagan king, who in his argument with the Church as a power structure discovers within himself a source of freedom, his ability to fly. The power it gives Heaney is perhaps indicated by the iconoclastic blow this revival of Sweeney inflicts on the Catholic-nationalist founding myth of Saint Patrick so prevalent in Lough Derg writing. "Station Island" is very much about overcoming through poetry a form of cultural incarceration. In it Heaney gives himself permission to use the powerful atavistic emotions generated by the Station as the fuel needed to launch himself, then swoop and soar through time and place. He dips into one hoard of Lough Derg memory, suggests some quick association, then flies away and dips into another repository: historical or literary or personal. Hence a new, highly individualized, nonideological, magpie construction of the identity of Lough Derg—and, by extension, of Ireland—is made as we read. Imagine Sweeney in the design created by his flight all over the whole island as rewriting the geographical and historical politics, the culture of Ireland, his levitated body acting as his pen. In earthing "Station Island" utterly in corporeal and emotional truth, and then and only then, lifting off into metaphysical and theological flight, Heaney guarantees that any potential overarching unities or continuities are also perceived as broken to begin with.

Largely perhaps because of the historical moment Heaney occupies and the slog work performed by his predecessors, the salient difference between his Lough Derg and theirs is the successful resistance he is able to mount against a received truth, while not depriving himself of valuable aspects of it. He can dispense with ideas of a false racial wholeness, continuity, and purity to embrace values of decency, accountability, and a predisposition to believe. Heaney manages to convert to self-possession the rebellious, often arrogant hostility unavoidable and necessary for Kavanagh and Carleton, each of whom revisited the nightmare of cultural determinism when they entered the Lough Derg "prison," be it the little church in Carleton's time, or the grandiose basilica in Kavanagh's. Both structures created spaces where the long hallucinatory vigil took place, a mini-episode in the nightmare of Irish history, a physical ordeal designed to erode personal resistance. Listen again to Rev. D. Canon O'Connor in the 1931 edition of his book implicitly correcting the impression left by Carleton's scathing description of the penal shrine on first sight. O'Connor with transparent point insists: "What wonder is it that the eye of the pilgrim is charmed, his heart elevated, his faith enlivened, nay, even his love for holy Ireland increased, when first the island of Lough Derg meets his view."[28] O'Connor, repairing here, as we have seen, the breach in Lough Derg reverence caused by Carleton's impiety, is very aware indeed of the power words can have to create and reinforce continuities of faith and feeling.

Reconsider in the light of assessing the load on Kavanagh's shoulders, a burden passed over to his successor, Heaney, the cultural valency of the following clerical strong-arming: "And what wonder is it that the Irish people should so love this Sanctuary? We love it because of the traditions, which enshrine it in the Irish heart; because of the numberless sinners here reconciled to God, and who here chose the better part."[29] Clearly, choosing the "better part" is indivisible from remaining one of the "Irish people." This spiritual bullying consists of a thinly veiled threat about the cost of not so choosing. Ostracism and perdition in Ireland after independence go hand in hand. No wonder resistance took so much time, so much accumulated history, so much confidence and experience outside Ireland. Heaney in "Station Island" emerges as a latter-day and revised Stephen Daedelus forging a conscience of rural Catholic Ireland—even more, of rural Catholic Northern Ireland. As the grown-up, guilty son in "Digging" or, later on, in "Making Strange," who feels shame for the relative ease of his literary life in contrast to his father's physical labor, Heaney does, in fact, obey an unflagging work ethic. In terms of our Lough

Derg conceit, he forces himself to stay awake through the entire night, hugging his self-possession, believing that the cost for letting go, lapsing into conformity, at this point in history will be vitiation rather than perdition.

Sifting through the countless historical allusions and suggestions buried within "Station Island," one soon realizes that all the layers of Lough Derg history are there, if only glimpsed partially, like gleaming artifacts protruding out of the bog. The poem opens on the fault line explored in "Sweeney Astray," where the Pagan meets the Christian. Sweeney, Simon Sweeney in this further incarnation in "Station Island," is a liminal figure from the author's childhood, someone who appears on the edges of memory, or daydream, or the coruscating space between sleeping and waking. This makes sense, because the Sweeney from mythology was always on the margins, a disaffected and ostracized figure in the community, attracting both fear and fascination, like the maligned "tinkers" of childhood memory with their assumed heathenish ways. Sweeney is a Virgilian artist surrogate, who, like his mythological namesake, is connected with the earth, with musky, bosky odors, with trees. Disembodied now, he reminds the poet of how corporeal Sweeney once was:

> When cut or broken limbs
> of trees went yellow, when
>
> woodsmoke sharpened air
> or ditches rustled
> you sensed my trail there
> as if it had been sprayed.[30]

From the first images applied to Sweeney, his pagan identity is hybridized by associating it with a dominant image from Dante, the circular template of hell. A still-spinning bicycle wheel, like memory itself, our modern hell, announces Sweeney's appearance. Soon the wheel transmutes, fragments into a lyre, implying a connection between outsider status and poetry. The lyre in turn becomes a hack saw, which cuts into a hazel bush and from there the resonances fly.

These amoeban images of the poem carry multiple connotations rather than a single meaning through their mutating lives. Here, for example, the echo of Yeats's "Song of Wandering Aengus" is sent up and with it a string of questions about Heaney's very complicated, ever-changing relationship with Yeats, questions that continue to surface and become more complex as the poem grows. Especially in regard to an iconic Yeats, Heaney exhibits how a deconstructive effort and growing independence go hand in hand. An intricate pattern of divergence and convergence between the two poets develops on a range of issues. On the one hand, Heaney openly shares with Yeats, as we have seen, a spiritual restlessness and appetite. He also shares a repugnance for a hard-line nationalism too often upheld in the name of one or another brand of Christianity. Heaney's tone is clear when Sweeney's lyre turns into a "harp of unforgiving iron."[31] Then again, Yeats's presumptive appropriation of the native inheritance of Irish mythology, especially of paganism, has been a bone of contention with nationalist critics of Heaney's generation. Seamus Deane, for example, as early as 1984 exposed this dubious borrowing in one of the first *Field Day* pamphlets, "Heroic Styles: The Tradition of an Idea." Joyce's ascendance over Yeats in today's cultural-nationalist politics may be traced arguably to this turning point, where Deane asserts:

> What I propose in this pamphlet is that there have been for us two dominant ways of reading both our literature and our history. One is "Romantic," a mode of reading which takes pleasure in the notion that Ireland is a culture enriched by the ambiguity of its relationship to an anachronistic and a modernized present. The other is a mode of reading which denies the glamour of this ambiguity and seeks to escape from it into a pluralism of the present.[32]

Yeats for Deane represents the former, Joyce the latter. It may be less a coincidence than in part the natural result of conversations bound up with the gestating of *Field Day* that Heaney, who was then central to the enterprise, gives this prominent role in "Station Island" to Joyce. Heaney parts company with Yeats presumably for this Romanticism, only to reconnect with him in "Joy or Night" because of a religious passion beyond a Romantic inclination. Heaney also, by including Joyce, breaches the Northern phalanx of the other literary precursors who precede him to Lough Derg, Carleton and Kavanagh. Heaney's purgatory occupies a ragged, uneven interface, where an urban, modern Ireland epitomized by Joyce meets a rural, still fetishized Ireland, in which Protestant, Catholic, and pagan beliefs and histories come together, meet, and jostle. Heaney manages through "Station Island" to make a distinction between his natural human attachment to his place of origin and any romantic, overzealous idealization of it. For example, he reminds us by indirection in "Station Island" that "Sweeney Astray" is hardly a nostalgic morality tale about the superiority of paganism. This less polarized truth comes alive in the original myth and in Heaney's rendition of it, when Ronan's Psalter, a symbol of Christianity, is rescued from the lake into which it has been angrily thrown by Sweeney, an act of defiance against the interloping Saint Ronan. Its recovery by natural forces shines as providential. Heaney reprises this image in "Station Island" in section x and expects the intertextual echo to resonate.

A hint of the reward to come from all this deconstructing and reconstructing of culture and the self, particularly their complex interrelationship, occurs in section x, where a fleeting moment of sublime integration is sensed. This section consists of a lyrical condensed poem about the gratitude felt, after the vigil, for simple food and the light of the sun. The moment locates a return to the domestic from the liturgical, nurturance from penance. The psychic and religious fallout of Heaney's ordeal begs comparison with Carleton's, particularly his fear that death or permanent insanity could result from the dark transport experienced performing the Station. Heaney reveals the individual at this point in Ireland's cultural evolution to be strong enough to withstand the ritual, even to be enriched by intimations of transcendence. Conveying the brand-newness, the restoration to oneself after emerging from "prison," Heaney implicitly compares his resurfacing to the recovery of Ronan's Psalter. Eliding Lough Derg and this other lake from "Buile Suibhne," Heaney implicitly, briefly, links himself with the otter who surfaced with the Psalter, and with the artifact itself, hinting further that that the poet cannot be divided from the poem, "as the otter surfaced once with Ronan's psalter / miraculously unharmed, that had been lost / a day and a night under lough water."[33] The wondrous coincidence is that the poet and the poem have returned to ordinary life "miraculously unharmed" after "a day and a night," the length of the Lough Derg vigil, submerged in self-doubt and self-hatred: "under lough water." Section x takes place in a refectory reminiscent of the light-filled kitchens of many of Heaney's poems recovering childhood, where a transporting and physical love for the mother is felt. That these kitchens are domestic chapels is appropriate given this ingrained fusing of sexual and religious love. "Station Island," where the homely indigenous ritual of Lough Derg is performed, is the place where Heaney makes his poetic cleave to the paradox of this originating revelation.

Perhaps the most extraordinary of the early poems that explore this illumination is "Sunlight" itself, ending with this pure perception of mother love embodied in hard, domestic work:

> And here is love
> like a tinsmith's scoop
> sunk past its gleam
> in the meal-bin.[34]

In adult religious experience, faith and doubt, light and dark hinge on the same experience of visceral attachment. Although the dominant ocular impression of that image in "Sunlight" is an arresting, "gleam," in fact the poem pinpoints the temporary loss of light, its submergence in the meal bin, ever so faintly suggesting that love, maternal and divine, is tested by fleeting sensations of loss. All of these poems prepare Heaney for a particularly earthed understanding of Dante's Beatrician vision; hence, any suggestions of Mariolatry in Heaney are rescued from the ether of theology by being grounded in an actual mother, the premise on which "Clearances" will rest.

In section x, a profound and subtle psychological and religious poem, the poet recalls an attachment he had to a particular vessel, a developmentally critical transitional object, both uterus and chalice and lowly mug, painted with a recurring floral pattern like the endlessly renewing earth of Heaney's early poems and secure childhood. The vessel, like a poem, becomes the symbol of an early receptacle for elusive feeling, a passionate love associated with home embodied in his mother but never fully realizable because other people are never fully possessed or even knowable. The defense against this distance is to transform the mug into an adored object always at a distance: "beyond my reach on its high shelf." One day, however, that distance perilously increases and then even more perilously collapses. The mug is borrowed by amateur actors as a prop in a play. The reigning conceit of theater suggests all performative events, from the ritualized movements of a woman in a kitchen to those of a priest on an altar. The ornate framing implied by the proscenium arch of that discrete memory suggests both the theatrical quality of Catholic ritual and a poetry enamored of high artifice. Both somehow fail for Heaney, whose epiphanies tend to come from the ordinary, the daily. In section x, the poet is exhausted by his vigil and grateful for his simple breakfast. He experiences, however, a religious moment not absolutely divisible from that prepared for by the official Lough Derg exercises, hence the allusion to Ronan's psalter, a relic of the official Church:

> And so the saint praised God on the lough shore
> for that dazzle of impossibility
> I credited again in the sun-filled door,
> so absolutely light it could put out fire." [35]

A heavenly light extinguishing the fire of hell, perhaps? This is an ambiguous and layered moment introducing the religious but not distinguishing it from the emotional, the psychological, and the physical. Where Carleton, for example, acts out his anarchic feelings, Heaney aims for self-reflection and integration. This is the nub of "Station Island." It is this merging and painstaking untangling of faith from feeling and reintegration of the two, along with even neurosis, which marks Heaney's unique contribution to the Lough Derg puzzle. "Station Island" can be read as a warning not to predict too categorically how faith happens or whether it will happen at all. The poem also registers the epistemological impossibility of differentiating divine from human love, the insight that will enable the truly purgative "Clearances."

One of the most resonant contradictions in section x is that the self-divided poet partakes of both Ronan's and Sweeney's identities. Two things appear to be certain. First, when the mug returns from its time away, it is newly perceived as damaged, though this seems to have been always the case. Now, however, it is "returned to its old haircracked doze." While away, absent, it has been the "loving cup," the shared vessel for a fictional couple on stage. The couple suggests any number of interdependent doubles, from mother and father to body and blood. The tableau of their commingling elicits from a distance the young child's jealousy, suggestive of oedipal rage toward the father for his usurpation of the vessel of the mother. Perhaps psychically, the mother and father at some level are distanced, as though they are actors in the drama of their marriage, particularly in bed, their private stage, beyond the insatiable gaze of this precocious child. The language of the poem ensures that this sexual reading does not invalidate a more literal reading about an actual theatrical event, nor does a religious interpretation of an epiphany at Lough Derg subsume an earlier transforming moment. At this point in Heaney's development, integration is all. What remains incontrovertible but ineffable is that the mug returns to its regular place "dipped and glamoured" by its experience elsewhere, whatever this elsewhere is among many possibilities, and "dipped and glamoured" carries as many overt sexual implications as it does religious and baptismal ones. As well, our entire being can be "dipped and glamoured" in a work of art, any transformative experience.

Although the epiphany at Lough Derg occurs in a frame, reminiscent of that proscenium arch and the theatricality of Catholic ritual generally, the frame of the humble adult epiphany is quite minimal, implying low artifice. The epiphany occurs in a door frame that, as distinct from a proscenium arch, implies a passageway as well as a stage. Perception, therefore, as well as spiritual intimation is presented in the poem as both bounded and bound to process. Heaney uses the later "Squarings" as a way to explore how continuous constructions of reality make it so fluent as to defy definition, a quite modernist stance, thereby extending the conversation Heaney begins about modernism in "Station Island." The later sequence demonstrates a limited indebtedness to modernism but also a deviation from it as being only partially fulfilling. "Squarings" resists all the way along the full logic of the nihilistic leanings of individual segments. More, the sequence appears to subsume modernism into a newer, more contemporary, and pan-European transformation in poetry that appears necessary "because there is the night," to quote Heaney's translation of Saint John of the Cross from "Station Island," section xi. In other words, as Heaney progresses, the light appears to gain more valency than the door within which it is framed. What is more, poetry that places too much self-conscious value on the frame, rather than gratefully regarding the poem as a receptacle for its own peculiar grace, is granted less validity. Heaney's increasingly strong leaning in this antimodernist direction after "Station Island" may be possibly accounted for by the increasing influence of Milosz. At one point in his correspondence with Merton, Milosz confides, "I am on the side of poetry which is nourished not by itself."[36] Later Merton adds, "We have to regain our sense of being, our confidence in reality, not in words."[37] It is a similar, though nascent, spiritual and moral hunger that makes "Station Island" necessary.

The lifelike splicing of various vital memories, beliefs, and sensations, some discordant, associated with that loosely centering mug predicts the approach toward meaning overall in "Station Island." Although the metaphors through their splicing create a surface continuity, it has no more reality or, crucially, sanction than the passage of time with its occasional epiphanies. It does not imply a unity and essentiality of meaning, since the harp, politics, jars absolutely with the lyre, poetry; this is a metaphorical way of indicating many unresolved conflicts at the heart of the poem. Similarly, the hazel branch, though carrying an echo of Yeats, echoes even more across Heaney's own oeuvre, recalling the poem "A Hazel Stick for Catherine Ann," also from *Station Island*. When Sweeney, a poet surrogate, therefore, cuts a hazel branch, it not only reminds us of Heaney's preoccupation with water divination, for sensing what is under the surface, but also with the vibrancy of the present, the layer on which we live. Within the image system of "Station Island," this hazel wand seems as much an instrument to locate a source of belief, the fountain of faith that will gush up in Heaney's translation of Saint John of the Cross, as it is a simple forked object, like the body itself and the riven consciousness trapped within it. Nowhere in "Station Island" is it implied that a healing essence of Irishness is found by digging down into a pagan past. Even the pagan source is splintered here, or better, expanded and enriched by its contiguity with Europe. The minute the Druidical oak appears, so too does the impulse to "loosen the toga for wine and poetry," [38] a line that sparks off an ironical pun with "Lough Derg wine," the colloquial term for the black tea drunk with the dry toast to break the fast after the vigil. Pagan Ireland, Catholic Ireland, and sybaritic Europe reverberate and jangle by means of this single allusion.

In the same way that Stephen knew the best route to Tara was via Hollyhead, so Heaney seems to recognize here that the only route toward personal integration is through a deliberate embracing of, not a Yeatsian anti-self, but the nonbinary, multiple selves that elude his too familiar one. This means, for one, opening himself to the mitigating influence of Europe, specifically in section xi where relief is found through that encounter with the imaginative, sympathetic monk "returned from Spain to our chapped wilderness." [39] In assigning for the scrupulous poet's penance, the translating of "something by Juan de la Cruz," [40] the surpassingly sensible monk suggests that Heaney's only sin may be a narrow and reductive idea of God. This is the deity who has been constructed over the course of Irish history to reflect the barrenness of the Lough Derg landscape, to match the quality of faith that often goes with it. The poem Heaney chooses by Saint John of the Cross advances the process created by his subtle and self-reflective spiritual pilgrimage precisely by revealing paradox as a means, rather than an obstacle, to faith. The refrain of the poem, "although it is the night," [41] constitutes the third, shorter line that follows on a string of couplets trying to do justice, often by means of enigma, to the incomprehensible purity of faith. Hence we have: "that eternal fountain, hidden away / . . . But not its source because it does not have one, / . . . So pellucid it never can be muddied," [42] etc. The penultimate stanza reads: "Hear it calling out to every creature, / And they drink these waters, although it is dark here / because it is the night." [43] The change in sense of the refrain provided by the change in conjunction from "although" to "because it is the night" is meant to underline the causal relationship between necessity and faith: the saving need for light is demanded by the certainty of darkness.

This interpenetration of light and dark, this eschewal of oneness, makes its presence felt in the eschewal, too, to a significant degree, of single authorship. "Station Island" accedes to the need for collaboration on every level. The resulting poem is part Heaney and part those who have guided him. Helen Vendler has made the case that the poem is about the different identities the poet might have assumed, given his upbringing, had he not become a poet. Although this is true, the assumption of different masks serves at a deeper level to define a spiritual as well as a psychological purpose. Experimentation with new identities happens just as much through acts of translation as through acts of ventriloquism with regard to the various ghosts. We have seen through the example of Denis Florence Mac-Carthy how integral translation is to the process of cultural self-discovery prompted by the continuous but various history of Lough Derg. Displaying the dependency on another that the act of translating must involve becomes a way for Heaney to discover true humility. The words of the great Spanish mystic and poet, his radiant self-abjection, is grafted onto section x and constitutes its greater part. The opposite proportions but the same hybrid, self-relinquishing method is used in "A Dream of Solstice," where Dante is grafted onto Heaney. In both cases this formal choice reflects a deeper collaboration. The implication is that the self is no longer sufficient to save itself. Spiritual, paternal guides are needed to lead consciousness beyond the ego, just as grace is said to visit a mortal body. In many instances throughout Heaney's oeuvre, other poets and other cultures enable him to take adept steps sidewise outside the conditioned and too familiar. These temporary displacements have a consistently beneficial effect.

This principle of operation is best illustrated by another incarnation of the lyre image in Heaney's poems, another deployment of a European poet, and another echo across Heaney's oeuvre. In this case the reverberant poem follows "Station Island." As a translation of a passage from the *Aeneid,* it evokes both Dante, who was guided by Virgil, plus Dante's indebtedness to Virgil for his narrative model, and finally Heaney's indebtedness to both in his use of them in "Station Island." The first poem in *Seeing Things* is "The Golden Bough," a translation of the *Aeneid,* book 6, lines 98–148. The central image here is that most associated with Lough Derg, the cave, but the lyre also appears in the hand of Orpheus, the mythological embodiment of the poet as pure lyricist. Given these many links with the earlier poem, surely another link, only implied, can be reasonably entertained. Aeneas expresses his most heartfelt wish, "I pray for one look, one face-to-face meeting with my father."[44] Really seeing the father would mean really seeing the self, wholly, clearly. But neither of these happy events occurs in "Station Island." It is worth recalling again that in the *Tractatus* the turning point in the living nightmare is the moment when the pilgrim speaks Christ's name in response to a revelation, an eidetic image, seeing before one the savior's face. But in keeping with the many-faceted and fragmented images produced by the kaleidoscope, which as a trope dominates the beginning of section x, Heaney's nightmare sequence, perception, including self-perception, remains prismatic throughout the poem. Even the kitchen epiphany in section x is divided between artifice and reality, the mug within the theatrical production and the mug at home, also framed, haloed, on a shelf. The wish for unity and full knowledge is always thwarted by history and the loss of innocence that entails a never fully recoverable separation from an originating love.

Heaney assigns to the mug a role significantly similar to and different from that which Wallace Stevens ascribes to a centering container in his "Anecdote of a Jar":

I placed a jar on hill in Tennessee
And round it was, upon a hill.
It made the slovenly wilderness
Surround that hill.[45]

The jar orders all the world around it. Crucially, however, and in keeping with the impact of Romanticism on Stevens's brand of modernism, this placement is both a subjective and self-conscious act, which gives the imagination full agency and assigns the jar this place. Heaney can't conceive of, let alone verbalize, a world preexisting this object of primal attachment: "When had it not been there?"[46] It seems to exist prior to himself, and its comings and goings are independent of his will. Hence the idea of the father, symbolically one half of an infinitely receding set of generating and regenerating dyads, becomes many fathers in this poem, and all perceptions of the self are partial and contingent. The idea of the mother is even more fugitive. Only a leap of faith into a realm beyond the ego can heal this primal rift and produce the liberating "Clearances." Within "Station Island" this move is foreseen but not executed.

This is truly a penitential poem where the usual assuagements of life are denied the author for a space. Section x is one of the few moments where the beneficence of maternal love, a resource as inexhaustible as the celestial light at the conclusion of the *Divine Comedy*, is allowed to shine down on the benighted poet. The most lurid, disturbing image of the poem, occurring in the related nightmare, is that "shed breast" floating down a putrid river, a distressing fragment of a portrait of the breastfeeding Madonna. One might see this almost pornographic image as the final consequence of that first hairline crack in the mug. This image of the violated breast sets up a Dantean echo recalling the final canto of the *Paradiso*, which Heaney incorporates in "A Dream of Solstice." In that canto, referring to the ineffability of the reception of grace, Dante says, in Heaney's translation, "an infant's tongue / milky with breast milk would be more articulate."[47] Grace transports the blessed to a place beyond words, just as the mirror image of such renewed innocence, a baby, resides in a preverbal limbo. Heaney has always been drawn to this purely gestational space, but in "Station Island" he sentences himself to an overdue weaning, confessing to himself and to the void: "I repent / My unweened life that kept me competent / To sleepwalk with connivance and mistrust."[48] Vendler, observing of those two sections, iii and vi, which foreground memories of girls or women, informs us that "the female presences were—according to the poet in conversation—later additions to what first presented itself as an all-male poem."[49] In "Clearances" part iii, taking stock after his mother's death, Heaney recalls a religious intensity that was a barely camouflaged, erotic attachment to his mother: "The ceremonies during Holy Week/ Were highpoints of our *Sons and Lovers* phase."[50]

"Station Island" is for the most part skeptical of this rapturous version of religion, largely sublimation, having little to do with rigorous self-examination. This protection of manly rectitude also formed a large part of Carleton's motivation. As well, Kavanagh's gruff, social satire is a way of resisting the pull of such conditioning. Heaney, picking up the baton passed on to him from Kavanagh, inherits the double challenge of rescuing Catholicism from this unthinking obedience and not depriving it of its mystical potential. So much of what might be construed as anti-feminist in this poem can be interpreted as a symptom of this inherited resistance; but it is also part of a dialectical process of constructing an autonomy that allows for the reintegration of the feminine and the visionary in a new, less stereotyped way. Not only is this inflected feminism a rectification of the feminizing effect of colonization, but also it is a correction of the antimystical, partisan bent of early postindependence nationalists like Curtayne.

In the opening section of the "Station Island," a contrapuntal set of images pit feelings associated with Sweeney against those associated with women, who appear as undifferentiated, a murmuring river. The poet cannot resist this current associated with maternal love and flows with it toward Lough Derg. Sweeney's final advice, predicting the urgings of Joyce at the end to preserve and assert autonomy, is the shouted order, "Stay clear of all processions." Cultural conformity is associated with the mother, the gentle scold of "Clearances," section ii, who spouts a litany of prohibitions—"Don't tilt your chair. / Don't reach. Don't point. Don't make noise when you stir."[51] Autonomy, accountability, moral authority, and psychic separateness are attached to the father. "Station Island" is a series of confrontations with father figures who all find Heaney coming up short. The poem is a reckoning with himself as a man, always being observed and measured, as he was in "Digging," against the implicit image of his father. The surest sign that Heaney has relinquished an essentialist mindset is the conspicuous absence of a single father figure, be it Saint Patrick or the monotheistic Yahweh. The self constructed amidst such a fractured sense of origin will be contingent, pragmatic, incomplete, yet still mysteriously receptive to faith. The more acute problem is to protect the self against the seduction of false and degrading epiphanies.

For Carleton, as we have seen, Lough Derg is a site where sanity can drop away in a blink and the boundaries that usually define the self dissolve. It is a place where one's masculinity is absolutely on the line. This liminal place is one, ironically, where a certain kind of perhaps spurious liminality must be resisted. Given this and the mythological weight of association with a devouring mother and the Lough Derg monster, it is even more remarkable that Heaney avoids female caricature. Although the significantly dual female presences in the poem are associated with a portal (the keyhole of her dress) and a receptacle (the grotto), cavelike forms that lead to or contain some secret, totalizing vision, in the end even this form of transport is resisted for a more virile, rational plurality. Only from this fully conscious starting point can any legitimate leap of faith be taken. As such, this position revises Denis Devlin in order to subvert the cultural sway of Mariolatry.

At the end, although the poet is urged by Joyce to return to a fluid medium that may suggest the womb, the spiritual rebirth urged is entirely self-induced. The open sea, far away from limiting islands, contains infinite possibilities for the self, identity. With this perception comes the division and proliferation of a totemic snake figure into countless "elver-gleams." Furthermore, the feared object becomes language itself, never absolute, always plural, contingent, fluid, and as such threatening to the identity of the poet himself who must open himself to such open-endedness. Language figured this way is leagues apart from the essentialist concept of a "mother tongue." As Joyce advises,

> fill the element
> with signatures on your own frequency
> echo soundings, searches, probes, allurements
> elver-gleams in the dark of the whole sea.[52]

The elver-gleams are immutably multiple, just as the father figures, like fleeting, fragmented glimpses in a mirror, are aspects of Heaney's unfinished self-image. This is a highly centrifugal poem that generates questions, rather than revolving around a preordained center. The elvers are the infinite, metaphorical progeny of the bloated maggot that Fionn slayed. Heaney in this poem is a slayer of received myth itself. His post-Freudian poem recognizes that any projection of a single sinewy enemy, be it mother or father or the devil, is untenable, as perhaps is the belief in God. The divine, however, is the only absolute that it is worth the adult struggle to discover, or to keep in view as we live somewhere between it and compromise, in purgatory.

The demons Heaney confronts in the poem are internal and plural, their constant shifting identities the quick, Sweeney-like calligraphy of poetry, a language emanating from no single tribal or national source. It is important that none of Heaney's ghosts are called in the poem by name, that we only know their identities from biographical and critical studies of Heaney's work. This is a strategy reminiscent of Yeats's up to the final lines of "Easter 1916", where at last "this man," "this other," and "this other man" and so forth are given names; "MacDonagh and MacBride / Connolly and Pearse." Yeats's reason for keeping the men nameless until the end is that the poem finally returns to multiplicity and individuality the impenetrable, fused, anonymous collectivity of "the stone in the midst of all." Heaney, too, is bent on breaking down the same stone of nationalism and Catholicism conjoined. Kavanagh, Carleton, and Joyce have no names, are all actors in a collective effort to dismantle the same calcifying myth. This is a poem of numerous shifting identities, none of them fixed, least of all the national or religious, and the interpenetration of European and Irish, Pagan and Christian texts and allusions is crucial to this eclectic reconstruction of Lough Derg. All the fathers, all the ghosts and guides, contribute to the remaking of the poet, who, in common with Lough Derg, remains ever more kaleidoscopic, elusive, and potentially whole.

8

Heaney's Ghosts

And Maybe There's a Lesson There for You

"STATION ISLAND" opens and closes with symmetrical spectral father figures, both outsiders to Christianity: Sweeney and Joyce, both of whom urge irreverence and independence on the poet. Their words almost echo each other. "Stay clear of all processions," Sweeney's last words, seem to be taken up by Joyce and expanded upon for their bearing on the practicing contemporary Irish writer:

> You are fasted now, light-headed, dangerous.
> Take off from here. And don't be so earnest,
>
> Let others wear the sackcloth and ashes.
> Let go, let fly, forget.
> You've listened long enough. Now strike your note.[1]

Even Heaney indirectly urges greater sacrilege against the then prevailing pieties of academe, the delvings of *Field Day* itself:

> The English language
> belongs to us. You are raking at dead fires,
>
> a waste of time for somebody your age.
> That subject people stuff is a cod's game,
> Infantile, like your peasant pilgrimage.[2]

This moment, however, is by no means conclusive, because we do not hear the poet's resolve in his own voice. What we do know, given the revisionist bent of the poem as a whole, is that this advice will not be passively received. Joyce's word "infantile" really cuts, for this is a poem about taking on the full responsibility of adulthood, chiefly for making choices, artistic and moral, and accepting consequences. One of Heaney's most trying challenges is to take the infamous Joycean defiance, by now the sine qua non for the free Irish imagination, and integrate this credo into his own time and disposition, which may include a need to yield as well as to fight.

All we know at the end of "Station Island" is that the perpendicular certainties of Joyce immediately vanish behind a scrim of rain. A double image of renewed confusion and equal determination reverberates in the last line of the poem: "the downpour loosed its screens round his straight walk."[3] In its irreducible ambiguity this line sums up every inch of what has come before. Far from regarding Joyce's words as definitive, therefore, it is necessary to take into account all the other ghosts who confront the poet, as he moves through the various set exercises of the Station. Weaving in his mind between an imposed order of exercises and his own thought, like a dialectic of determinism and free will, the poet, ever processing the advice and reprimands received en route, rehearses his perennial conflict between submission and rebellion. These are choices with far-ranging consequences. Part of accepted myth about the pilgrimage is that Saint Patrick, frustrated by the recalcitrant paganism of the Irish, asked God to provide him with a pedagogical tool for conversion: physical proof of what would happen to these robust sinners, if they did not repent. A round-trip ticket to hell was the perfect answer. The Irish had been granted a unique privilege, the right to enter the underworld, witness its tortures firsthand, pay their pre-estimated dues, and, if they survived the temptations experienced there, mainly to despair, emerge alive with some remaining time on earth to reform.

The attitude, however, inculcated at Lough Derg for the last two centuries, as we have seen, is in direct opposition to Stephen Dedalus's defiance, itself a limiting posture. The combination of the appearance of Joyce at the end of the poem and the use of Dante, "the chief imagination of Christendom," in Yeats's words, as the author of the dominant narrative paradigm for "Station Island," creates its own potential conflict. The reader cannot help being reminded, if only subconsciously, of the famous Christmas dinner scene at the opening of *A Portrait of the Artist as a Young Man,* where the indignant, pious aunt who has to leave the impious table is, of course, Dante Riordan, "Aunt Dante." Early into the scene, before the anticlerical heat has risen to a degree absolutely intolerable to her, she warns that certain sacrilegious words will be overheard and remembered by young Stephen, the young Joyce. Stephen picks up by osmosis from the vituperative anticlerical remarks of his father, Mr. Dedalus, and his friend, Mr. Casey, a lifelong conviction of the necessity to separate church and state. The two men, after all, are discussing the culpability of the clergy in the downfall and death of Parnell. "If they took a fool's advice they would confine their attention to religion,"[4] observes Mr. Dedalus, who sums up the Irish, in their sorry condition under the political thumb of the Church, as "a priest-ridden, Godforsaken race."[5] It is up to Mr. Casey, however, both to trot out the damning, specific, historical evidence and to give voice to the most provocative declaration possible at a bourgeois Irish Catholic Christmas dinner:

Didn't the bishops of Ireland betray us in the time of the union when bishop Lanigan presented an address of loyalty to the Marquess Cornwallis? Didn't the bishops and priests sell the aspirations of their country in 1829 in return for catholic emanci-

pation? Didn't they denounce the Fenian movement from the pulpit and in the confession box? And didn't they dishonour the ashes of Terence Bellew MacManus?[6]

Finally, reaching a crescendo of anger, goaded by Dante's furious refrain, "God and
religion before everything," Mr. Casey declares, "No God for Ireland. . . . We have
had too much God in Ireland. Away with God."[7] Mrs. Riordan's response to this is
"Blasphemer! Devil!" and at this point she leaves the table.

Her physical departure is a symbolic demonstration of the inability of Catholicism and nationalism to coexist in Ireland, without the transgression of boundaries
represented by the Parnell tragedy. It is important to note that Aunt Dante is presented as "for Ireland" too. Wasn't she seen "hitting a gentleman on the head with
her umbrella because he had taken off his hat when the band played God Save the
Queen?"[8] Yet, just as the Church is depicted by Mr. Casey as colluding with the
British to the detriment not just of Ireland but the welfare of its people, so Dante's
mind is colonized by the Church at a moment in history when nationalism acutely
needed to be free of Catholicism. For writers of generations following Joyce, the
repercussions of this dinner table fracas reverberate as much as they did in the
young Stephen's consciousness. Helen Vendler is invoking this historical conflict
when she insists on Heaney's essential secularism, except that Heaney, in the context of the Troubles, is responding perhaps more to the use of the collusion of
Catholicism and Republicanism to justify violence than to the Church's betrayals of
Ireland. Still, the fundamental question for Heaney is whether Catholicism and nationalism can be reinvestigated for their own separate and intrinsic merits. The degree of complexity and conflict Heaney faces is indicated by his espousal of Joyce at
this juncture, and then Milosz at a later: one man fighting to rid Ireland of God, the
other arguing to include God in poetry. By enlisting the examples of such divergent
positions, Heaney is reconstructing and realigning for his own purposes a multi-
faceted problem already bequeathed Ireland by history.

One of the basic questions asked by "Station Island" is how much Heaney's use
of Dante Alighieri represents an adherence to or deviation from doctrinal Catholicism. In the next chapter, I will examine the substance of the link between Heaney
and Dante by investigating the bearing of the *Purgatorio* on "Station Island." There,
too, I will more fully reckon with Joyce's ghost and the specter of modernism,
which offers a historical precedent for representing the psychic fragmentation and
doubt about God that pervades this poem. For now, Dante can be regarded as the
ghost behind the entire sequence. His presence is felt more or less directly in every
poem and, if only by ironic contrast, to every message conveyed by Heaney's particular ghosts, be they literary or everyday figures. All the literary ghosts urge the
opposite of what we have come to expect from Dante: recognition of sin and of its
wages, horror at its intrinsic vileness, and a firm resolve to reform. Heaney's ghosts

if anything attempt to free him from his excessive scruples. Their impatience and aggressiveness only underscore the necessity for the Irish artist to fight without crippling ambivalence the domination of the Church, but the covert ghost of Dante, especially for the learned poet, offers perhaps a more integrated approach. The relationship with Dante is far from simply emulative or combative. Not only on the level of borrowed narrative devices and motifs, but on the overall moral level of the making of the soul, Heaney is following, as Dante did with Virgil, in his teacher's footsteps, yet telling his own highly individual story of repentance. Heaney, however, also knows through his intimacy with Yeats (and must be reassured by the knowledge) that the biographical Dante offers no straightforward moral example. Apparently unscathed by the doctrinally airbrushed, 1940s image of a Catholic Dante, Heaney turns to the sinner-philanderer-poet of Yeats's "Ego Dominus Tuus." Yeats presents the *Divine Comedy* as being born of an imaginative striving toward an antiself: the pure lover of Beatrice emerging like sun from behind a cloud of corruption: "Being mocked by Guido for his lecherous life . . . he found / The most exalted lady loved by man." [9] While detailed allusions to Dante, beyond the broad structuring of "Station Island," crop up with every ghost who appears, mentioning a few of these echoes at the onset demonstrates how, as with every feature of this poem, the end result is further complication and contradiction, the staples of what Milosz calls "striving toward Being." [10]

First, there is the matter of Beatrice. Dante's poem is entirely engineered to build toward the final revelation of this embodiment of divine love. At first glance, Heaney's much, much shorter poem, more a snippet, a fragment of a *Purgatorio*, seems to end on an opposite note with the revelation of Joyce, a father figure recommending defiance, especially against the mother—Mother Ireland, Mother Church. At the end of the *Purgatorio*, when Beatrice finally appears, after playing the sort of cat-and-mouse game Jane Eyre plays on the blind Rochester in their famous reunion scene, Beatrice, not unlike Jane, puts her lover to the test, dressing him down for his former faithlessness and obtuseness. Dante registers the rebuke as a shameful, chastised child. Beatrice for a split second, according to his simile, is the bad mother: "So does the mother seem harsh to her child as she seemed to me, for the savour of stern pity tastes bitter." [11] This is also a moment when Dante feels especially vulnerable to a mother figure, having moments before this conversation providentially lost his paternal guide, "Virgil, sweetest father, Virgil to whom I gave myself for my salvation." [12] The revelation of Beatrice makes it clear that Virgil, the father, while an essential aide for the journey, is redundant at its conclusion, when a reunion with the mother, as private and close as birth, must occur. This may be the moment of final yielding Heaney faces in "Clearances," ironically at the death of his mother. It is not contained, however, within "Station Island," which, while not fully endorsing Joycean rebellion, also, despite lapses, manfully resists the submission Dante performs for the sake of his soul. The conclusion of "Station Island" by featuring yet another father figure signals nonconclusion, which is appropriate given the relativist, highly intertextual climate in which the poem exists. The *Divine Comedy* is always rumbling in the distance, predicting an ominous clash between Dante and Joyce.

While the full liberating impact of a confrontation with the mother will be explored in the succeeding chapters, especially the last, it is enough here to note that the two sections added to "Station Island" in order to include a female element only reinforce the revisionist selectivity of this referencing of Dante. These two poems, sections iii and vi, explore the two sides of a dichotomous love borne by men toward women: metaphysical and physical, sacred and profane, the first focused on death and the other life, the second on sexuality and this life. The order of this spiritual discovery in the poem may be the opposite expected by a reader familiar with Christian morphology, but for the Irish Catholic male of a certain generation, a freeing from the metaphysical into the physical is a much more challenging journey than the reverse. Heaney has been insistent in his career, like Joyce, on challenging head-on the sexual repression innate in the Irish Catholic culture he knew as a young man. Although over the course of the *Divine Comedy* the physical becomes integrated with the metaphysical, in the *Inferno* matters are more dualistic because we are dealing with extremes. As Dante enters the second circle of hell, he comes upon a place of complete darkness and hideous sounds of suffering. He tells us: "I learnt that to such torment are condemned the carnal sinners, who subject reason to desire."[13] A pivotal moment in every Lough Derg pilgrimage is standing before a cross on the lake shore and publicly renouncing the flesh. Section iv of "Station Island" begins with this moment in the liturgy. Heaney mouths the automatic words, "I renounce"[14] and immediately drifts off into a subversive reverie about the fraudulence of the vocation of that young priest he knew at home. The most pointed refusal to mortify the flesh, however, occurs in section 6, where his childhood initiation into the wonder of sexual feeling, a rapture surpassing the conventionally religious, is retrieved.

Section vi opens with a string of natural metaphors to describe the object of this childhood attraction: "Freckle-face, fox-head, pod of the broom / catkin pixie, little fern swish." This nameless girl, who may be around the age of Beatrice when Dante met her, is meant to set up a Beatrician resonance as an unforgotten object of early worship. The difference is that Heaney's worship is physical, and the entire poem works at some level to rescue the vital mystery of sex from the sin against life of lust, since the allure and warmth of this remembered moment is far from the coldness and dullness associated with that lackluster sin. Such insistent appeals to nature, including human nature, carrying with them a suggestion of being restored to a fluent wholeness through sex, return the reader to Sweeney and his values. The consoling, life-enhancing legacy of paganism is most consistently indicated by images that might be described as anti-anthropomorphic. Instead of projecting man onto nature, they project nature onto man and the reversal is health-giving and ego-diminishing, just as Tsvetaeva's assumption of Christ's identity freed her, according to Brodsky. Also, similar to the way Tsvetaeva sees the love of God as connected to sensual experience, Heaney in section vi of "Station Island" recalls a young self vivified by desire, a memory that makes him ignore the doleful tolling of church bells even in the present. The point is that this state of youthful infatuation is conveyed by depicting a body that is all but imbricated with the natural world. Remembering how he tried to keep his verdant secret from authority figures, he confides, "I shut my ears to the bell / Head hugged. Eyes shut / leaf ears."[15] Years later and sexually mature, he is aroused by the keyhole cutout on the back of his loved one's dress, seeing a counter salvation, a proverbial promised land through that aperture: "Her honey skinned shoulder blades and the wheatlands of her back."[16] Once again the love object merges with the natural world, less imposition than fusion. On balance, in "Station Island" Heaney is revising his attachment to nature less for its transcendent than its Manichaean properties. "Station Island," even on its level of defying Catholicism, is not a paean to guiltless sexuality and pagan simplicity.

The central object in pagan worship is also central to this section: the sun. And yet the two references to the sun each in different ways create complication. The first, an allusion to Horace, *"Till Phoebus returning routs the morning star,"*[17] appears as a sardonic private joke that the worn-down pilgrim mutters to himself, feeling a hostility he himself does not fully understand, as he reenacts this "peasant pilgrimage."[18] The brunt of Heaney's ironic intent can be felt in the droll remark, "Shades of the Sabine farm / On the stone beds of Saint Patrick's Purgatory."[19] References to light in "Station Island" always occur when there is an amelioration of penitential pain sought or found. The reference to Horace, in part sincere, follows directly on the sarcastic "Loosen the toga for wine and poetry." Somehow these lateral appeals to other pagan cultures as a means to loosen the grip of Catholicism and Romanticism on the poet backfire: Lough Derg is no place to "loosen the toga," become unzipped.

The second quotation, taken from Dante, makes this conflict even more apparent. These lines, beginning, *"As little flowers that were all bound and shut"*[20] occur in the *Inferno* when Dante is losing faith. The innocent floral image represents a prefiguring of the later appearance of Beatrice, who in her totalizing love and beauty will completely heal the pagan-Christian divide, in addition to realizing a synthesis of carnal and religious feeling. Those lines by Dante, where he gains a second breath in purgatory, conclude *"So I revived in my own wilting powers / And my heart flushed like somebody set free."*[21] Heaney then describes his own freeing thus: "translated, given, under the oak tree."[22] This line, however, splits along several seams. The oak tree is the sacred tree of pagan worship, and the word "translated" is being used for its entire rich range of meanings, but especially for two that are quite divergent: first, to translate a text, a human operation, that leaves us with two objects and a sense of imperfection, and second, to translate a person, a divine operation which removes the soul from earth to heaven without death. A complete redemption is both implied and denied. In cultural-historical terms, the role translation has played in Ireland to achieve a spiritual redemption is both acknowledged and judged as once again frustrated.

Such undermining is the retrospective result of rereading section xi, particularly after we have heard Colum McCartney's censuring of the poet for drawing the "lovely blinds of the *Purgatorio*" over a still resonating, difficult memory. Heaney here is not just recovering the pleasure of a sexual awakening, but the first stirrings of sexual guilt. Also, the poem juxtaposes ordinary demotic speech with the canonic, just as it juxtaposes the literary ghosts with those of ordinary people. Crucially in "Station Island" overall, the force of lived experience is always more powerful than book learning is. A cited passage from Horace or Dante might as well be a "rubbed quotation"[23] of the former schoolmaster recalled with tender irony in the previous section v. Such burnished, unoriginal words stand in weak opposition to the indelible, remembered, spoken words of his first furtive love, *"Don't tell. Don't tell."*[24] The very word "don't" has the power of the mother behind it. The reader must wonder how much this specific internalized prohibition resonates within the work, determining certain secrecies, unspoken sources of pervasive guilt. What does surface with absolute clarity is the way certain words, like Ronan's psalter, recovered from the dark hoard of memory, are themselves "dipped and glamoured":

> I felt an old pang that bags of grain
> And the sloped shafts of forks and hoes
> Once mocked me with, at my own long virgin
> Fasts and thirsts, my nightly shadow feasts,
> Haunting the granaries of words like *breasts.*[25]

That one word *"breasts"* resonates, along with *"Don't tell. Don't tell,"* throughout "Station Island," never more so than in the nightmare sequence, where a mutilated, solitary breast suggests some horrible distortion, perhaps accomplished by guilt, or misogyny, which is its corollary. Then at the very end of the sequence, Joyce's prescription includes this advice: "Cultivate a work-lust / that imagines its haven like your hands at night / dreaming the sun in the sunspot of a breast."[26] Suddenly the breast is restored to its innocence and the word "lust" deprived of its sinister overtones, redeemed by a work ethic. As well, the pagan sun shines through every act of writing that integrates mind and body. The poem's method of being minutely true to human consciousness or, more, subconsciousness, with its obsessive repetitions and surprise surfacings, all attached to language, is our surest clue to the process of faith it foresees. This use of language, the basic platform of Heaney's poetic, is organic and animist, words for Heaney being both concrete and numinous. The more integrated with the ordinary, the more revelatory. True change can only come to the poet through words that, like leaves on trees, are attached to vital, rooted memories. Certain keyhole, revelatory words are part of the edifice of life itself.

The second poem where a female is the center of attention, though not a spectral voice in this highly dialogical poem, is section iii, which begins, "I knelt. Hiatus. Habit's afterlife."[27] Existing roughly, but only roughly, in opposition to section vi, this is a poem where death in relation to a female, not sex, is the focus, in conjunction with an entirely rapt spiritual but repressed sexual fascination, indistinguishable from religion. Here we have another possible Beatrice surrogate, an aunt who died before the poet was born and whose memory is kept, indeed fetishized, by the young Heaney. This thanatoptic fixation also elides effortlessly into a chthonic fantasy, a childhood experience that presages the Lough Derg pilgrimage later in life. The young boy attaches his musings about this lost, idealized girl to "A seaside trinket . . . / a toy grotto with seedling mussel / shells and cockles glued in patterns over it."[28] This grotto, like the opening of a cave, is replicated and magnified by the child's hiding place, a sideboard, where he can locate this treasured taboo image, female and genital in suggestion, as he unwraps the material reminder of his dead aunt and holds it—her—in his hands. Layers and layers of enclosure structure the following:

> pearls condensed from a child invalid's breath
> into a shimmering ark, my house of gold
> that housed the snowdrop weather of her death
> long ago. I would stow away in the hold
>
> of our big oak sideboard and forage for it
> laid past in its tissue paper for good.[29]

The old sideboard and even the grotto, where the mind can hide, replicate all those "secret nests" Heaney mentions as early as the essay "Mossbawn": the "fork of a beech tree," "the throat of an old willow tree," "the caul of veined light" that was a pea-drill.[30] As the word "caul" gives away, all this ritualistic hiding and emerging is rebirthing, the psychological experience that resonates at the heart of the pagan myths about Lough Derg and early Christian practice there, which centered on the cave and nude bathing. For Heaney these immersions in the feminine carry with them both a feverish, exciting anxiety and an opportunity, which draws on discipline and detachment.

These moments present the threat of a loss of individuation and the chance for the birthing of mysterious poems larger than the ego. In section iii of "Station Island," this tension expresses itself through two species of words, whose provenance is in two separate corners of the heart. Liturgical language, the mantras of his Catholic past, lure the poet toward the stream of collective experience epitomized by a procession of praying women. The other kind of language, utterly secret and personal, is taken from the world of touch and things. It is the repetition of phrases such as *"pray for us"* and "Health of the sick" that constitute the "habit" referred to earlier. A word such as the innocently tactile, indeed sexual, *"wreath,"* which he associates with his dead aunt, is from another category of experience. It is the word that comes to him when he thinks of unwrapping that trinket: "It was like touching birds' eggs, robbing the nest / of the word, wreath, as kept and dry and secret."[31] The word in this authentic attachment is utterly inextricable from the feeling it embodies. One cannot help speculating further that Kavanagh's resonant use of the word "nest" in "Canal Bank Walk" is influencing Heaney's word choice, arising, however, first from experience. This seems especially possible given that the word is being used to articulate a similar inherence of grace in the actual. Kavanagh refers to "a bird gathering materials for the nest for the Word / Eloquently new and abandoned to its delirious beat."[32] For Heaney, these passing moments of complete, radiant integration prefigure an autonomy indivisible from a religious impulse. These moments are, however, like the hiding boy: interstitial, tucked between, inside, under the words of habit—"Habit's afterlife"—and cannot exist, cannot be recovered, without a recovery of the less authentic. This section from "Station Island" makes it patent that Catholicism is so enmeshed with the poet's possession of words that any spiritual reckoning through words will involve Catholicism, either vestigially or vitally.

At the most broadly mimetic level, there are any number of images that recall Dante, especially the *Inferno*. If you let the imagination play with certain basic associations with Dante and Saint Patrick, they concatenate into a shadowy amalgam of Lough Derg. The site, with its legendary cave, its underworld, although not the mountain of Dante's *Purgatorio*, still feels connected to it via that other Patrician site, Croagh Patrick. Not that far southwest of Lough Derg is the mountain where Saint Patrick, according to legend, banished the snakes, those prefigurements of the Lough Derg maggot and ultimately Heaney's elvers. Also according to popular legend, a *souteraine*, through which the snakes wriggled, connects the mountain to the lake. Even more specifically, the Caora, the devil's mother and mother of all snakes, slain by Fionn MacCool, is said to have arrived in the lake by this route. Croagh Patrick, what is more, with its perfectly conical shape, is not unlike illustrations of the schematic mountain Dante chose for purgatory. In keeping with this loose fit, Station Island in Lough Derg is approached by boat, a crossing reminiscent of the crossing of the River Styx. In Canto vii of the *Inferno*, Dante and Virgil, entering the fifth circle of hell, come to

> water of the blackest purple, and following its murky waves we entered the place below by a rough track. This gloomy stream, when it has reached the foot of the malign, grey slopes, enters the marsh which is called Styx; and I, who had stopped to gaze intently, saw muddy people in that bog, all naked and with looks of rage. They were smiting each other not only with the hand but with the head and breast and feet and tearing each other piecemeal with their teeth.[33]

Not only does this image as a whole evoke the finally self-destructive maelstrom of the Troubles, but more specifically recalls Colum McCartney in section x who appears to the poet first as "a bleeding, pale-faced boy, plastered in mud."[34] Indeed, Heaney's translation of Saint John of the Cross includes the line, "so pellucid it can never be muddied," to evoke the inviolability of God's infinite grace. When McCartney speaks, we hear the anger in which he is still mired, though nothing in Heaney's unorthodox, eclectic beliefs, as they appear in the poem, suggest that McCartney is in an old-fashioned, literal hell, more an underworld of unresolved rage.

Heaney is adamantly resisting the schematic, mathematical exactitude of Catholic doctrine and even Dante's historically determined practice of consigning sinners to their precise and just geographical-moral position in hell or purgatory. More, Heaney will not be deflected from his focus: self-accountability.

Hence Heaney assiduously avoids adjudicating the rights and wrongs in Northern Ireland. For example, the filth and mutilation characteristic of the fifth circle of hell is not unlike the "swirl of mucky, glittering flood" in section ix,[35] where Heaney sees the "shed breast" and perhaps encounters his own self-mutilating anger. There is nothing, however, to suggest that the poet feels himself literally damned. All is associational, a nightmarish, unseemly coupling of images from life and books, fused under the pressure of the pilgrimage. Sweeney, for example, also finds his echo in Dante, but the telltale images announcing Sweeney come from different parts of the *Inferno*. His connections with trees, where in myth he roosted, associate him with the first circle of hell, or limbo, where the unbaptized spirits dwell: "the forest . . . of thronged spirits,"[36] in Dante's words. This is the innocently pagan view of Sweeney; the demonized view of him comes through by means of one key point of resemblance with Charon, the boatman, who ferries the damned souls into the underworld. In this connection, it is also noteworthy that the job of ferryman in the Middle Ages was hotly contested at Lough Derg, it being a lucrative sinecure that stayed in families, notably the Muldoons, for generations. As we have seen, the payment given to the Lough Derg boatman by pilgrims was one more proof to Protestant critics of the corruption of the pilgrimage. Even the Catholic hierarchy, eager to defend the Church against such damaging allegations, ruled that the practice smacked of simony and must be stamped out. Given the association of the Dantean wheel with Sweeney, his demonization as a heathen might be signaled by an implied association with Charon, "about whose eyes had wheels of flame."[37]

These perhaps chance points of similarity are endless, but what is most kindred and deliberate is the spiritual torment suffered by the analogous poet pilgrims. There is a very affecting juncture in canto viii of the *Inferno*, when Dante undergoes precisely the central emotional crisis that lies behind "Station Island." This speech, a prefiguring of Christ as the savior, occurs when Virgil has announced his intention to leave Dante's side in hell temporarily. This is how Dante says he felt at hearing he was about to be abandoned in this place of no return:

> Judge, Reader, if I did not lose heart at the sound of the accursed words: for I did not think I should ever return hither. "O my dear leader who seven times and more hast restored my confidence and drawn me from great peril confronting me, leave me not," I said, "so undone; and if going farther is denied us, let us quickly retrace our steps together." And my Liege, who had brought me there said to me: "Do not fear, for none can hinder our passage, by such an One is it granted us; but wait for me here and comfort thy weary spirit and feed it with good hope: for I will not forsake thee in the nether world." He goes away and leaves me there, the gentle Father, and I remain in doubt, ay and no contending in my head.[38]

Virgil is prophesying the coming of Christ and is reminding Dante of the covenanted, providential pact behind his descent into hell. Dante has already been told that Virgil has been sent directly by Beatrice to help him: "I am Beatrice who bids thee go; I come from the place where I desire to return; Love moved me and makes me speak."[39] Dante's feelings of desolation and doubt, of not being sure he was predetermined to experience this nightmare, in short his panic, can easily be understood through other similar moments in religious literature; for example, Saint John of the Cross's dark night of the soul, or, as Thomas Merton refers to it, his Job experience. Heaney, too, must rely on a belief that good, liberating cultural work has already been done, that he has added to it, and that "none can hinder our passage." In Heaney's case all the other Lough Derg writers and courageous souls he has known are his guides, the guarantors of his reemergence.

One reassurance for Heaney that he will not be forsaken in his underworld is that he has a steady, if questioned, guide in Dante and, closer to home, all those writers who have preceded him to Lough Derg. Dante has Virgil for his scout into this unknown territory; but Dante may have also had a slighter literary example, and a Christian, H. of Saltrey. As we have seen, this is the monk who on the basis of a report from another monk, Gilbert, a Welshman, told the story of Knight Owen, who descended into the Lough Derg cave. The twelfth-century text, which describes the knight's episodes underground and the divine judgment on his ordeal, was, as Shane Leslie puts it, "one of the best sellers of the Middle Ages."[40] The legendary proof that Dante read the *Tractatus de Purgatorio Sancti Patricio* rests on a slim allusion "to the red, seething wave"[41] in relation to Lethe. More generally the argument goes that Dante's presentation of hell as being freezing as well as fiery shows a debt to the *Tractatus,* which reflects Celtic mappings of the underworld that typically include a cold corner. Heaney would have been taught as a schoolboy of this legendary indebtedness, as it bestows a halo of fame on the by-then provincial pilgrimage site not far from Derry. Whether Dante knew the *Tractatus* or not (and Jean Michel Picard, one its recent translators assures us that "not less than a hundred and fifty manuscripts containing the Tractatus and written between the twelfth and seventeenth century lie between Dublin and Moscow"[42]) there is a continuity of key motifs that find reiteration in Heaney. So, although Heaney did not read the *Tractatus* as preparation for "Station Island,"[43] his reliance on Dante assures that his version of the *Purgatorio* echoes the *Tractatus* and countless other examples of the highly conventionalized underworld genre.[44] This unintentional splicing of Heaney's twentieth-century narration of a Lough Derg pilgrimage with that of Knight Owen only emphasizes how collective the effort has been to commit to language the extraordinary effect of this still-testing pilgrimage. Over time, however, the danger has evolved from the physical to the psychological, a transition signaled as early as Carleton and consummated in Heaney. Knight Owen undergoes ten torments in the underworld, and many of them feature agonies and forms of torture that flash as images through Heaney's poem, again by coincidence, or more accurately, the osmosis that is cultural history.

Listen to Picard's translation of the fifth torment, the torment of the cauldron: "Some were suspended in fires with iron nails stuck in their eyes, or ears, or nostrils or throats or breasts or genitals. Others were dripping with various molten metals." [45] The mutilation of section x of "Station Island" seems less than eight centuries away from this similarly graphic language. Also, the extreme, hellish heat in the rain forest in section iv of "Station Island," where the young, pettish priest lost his health and innocence, is reminiscent of the Knight's fifth torment, as is the priest's physically repellent, bestial view of his fellow human beings: "Bare-breasted / women and rat-ribbed men." [46] Further, the Knight's tenth torment features "a wide and stinking river," [47] a body of water threading straight out of Virgil, through early medieval literature, through Dante, and up to Heaney. As well, there is the common phenomenon of salvation being viewed through an aperture. In H. of Saltrey the aperture is a magnificent, glittering door: "And the door opened in front of him and a fragrance pouring from it wafted up to him. It was so sweet that, if all the world was turned into spices, it would not surpass the intensity of this sweetness." [48] For the subversion and continuance both of this convention, compare it to the passage in section vi of "Station Island" where salvation is glimpsed through "the keyhole of her keyhole dress." [49] The double reference to a constricted aperture suggests the furtiveness of a still-inherent sexual guilt. Then, as the poet feels emboldened and freer, "a window facing the deep-south of luck / Opened and I inhaled the land of sweetness." [50] Earlier on Heaney referred to the "sex-cut of sweetbriar after rain." The land of spices is arrived at here by another, perhaps heretical route, but a conventional destination is found.

One final inadvertent echo of the *Tractatus* relates to the image of a fountain in the ninth torment of Knight Owen. This fountain, however, symbolizes everything opposite to divine love: "But the devils, not yet tired of ill-treating the soldier of Christ, came to him and dragged him toward the south. And suddenly he saw in front of him a horrible flame stinking of foul sulfur which shot up as if from a well . . . the devils said to the knight." This well, belching flames, is the entrance to Hell.[51] In the story Owen falls into the well, which has an endlessly renewable capacity like the fountain of God's grace, only the reverse: the well becomes wider and wider the more one descends into it. Owen is saved only by remembering the name of his savior. Heaney, sidestepping this injunction for personal speech, translates the poem by Saint John of the Cross, which is suffused by mercy, not torture. Indeed, the affect of this mystical poem about the beneficence of grace is opposite in every conceivable way to the vision in Knight Owen's underworld. For Saint John of the Cross the fountain dispenses God's infinite love: "How well I know that fountain, filling, running, / although it is the night." [52] Once again, however, Heaney translates more than a text by his penance of rendering Saint John of the Cross in English. He also translates himself, placing himself on a border, halfway between his pedestrian self and the Spanish mystic. His encounters with the ghosts who appear to him in his pilgrimage involve a similar ambiguity. The ghosts in their noncorporeal insinuation pass into, through, and then out of him again, as separation from them and the reconsolidation of the self occur. Each ghost leaves the poet both changed, and more himself. Heaney's view of the Lough Derg tradition emerges as both centrifugal and centripetal, open-minded and selective, but above all fraught with ambiguity.

That Heaney uncannily resembles Hamlet through much of anguished "Station Island" turns out to be more than a coincidence of temperament. It is also one of history. Shakespeare's tragedy and "Station Island" share a common point of reference: Lough Derg. Stephen Greenblatt's *Hamlet in Purgatory* demonstrates how Knight Owen's experience in the *Tractatus* is a major historical layer in the religious foundation of the play. The medieval narrative bears in particular on the ontological status and message of the ghost, both to remember and to act. Heaney's ghosts, like Hamlet's father, all demand the conversion of melancholia, an excess of memory, into robust action. In "Station Island," Carleton, Kavanagh, Strathearn, and Joyce all address in their separate ways the poet's Hamlet-like "blunted purpose" (3.4.101). McCartney even specifically urges an act of revenge for his death. Greenblatt calls special attention to those passages in *Hamlet* that imply the existence of purgatory in the prince's mind, as he struggles to grasp the full range of questions and implications presented by his father's specter. Greenblatt calls our attention to the fact that various lines spoken by Hamlet from the first act address the double conundrum of the ghost's essence and provenance: "There are more things in heaven and earth, Horatio, / than are dreamed of in our philosophy" (1.5.166–67); and "Rest, rest, perturbed spirit!" (1.5.182). Of course, above all, the ghost himself specifically denotes purgation as the agonizing process he is undergoing:

> Doomed for a certain term, to walk the night,
> And for the day confined to fast in fires,
> Till the foul crimes done in my days of nature
> Are burnt and purged away. . . . (1.5.9–13)

Finally, when Horatio apologizes with, "There's no offence, my Lord" (1.5.135), for his comment about Hamlet's "wild and whirling words," the prince's first words to a mortal after seeing the ghost on his own, Hamlet rounds on Horatio with the even more cryptic:

> Yes, by Saint Patrick, but there is, Horatio,
> And much offence, too. Touching this vision, here,
> It is an honest ghost, that let me tell you. (1.5.139–42)

Hamlet is reflecting on a far greater offence than Horatio's barely perceptible slight. Hamlet is suddenly in the throes of an eschatological crisis that can lead to everything from the confused transport indicated by "wild and whirling words" to the equable acceptance of an "honest ghost." These poles of perception with their respective impact on language correlate with the diametrical poetics of self-referential, abstract complexity as opposed to the incongruously mimetic simplicity of vision.

The deepest echo within "Station Island" of *Hamlet* concerns the relationship between belief and poetry. We are accustomed to asking whether poetry is belief but less whether belief is poetry. Referring to Protestant attacks in the sixteenth and early seventeenth centuries on the developing concept of purgatory, Greenblatt reminds us that these subversions were "focussed on the imagination. . . . Purgatory . . . was not simply a fraud; it was a piece of poetry." [53] Greenblatt's Hamlet is a poet not unlike Heaney, and the history of purgatory conceptualized and constructed as poetry includes discernments and decisions close to those Heaney makes in his career. The growing suspicion Heaney has of a self-preening, Parnassian poetry, his gradual embrace of poetry as "transformational," as having an effect on the world beyond it, are reflected in Greenblatt's words about the *Tractatus*. This piece of vision literature, according to Greenblatt's analysis, possesses what Heaney, the poet who digs into the vital substance of memory, might call an "artesian" effect:

> Far from occupying a self-enclosed space, this text attempts to drive its fantasies directly into the earth where it locates the actual cave entrance that leads into Purgatory. It has nothing to do with the pleasures of suspended disbelief, a toying with the world and the mind that enables one to pretend that something is real that one knows is actually an invention or a clever hypothesis. . . . The central creative act is to assert that this place actually exists.[54]

For the reader of Heaney, this indirect reference to Saint Patrick striking his staff on the ground and locating purgatory reminds one of Heaney's "poetry of divination, poetry of revelation," [55] discoveries no less belonging to the "visionary." So, a burden of proof also falls on the shoulders of Heaney, who defends this poetic in part by invoking the example of precursors and peers, like Wordsworth and Milosz. Similarly, because so much in Knight Owen's fantastical adventure depends on belief in what might seem a fiction, Greenblatt further points out that noticeable care is lavished on establishing the bona fides of the narration and narrator, establishing proof of the authenticity and veracity of Knight Owen's experiences as related to Gilbert and passed on H. of Saltrey. Echoing Heaney's nightmare in "Station Island," however, the *Tractatus* appears to betray this quest for factuality by assigning a central place in the story to a dream experienced by Saint Patrick, which reveals this antechamber to the underworld. Greenblatt discloses this narrative choice as only the beginning of a chain of seeming contradictions, an accumulation of distancing illusions, adding up to the crowing paradox, which the reader has been led to embrace as truth: "Saint Patrick dreams a dream; the dream becomes the reality of the black hole; the hole is said to be the entrance to Purgatory; and Purgatory turns out to have the structure of a dream." [56] Knight Owen's journey, within this deliberately constructed hall of mirrors, which miraculously reverses solipsism and narcissism in the end, becomes, according to Greenblatt, "a model for the imaginative experience, as it subsequently came to be developed." [57] Heaney's ghosts, however, in "Station Island" are, perhaps still primarily grounded in literary convention rather than in the ontologically exact "middle

ground" of purgatory, but as the poem progresses through nightmare, a nightmarish mirroring of the self, and a translation of Saint John of the Cross that translates
the translator almost in the theological sense into the realm of grace, the status of
the ghosts, of poetry itself, transmigrates in a direction anticipating Heaney's later,
more metaphysical work.

Greenblatt asks what might have happened spiritually to Knight Owen, if he
had turned back in the cave. Greenblatt, essentially advocating for poetry, judges
such a choice as error, "a compromise," which would have led to "a chastened,
unimaginative life, . . .the alternative that the bishop of Ireland initially urges on
Owen."[58] In Irish culture there are many texts that iterate the bishop's behaviorist
position, one held latterly by Curtayne and O'Connor, and one consummately contained in the genres of medieval writing called "Penitentials." The tenor of these instructive writings is the methodical chastening of the soul to the point that to claim
experience of the visionary is an impossible arrogation of divine power. Consider
for example, for the way they echo Heaney's most self-lacerating moments in "Station Island," these words on the correction of envy from the *Penitential of Cummean:*

> The envious shall make satisfaction to him whom he has envied; but if he has done
> him harm, he shall satisfy him with gifts and shall do penance. He who for envy's
> sake defames (another) or willingly listens to a defamer shall be put apart and shall
> fast for four days on bread and water. If the offence is against a superior, he shall do
> penance thus for seven days and shall serve him willingly thereafter. But, as some-
> one says, to speak true things is not to defame.[59]

The entire thrust of these prescriptions, though they might lead to a self-
flaying scrupulosity, is to remedy such subjectivity with practical, quantified action, that or the unlikely articulation of utter truth. The quantification of the
designated penance foresees the mechanistic certainties of devotionalism. This re-
medial emphasis on action, however, is a rebuke in itself to the Hamlet in Heaney.
The mental posture fostered by the Penitential tradition ironically can lead to the
hair-splitting, cerebral pride these recipes for humility intend to counteract. As
such, the mindset inculcated can be acutely self-divisive. Greenblatt refers to *Hamlet* as "a play of contagious, almost universal self-estrangement,"[60] an apt encapsu-
lation of Dante's *Purgatorio* as well. This evokes Heaney staring into the shaving
mirror in "Station Island" and seeing an image of himself not only reversed by
transmogrifying self-hatred but itself "half-composed."[61] Somehow Heaney's dai-
mon is calling for a transformational journey through the cave of his own subjectivity, which will lead paradoxically to clarity of purpose. This conversion will
hinge on an acceptance of the truth of paradox and, very like with Hamlet, on his
response to the death of a parent, who somehow doesn't die. That the parent in
Heaney's case is his mother is prepared for by the mire of gender issues in which he
finds himself in "Station Island."

Ultimately, this unresolved puzzle of gender insists on a truthful deviation
from Dante. This independence, however, is echoed in every encounter with the

ghosts in "Station Island." Also, the relative power afforded two distinct species of ghost is a decisive factor in Heaney's weighing of his own soul. The discrepancy in message between the literary ghosts and the ghosts from ordinary life asks one of the most basic questions of "Station Island," and of all Lough Derg writings, namely: is there something simply in being an artist that puts the soul in jeopardy? This question, which ironically may as well have been poised by a reformationist objector, is felt with almost lethal sharpness when the artist is Irish, facing submission not just to the Church but to the idea of the nation. Colum McCartney, as we've seen, makes this diametrical choice seem intractable. But there are more forgiving, easygoing, nonjudgmental ghosts who, through the examples of their well-conducted lives, leave Heaney even more stumped, almost tongue-tied. Once again, the ultimate struggle in the medieval Lough Derg texts centers on a verbal challenge: to find the one word that will save the soul. That word is "Jesus" for these Christian penitents, but for this lapsed Catholic poet, steeped in language and at the far end of the twentieth century with a head full of echoing, competing texts, the task is even more daunting, though it still seems to center on finding one true word to say. The vanity of most language, especially literary language, is one of the apprehensions that results from exchanges with these effortlessly honest ghosts, be they writers or not. Indeed, one of the mysteries of the poem is that the poet agonizes about his verbal evasions and embellishments, and yet creates characters who speak hard truths without flinching or balking. Heaney seems to be waiting to be translated into his fullest self and can only imagine his completed, polyphonic voice through the internalized voices of others. This irony is never greater than in section vii, about William Strathearn.

The poem gains its power by sticking absolutely to plain speech. Interestingly, in keeping with the poems composed of translations from other texts spliced to Heaney's own language, this one begins and ends with Heaney's narration. The middle, however, is entirely in Strathearn's words, treated as another text that reverberates as much, if not more, than official literature, indeed is made so by Heaney's empathic words. As the shopkeeper relates the story of his last night on earth, his tone is without regret, resentment or even self-reproach. He seems sublimely free. Even his memory of being short with his wife is explained with such honesty we know he has forgiven himself:

> She started to cry then and roll round the bed,
> lamenting and lamenting to herself,
> not even asking who it was. "Is your head
>
> astray, or what's come over you?" I roared, more
> to bring myself to my senses
> than out of any real anger at her
>
> for the knocking shook me, the way they kept it up,
> and her whingeing and half-screeching made it worse.
> All the time they were shouting "Shop!" [62]

"Whinge" is a word Joyce (section xi) uses (notably in the revised version of the poem in *Opened Ground*) to describe the infantile practice of complaining about the colonial imposition of the English language on the Irish: "rehearsing the old whinges at your age."[63] In both instances the response is perceived as offensive to a manly sense of self-assertion, even self-composure. Strathearn in the end makes Heaney feel effete in his inability to face himself and life squarely. Heaney's apology comes across as a whinge: "Forgive the way I have lived indifferent— / forgive my timid circumspect involvement." "Forgive / my eye" is Strathearn's not entirely hostile but somewhat impatient retort, "all that's above my head."[64] The pun alerts us to the actual, still-bleeding wound above his eye but also makes the poet, because Strathearn's wound is not above his head, seem overly intellectual, overly scrupulous. And yet, despite the masculine authority of Strathearn, his reply seems a little curt, lacking in compassion. Also, the reader is not convinced that the poet, made to appear effeminate by his apology, may not be performing the strenuous moral and psychological work of gradually integrating the feminine in himself. In the meantime, Strathearn's rebuke severely challenges the poet's masculinity, as his own Beatrice's injunction, *"Don't tell. Don't tell,"* challenged his sexuality. This plain speaking is endowed with great power, a value that challenges the verbal complications of modernism.

Silence resonates with even more forbidding force. Heaney describes with self-flaying honesty his failure to find the words required at the deathbed of a friend, yet another person he feels he gave too little to in life. Everything about the hospital visit is visual, usurping language though rendered in it:

Those dreamy stars that pulsed across the screen
beside you in the ward—your heartbeats, Tom, I mean—
. . . .
I could not take my eyes off the machine
I had to head back straight away to Dublin.[65]

Once again, the self-muzzled poet speaks with another's voice, out of an otherwise inaccessible part of himself. Were it not for these multiple masks producing a highly dialogic poetry presaged by Carleton, Heaney would not be able to approach integration. Indeed, the more spiritually trenchant Heaney's introspection becomes in his career, the more the silence beyond polyphony becomes his hermeneutic key. Here, in "Station Island," Heaney remembers how he could not bring himself to speak to his dying friend about what was actually happening to him, let alone about the injustice of his dying so young. Yet the archeologist friend, instead of gliding over this failure of courage, confirms it. With a cool honesty devoid of malice he explains that, although Heaney offered no consolation, he, the archaeologist, had come to expect none, not only of Heaney but of the world. This man's work with remote, mute stone objects had prepared him for the galactic silence of death. Yet as a ghost he speaks some hard, even heated words, registering his sense of inadequacies in their friendship. He highlights the propensity for banter between them rather than real talk, which, in the context of the sequence, touches on the theme of the paradoxical abundance and paucity of language. Most of all, however, Tom speaks his own resentment, perhaps the one flaw that keeps him in purgatory despite his overwhelming courage and taciturn manliness—"His scribe's face smiling its straight-lipped smile."[66] Again, like Strathearn's parting shot and that of Heaney's "catkin-pixie" childhood love, Tom's last words inflict a wound as much on target as Strathearn's gash over his eye. Tom laments: "Ah poet, lucky poet, tell me why / what seemed deserved and promised passed me by?"[67]

This is an impossible question, and such is the moral discernment of "Station Island" that even the all-too-human presumption of deserving or being promised something from life comes under an implied, distant lens of scrutiny. It seems right that the poet has no answer at this impasse. Yet his inability to reply rests not just on the genuine magnitude of the question but on a fear of the explosive emotion from the direct hit of "poet, lucky poet." On the one hand, the torment of the friend is sensed and by projection the terror of one's own mortality. As well, the poet recognizes fully his own failings, producing an incendiary shame and self-hatred that might be sparked by this confrontation. Once more the poet can only render this sense of a menacing ineffability with a visual image accelerating quickly from the stone age to the nuclear:

> I saw a hoard of black
> basalt axeheads, smooth as a beetle's back,
> a cairn of stone force that might detonate,
> the eggs of danger.[68]

The irony is that, while these quick sidesteps from the verbal to the visual might seem evasions, they are also the most direct route for the poet to a truth that has heretofore eluded speech. They create a space, like Yeats's laugh in conversation with Wellesley, where things can begin to move again. These gestational, nonverbal spaces have always been the potent heart of Heaney's poetry and perhaps his residual, not fully articulated faith. The journey up into speech is so long that still another visual image must intervene to focus his thoughts and feelings. Suddenly he remembers

> a face
> he had once given me, a plaster cast
> of an abbess, done by the Gowran master,
> mild-mouthed and cowled, a character of grace.[69]

Observation of this pure image of feminine, maternal, yet virginal love instills in the poet some form of faith, both expressed and distanced by being couched in metaphor, not plain speech: "Your gift will be a candle in our house. / But he had gone when I looked to meet his eyes."[70] The image of the candle, a frail illumination, stays with the poet, however, and becomes his temporary salvation. It resurfaces in the nightmare sequence as a return of self-belief, masculine dignity, and perhaps even faith. It appears to grow out of the magnolia bloom, to supplant the image of the "shed breast": "like a pistil growing from a polyp / A lighted candle rose and steadied up."[71]

The murky sexual depths of this poem are most sounded by this phallic image, directly produced by the beatific, virginal smile of the abbess, which in turn is the direct product of the Gowran master. One way of seeing this evolution is as a variation on the process described by Brodsky in reference to Tsvetaeva and Pasternak. Only in this case the transfer of energy is from one male artist to another, via a created female image, which epitomizes "grace." While there are worrying gender implications in this process, in its use of the female as objectified and silent, the end result mysteriously appears to be a routing of a hideous image of female mutilation flowing down the river of nightmare. It is arguable that in the way Heaney previously used femininity less to denote actual women than to locate a fertile, gestational part of himself as a poet, "Station Island" is involved with cleansing himself of a degraded femininity in favor of one more allied with a chaste but manly belief. This restoration is not without postcolonial implications, a redressing of feminization. As a process it also bears a kinship to that which Yeats went through transforming what he regarded as his effeminate early style to the masculine diction of *In the Seven Woods.* To make matters more complicated, however, Heaney's epiphany does not depend on a rebellious, though covert, assertion of the power of art and with that of stereotypic male strength, for the candle reappears only after the truest act of repentance, of self-abnegation in the poem. Speaking finally not to another person, whom he is bent on pleasing or assuaging, Heaney addresses either his deepest, blackest self or a distant, inscrutable God: "And I cried among night waters, 'I repent / my unweened life that kept me competent / To sleepwalk with connivance and mistrust.'"[72] The female source of nurturance to which he has been attached for an unnatural, unhealthy length of time may be the feminized idea of the nation, the Church, even of an idealization of the mother that prevents growth, change, full subjectivity in both directions. In this poem the restoration of male, moral potency implies a reciprocal recovery of the female.

At every point in the poem freedom from the wrack of self-doubt and shame appears in the form of a bird. "Station Island" at times reads like an aviary. These are all fleeting images of Sweeney, like a recurring melody in an opera, flashes of beauty and sunlight reminding the poet of another self, another life, beyond this enervating complexity. They appear in the way Sweeney was propelled: by emotion so strong that it breaks the bounds of ordinary behavior, conventional expression. So the poet's infatuation with his dead aunt becomes "the white bird trapped inside me."[73] Likewise, just before the deeply sorrowful visitation by the archaeologist friend, a magpie "flew from the basilica,"[74] sending up with it an echo of that proverb associated with the magpie: "one for sorrow, two for joy." And the archeologist himself is remembered in terms of a bird, with a "wing / of woodkerne's hair fanned down over his brow."[75] This association with Sweeney is appropriate in relation to a man whose life was devoted to unearthing artifacts from an early Chris-

tian, still substantially pagan era, and who loves "the small crab-apple physiognomies / on high crosses,"[76] vestiges of a nature-worshiping people. All these objects, images, and folk sayings reverberate as texts in the poet's head, which
cumulatively articulate a cultural understanding. They also embrace private religious apprehensions, all of which elude definitive speech. The words of writers before him, who have faced these same complications and contradictions, echo also in
"Station Island," but resonate with a different meaning than the ghosts of friends
and relations, who on the whole plunge the poet further down into his personal
hell.

Heaney uses the ghosts of past Lough Derg writers most to help him traverse
this morass of gender. It is as though Heaney senses the gender problem as pressingly cultural too. He seems to know that this is the terrain that a man of his generation and background must negotiate in order for his spiritual condition to be first
assessed, then redressed. The most obvious instances of Irish intertextuality in the
poem center around the figures of Carleton and Kavanagh, the former especially.
Both leave the poet feeling wanting in his masculinity. This slide into effeminacy
begins when Heaney implicitly joins the procession of women moving on foot to
Lough Derg. A large part of the humility necessary for the penitence of the pilgrimage derives literally from the ground up: the contact of bare feet on rock, since
walking around and around is a crucial part of the penance. It is significant, therefore, that Heaney squares up to his verbal duel with Carleton from the more manly
position of sitting in his car. The poet Medbh McGuckian, in a rare foray into critical prose, has written a pithy, wickedly funny essay on Heaney and driving entitled, "Horespower Pass By! A Study of the Car in the Poetry of Seamus Heaney."
McGuckian's unrelenting humor is made possible by her affectionate exposure of
the absolute link not just between the male posturing of two Irish poetic icons, but
for Heaney specifically, between driving and masculinity: "His narrative stance is
so often that of a driver, even in his prose or interviews, that his artistic/sexual
drive itself may be seen in places to fuel and animate a car-body which is a physical
extension of him."[77] Given this connection between the male body and the car, it is
further significant that Heaney first glimpses Carleton (no pun involved) when
Heaney is behind the steering wheel. Carleton, in section ii, is first sighted "in the
driving mirror,"[78] an appropriate frame and perspective, since the poet is taken
back to Carleton's pilgrimage two hundred years ago. What is more, Heaney, on his
way to the lake, has stopped his car right on that same hill where Carleton in the
"Lough Derg Pilgrim," as Heaney puts it, "overtook the women." It is Carleton's
confidence, however, not his emasculating confusion, that Heaney, reflecting his
particular reading of the Tyrone writer's works, chooses to foreground. His ances-
tor's assertiveness is eviscerating, particularly as it compares to the poet's meek-
ness. Heaney, still in the position of looking up to and therefore distorting a father
figure, fails to include a perception of Carleton's depressive, vulnerable side.

Heaney seems to occupy a moment in cultural history when the revision of the Catholic dismissal of Carleton voiced by O'Connor and Curtayne is crying out for further revision. After all, the process of correction was set in motion by Yeats, who wrote the admiring introduction to the 1889 edition of *Stories from Carleton*, then continued but also revised by an act of reappropriation by Curtayne's contemporary, Kavanagh, who proudly identified Carleton as a direct precursor. Carleton talks in "Station Island" of his moment in history, which is both similar to and different from Heaney's:

> If times were hard, I could be hard too.
> I made the traitor in me sink the knife.
> And maybe there's a lesson there for you,
>
> Whoever you are, wherever you come out of,
> for though there's something natural in your smile
> there's something in it strikes me as defensive.[79]

This self-authored abuse enacts a penance. On hearing it, Heaney takes an instant inventory of crucial decisions in his own life that compare to Carleton's. To perform this reckoning he has the voice of Carleton recall his conversion to Protestantism, along with his exposure, say in "Wildgoose Lodge," of the horrors perpetrated by land agitation, equally of his resistance to it:

> I who learned to read in the reek of flax
> and smelled hanged bodies rotting on their gibbets
> and saw their looped slime gleaming from the sacks—
>
> hard-mouthed Ribbonmen and Orange bigots
> made me into the old fork-tongued turncoat
> who mucked the byre of their politics.[80]

Heaney tries to explain that the Ulster he grew up in was quiescent, that displays of Catholic piety on nationalistic occasions were relatively innocuous. At the same time he points to shared experiences, instances of cultural continuities ("And always, Orange drums"[81]), and especially in Heaney's later years in Derry, signs of impending violence ("neighbours on the roads at night with guns"[82]). He also recites a litany of rural and farmyard images ("The alders in the hedge . . . mushrooms / dark-clumped grass where cows or horses dunged / . . . old jampots in a drain clogged up with mud—"[83]). Just as these images are not uniformly beautiful but all mnemonic, so Heaney does justice in this searching exchange both to similarities and to differences between him and his predecessor. Carleton's final advice is directed exclusively at the artist in Heaney: that everything is material for one's art: "We are earthworms of the earth, and all that / has gone through us is what will be our trace."[84] Carleton, however, also recognizes the inevitable pain of the artist's life, offering no cure other than the no-nonsense continued doing of it, of writing. The relationship between the artist and unmediated life assumes a Manichaean diagram for Carleton, of a matter-of-fact acceptance of evil, which serves its paradoxical, saving purpose for the artist: "All this is like a trout kept in a spring / or maggots sown in wounds."[85] In other words, everything is of use. Such an attitude does indeed add support to Helen Vendler's argument that Heaney himself uses his religious background for his art. The rest of "Station Island," however, puts Carleton's brash certainty in perspective, revealing it as not the necessarily individualized answer for Heaney. What Carleton does not address is the spiritual hunger that persists throughout "Station Island," indeed, throughout his own "Lough Derg Pilgrim."

Still, Heaney, explicitly recalling Carleton's infamous first viewing of Lough Derg, perhaps inadvertently resurrects other resonant details from Carleton's first story. He reminds the reader, for example, that Carleton's own work too is intertextual. As Heaney inserts Horace, Dante, and Saint John of the Cross, so Carleton, as we've seen, enlists the rabidly anti-Catholic Caesar Otway and Bishop Henry Jones, stern reminders of the hybrid meaning that accretes to Lough Derg. Heaney also makes the reader remember Carleton traveling to Lough Derg in the costume of a priest and in the process slowly shedding any fantasies he might have had about actually having a vocation. Heaney recovers his early fears about the stifling, stunting personal consequences of choosing the priesthood through the remembered image of the priest returned from South America. Carleton's ghost, too, stirs up all of Heaney's anxieties about the castrating effect of Mother Ireland. He may have at the back of his mind the image of Nell McCollum trotting off in the putative priest's garb, leaving the stripped Carleton with nothing but the asexual motley left behind by this "Old Woman of the Roads." Above all, the stringent, deeply felt argument at the heart of the "Lough Derg Pilgrim" about the renunciation of reason required by Irish Catholicism, epitomized by the pilgrimage, brings up Heaney's own protectiveness of his, as Carleton put it, "free, manly, cultivated understanding." Heaney would also be aware, however, of a competing text, the *Divine Comedy,* and especially of the damned inhabiting the last, eighth circle of hell, including sinners who betray those with rightful authority over them and those who have been good to them. Is Carleton so damned for the pragmatic treachery represented by his conversion? Has he sinned against God? Or has the accommodationist Heaney sinned against his master, Carleton, by living, as his precursor sees it, with timidity?

When Kavanagh appears, his accusation aims at a slightly different area of weakness, less the poet's handling of conventional politics than a wary conservatism in regard to Irish culture and literature. Kavanagh, before leveling a parting shot that is a sexual barb, "In my own day / the odd one came here on the hunt for women,"[86] finds broad fault with his scion's unoriginal behavior in taking on the Lough Derg theme. This choice signals a redundancy, Kavanagh suggests, in Heaney's generation: "Sure I might have known / once I had made the pad, you'd be after me / sooner or later."[87] Heaney is accused of trudging along a preworn cultural path, of rehashing the revision of the revival accomplished by Kavanagh, of not sufficiently breaking with the past and swimming out on his own, as Joyce urges him to do. In fact, all three literary precursors leave Heaney with a similar sense, that the time has come for departure, breaking away, inventing a new, independent response to the pressures of Ireland. The fact that "Station Island" can read as an echo chamber of allusions from all quarters—Europe, Ireland, the medieval period, the pagan, the contemporary, from the world of artifacts to literary quotations—can make it reverberate as a nightmare of hybridity out of control. Its polyphonic energy can veer in so many directions at once that it sounds like Heaney is having difficulty finding a voice of his own. This is an extraordinary pass for the poet who gave such eloquent expression early in his career precisely to the phenomenon of finding a voice. Regarded retrospectively from the vantage point of "Station Island," the following reads as psychological essentialism:

> Finding a voice means that you can get your own feelings into your own words and that your words have the feel of you about them; and I believe that it may not even be a metaphor, for the poetic voice is probably very intimately connected with the poet's natural voice, the voice that he hears as the ideal speaker of the lines he is making up.[88]

When these words from "Feeling into Words" from *Preoccupations* first appeared in 1980, their confident simplicity promised recovery from the psychological and cultural depredations of colonialism. Here was an untortured self-possession, an easy, unselfconscious translation of the self into words without all the warping intermediaries of competing hegemonic voices or texts. Somehow, further into that decade this sureness breaks down. The belief in a single, unified voice vanishes, perhaps in response to a growing understanding of the necessity for true pluralism, or in the face of such moral and political breakdown that a recognition of the difficulty of saying one true thing emerges. Add to this the historical and political obstacles to finding an inner simplicity, and one appreciates how the radical revision of Heaney's poetic becomes understandable, necessary. This, indeed, is the crisis "Station Island" addresses, where the cultural inheritance is so vast and various that the only sense to be made is by the individual conscience, the individual artistic judgment, and, like Hamlet's, it falters. The choice of Lough Derg, especially, with its hybrid Irish-European background, makes it the perfect vehicle for exploring Ireland in the 1980s, as it once again began to be Europeanized. Also, the degree to which Catholicism is conceived as universal relegates it to an inappropriate prop for Irish nativism. At the same time, the unbroken tradition of the pilgrimage in both its European and Irish phases gives the lie to narratives of complete rupture that preside in postcolonial theory. Still, the problem remains for Heaney to decide how much rupture and fragmentation will rule his historical view and how much an unbroken progress will dominate. These questions are deeply related to metaphysical questions, specifically whether human beings enjoy a continuity with a divine source, interrogations all central to modernism. This concatenation of intransigent issues is conjured by the appearance of Joyce, a ghost who also becomes one of many guides through this maze.

9

Heaney's Guides

"Do Not Waver"

HEANEY HIMSELF has achieved the stature of being a guide for the next generation of Irish poets. He has also guided himself through the penitential ordeal of "Station Island," to the affirmation of "Clearances," and on to the reinterrogation of "Squarings." Guided by other literary examples as much as by his own, one of his tasks, in assessing the use of possible mentors, has been to interrogate both Romanticism and modernism, an activity that is part of a broader self-conscious placement of his creative principles in relation to the past, itself a modernist stance. The question of modernism especially—how much houseroom to grant it—is vexed for writers from cultures removed by history from the very history that gave rise to that influential movement. I am thinking particularly of colonized or conquered cultures, including Poland, where a strong religious, oral, rural base is still extant, though threatened and threatening. Ireland, for example, was going through a revolution for political independence when much of the rest of Europe was engaged in World War I, which revolutionized Western culture. On the one hand, modernism gave Joyce a formal and philosophical means to voice his alienation as a cosmopolitan iconoclast from the narrow pieties of Irish nationalism and Catholicism, made narrower by being fused. It gave the similarly urban Devlin the platform from which to critique the new theocratic nation. For Heaney, however, the problem is compounded by a double alienation from, and sense of belonging to, native and secondary cultures.

Fierce tribal loyalty in the face of losses, vestigial Catholicism, the tug of preverbal memory, plus a gravitation toward the symbolic properties in language all distance Heaney from the skepticisms and dislocations of modernism. His treatment of Larkin in "Joy or Night" is less an assault on contemporary English secular culture than a brisk questioning of the literary legacy of modernism. At the same time, Heaney's preference for Holub betrays an affinity for artists from cultures where belief has been under siege, bullied by a brutal positivism. Yet, Heaney's implacable defense of artistic freedom, his own fractured sense of identity as a Northern Catholic educated under and rewarded by an English system, his lapsed Catholicism, not least his peripatetic professional life in middle age, but most his repugnance toward atrocities committed in the name of the nation and the Church draw him toward the transnational sophistication of modernism. Heaney's troubled example may prompt the speculation that a postcolonial background in itself inclines the artist toward a unique brand of postmodernism, indebted to but not claimed by modernism, operating both inside and outside it.

In trying to place Heaney in relation to modernism it is useful to consider his relationship to Romanticism, from which modernism springs. David Lloyd, in "Pap for the Dispossessed," takes Heaney to task for his allegedly retrograde embracing of the English Romantic tradition.[1] Lloyd faults Heaney not for the built-in time lag that inevitably delays a postcolonial writer's confrontation with the various phases in the imperial tradition but for the misrepresentation of Ireland's fractured history, which the transcendent wholeness at the heart of Romanticism falsely heals. I would contend that this major depredation of colonization, an eternally disjointed relationship simultaneously with hegemonic culture and one's deracinated own, may be redressed in more than a single way. Reestablishing a meticulously true, complicated alignment with history may be one response, but a more anarchic, eclectic, perhaps poetic impulse to play within the space, the "elbow room" created by this ambiguous freedom, may be another. It is important to see Heaney as not at all naïve about the hopeless fragmentation and meaninglessness inherited by the late-twentieth-century artist, but as even more determined to choose consciously what to do with this bleak bequest. Notice again in "Joy or Night" his comparison of Larkin and Beckett: "Indeed, Beckett is a very clear example of a writer who is Larkin's equal in not flinching from the ultimate bleakness of things, but who then goes on to do something positive with the bleakness."[2] This "something positive" in Beckett includes his sense of comedy, an absurdist slapstick that makes the void grin. In retracing the path of modernism, Heaney, too, will impose his own footprints, including a heel mark determined as much by his rural Irish upbringing as by his cosmopolitan adult experience. Increasingly, Heaney has taken upon himself the role of literary executor of the hybrid cultural inheritance of Northern Ireland. He has assumed an independence that enables him neither to accept nor to reject either tradition in totality but to pick and choose, deconstruct, and accept each part by part. Heaney's relationship with Wordsworth has provided him all along with a subtle way to negotiate his memories of a rural past from the perspective of a cosmopolitan, educated, international present. At one level, he is as distanced as Wordsworth is from rural simplicity. At another level, Heaney is still a mental resident of Mossbawn, having never fully left. Increasingly, his use of recollection has been refracted by this difference from and similarity to both his points of origin and arrival. Far from lapsing into a nativism, Heaney's selective use of Romanticism eventually has allowed memory to root but not confine, in fact to complicate adult growth, which is invariably hybrid. Hence an Irish poet gravitates toward an English Romantic. In his later works, however, even this modulated relationship with Wordsworth has been radically revised.

Similarly, Heaney's relationship with modernism is ambivalent, quite unresolved. Perhaps the most useful vantage point from which to view this Augean cultural labor on Heaney's part is precisely to examine his relationship with Dante. Given Dante's assumed, legendary use of the *Tractatus,* Lough Derg locates the intersection where rural Ireland meets the Great Tradition. Heaney is aware that placing oneself in relation to Dante is a standard, modernist project. He has witnessed Pound, Eliot, Yeats, and Joyce all making their separate pilgrimages to Dante. Occupying a different historical moment and ethnic profile, however, Heaney has to revisit these modernists and their responses to Dante in the process of reading and reinscribing the medieval poet for himself. As well, writing from a distinctly Irish Catholic, Northern corner, Heaney consults Dante for very urgent personal reasons: questions of faith and moral responsibility equally for the individual and the state.

In stressing the importance of poetry as a necessary assuaging force in the Troubles, Heaney has often turned to Wallace Stevens. For example, in "The Redress of Poetry," Heaney quotes Stevens's description in "The Noble Rider and the Sound of Words" of the agency imagination possesses: "It is a violence from within that protects us from a violence without."[3] Stevens, however, begins that essay with a passage that may have been less to Heaney's liking. Stevens invokes Plato's "Phaedrus," the conceit of "a pair of winged horses and a charioteer,"[4] which figures the triadic, finally unified composition of the soul. Summarizing the passage, Stevens begins, "We recognize at once in the figure Plato's pure poetry; and at the same time we recognize what Coleridge called 'Plato's dear, gorgeous nonsense' "; then with a stab of Stevenesque, metaphysical candor he adds, "We remember, it may be, that the soul no longer exists and we drop in our flight and at last settle on solid ground."[5] Whether Heaney, too, experiences this deflation every time he finds himself floating close to the existence of the soul is the key question to ask of his later, increasingly airborne poetry. Put more simply, can we imagine Heaney ever uttering Stevens's flat, apostate words? I cannot.

A closer look at the later poems discloses the ineradicable doubleness of Heaney's language when he entertains spiritual concerns. Take the last sonnet of "Clearances," which revolves around the dual image of a chestnut tree: the living plant rooted in the ground during childhood and the memory of it rooted in adult consciousness. This is the same conceit that opens Heaney's later, second prose assessment of Kavanagh, "A Placeless Heaven." This essay is studded with phrases that convey the radiant intensity of Kavanagh's vision, "the white light of meditation"[6] that suffuses his later poetry. Yet Heaney must acknowledge a lack of resolution even in the late Kavanagh, whom he depicts as "preparing to be spirited away into some transparent, yet indigenous afterlife."[7] Heaney's words both line up and diverge, heading in two separate directions: "spirited away," "transparent," and "afterlife" point toward the sky; "preparing," the qualifiers "some" and "yet," and the emphatic adjective "indigenous" toward the earth.

Heaney's later poems often hang on the trope of actual scales or the shape of scales, anticipating the moment of the soul's "particular judgement": "Two buckets were easier carried than one. I grew up in between,"[8] he tells us in "Terminus"; but think also, among others, of "Saint Kevin and the Blackbird" and "Weighing In," as well as "The Spirit Level," featuring another tool of alignment. In "Saint Kevin," while the poet wonders at saintliness, he even more imagines Kevin as a man with a body capable of fatigue; the life he lets thrive at the end of his extended mythical arm is a warm-blooded bird. "Weighing In" sardonically celebrates the slippery magic of balancing, but nearly gives in to exhaustion from this tension. Like Hamlet desperate to be freed of ambivalence, Heaney nearly advises throwing one's weight around when exasperation calls for it. Yet, for all these images of more or less equilibrium, there are as many appeals to unity. These moments most often culminate in that word, "transformative." The "diamond absolutes"[9] that sparkle in "Crediting Poetry" refer to such transubstantiated matter, but being plural even these metaphysical jewels fail to capture a lapidary oneness. A light-trapping diamond is, however, the ideal metaphor for the illumination Heaney is projecting, for a verbal coruscation enters his poetry when he glimpses transcendent possibility, and beatific light is the guiding simile of similes that eliminates all others for Dante in the *Purgatorio*—"I saw a light come speeding o'er the sea / So swift, flight knows no simile thereof."[10] Revelation routs comparatively lackluster language, thereby making such moments of transcendence a dubious gift for a poet, but the distinct possibility of false transport gives words the responsibility for truth, for resisting the seduction of appearances and the insistence of the will.

Heaney resists transcendence, I believe, not cynically to insure the longevity of language, but rather emotionally and spiritually because honesty demands this tiring, unending balance. It is tempting, in drafting a crude diagram of Heaney's oeuvre to date, to take that oscillating, now-you-see-it-now-you-don't chestnut tree as a model and divide that Siamese twin at the hip, assigning the material tree to the first half of his career and the metaphysical double to the second. The temptation is strengthened if you consider, say, a further symmetry, another mirror image. In *Field Work*, the volume preceding *Station Island*, Heaney tells the story of Count Ugolino from the *Inferno*. Then, more recently, we have Heaney's incorporation of the beginning and end of canto xxxiii from the *Paradiso*. Dante's lines in fact constitute the beginning and end to Heaney's millenial poem. The absolute conclusion to the *Divine Comedy* relates the ultimate stage of spiritual purgation, where even the innate corruption of the lustful eye copulating with physical images is cleansed, corrected, or almost so. This is, after all, the place in Dante, and Heaney is faithful to the moment in the last lines of "A Dream of Solstice," where the most profound of corporeal similes occurs. As we have seen, Dante's trope locates the human being's initiation into touch and love: the infant sucking at the breast, the common ground of all humanity, the common subject of sacred painting. Dante's theology on love seems congenial to Heaney, namely, that adoration of the divine integrates and purifies rather than eliminates and nullifies human love. This is the view that Brodsky ascribes to Tsvetaeva and that Curtayne denounces. This is also the inter-pretation of Dante's theology as read by Dorothy L. Sayers, the translator in the fifties of Dante for Penguin, Heaney's introduction to the poet. Dante's earthed ide-alism should caution us against positing a dichotomous Heaney oeuvre. When Heaney translates Dante's famous final simile as "an infant's tongue milky with breastmilk would be more articulate,"[11] he is also integrating his own poetic career, harking back to that preverbal resource, so much the ground of his being in the early poems, and identifying that beginning as also his ending: the font of free-flowing grace and inspiration. But even here, Heaney holds back from epiphany. His attraction to Dante comes from the built-in incompleteness of vision guaran-teed by the central conceit, that Dante is still mortal. In "A Dream of Solstice," Dante "lives with the aftermath of a dream," since what he saw "departs." "A dis-tilled sweetness," however, remains and infiltrates his "heart." In translating and then responding to these lines in the body of his own poem, Heaney both confronts and backs off from a major question. Is the "dream" a vibrant Wordsworthian memory or a metaphor indicating deep-down faith?[12]

Heaney has never relinquished the tension between "Truth and Intellect" that marks for Dante the purgatorial struggle, but, while never yielding to what Stevens would call the "first idea" or the nihilism of "zero green," Heaney equally has never settled for the cerebrality in an oxymoronic "Supreme Fiction." He retains a vestigial link to intuitive belief. This quite unique state of betweenness is, in fact, best captured by the *Purgatorio,* where a compromised light is the norm. Dante's unique bodily presence among shades makes him cast a shadow that visually dou-bles him, producing a fracturing of sunlight: " 'See, the rays do not seem to shine on the left of him below and he seems to bear himself like one alive.' I turned my eyes at the sound of these words and saw they kept looking in amazement at me and the light that was broken."[13] Broken light as an image might well convey the crisis of faith at the heart of modernism and "Station Island," though already here Heaney seems to favor the second term in this spiritual paradox.

In an essay written in 1985 about readings of Dante by modern poets, Heaney notes their reflexive projection of themselves onto Dante. Speaking indirectly of Eliot, Heaney observes: "Dante may be writing about a mid-life crisis within the terms of the allegory, but he is also writing about panic, that terror we experience in the presence of the God Pan, numen of the woods."[14] Note that Heaney invokes both the psychological and the spiritual, and that his spiritual focus is not on the god but on *a* god. Christianity is sidestepped. Yet, despite retaining this attachment to the pagan substratum of Irish culture as a site naturally blending the aesthetic and the spiritual, that strategy in "Station Island" is viewed as also morally per-ilous. In the *Purgatorio,* where Virgil after all is Dante's guide, the virtuous but unshriven figures from the classical age, such as Cato, reside in ante-purgatory, a modified, upscale limbo. Moral movement is what Heaney craves at this juncture. Speed is of the essence, too, in Dante's purgatory. "Station Island," as noted, is the first major volume of Heaney's to be published after the hunger strikes, and, for all its stasis, reads with a terrible urgency. Heaney confronts himself with substantive, unavoidable, overdue questions of conscience, like his response to Colum McCartney's assassination. All this self-flagellation is suffered for the belief that the state has little hope of being cleansed until the individuals within it are purged. All of the self-reflexive ironies surrounding McCartney's presence in "Station Island"— Heaney's recommitted sin of quoting Dante to ameliorate pain, his moral confrontation with himself performed through a character of his own making—add up, however, at one very dark level, to a digging of one's own moral grave deeper and deeper.

The more Heaney does to rectify matters through poetry, the more he can appear to recommit the sin of using poetry to evade life. Dante offers the hope that all this mirroring may not add up to fatal narcissism, that the *Purgatorio* may be both the source of sin and its eradication because the prescribed penance is always a wickedly literal reflection of the sin it cleanses, a metaphysical legerdemain reminiscent of that wielded in the *Tractatus*, where a dream within a dream within a dream becomes a new reality. Hence the penance for the wrathful is to be encased in suffocating, black smoke. Furthermore, Dante is so psychologically astute that he uncovers even the elusive lapses of a good man. Hard as it is to credit of one so hard-working, Heaney's self-perceived sins may come under "sloth," which includes, oddly, the excessive worrying that makes simple virtuous action more and more fugitive. Self-absorption, passivity, excessive soul-searching, all the attributes of the "artful voyeur" in the controversial bog poem "Punishment," go under sloth. There is, however, a fine line between preoccupation and the contemplative life, which in turn requires, according to Dante, integration with the active life. The parable in canto xxvii in the *Purgatorio* of Leah and Rachel, the two symbolic wives of Jacob, illustrates this: Leah being blind but fertile, Rachel beautiful but barren.[15] The parable indicates the absolute interdependence of the aesthetic and metaphysical, beauty and belief, prayer and action. Dante also identifies the barrier to self-perfection most daunting for him, perhaps all poets. Under pride he includes the pride of achievement. I think of Yeats, musing in amazement about Thomas MacDonagh's sacrifice in 1916, "He might have won fame in the end."[16]

The *Purgatorio* also has wisdom to offer about the Northern situation. Part of the divine integration it foresees is on a civic level, a moral system that makes the state accountable to the individual and, more importantly, the individual accountable to the state. Heaney reveals the fruits of this moral reading of Dante in his more recent poems. In "Mycenae Lookout" the figure of the watchman is a reincarnation of the artful voyeur of "Punishment," yet in "The Nights" Heaney's watchman persona goes on record without equivocation as personally accountable for his sins of omission. Heaney may also identify with Dante as a lifelong exile, even though

Dante left Florence because the Pope forced him to and Heaney left Belfast by choice. Heaney bridges this difference in "Station Island" through the concluding figure of Joyce, who left Dublin for personal reasons, not least the bane of Catholicism. In his essay on Dante, referring to Eliot, Heaney expresses dismay that in the wake of World War I Eliot paid so little attention to the political content of Dante, who did combine the contemplative and active lives. Dante's activities as a prior of Florence, belonging to the anti-papal White party (the Florentine Blacks and Whites being a paradigm for partisan strife) led to his imbroglio with the Pope. Comments Heaney of Eliot, "It is curious that this born-again Anglican and monarchist did not make more of the political Dante, the dreamer of a world obedient to the spiritual authority of a cleansed Papacy and under the sway of a just emperor."[17]

Heaney openly distances himself here from Eliot, the one modernist who made room for a religious system. Again, Heaney looks to Eliot's response to Dante and finds it wanting, mark, for its religiosity. Heaney, the lapsed Irish Roman Catholic, is less suspicious of Eliot the Englishman manqué than of Eliot the High Church zealot. It is a matter of the doubting born Catholic being wary of the ardent convert. This distaste filters into Heaney's assessment of the Eliot canon, rejecting, to use Eliot's term, the "high dream"[18] of the "Four Quartets," mimetic in its transformed somnambulism of Dante's pageantry at the end of the *Purgatorio,* in favor of the Low Church, resolutely ambiguous, earthed dream of the "Wasteland." And yet, Eliot's attraction to this high dreaming was the release it offered from the purgatory of egoism. The author of "Station Island" might have been drawn to Eliot on these grounds; he might even have sympathized with Eliot's poignant admission in 1929, after his mental breakdown, that he found it hard to accept Dante's "prejudice that poetry not only must be found through suffering, but can find its material only in suffering."[19] Also, writing from the edges of the rubble of World War I, Eliot leaps on the universal in Dante in order to set him up as a beacon for an international, albeit European, poetry. All this might have appealed to a poet in the midst of sectarian strife, caught in the crossfire of competing narratives, competing discourses. Instead, Heaney diverges radically from Eliot precisely on the matter of remaining true to one's local speech, local politics, and spirituality as a process rather than a fait accompli. However much he endorses poetry as transformative, Heaney prefers a symbolic rather than transubstantiated reality, one that protects the integrity of words rather than jettisoning them for an a priori spiritual salvation.

Heaney's model as a precursive reader of Dante is the Russian poet, Osip Mandelstam. He attracts for his sturdy independence in relation to Dante, his refusal to lose a sense of his own needs by simply being awed. Heaney's response reflects his own wariness of the sway of modernist canonic taste. Heaney is distinctly impatient with Eliot and Pound for their academic, reverential, and finally, in his view, provincial readings of Dante. Referring to the two modernists as "two Americans," Heaney notes their service to Dante and undermines it by means of Mandelstam: "The two Americans at once restored and removed Dante in the English speaking literary mind because they both suggested what Mandelstam was at pains to mock, that Dante's poem was written on official paper."[20] For Heaney, like Kavanagh, the most provincial position is the self-consciously cosmopolitan, and the true parochial is the true cosmopolite. Mandelstam, in contrast to Eliot, finds in Dante a savior, not of his life but of his soul as an artist. Heaney, having endured a lesser pressure than Mandelstam to mold poetry to the exact contours of politics, identifies with the Russian poet who survived and thrived as a poet under the Stalinism that took his life. I read Heaney's poem "Chekhov on Sakhalin" as an encoded elegy for Mandelstam. In the poem, the much praised and pampered Chekhov, who remembers always with guilt, much as Heaney does, his humble origins, undertakes a penitential journey to the penal colony on Sakhalin, which is north of Vladivostok, the closest city to the camp where Mandelstam died as a political prisoner in 1938.

Yet, while there are a few surprises in the Mandelstam alliance, there are many interesting angles to Heaney's differences with Eliot. On the one hand Heaney criticizes Eliot's elevation of Dante's language into a universal discourse, which the American prizes for being amenable to translation in a way Shakespeare's recalcitrantly individual style is not. Whereas Eliot praises Dante for wielding a language of Latinate neutrality, Mandelstam reads Dante as serving no master other than his utterly individual vision: "Dante is irreplaceable precisely because he is unnecessary."[21] We could have anticipated where Heaney would weigh in on this debate. Although torn himself between being "adept and dialect,"[22] it is this vital tension between archeological layers of language, from the local to the universal, that partially locates Heaney's linguistic verve. Heaney, himself a digger into dialect, celebrates, as Mandelstam does, Dante the rebel stylist who clung to the vernacular. Likewise, Heaney defends the indissoluble particularities, the local texture of Shakespearean speech. On the other hand, perhaps as one who has at times felt a debilitating allegiance to the parish, Heaney is drawn to Mandelstam, the assimilated Jew in late-nineteenth-century St. Petersburg, who reveled in his mother's perfect Russian and was embarrassed by his father's Yiddish. Mandelstam even shares some of Carleton's fearless treachery, as Mandelstam in "The Noise of Time" refers to Judaism as "chaos."[23] He, like Carleton, embodies the conflicts and betrayals, the often ugly pragmatism necessary for survival, especially the survival of the creative imagination. Every major decision in Mandelstam's life was taken to preserve a life in language rather than in the flesh, however interdependent in fact the two are. His acmeism, as distinct from modernism, places a premium on the absolute value of poetic language, finding in it a haven from Stalinist politics, all politics. Mandelstam's dynamic vision of how poetic speech works constitutes it as an agent that makes its own inviolate space. The redemptive power of words resides in this self-generating autonomy, the asylum Mandelstam finds in Dante. In the Russian poet's gnostic "Conversations about Dante," where he limns by rapid strokes a theory of poetry as a constant reinvention of itself, he likens the infinitely symmetrical, geometric, exponentially expanding structure of the *Divine Comedy* to the architecture of a beehive—perfect, inevitable, organic. This view is not the cliched, Arnoldian one of religion as poetry; it is more a faith that words themselves perform the primal act of creation, that a divine force inheres in the impulse to create order. We know the impact of Mandelstam on Medbh McGuckian, whose linguistic dynamism is truly Mandelstamian. Her startling simile in the "Dream-Language of Fergus," "as if an aeroplane in full flight / launched a second plane,"[24] is lifted straight from Mandelstam's "Conversations";[25] likewise the phrase "trans-sense language" in "Elegy for an Irish Speaker."[26]

For his theory of form alone Mandelstam provides a model of resistance, useful for poets living actually or imaginatively in the midst of chaos, for he regards form as emerging from language itself, not imposed by tradition, hence his immunity to the reverential and hegemonic at once. What he says about form echoes Heaney's words in the conclusion to "Clearances," where "the space we stood around had been emptied into us."[27] As Mandelstam puts it observing Dante, "space virtually emerges out of itself,"[28] as one plane emerges from another, as the poem grows out of itself, an extraordinary image of autonomy. The beauty of this idea, for the artist pressured by the literary conventions and forms of a non-native culture, is its relegation of the creation of form to a process carried on within the generative domain of language. The politically beleaguered Heaney seems to be won over entirely by Mandelstam's antipolitical assertion that the final value of the *Divine Comedy* is that it serves no purpose: it simply is, like a plant or an animal or an individual.

From Heaney's earliest sensuous poems, before the shadow of sectarian violence fell over his every measured utterance, he has subscribed to the incontrovertible logic of natural processes, as though each person's freedom to pursue a natural destiny were the measure of true liberation. His assimilation of each manifestation of literary tradition obeys this rule: how well does it serve his own, self-perceived destiny? So it is with Dante and modernism. An utterly sincere, necessitous purpose underlies Heaney's borrowing from Dante for "Station Island." It is true that enlisting Dante restores centrality to a marginalized culture: that of Northern Catholics. Writing a poem set in the exact place where the entrance to hell through purgatory could be found is locating, as Heaney might call it, the omphalos itself at Lough Derg, but this oracular center is always for him the poetic imagination, when it is rooted in place. Heaney, therefore, will bring Dante to Lough Derg, not vice versa. This is done not for provincial justification but for the importation of those perennial questions of faith and morals, which the *Purgatorio* above all addresses most subtly. So Heaney also reads other poets, predominantly modernists with a religious proclivity, who have come to Dante in the same searching spirit. All participate in the irony of seeking the poet of sublime order from a perspective of apparent fragmentation and abysmal subjectivity. Dante guides Heaney particularly out of the vanity of being a poet, the attachment to excessive self-scrutiny, which thwarts simple, virtuous action. It is for this reason that Yeats does not enter Heaney's deliberations about former readers of Dante. Ultimately, the Pre-Raphaelite fixation on an attenuated femininity located by Yeats in Dante's Beatrice exists at the opposite pole from Heaney's pressingly male concerns at this point.

For all this attachment on a level informed by a past, undervalued religion, Heaney's excursion into Dante also reinforces certain modernist doubts and strategies. The consummate fictionality in Dante's poem, a mortal surviving the other world, anticipates Wallace Stevens's "Supreme Fiction," yet Heaney never fully subscribes in his poem to the ontologies of faith or fiction. He remains resolutely in between, in purgatory. So it is that Heaney can take Dante's moral lessons seriously and yet invent his own parade of ghosts, many of whom prompt defiance. Heaney's deviation from and emulation of Dante is reflected in formal decisions throughout "Station Island," which, with the exception of one out of twelve sections, refuses to cleave to terza rima, a form that echoes the triangulation of the Trinity and, for a rural Irish Catholic, might imitate the circularity of the rosary, too. The only section of Heaney's poem that does conform to terza rima is ironically the anticlimactic conclusion. Here Catholicism is never more subverted. This is equally true for nationalism. As Heaney, on leaving the island, lifts himself from the boat by accepting the extended bony hand of what turns out to be Joyce, the reader is reminded of another famous moment in Lough Derg lore. The tableau is a replay of that fabled moment when Turlough Carolan (1670–1738), the blind harper and romantic symbol to later generations of the lost Gaelic Ireland, climbs out of the boat and recognizes by feel the hand of the woman he cannot see as that of his lost love. The woman in the tale is yet another *aisling* figure, a personification of "Romantic Ireland." It may be significant that revisionist history today paints a portrait of Carolan not unlike that of Heaney, particularly in the context of Northern politics. Carolan, living through his own painful history, predominately the imposition of the Penal Laws, is said by R. F. Foster to have "sedulously avoided either political or religious controversy in his lyrics."[29] The indirect presence of Carolan, a ghost of a ghost, marks yet another iconoclastic, revisionist moment in "Station Island," appropriately announced by the appearance of Joyce urging his heresies. It is also where a return to everyday hell is carried by the imagery: "The shower broke in a cloudburst, the tarmac / fumed and sizzled."[30]

By directly confronting, confessing, and assessing his culpability in relation to public suffering in "Station Island," while still maintaining self-possession, even from the inherited poetics of others, Heaney regularly returns to this kind of situation, where a rededication to the demands of poetry is required in the face of competing demands. In "The Flight Path," from his 1996 collection *The Spirit Level,* he recalls an incident where he is directly accosted by a Catholic terrorist, an old schoolmate, who asks the poet point blank when he is going to write something that "weighs in" with their side, something that does not equivocate or strike once again the balance for which Heaney is famous, and, to certain others, infamous. I quote part 4 of "The Flight Path" in full, since this section threads back to "Station Island," not least by revisiting the discomfort of having one's manhood questioned. It also contains a mention of Pettigo, the border town nearest Lough Derg, and an allusion to, in fact a direct translation of, Dante:

The following for the record, in the light
Of everything before and since:
One bright May morning, nineteen-seventy-nine,
Just off the "red-eye special" from New York,
I'm on the train for Belfast. Plain, simple
Exhilaration at being back: the sea
At Skerries, the nuptial hawthorne bloom,
The trip north taking sweet hold like a chain
On every bodily sproket.
    Enter then—
As if he were some *film noir* border guard—
Enter this one I'd last met in a dream,
More grimfaced now than in the dream itself
When he'd flagged me down at the side of a mountain road,
Come up and leant his elbow on the roof
And explained through the open window of the car
That all I'd have to do was drive a van
Carefully in to the next customs post
At Pettigo, switch off, get out as if
    I were on my way with dockets to the office—
But then instead I'd walk ten yards more down
Towards the main street and get in with—here
Another schoolfriend's name, a wink and smile,
I'd know him all right, he'd be in a Ford
And I'd be home in three hours' time, as safe
As houses . . .
    So he enters and sits down
Opposite and goes for me head on.
"When, for fuck's sake, are you going to write
Something for us?" "If I do write something,
Whatever it is, I'll be writing for myself".
And that was that. Or words to that effect.
The gaol walls all those months were smeared with shite.
Out of Long Kesh after his dirty protest
The red eyes were the eyes of Ciaran Nugent
Like something out of Dante's scurfy Hell,
Drilling their way through the rhymes and images
Where I too walked behind the righteous Virgil,
As safe as houses and translating freely:
When he had said all this, his eyes rolled
And his teeth, like a dog's teeth clamping round a bone,
Bit into the skull and again took hold.[31]

The place where the dream occurs, "at the side of a mountain road," near Pettigo, could easily be where Carleton appears to the pilgrim-poet in "Station Island," itself a dream-like occurrence. The connection with Carleton is enforced by the evocation of a terrorist descendant of the Whiteboys in Carleton's "Wildgoose Lodge." The difference between these two moments in Heaney's poetry, "Station Island" and "The Flight Path," is that here, in the latter, Heaney strikes back at his challenger with equal verbal force. After all, although the actual incident of being confronted in the train, anterior to the dream of being accosted, occurred in 1979, the poem is written some fifteen years later, with accumulated time at Harvard and international recognition in between. The poem, however, particularly as it leads up to the confrontation, registers the ambivalence about the North that still persists in Heaney: "The trip north taking sweet hold like a chain / On every bodily sproket." Beginning in pleasure, soon, as the monosyllables mount, this visceral sensation resembles, given the word "sproket," being stretched on the wrack. Once again, as in "Station Island," there is the acrid taste of guilt in Heaney's mouth, despite the forthright, assertive response to bullying, because of his privileged literary life: "Where I too walked behind the righteous Virgil, / As safe as houses and translating freely." In a society ruled by the bomb, the irony attendant on the colloquialism, "safe as houses," gathers force here as Heaney's literary life is portrayed as hardly sheltered. Physical danger and mental anguish both can result from proximity to paramilitaries. Notice again the prominence of translation as a paradoxical way of maintaining a remove from politics and getting to its core, translating it in the theological sense to another level. This Dantean insertion prefigures the role other non-English poets, prominently Milosz, will play in helping Heaney to translate the Ireland of his times. Paradoxically, the very inexactitude of translation provides the space in which meaning can assume dimensions not generated by flat, political discourse. This revisiting of a "Station Island" moment fifteen years after that sequence reveals both a continuation of its moral and poetic dilemma and significant progress in dealing with it. This advance is in large measure achieved by the act of translating, of tacking on translation to a poem resolutely written in the vernacular. This addition reaffirms a resolve both to preserve a distance and to be engaged on one's own terms, as a poet plumbing the universal in the local.

As a further reminder of "Station Island," there is another repetition of one of its ploys: the use of a cross-reference within Heaney's own oeuvre. This one, however, has an especially complicated ring because it is a repetition of a translation taken from a larger poem-translation. The concluding lines of section 4 from "The Flight Path" reprise lines from Heany's "Ugolino" from *Field Work,* a volume from 1979, not coincidentally the very year in which the incident from "The Flight Path" is said to have occurred. The cross-reference, therefore, dredges up an entire period of the poet's life, one when the idyll in Wicklow, culminating in the "Glanmore Sonnets," underscored a determination to be true to the poet in himself first. This interlude in lush east Wicklow brought a reimmersion in the umbrageous and fertile as relief from the strobe-lighted and barren horrors of the dirty protest and the hunger strikes. "Ugolino," however, which translates the end of canto xxxii and beginning of xxxiii from the *Inferno,* marks a return to the hell of Northern Ireland from the double distance of Wicklow and Dante, and paradoxically, brings Heaney to the bottom, the center, the ninth circle of his own hell. By reinvoking these lines, a repetition of a translation, from the even greater distance of transatlantic travel and years beyond the incident mentioned on the train, Heaney is once again both placing a protective barrier between himself and too painful material and leaping that barrier to an essential reality.

By departing a necessary measured distance from the local and actual, Heaney is able to create layers of meaning not conveyed by bare anecdote. Such distancing also creates room for the poet to translate himself, consolidate his subjectivity, rather than merely to react to certain cultural givens. Above all, translation can refract the givens into new patterns of association. By invoking his own "Ugolino" and the two penultimate cantos from the *Inferno,* Heaney by implication places not only his interlocutor and his ilk in the ninth circle of hell, but also does not spare himself. As compared to the "righteous Virgil," the Irish poet, now completely identified with Dante, beside whom he walks, suffers in his subconscious, his dreams, from an ineffable sense of sin. The common material that creates the triple overlap of this part of "The Flight Path," Heaney's "Ugolino," and canto xxxiii of the *Inferno* is a sinister, prophetic dream. As Heaney translates it, "the bad dream" of Count Ugolino is about a hunt conducted by expert huntsmen that results in a slaughter: "My hallucination was all sharp teeth and bleeding flanks ripped open."[32] Heaney refers to the "wolf and wolf cubs" as the dead prey. Dorothy L. Sayers, more explicit about the prefiguring potency of the dream, refers to the "wolf and wolf cubs" as a father and sons, anticipating the grotesque deaths of Ugolino and his children and grandchildren. Heaney's dream in "The Flight Path" is of being enlisted as a terrorist, a bomber, a role he subconsiously associates with himself because his past included schoolmates who as men became terrorists. There is a guilt by association and a survivor guilt beyond the margins of the dream, which Heaney can only purge by the independence and integrity of his poetic stance, justifying both his intimacy with this *Inferno* and his distance from it.

The inhabitants of Dante's ninth circle of hell could easily be exchanged for men Heaney knew firsthand and who became involved with terrorism in Northern Ireland. If we turn to Sayers's translation of canto xxxii, we see how Dante would have offered himself to Heaney as a means of getting close to the incestuous, seditious violence of the North, especially in the late seventies and early eighties. First of all, for Heaney to read in the introductory gloss to the canto that "The Ninth Circle is the frozen Lake of Cocytus, which fills the bottom of the Pit, and holds the souls of the Traitors"[33] might have immediately suggested an analogy because, as we have seen from the *Tractatus,* the frigid center to Dante's underworld is borrowed from a Celtic, pagan archetype. Then to read Sayers's footnotes on the identities of the various traitors included might have sealed the analogy. Their ruthless, bloodthirsty, unnatural acts square with conduct on both sides of the sectarian divide in Northern Ireland. Here are Sayers's notes on just three typical traitors:

> Foccacia: one of the Cancellieri family of Pistoi. He is said to have cut off the hand of one of his cousins and cut his uncle's throat, and thus to have started the family feud from which the Black and White Guelf factions had their origin.
>
> Sassol Mascheroni: One of the Toschi of Florence, who treacherously murdered his uncle's only son and seized the inheritance.
>
> Camcion de' Pazzi: of Valdarno, murdered his kinsman Ubertino. . . . It will be noticed that the shades of the Traitors, though inclined to be reticent about their own affairs, are only too eager to denounce each other, and pour out strings of names without even being asked.[34]

These are men possessed, in Sayers's words, of a "cold and cruel egotism, gradually striking inward till even the lingering passions of hatred and destruction are frozen into immobility—that is the final state of sin."[35] We know that immobility, being stuck, as these sinners are in ice as hard as glass, is Heaney's great fear in "Station Island," a specific worry that revolves around a perception of the artist's egotism. Dante's depiction of the final circle of hell also includes a detail that strikes a chord within Heaney's own early work, where carnality itself is feared as a self-destructive, devouring force. Dante's simile for these foulest of sinners, sunk to the neck in ice, echoes a favorite Heaney image from postlapsarian nature: "Muzzles peeping from the stream / The frogs sit croaking."[36] Heaney's almost stern reinvoking in "The Flight Path" of the prerogatives of the poet risks deepening that egotism but also holds out the chance of hauling oneself up out of the pit. Release takes the form of being able to see beyond the self, even competing selves, the discordant voices echoing in the hell of the Northern situation. In fact, Heaney's imaginative leap into the Dantean conceit makes this larger vision possible. Reading cantos xxxii and xxxiii sets in motion a vortex of analogical thought and association about Irish history larger than the whirlpool of the Troubles, and it is this larger historical sense that gives the "Ugolino" its resonance as a poem. In fact the strategy parlays an anecdote into a poem. This borrowing from the "Ugolino" rescues "The Flight Path" from being a depiction merely of one ego pitted against another.

The dominant image Dante employs of these traitors in the ninth circle is that they are paired off with an old enemy, also locked into the frozen lake of the ego, each cannibalizing the other, the implication being that egotism is insatiable. A further irony is that these egotists are paired off, sunk together into the same hole, despite their delusion of being unique. Dante, therefore, offers Heaney a way of bringing moral focus to the chaos of the North, where blame is endless and responsibility endlessly fugitive. Dante places moral responsibility firmly on each individual, demanding individual accountability, if personal eternal suffering is to be avoided. Also, the fact that an unappeasable hunger reigns as the prevailing energy, a constant gnawing at another, cannot help but create further connections with Irish history, especially since Count Ugolino tells us that the tower in which he, his sons, and grandsons were imprisoned was later named for them as the Tower of Famine. One wonders if Heaney could make such reverberant connections within Irish history without the assistance of his analogue, his translation. Above all, the Ugolino story, with its undercurrent of cannibalism combined with infanticide, allows Heaney to brush lightly up against some of the most repressed and horrific images of famine. Actually, Sayers translates lines 22–24 of xxxiii as: "A narrow loophole in the dreadful den / Called 'Famine' after me, and which, meseems, / Shall be a dungeon yet for many men."[37] The eternally damned Ugolino sees the tower as named after him, as though he alone starved there and this were the worst horror imaginable; this is the same eternally unregenerate man whose traitorous act was to plot with Archbishop Roger, the man to whom he is now locked in frozen bondage, in order to topple his own grandson from power. Heaney translates the same lines in the "Ugolino" as "Others will pine as I pined in that jail / Which is called Hunger after me."[38] He begins the poem with an image of another symbiotic pair:

> two soldered in a frozen hole
> On top of other, one's skull capping the other's,
> Gnawing at him where the neck and head
> Are grafted to the sweet fruit of the brain,
> Like a famine victim at a loaf of bread.[39]

The deft use of the words "hunger" and "famine" both in the same poem is Heaney's way of connecting the local horror of the Troubles with the greatest cataclysm in collective Irish memory. The two words side by side also anticipate with eerie prescience the hunger strikes of 1980–81, which were on the horizon in 1979, and in fact not only revive a traditional tactic of resistance in Irish history but revive with a terrible poetic logic the place of starvation in Ireland. As well, locating this translation at the point in the *Inferno* where Dante and Virgil reach the "great fundament of Hell,"[40] evokes the Dirty Protest going on at that time and recalled much more explicitly later in "The Flight Path": "The gaol walls all those months were smeared with shite." Miraculously, such expansive reflection happens because of the oblique reach and ramifications of the Dante translation.

In linking this squalor with that of the famine—the specter of children dying of starvation with parents, and of hitherto unspoken, vile acts—Heaney is doing much more than reporting from the front in Belfast. As a poet, he is translating the present into the past and vice versa by means of continuous images of atrocity. Because of the horrifying repetition of these images and their patterning, past and present seem as incapable of being separated from each other as these sinners. Heaney even hints at the well-documented sense of personal guilt and shame stemming from a belief, pervasive in Famine literature, that the Famine was a punishment from God. Furthermore, his resorting to translation calls up the profound truth that lies behind all these sidesteps into translation: that part of the invention of Ireland is the task of finding an adequate translation of the past in terms of the present, a transposition that will never fully occur. The provenance of such a poem, therefore, reaches straight back to the restorative efforts conducted in the mid-nineteenth century by "Davis, Mangan, Ferguson," and MacCarthy. By resorting to the Dante translation, however, Heaney also resists the provincialism and isolationism still imposed, particularly on Northern Catholics, by a nativist Republicanism. Uncannily, Heaney's reaching back here to the Famine makes the reader hear another language, not just Italian but Irish, rumbling beneath the surface of the poem's English. Appealing to a foreign culture, as MacCarthy did, is a way of gesturing toward but not pretending to capture fully this fugitive otherness. The foreign language in itself provides a salutary difference, reminding the reader of the primary otherness of all poems, their intrinsic untranslatability, like the opacity of the past. Dante and his Italian becomes the veil of memory itself that will always occlude history, especially its most traumatic episodes. More than anything, at this mature point in Heaney's oeuvre, literary allusion, especially via translation, is emphatically not a gratuitous touch of sophistication but another means of digging. His "Ugolino" and "The Flight Path" in its turn, taking off from "Station Island," are part of an ongoing translation of self and culture, a never-perfected text with countless, ever proliferating versions, like Lough Derg itself.

Heaney has written in his prose about translation in the abstract and about individual acts of translation. His words on the subject help us to understand why poets in another language, such as Dante and Milosz, serve Heaney so strategically as conduits back to a buried, Irish truth and forward toward a new poetic with which to express these retrievals. From Heaney's own ruminations on this subject, it becomes clear that he perceives Irish culture as proceeding by a sequence of translations. It is precisely the Irish language shards, some so local and idiomatic as to be perhaps untranslatable now, in Carleton's prose that give it the archeological value Heaney treasures. Carleton's Hiberno-English embeds a lost world. The irretrievable quality of Irish and the history associated with it come across in a review Heaney wrote of *An Duanaire: 1600–1900,* an anthology of Irish poetry translated by Thomas Kinsella and edited by Sean O'Tuama. Heaney opens this essay by recalling "a dark green cliff of books . . . a complete range of the Early Irish Texts Society's publications" that sat ominously and opaquely on bookshelves in the room of his confessor at Saint Columb's College in Derry. Heaney regards these translations by Kinsella as improvements on older translations, because these newer versions capture the tone, the context of a world in such a living way that "a community of feeling between us and our forebears"[41] is restored. In a sense Kinsella's translations, even to an Irish speaker, are the latest chapter in a narrative of English translations, each judged against the others for success. It is this parallel history, the perpetual process of translating the past, that provides writers in English and Irish alike with a sense of "the direction Irish poetry should take, now and in the future." Heaney here betrays both his sense of how cultural work is done incrementally, but also his conviction that there are more and less fruitful directions in which to proceed. Translation practiced at the level where Heaney deploys it achieves the paradoxical magic of healing an old rift by creating a new, more benign one. It allows the writer to experiment relatively safely with ways of proceeding, because nothing literal or final has been said.

Creating "elbow room," space for experimentation, especially with poetics as they ramify, determined by and determining perception, is the expressed concern of Heaney's extraordinary later sequence, "Squarings." Owing its inception to a spirit of detached inquiry, which necessitates a departure from the lyric in "Station Island," "Squarings" in its self-conscious mutability of philosophical positions and sustained, cerebral tone is arguably Heaney's most modernist writing. Much of the live connective tissue between the two sequences is exposed by the common presence of Dante, who reappears in section xxxvi of "Squarings," appropriately the closing poem of the section entitled "Crossings," Dante's great theme. Evoking specifically the passage over the River Styx, the poem makes the connection between the hell of the Troubles and Dante's *Inferno*. The scene in Heaney's poem is a dispersal of demonstrators after a political march in Northern Ireland. In that atmosphere of incipient danger, the unreliability of "help" offered by the Royal Ulster Constabulary is foregrounded, their "torches" being compared to "fireflies" that "clustered and flicked and tempted us to trust / Their unpredictable, attractive light."[42] The passage where this comparison is launched begins with the direct reference to Dante: "Scene from Dante, made more memorable / By one of his head-clearing similes—."[43] Note the double illumination produced, physical and metaphysical, the actual light of the flashlights and that provided by simile. This second light source in its turn splits, between the unparalleled precedent set by Dante, famous for his similes, and the homage to him here. Highly reflexive, therefore, Heaney's simile is an allusion to a poetic based in simile, another echo of the reflexive dreaming in the *Tractatus*. All this ambiguity and layering is the perfect accompaniment to a scene dominated by doubt and fear. So, when the transition described is complete, literally moving from the danger of the street into the relative safety of the car, it is as though one of the legs of the journey undertaken by Dante and Virgil has also been accomplished:

> We were like herded shades who had to cross
>
> And did cross, in a panic, to the car
> Parked as we'd left it, that gave when we got in
> Like Charon's boat under the faring poets.[44]

There is a movement from panic, the same debilitating terror in the woods associated with Eliot, to the restoration of relative safety in the car, a moment McGuckian might relish. Yet, as this vehicle gives with the weight of its passengers, so their mortality is seen to be resting in the scales of fate. The poem, therefore, balances ultimately a certain security provided by the power of making the poem and drawing on the mastery of a predecessor, against the perpetual danger of simply being human, constantly facing one threat or another. Reflecting all this ambiguity, this poem and the entire sequence is composed entirely in tercets, but not terza rima. We are reminded that the tercet was used by Wallace Stevens in "Notes Toward a Supreme Fiction." It is also the chosen form of Walcott, for his postcolonial revision of and homage to Homer in *Omeros*. Heaney's own departures from Dantean form in "Squarings" are telling, especially if, as poets tend to believe, everything is innate in form, hence Mandelstam's belief in the sublime architecture of the *Divine Comedy*. Heaney's "Squarings" consists of forty-eight rock solid, four-square poems of four stanzas each; however, there are twelve poems in each section. Since three times four equals twelve, the Trinity makes a secret showing. There are, however, only four sections, a truncated version of a complete, celestial whole, which would have involved twelve sections, one hundred and forty-four poems. A mystical multiple of three is withheld. It is as though Beatrice never appears. The implication of this incompleteness is that Heaney is still trying to make it all add up, an impossible task when the remembered idea of the soul, everything and nothing, insists on counting.

The four sections—"Lightenings," "Settings," "Squarings," and "Crossings"—that make up the sequence are not categorically divided by theme, discrete unto themselves. Indeed, each section, implying a particular stance in relation to reality, telescopes all the others. If one thinks of "Lightenings" as sudden epiphanies, "Settings" as given circumstances, "Squarings" as attempts to control those circumstances, and "Crossings" as passages from one manifestation of being to another, then a preponderance of the poems make quicksilver shifts from one position to the next, and all those in between, often simultaneously. Also, continuing in the self-conscious spirit of "Station Island," where the dialogism alone signals not just an earnest search but a self-conscious, intellectual one, "Squarings" even more reflects this growing cerebrality. A greater acknowledgment in Heaney's poetry of the bearing of philosophy and theology on it bespeaks, more than the legacy of involvement in the eighties with the literary-theoretical probings conducted by the *Field Day* pamphlets (Seamus Deane, Declan Kiberd, Fredric Jameson, Terry Eagleton, and Edward Said among the contributors) and even the rarefied climate of Harvard. It indicates the influence of unabashedly intellectual poets such as Milosz, who by example and stated intention, aim to banish a squeamishness about philosophical and theological discourse in poetry.

Consider, for example, Milosz's poem with the arcane, precise title "Theodicy," an angry, Manichaean denunciation of Christian theology's failed attempt to reconcile the power of absolute evil with God's love. The frankly lesser but countervailing power of this otherwise quite abstract, discursive poem, its *bona fides* as it were, comes from Milosz's perspective as one who witnessed the Nazi occupation and must morally account for it. At such moments in Milosz it seems that any other diction, words in a conventionally poetic register, would betray the detached but impassioned spirit of this meditation on the repository of legitimately inherited thought and belief behind the poem, both drawn on and mocked. The sarcasm of the poem would fail without the inclusion of a targeted, specialized discourse, as normal to Milosz as Heaney's *"Health of the sick"* and *"pray for us,"* words exposed by poetry for their inadequacy:

> No, it won't do, my sweet theologians.
> Desire will not save the morality of God.
> If he created beings able to choose between good and evil,
> And they chose, and the world lies in iniquity,
> Nevertheless, there is pain, and the undeserved torture of creatures,
> Which would find its explanation only by assuming
> The existence of an archetypal Paradise
> And a pre-human downfall so grave
> That the world of matter received its shape from diabolic power.[45]

By allowing himself such latitude and inclusiveness of style Milosz refuses to cede to the experts responsibility for framing certain central metaphysical questions. The poet, too, is released from a confining range of experience, comment, and diction. The poem takes its brio from its confidence in wielding theological argument, and from the nail-in-the-coffin effect, prepared for by the word "grave" of the climactic final line, which sources evil in the creation of matter itself.

Returning to Heaney and "Squarings," consider merely the disruptive, provocative effect of two words included in poems that, though highly imaged and metaphorical, are not tied solely to figuration and the concrete. (For the purpose of reading this critical sequence closely and economically, I am confining myself to six sections from the first sequence, "Lightenings," which, in keeping with the syncretic method of the poem, anticipate or contain the often conflicting, differentiating postures of later sections.) These two words are "phenomenal" (xii) and "proleptic" (vii). In the first instance, Heaney is using the word "phenomenal" with the full freight of the philosophical movement of phenomenalism behind it. So, while he asks us to consider the phenomenalist's position of resolute in-between-ness, between consciousness and things, that vibrant, shimmering interface, he is equally latching onto the specific idea of intentionality in phenomenalism, which holds that, while reality beyond consciousness may not be exactly denominated, consciousness nonetheless attaches to something. One is reminded further by the overtly religious context surrounding the word in Heaney—"A phenomenal instant when the spirit flares / With pure exhilaration before death— / The good thief in us harking to the promise"[46]—of the recently beatified Saint Edith Stein, the controversial German Jewish convert to Catholicism. Stein, who became a Franciscan nun and died in the gas chambers, gained her first purchase on Christianity through, ironically, her work as a student of and amanuensis to Edmund Husserl, the German father of phenomenology. "The promise" may precisely be innate in the idea of intentionality: the unprovable but sensuous attachment to a greater life than the self. The point regarding Heaney is that he uses the word to underscore a secular philosophy, one heavily implicated in current literary criticism, especially in relation to modernism, but also to stipple in the not unbroken, still perceivable link between philosophy and faith. Significantly, Heaney uses the word "lightenings" not "lightnings," thereby embracing both a liberation of the soul from the body and the scientific phenomenon of illumination rendered in an archaic spelling. The second word, "proleptic," similarly unbends into a variety of very different philosophical postures, as a thinking person can embrace mutually contradictory positions at once. I sense here that Heaney is also deliberately, impishly using a learned discourse to expose the limits of learning. Nonetheless, he has always sent the humble reader scurrying back to the dictionary, a response conditioned in us early on by Heaney's etymological and philological preoccupations in *North*, part of his reckoning with the multiple, much more than double, language tradition of Ulster. Webster's identifies three main meanings for the root noun, "prolepsis," the second meaning having important submeanings. "Prolepsis," therefore, can mean:

> 1. The representation or assumption of a future act of development as being presently existing or accomplished . . . 2.(a) a figure in which a matter is set forth in summary before being stated or related in detail; (b) a figure by which objections are anticipated in order to weaken their force; (c) the use of an attribute to denote a future condition or development as existing or occurrent while it is actually consequential. . . . 3. A conception or belief derived from sense perception and therefore regarded as not necessarily true. [47]

In short, prolepsis can qualify as anything from prophetic moments in the Old Testament anticipating the New, such as the salvation provided by Jesus in the image of the dove who comes to Noah's aid, to bogus or deliberately misleading instances of such prediction. It embraces the use and misuse of faith and reason both. The way in which Heaney uses the word displays the range and accuracy of his formidable vocabulary, but most his ability to tap all at once the multiple, even opposing meanings in a single word. Even on the level of individual words, therefore, the fugacity of single truth is demonstrated.

The word "proleptic" occurs in section vii, the second poem written about Thomas Hardy. This poem and its companion piece both focus on a trick that Hardy as a child, prophetic of the young, reclusive Heaney, played on the grownups responsible for his welfare. In the first poem of this pair, we are told that Hardy laid himself down in a field of sheep and pretended to be dead. The irony of this poem is that in anticipating proleptically his demise, his total disappearance, the young Hardy performs as the protowriter, making himself the vital center of the universe, the omphalos. The poem climaxes in the presentation of waves of consciousness emanating from his resonant center. First we hear that "his small cool brow was like an anvil waiting / For sky to make it sing the perfect pitch / Of his dumb being."[48] That first act of total self-attentiveness and awareness of a vastness radiating out from the self, reminiscent of the fiery energy emanating from Heaney's "Door into the Dark," predicts Hardy's life's course and end: "A ripple that would travel eighty years / Outward from there, to be the same ripple / Inside him at its last circumference."[49] The system of correspondences implied suggests the validity of faith, particularly in the self, a Romantic stance. This isolated but defining moment in childhood is proleptic in the sense of reinforcing faith.

The second poem, placed right beside the first, graphically on the opposing page, creates a more complicated picture. Cast as parenthetical, the poem contains a nihilistic perception perhaps too threatening for full unbracketed consciousness. Less a romantic musing, however, than a factually revised, clear memory, as supplied by a relative of the English poet, this version features Hardy coming face to face with the animal, not the God in himself, by looking the sheep directly in their eyes. What he sees is his own nascent, animal terror of death:

> Their witless eyes and liability
> To panic made him feel less alone,
> Made proleptic sorrow stand a moment
>
> Over him, perfectly known and sure.[50]

These animals reappear in the end as the meek, adoring acolytes who sheepishly trail the famous writer as an old man at a party. To avoid them, their panic, their displacement of fear onto a myth of his immortality, Hardy once again pretends to be dead. This time, however, death does not make him the potent center of creation; it puts him on its edges: "he imagined himself a ghost / And circulated with that new perspective."[51] Less a lightening and more a squaring, a circling, this circumambulation encompasses a nonresonant emptiness. "Proleptic sorrow" can weaken the brunt of death by anticipating it, a different role from prophecy, determining a decidedly different poetry from Romantic.

As it turns out, the very act of looking up "proleptic" in the dictionary produces its own proleptic moment. One of the examples of usage provided for the word cites, of all literature available to the compilers, lines by Denis Devlin; the lines come from his poem "Est Prodest," which, of course, Heaney would know and which, as its erudite title predicts, shares with Milosz an engagement with weighty matters. One can see at a glimpse Devlin's jarring, distinctly European mixture of a postsymbolism reminiscent of but not as extreme as Celan's— elliptical, cryptic, associational—with the discursiveness of Milosz in, say, "Theodicy." One could slice in anywhere in Devlin and find the same essential, modernist effects of disrupted syntax, spliced fragments, atomistic but enjambed lines. The lesson for the reader of Heaney as a historiographer of poetics is that modernism, as the late Eliot illustrates, does not exclude religious belief.

> Frightened antinomies!
> I have wiped example from mirrors

I have brought to heel my shadow—
Soul from her rebel Heavens
My mirror's face and I
Are like no god and me
My death is my life's plumed gnomon,
Is a bride's embrace cruciform.[52]

Devlin's poem ends with the almost double prolepsis of two word coincidences that anticipate Heaney's involvement with the religious issues that have come to suffuse his later work, also the more obviously European bent of these poems. The final, cryptic lines of "Est Prodest" read:

And he will move breathing
Through us wing-linked
Proleptic of what Eden
Quiet blown in air
Lightened as if we were[53]

The poem's last line ends without the conclusive punctuation of a full stop, as the process of salvation is envisaged as going on and on into infinity. To note the co-incidence that Devlin experienced moments of consciousness proleptically, that he experienced as well a freeing within and knew it as a "lightened" sensation, does not, of course, imply a further similarity with Heaney. It does, however, point to a common need to adopt selectively European, stylistic strategies that assist in lever-ing problems closer to home. Heaney, however, stays, both in "Squarings" and in the even more numinous poems of "Glanmore Revisited," closer to a more conser-vative, less self-conscious poetic diction, relying predominantly on the sensory ap-peal of image and metaphor, indicating divergent ontologies while maintaining a continuous, clear narrative line and predisposition toward symbol. Lucidity still enjoys sway, less from Aristotelian principles than from the desire to leave the channels open for illumination.

Having said that, many of the poems in "Squarings" line up in dialogic pairs, like the two Hardy poems, speaking to each other from separate but neighboring pages across the fence of the book's spine. The debate set up, however, while mini-mally discursive in tone, works much more by showing than telling competing ver-sions of felt, interpreted experience. I would like to look at sections i and ii, then viii and ix of the first section, "Lightenings," to demonstrate how this contrapuntal strategy plays out, and how images largely do Heaney's arguing for him. Turning to section i to track the journey of light in its transmutations through the poem is to follow Heaney in a dense, compressed meditation. The poem achieves liftoff im-mediately, its first line announcing its central conflict between light as a vehicle for both faith and nihilism. The dramatically halved line foreshadows the ease with which Heaney in translating Beowulf will adapt to the caesura as a constant in every line. The halved and balanced line was already a habit, a tactic used to pro-duce the cadence of dialogue: "Shifting brilliancies. Then winter light."[54] Those brilliancies, tantalizing shards of transcendence, seduce and caution, being obviously ephemeral. Devoid of such false promise, "winter light" is clear, stark, and constant. The first words of the next enjambed line insert a crucial concept, that the experience following is perceptually framed: "Then winter light / In a doorway, and on the doorstep / A beggar shivering in silhouette."[55] This reprise of the doorway, the frame responsible for the epiphany in "Station Island," where a flood of memory returns the poet to the sensation of maternal love in a contained, domestic setting, concretized in a cup, here signals much more the empty vessel of the earlier poem.

"Squarings" is the juncture where Romanticism in Heaney, I believe, finds its most aggressive revision through a partially embraced modernism. Here the subjective framing of the self no longer works as a unifying assertion. On the contrary, the framing now strips the self of power, leaving it mendicant and emptied of vital substance, a "silhouette," all frame, no flesh. The next line, however, alerts us to an irony in this otherwise despairing perspective: "So the particular judgement might be set." No longer using the frame of subjectivity to unify and essentially create reality in an omnipotent fashion, here the poet frames himself as severely limited, but this ultimate frame is also sketched as the way God sees man. The poem enacts a view of the self from a position of supreme detachment, almost a perch in heaven. Yet to the earthed, forked creature captured by this quick, metaphysical snapshot, the sensation of being so essentially seen and judged feels like total despair: a world devoid of meaning—"Bare wallstead and a cold hearth rained into— / Bright puddle where the soul-free cloud-life roams."[56] In this single compound image of a "bright puddle" over which a cloud passes and is reflected, the reader is sent back to Wordsworth's and Heaney's profound but also evolving relationship with Romanticism, and by historical indirection, modernism.

It is at such moments that Heaney's relationship with Romanticism is explicitly revised. "Soul-free" states a terrible loss, a painful admission, if only for the moment of this particular poem, which claims only partial truth in a long sequence. Nonetheless, Heaney at this moment is asking for a direct comparison to be made between this perception of unmitigated bleakness and Wordsworth's mitigated despair in "I Wandered Lonely as a Cloud." First of all, Wordsworth identifies with the cloud and, for all his aloneness, imbues the cloud with the capacity to observe and frame and idealize "a host of golden daffodils." The golden, waving flowers acquire the coruscation of "sparkling waves"; in fact, they "out-did the sparkling waves in glee, because their vitality inheres, is more than a reflection. So, when they are reflected, "flash upon that inward eye," they can induce albeit the "bliss of solitude" because they once were real. "I gazed—and gazed—but little thought / What wealth to me the show had brought." The more Wordsworth looks, the more consolation he accrues. This is true because Wordsworth retains the ability to fuse totally with the seen thing, jumping over even chasms of destructive, distancing time: "And then my heart with pleasure fills / And dances with the daffodils."[57] For Heaney, from "Station Island" on, such fluent fusions and identifications prove increasing untenable. See how he revises here the Wordsworthian gaze into a perspective bound to absolute solitude, beyond mitigation: "And after the commanded journey, what? / Nothing magnificent, nothing unknown. / A gazing out from far away, alone."[58] Again, however, underneath the despair, the eschewal of fusion, is the hint of an unthinkable identification, a perspective so stripped of corporeality and desire, so totally remote and removed, it might be God. Yet one is forbidden by the language with its nuance and ambiguity to reify this barest brush of the divine. The poem resolutely holds with its nonresolution, embracing bravely the two extremes of belief and atheism. The line "And it is not particular at all"[59] can be read simultaneously as a dismissal of a juvenile belief in the doctrine of the "particular judgement," and as a dismissal, too, of the Romantic doctrine of the self, but also, less in protest and more in faith, as a yielding from, a freeing of the ego. After all, the phrase "soul-free, cloud-life" also holds out such a cold promise. "Free" might imply liberation from the mental torture that a half-belief in the soul creates. Given this precedent of sustained doubleness, the ending is like forked "lightening," totally splitting, indeed cleaving consciousness, itself riven: "Just old truth dawning: there is no next-time-round. / Unroofed scope. Knowledge-freshening wind."[60] In the concluding line, the caesura doubles on itself, creating two halved lines in themselves halved. "Unroofed scope" implies both exposure and opportunity, being gazed at and gazing with a new expansiveness. Similarly a "Knowledge-freshening wind" will chill an already shivering beggar to the bone, especially given its flaying of all hope, but also of old illusions. This radical purgation creates the possibility for belief in something real. The poem ends not entirely rejecting atheism but making way for a new, chaste level of belief, stripped to a naked faith.

These rapid perspectival shifts are born of the dialogism of "Station Island," where, above all, a received body of faith is being perforated through a series of points of view. The confrontation and examination continue, become more and more refined, and are filtered in changing ways into the poetry itself. Indeed this continuous enquiry becomes inseparable from the activity of the poetic imagination; therefore, its first prompts are always feelings. Take the beginning of "Squarings" ii, following directly on the opening poem: an interrogation of outmoded means of spiritual warmth conducted in subzero emotional and philosophical conditions. This second section begins with rapidly telegraphed commands to the self, survival tactics: "Roof it again. Batten down. Dig in."[61] Embodying a steadying purpose, stability is gained from a line that departs from being halved. The tripartite division makes it stable as a three-legged stool. Indeed, the trajectory of this poem seems to be toward a fresh espousal of materialism for sanity's sake. Unmediated transparency, as opposed to the opacity of things, is associated with the alternating perceptions of everything and nothing. This assertion of virile factuality, leading to a stoic honesty reminiscent of "Vain My Visit to Lough Derg," also recalls the spiritual correctives urged by Curtayne, an admirer of that unembellished cry from the Gaelic past. The difference Heaney makes is that he goes beyond this revisionism of a knee-jerk transcendence to make room for the possibility of a new, earned transformation. At this corrective crux, however, this poem from "Squarings" emerges as the sum of urgent imperatives, all directing the self toward the solidity of objects: "Touch the cross-beam, drive iron in a wall."[62] But just as the "cross-beam" hints at a crucifix and abiding conflict, so the freshly dusted-off architectural words, "coping-stone and chimney-breast," are used for their terse but tender articulation of how much feeling human beings invest in objects. Such compound words also reveal, not least through their very hyphenation, the potential for loss between the cracks created by such displacements. While suggesting, therefore, that things may fail us, the words also carry with them the sense of human fortitude, of how well human beings can cope and, in fact, retain hope in their breasts, warm themselves, in the face of intersteller coldness, the inhospitable reality that Tom the archeologist grasped.

"Squarings" ii is a poem about discipline, about resisting false faith, about beginning at the beginning, the purgatorial point of departure in "Station Island." Now Heaney advises himself: "Make your study the unregarded floor," as though looking down while he walks on those Lough Derg stones. His final order to himself, a variation on creating ghosts to confront the self, is contained in the final stanza: "Sink every impulse like a bolt. Secure / The bastion of sensation. Do not waver / Into language. Do not waver in it."[63] Of course, what lurks for the reader behind such desperate measures, as though securing a house for a hurricane, is that the flaying wind of the preceding poem still sweeps through this one. However, this poem argues for inclusiveness of perspective. The floor is "unregarded," underinspected and undervalued because transcendence can be too eagerly sought, found when it's not really there. The "shifting brilliancies" that opened the first poem are circled back to in the ending of the second, where such coruscation, such wavering, is viewed with suspicion, even dread. In that direction can lie not just transcendence but extinction. The most crucial detail of this final command, however, is the way it absolutely links the use of language with the creation or falsification of truth. If Heaney's poems are prayerful, they also obey an inner injunction, adumbrated by the medieval Penitentials, to be truthful. The poem openly rejects plays of transcendence, placing a halo of radiant light around one's own head, becoming too easily transformed to substanceless reflection itself, the soul-free cloud in the bright puddle, not a man still wrestling, as Devlin did, with an opaque body and a transparent idea of God, more permanent than mere reflection.

Sections viii and ix of "Squarings" together provide a culminating moment of religious intuition and skeptical argument. They are also two of the most beautiful, radiant, and lucid poems in the sequence. Section vii has already gained canonic status as a poem on its own, beyond its place in the sequence. While this poem is genuinely one of Heaney's most elegant, creating great complexity through sublime simplicity, one fears that its place of favor may partly result from a simplification, a misapprehension of the poem as being both more Irish and Catholic than the aftertaste of its ironies allows. The poem begins in a way that might locate it within the ambit of an anachronistic cultural nationalism:

> The annals say: when the monks of Clonmacnoise
> Were all at prayers inside the oratory
> A ship appeared above them in the air.[64]

"The annals say" can be heard as Heaney invoking a source of biblical author-ity, but this very distance from a personal voice also begins to register as detach-ment from the miraculous content of the disclosure. Both of these poems, viii and ix, again arranged on facing pages, center on the image of a boat, a vehicle for some significant "Crossing." The poems interrelate, indeed interlock, by means of a cen-tral irony: that the first poem (viii) about Clomacnoise slowly implodes into rela-tive rather than absolute truth, while the second (ix), which takes an actual boat and actual memory as its starting point, travels far less ambiguously because de-parting from solid ground—the boat is beached!—toward transcendence.

The Clonmacnoise poem takes as its starting point a medieval congregation of monks praying, an epicenter of belief. The prayers of these holy men are also, cru-cially, contained within a resonating space, an oratory, a variation on all the enclo-sures Heaney has returned to regularly as spaces for the play of imagination. When the ship appears, therefore, it is both miracle and illusion, a vision in both senses. The poem proceeds to multiply this doubleness into numberless spokes, producing an antidiadem radiating out in interrogating directions. First, the vision partakes of an extraordinary verisimilitude in relation to this world, enough literal detail to plant a seed of doubt concerning the true otherness of this boat, replete with an-chor, rope, and crew. Yet, not to be itself anchored solely in this world, the poem al-lows us to entertain the possibility of true miracle. This process of ascent starts ironically with our observing that the literally overriding conceit of a hovering boat, riding on the surface of the ocean, relegates the monks, and us, to the bottom of the ocean. This submerged position, like that of Ronan's psalter, nods toward perennial perplexity and doubt, the necessary precursors of true faith. On the other hand, the conceit as it is sketched places man in the kind of inveterately needy pos-ture that easily produces optical illusion instead of legitimate vision. When one's eyes are not on the "unregarded floor" but on the too-regarded sky overhead, mis-takes can occur. What we are left with is a mirror image of our world, to the extent that, as the wise abbot says, these supernatural visitors, who like us yearn for an-other world, also cannot survive in it. They are unfit, in fact, for any element other than their own: "This man can't bear our life here and will drown,"[65] says the Ab-bott of an angelic crew member who has "shinned and grappled down the rope"[66] (the same action in the opposite direction as Dante's escape from hell) to release the anchor that has snagged on the altar rails. Again, the implications split and scurry off in opposite directions. Because of the initial anthropomorphic projection, we identify with the visitors and by implication see our lives as finally untenable in the

alien element of our own mortality. On the other hand the poem posits the possibility that all nature, even the so-called supernatural, strives for what it is not, and
therein lies extinction. In this poem, which makes the marvelous ordinary and the
ordinary marvelous, we are left sitting on a line, perhaps the surface of the water,
and wondering in which place we really do belong or whether these realms are divisible at all.

Accordingly, "the man climbed back / Out of the marvelous as he had known
it." [67] This is the ironic ending of the section viii, the first half of this critical dialogue.
The conclusion suggests that our daily world can be perceived as marvelous, if also
perceived as other. In a sense this is what the second poem achieves, this transformation of the ordinary into the marvelous. Following the precedent established in
this sequence by previous dialogues conducted through deliberately paired
poems, this exchange appears to move broadly from the ethereal to the material,
but, of course, this is just an illusion. Nonetheless, section ix begins with the kind of
back-to-bedrock mentality that initiates section ii. The former opens:

> A boat that did not rock or wobble once
> Sat in long grass one Sunday afternoon
> In nineteen forty-one or -two. The heat [68]

"The heat" instantly differentiates the mood here from the chill atheism of section i, where all belief except some almost intolerable, final one is extinguished. Yet
here, where the warm beginning of a life is contemplated rather than its cold end,
there is still a resistance to mere illusion, memory as falsifying palliative. The very
fact that the year is debated, is rendered as inexact, argues for a scrupulous honesty.
This is a true memory; the verisimilitude here is of lived experience, as with the second, revisionist Hardy poem. Echoing, therefore, "Do not waver / Into language.
Do not waver in it," [69] this poem begins with "a boat that did not rock or wobble
once," [70] as distinct from the angelic curragh, of which "the big hull rocked to a
standstill," [71] as though embodying the sensation of vision returning to common
sense. This second boat, too, is not in water but "long grass," an image that carries
us back to "Station Island" and the Ruth-like women who "were wading the young
corn, / Their skirts brushing softly." [72] The seductive sibilance of "long grass"
makes this poem drift slowly back toward the warm sources of a belief that pre-
cedes speech, a faith utterly rooted in the sensation of maternal love. In this poem
Heaney approaches naturally, without philosophical self-consciousness, the totally
embodied but heavenly love Dante ascribes to Beatrice. Perhaps the death of his
mother gives birth to this very early memory of his own life being sustained by
hers. The poem on the surface is a memory of a summer day on the shores of Lough
Neagh, when the poet's mother and her two sisters sat and talked in this stationary
boat together, the poet as a very young child held like a bird in the nest, in the crook
(like the *"wreath"* in "Station Island") of his mother's arm. The poem in other's
hands might have been a memory of simple, creaturely security, but in keeping

with his vision in "Station Island" of the haloed mug, another idealization of containment, this poem too carries with it the shadow of separation, breakage.

The age of the child is crucial and the images, plus the speculation about the year, suggest perhaps two or three: "The heat / . . . Grew redolent of the tweed skirt and tweed sleeve / I nursed on."[73] The image of a child nursing on wool suggests a time after weaning but before a more definitive psychic separation. Of course, as the middle-aged poet laments his "unweaned life" in "Station Island," this dependence on the physical security of the mother and the way the threat of its loss inhibits autonomy is a persistent theme and problem. Here, however, with his mother's actual death between him and "Station Island," a leap is made that was impossible before. The centralizing, luminous, primal image here recalls that in Dante's last canto to the *Paradiso,* which Heaney, as we have seen, has translated. The image of the sucking child is one of the culminating similes there for Dante. Heaney may have been compelled to translate this concluding canto precisely for this simile, which most certainly has an artesian effect, digging down into his own earliest memories. His translated lines, once again, where Dante attempts but shies off from describing the heavenly vision are, to repeat, "And now my speech will not / Match what I remember: an infant's tongue / Milky with breast-milk would be more articulate." This warm, secure, sensuous memory from "Squarings," the kind of religious feeling Brodsky ascribes to Tsvetaeva, may be just such an attempt to describe ideal love, a love anchored in this world, which is assumed, translated like the virgin, into the divine. This tone of earthed transcendence, however, is not sustained. The poem ends with perhaps the most recalcitrant and rooted paradox in Heaney's work, since this literary moment is so grounded in lived experience. Not only is this poem rooted, it is also about a futile rooting for love, the nonproductive suckling of a hungry child on "tweed." This word, with its Scots-Presbyterian tinge and hinting at the carnage of the Battle of the Tweed, anticipates violent rupture, loss.

The poem ends with an equally early countermemory not of security, of being held, but of emptiness and perhaps the nascent belief that beckons beyond and heals that abysmal rift in security, the spiritual opportunity explored in "Clearances." Again, however, Heaney locates this moment of high consciousness in the grounded fact of being a physical being, an actual child, lying back in his mother's arms and looking up at the sky. Suddenly in this moment, a flash out of the depths of memory, the easy, reassuring chatter of his mother and her sisters dies away, and the child is left wide awake and alone:

> Open now as the eye of Heaven was then
> Above three sisters talking, talking steady
> In a boat the ground still falls and falls from under.[74]

So easy is it to violate the ineffable complexity of this poetic moment, one hesitates to venture into crass paraphrase, except to suggest all the multiple directions in which this ending gestures: toward a recognition of uninterrupted vastness, looming both as vacuum and heaven; toward a sensation of the steadiness of the women not availing finally to withstand the rocking of a boat, which inevitably must leave solid ground, must go to sea, according to its purpose, as a child must separate from the breast; toward a sense of how this final rocking at the end both returns the poet to his mother's arms and simulates the grief produced by her death; toward the sensation of falling and falling through space placing the poet somehow in the ship sighted at Clonmacnoise; toward the glint of possibility that the unreal, so apparently antithetical to the solidity and warmth of human love, might possibly be innate in it, as real as Beatrice.

10

Heaney and Milosz

Striving Toward Being

SIMILAR TO HIS FIRST ENCOUNTER with Dante, Heaney had a moment of both kindred feeling and prophetic sensation when, in the seventies, in Berkeley, he heard Robert Pinsky read a translation of a Milosz poem, "Incantation." The poem immediately made Heaney aware of the Anglocentric provincialism of the aesthetic climate he had grown up in, one fed largely on the outmoded pieties of British poetics. It is precisely these conventions that Milosz flouts in this poem, which, while not devoid of imagery, unabashedly plumps for statement. Here is how the poem opens:

> Human reason is beautiful and invincible.
> No bars, no barbed wire, no pulping of books.
> No sentence of banishment can prevail against it.
> It establishes the universal ideas in language,
> And guides our hand so we write Truth and Justice
> With capital letters, lie and oppression with small.[1]

There is a lack of hesitation in speaking directly here of "Truth and Justice" in "capital letters" and of relying on the patent failure of the world to live up to this towering ideal as enough pathos for the poem to rest on. Milosz presents Heaney with a way to be political, which, in its unabashed deployment of the discursive, is alien to the legacy of English-language modernism. Heaney is already positing in print that even the highly evolved practices of modernism, with its emphasis on object and image, are somewhat obsolete: "Many contemporaries writing in English have been displaced from an old at-homeness in their mother tongue and its hitherto world-defining poetic heritage."[2] In this essay, "The Impact of Translation," Heaney begins to pencil in the growing attraction of eastern European and Russian poets for certain English language poets, who, "with a kind of hangdog intimation of desertion, . . .have felt compelled to turn their gaze East and have been encouraged to concede that the locus of greatness is shifting away from their language."[3] What separates these eastern poets from the "ironists and dandies and reflexive talents"[4] of the West is precisely the way the pressure of unmediated reality makes these stalwart witnesses "introduce us to new literary traditions but also to link the new literary experience to a modern martyrology, a record of courage and sacrifice which elicits our unstinted admiration."[5]

The word "martyrology" immediately makes the reader familiar with Irish history think of Pearse. In fact, the theme of martyrdom threads back in Heaney's prose writings to an approving mention of Patrick Pearse in "The Poems of the Dispossessed Repossessed," his review of Kinsella's translations in *An Duanaire*. As a Northern Catholic accused of inadequate politics by those on both sides of the sectarian divide, Heaney is aware of the minefield to be crossed in even approaching Pearse. He is accordingly circumspect. Heaney refers to Kinsella's "advocacy of Pearse as a translator," which is "based on thoroughly literary criteria—fidelity to the originals, lack of interference with the texts."[6] Yet, Heaney adds, "one senses that Kinsella would see this integrity as the natural concomitant of Pearse's extreme, uncompromised, and by now unfashionable political ideals." Heaney manages, therefore, to lodge an endorsement essentially of a poetic rather than any particular political agenda, especially a violent one. By appealing to certain Eastern European poets whose courage exhibits itself by not colluding with totalitarianism, Heaney occupies a stance against oppression as he knows it best, as the pressure to endorse a politics of violence: "It is not so much their procedures on the page which are influential as the composite image which has been projected of their conduct. That image, congruent with the reality, features a poet tested by dangerous times. What is demanded is not any great public act of confrontation or submission, but rather a certain self-censorship, an agreement to forge, in the bad sense, the uncreated conscience of a race."[7] That is precisely what Heaney in "The Flight Path" is being asked, nay told, to do by his former school mate, to write the text to accompany the ongoing translation of Ireland into itself and in the process to censor himself. Heaney's resisting the fascistic demands of the terrorist, an act of defiance and a bid for freedom, is also an emulation of these poets of Eastern Europe. Invoking the value of poetic courage by means of these poets, Heaney not only avoids the misunderstandings that can readily arise from addressing his local situation but also locates the moral nub of the question.

The grave consequences of such explicit collusion move more and more to the forefront of Heaney's consciousness. Embracing poets who come to him through translation heightens these matters of conscience, the act of translation itself creating an anxiety about fidelity, as we have observed with Denis Florence MacCarthy. Personal accountability has been Heaney's focus from "Station Island" on. He no doubt sees a similar rectitude and anxiety in Dante, who, for example, toward the morally definitive conclusion of the *Inferno* at the beginning of canto xxxii, the penultimate, asks the muses to help him, "lest from the truth my wandering verses stray."[8] One recalls that even the Irish Penitentials grant immunity from the sin of pride to anyone who simply speaks the truth, though such unembellished, measured, and precise speech is difficult to achieve in poetry. Dante has begun this con-

cluding canto on a note of marked self-doubt as a poet, as though poetry itself finds
it difficult, if not impossible, to approach the grotesque truth of this final circle of
hell. Dante's opening lines to the canto muse wistfully,

> Had I but rhymes rugged and harsh and hoarse,
> Fit for the hideous hole on which the weight
> Of all those rocks grinds downward course by course,
>
> I might press out my matter's juice complete;
> As 'tis, I tremble lest the telling mar
> The tale; for, truly, to describe the great
>
> Fundament of the world is very far
> From being a task for idle wits at play,
> Or infant tongues that pipe *mama, papa.*[9]

Dante, as usual, lays out the problem with clarity. The adequate poetic, moral,
and developmental position from which to write is almost impossible to inhabit.
On the one hand, one cannot be a replica of Heaney's decadent, sophisticated western "ironists and dandies and reflexive talents," the "idle wits at play" of Dante's
poem. On the other hand, the naïveté and rudimentary language skills of the babe
are inadequate from the opposite developmental extreme on the spectrum. One
must "regret one's unweaned life" and grow up fast, because no naïf can meet these
moral and verbal challenges, which also require a break with verbal foppery, effeminacy, in favor of "rhymes rugged and harsh and hoarse." Heaney is champi-
oning a Spartan aesthetic, not unrelated to the virile, spiritual values Curtayne
privileges. Heaney deploys this pared-down style in "Mycenae Lookout," indeed
throughout *The Spirit Level.* Dante's concern at the end of the *Inferno,* to find a language adequate to a repellent environment, is echoed in "The Flight Path." Heaney,
just prior to quoting Dante from canto xxxiii, sets the hellish context of the Dirty
Protest with, again: "The red eyes were the eyes of Ciaran Nugent / Like something
out of Dante's scurfy hell, / Drilling their way through the rhymes and images."
The reality, like that of his valued Eastern European poets, and Dante in the midst
of brutally divided Florence, determines, literally colors, incarnadines language.

Similarly, it is to these writers from "the Soviet Republics and the Warsaw Pact
countries, whose poetry not only witnesses the poet's refusal to lose his or her cultural memory, but also testifies thereby to the continuing efficacy of poetry itself as
a necessary and fundamental human act,"[10] that the Irish poet in English turns
rather than to poets admired for other reasons from the English language tradition.
Heaney underlines the limitations imposed on poetry by "England's island status,
its off-centre European positioning, its history of non-defeat and non-invasion
since 1066."[11] He ascribes other limitations to poetry in the United States where a
"grant-aided pluralism of fashions and schools, a highly amplified language of
praise which becomes the language of promotion and marketing"[12] prevail, as well
as "a conditional, indeterminate mood,"[13] in poetry, conditioned not least by a hot-

house environment opposite to the raw reality that necessitates the creation of Milosz's direct and urgent "Incantation." History, as much as the artist himself, is responsible for those precious, necessary qualities of the "creditable, desolating and resuscitative"[14] that Heaney finds in Milosz and other Eastern European poets.

Milosz's struggle to integrate the religious and poetic impulses offers the closest analogy I know to Heaney's. In Heaney's latest poetry collection, *District and Circle*, there is an elegy to Milosz. The title of the poem, "Out of This World," gestures in two directions, high and low, toward where the Polish poet may be in death and where he was in life, some extraordinary place, quite out of this world.[15] In the essay "Atlas of Civilization" Heaney refers to Milosz as "sky-worthy,"[16] high praise. I believe Heaney respects and lauds this value because it is not at the expense of the Antaeus in Milosz. In an exchange with Thomas Merton from one of the letters collected in *Striving Towards Being*, Milosz notes, addressing Merton, "You said very justly that I am best when I touch the earth, nature, when I am vegetal."[17] This ferocious devotion to the earth, the "vegetal," forms the tangible center of Milosz's *The Issa Valley*, about growing up in Lithuania. Moreover, it is this autochthonous authenticity combined paradoxically with a sky-worthiness that creates his strong link with Heaney. In a review of Milosz, Heaney refers with apparent perversity to Milosz as "secular." This piece, entitled "Secular and Millennial Milosz" is the last essay, the last word, so to speak, in Heaney's selected prose, *Finders Keepers*.[18] As Heaney regularly heightens our consciousness of language in his poems by deploying words in a way counterintuitive to ordinary usage, so he is instructing us with his incongruous choice of "secular" to describe Milosz. This word is meant to ally itself with "millennial," one of its arcane meanings, and subconsciously to rub up against etymologically related words from the Latin mass: *seculae seculorum*, that is, "world without end." Heaney is presenting Milosz to us as a lay person who in his fortunate longevity renders an epoch to us, interpreting history as a priest or rabbi would sacred text. He is both hieratic and ordinary. It is within the vibrating space of this double perspective that a poetic inclusive of religious instincts but resistant to religious posturing finds its conception.

As Milosz has been a guide for Heaney, so Merton was a guide for Milosz. As Merton revealed to him, so Milosz reveals to Heaney that the dialectic of faith embraces as many negations as affirmations. This paradox is possibly the key to the Lough Derg puzzle. As the correspondence between Milosz and Merton discloses differences as well as similarities, so Heaney's relationship with Milosz is far from imitative. Indeed, as Robert Faggen, the editor of the correspondence between Merton and Milosz points out, the order of power shifts midway in the relationship, with Milosz acting much more as a mentor to Merton. The two make a surprising but utterly logical pair: the monk who is a poet, the poet with monastic leanings. One can easily use imagination to insert a third, monastically minded, invisible listener to this dialogue: Heaney "bent over a prie-dieu." Milosz, in fact, expresses a profound respect and affinity for the solitude his friend Merton espoused by entering the closed, Trappist order. Merton, during the ten-year interval of the friendship, from 1958 to 1968, when he died, is struggling, however, to find a way to translate his faith into activism, being particularly exercised about nuclear proliferation. Although naturally predisposed to seeing a harmony between prayer and poetry, Milosz is also increasingly dubious of the efficacy and honesty of language and contemplates entering a period of complete silence. Both men share an interest in Buddhism and an attraction to an idea of resonant emptiness. As Faggen describes this important connection: "Guided by Milosz, Merton saw the vocation of solitude as leading to that 'emptiness' in which one 'does not find points upon which to base a difference between himself and others,' a nothingness in which all being and love begin."[19] The reader of Heaney thinks of those lines from "Clearances," the concluding lines to sonnet vii and the opening lines to sonnet viii, linking the two poems in a sustained meditation on the opportunity for belief created by death, the greatest threat to belief:

> The space we stood around had been emptied
> Into us to keep, it penetrated
> Clearances that suddenly stood open.
> High cries were felled and a pure change happened.[20]

So sonnet vii concludes. Immediately, sonnet viii begins:

> I thought of walking round and round a space,
> Utterly empty, utterly a source.[21]

The word "clearances" with its painful resonance within Irish history, particularly that of Northern Ireland, referring to the confiscating and clearing of land for the purposes of plantation, inserts the cruel arbitrariness of history and death into this meditation centering around awe. The central paradox of loss and gain, emptiness and fullness, is presented on many levels simultaneously. As a poet who cannot extricate history from the personal, who also cannot extricate faith from politics or finally from the self, Heaney, too, has been led naturally into conversation with Milosz. This conversation, which at this point in literary history has not yet surfaced in the form of letters, is embedded, at least on Heaney's side, in his later poems. Compare, for example, Milosz's observation to Merton that we live "in a period when the image accepted by the majority is clear: empty Sky, no joy, stone wasteland, life ended by death."[22] This is the chilling world view expressed in Heaney's opening poem to "Squarings" ii, where "winter light" dominates the spirit. Heaney, as we have seen, is similarly susceptible to seeing nothingness as just that, rather than a radiant space.

As a poet and a man, Milosz wrestles with faith and despair both. Referring to his relinquishment of a diplomatic position as an envoy of the People's Poland in the United States, a mouthpiece for a monolithic ideology, he confesses to Merton in 1960, "Ten years ago I escaped from America, being afraid of life without purpose and of acedia."[23] Milosz is convinced that conflict is innate, that opposites are inseparable and necessary for each other, though also conducive of steady pain, and poetry. This is not a poetry feeding cynically off faith, it is a poetry steeped in contradiction, not only able to bear, but bound to bear such torque in its language to qualify as art. Milosz expresses to Merton the value he finds in Simone Weil's belief that faith occurs only in conditions that systematically deny it: "for her everything was Necessity and Grace operated so to say through what seems to us as pure impossibility and contradiction."[24] Milosz is writing about this principle in the broader context of questioning Merton's romanticization of nature, his pantheistic tendencies. I see Heaney as particularly attentive to this debate, given his tendency from the beginning to associate both romantic possibility and evil foreboding with nature. Following the span of this decade-long correspondence between Merton and Milosz, the reader comes to sense that there is perhaps no means other than poetry by which to explore faith and no poetry for these men that does not explore faith. On the one hand, the maintenance of metaphor seems paramount, though its separation from religion untenable. Also, nonbelief seems an intrinsic part of belief, the very contradiction Weil sees as necessary for the surprise intervention of grace. Is there any form of linguistic utterance that can accommodate such boundless complexity and contradiction other than poetry? Is there any form of utterance other than poetry that encompasses a flux of meanings without end, more process than final statement? Milosz, trying to describe a Marxism not without positive qualities, in contrast to the system he found ignorantly demonized in cold war America, says Marxism has a Heraclitan energy. Section xxvii of "Squarings" begins, "Everything flows." It is this flow of a life of dialectical, spiritual search that Heaney and Milosz both seek to express in poetry.

Nothing, however, is further from Milosz's intentions than being perceived as or behaving as a "Catholic" writer, and that is key to his appeal for Heaney, given the sectarian pressure the Irish poet has suffered. In his exchange with Merton, Milosz is scathing about writers with such a limiting and, as he sees it, antiquated tag. In responding to Merton's *Sign of Jonas*, Milosz begins by establishing the premise that "Catholic literature rarely comes across the barrier to reach domains of 'lay' literature."[25] Merton's book also fails to make this passage for Milosz, who is totally dismissive of conventionally Catholic writers such as Graham Greene and François Mauriac, who "belong to the past (in them religion is added, as a deus ex machina)."[26] The desired aim, therefore, is for religion to be completely integrated with ordinary life. Milosz shares with Merton, however, a fear that, because everyday language can impose such deceptive dichotomies, perhaps poetry is the only use of words subtle and inclusive enough not to effect such falsifying splits. For Milosz explicit speech about belief is anathema: "I do not know whether by using the highest name we do not commit an act against piety."[27] For these reasons, to stay indirect and disguised, he is glad to go unrecognized as some form of Catholic by what he has written: "In any case few people suspect my basically religious instincts and I have never been ranged among 'Catholic writers.' Which, strategically, is perhaps better. We are obliged to bear witness? But of what? That we pray to have faith? This problem—how much we should say openly is always in my thoughts."[28]

As his questions proliferate, the solutions they inversely beg become increasingly both untenable and tenable. The interrogative mode, both naming an issue and wondering what to do with it, is not that far removed from the means by which poetry investigates problems. There are two points in the correspondence where Milosz, sketching how to speak accurately of faith, actually can be seen as describing poetry in his terms, so much are the two realms coterminous. He speaks of a hypothetical book that has never been written treating religion with "great simplicity: what I believe and not why I believe but how I believe, namely to draw a contour around what is hardly formulable, by images taken from a religious experience."[29] Notice his deft movement from "what" to "how," doctrine to process, ultimately, dynamically, "to draw a contour around what is hardly formulable." How is it again that Heaney puts it? "Circumambient"? Then in a second instance, echoing this attachment to poetry as spiritual process and with brutal honesty finding Merton failing to achieve this level in *The Sign of Jonas,* Milosz demands "answers to theological questions but answers not abstract as in theological treatise, just on the border between the intellect and our imagination."[30] Indeed, in another letter Milosz refers to theologians who "swim in the vague."[31] Poetry is appealed to primarily for its exactitude, integrative energy, and resistance to stasis, all chief Mandelstamian values. This is very close to the poetic on display in "Squarings," where "swimming in the vague" is strictly forbidden: "Do not waver into language, do not waver in it." What better way to describe these poems by Heaney, drawing as much on philosophical discourse as luminous memory, poems that flow from one to another, defying boundaries, than as an exploration of the "border between intellect and imagination."

Milosz would probably be of less use to Heaney if they did not also share certain temperamental and cultural similarities. It is interesting, given Frazier's description of Heaney as "weak of faith" that Milosz describes himself to Merton similarly: "It does not mean I am tepid but of little faith and loathing of my nature (which is a pretext not to see certain sins)."[32] This parenthetical comment might serve as a trenchant criticism of "Station Island," where one feels a blanket self-loathing may in fact obscure certain more common failings. Milosz, too, laments at length to Merton an ineradicable egotism in his nature. He even sees with his inveterately complicating eye how Marxism aims to uproot this particular evil, observing that the "Marxist psychology of bourgeois individualism is not too far wrong when it condemns the perpetual turning around and around in circles of guilt and self-analysis."[33] These closing words might serve, especially the reference to turning round and round, as a description of the ritual movements and mental gyrations performed in "Station Island." Yet, Milosz, aware of this pitfall of individualism, staunchly resists the opportunity in Catholic practice to relieve the individual of personal responsibility, Heaney's abiding concern in "Station Island." In a diatribe about Russia determined by, indeed probably blinded by, his own anger as a Pole toward that country, Milosz accuses Russian soldiers during the Stalinist occupation of Poland of killing the innocent with a sense of sin but not guilt, guilt entailing personal responsibility in his eyes.[34] The primary guilt that Milosz confesses to Merton is for his self-exile from Poland. After he resigned his position in Washington, D.C., he first moved to Paris and later to Berkeley, a pattern of migration echoed by Heaney's moves to Wicklow and Dublin from Belfast, then on to Cambridge. What might catch Heaney's ear, too, in this disclosure of guilt is the poet's egotism behind it: "It is possible that I am guilty of having left Poland, guilty toward my own possibilities and gifts. Perhaps I paralyzed myself in that way."[35] Such a finely honed guilt suffuses almost every word of "Station Island."

Only a poet with the background of someone like Milosz can understand what it means to come from places like Ulster and Poland where Catholicism is absolutely welded, as though obeying the commonality of ship building in each economy, to nationalism. So untranslatable is this fused identity that Milosz hesitates even to broach the subject with Merton, born in relatively secular France and now living in a monastery in Gesthemene, Kentucky, a life of clear demarcations. For Milosz the history of Poland is impossible to unbraid from the history of religion. He explains the brutal suppressions of the Soviets by reference to an ancient rivalry between the Orthodox and Roman faiths. We can almost feel Milosz's exhaustion in having to fill in so many blanks for Merton:

> I don't know whether you are familiar with the history of the Greek-Catholic (Uniate) Church. It is strange to think that big planetary issues of today depended once on the success or failure of what Russia considered the greatest threat to its power: the spread of the Church fostered by the Vatican and the Poles. The last act was staged in 1944/45 when the Soviet authorities converted by force the last areas where that Church was rooted and killed its bishops.[36]

Imagine Heaney similarly trying to trace for some sophisticated but culturally remote interlocutor a fused narrative from Cromwell to Northern loyalism and the correlative and opposite justification of Catholic loyalty on the Republican side. Both poets, however, also share a determination not to be determined absolutely by the weight of such histories. Speaking of Russia but expressing a broader aversion, Milosz rejects the efficacy of religious or political martyrdom for the sake of the nation: "A collective body, a human society, cannot be the Saviour. A dream about collective purity achieved thanks to collective suffering is just a dream and in practice it leads to bestiality."[37] One can imagine the writer of "Punishment" assenting to this axiom.

The correspondence between Milosz and Merton is a revelation of the latitude for doubt and honesty that this more intellectual, more catholic form of the faith allows. How liberating to hear Milosz confessing with perfect candor that his confessions are chronically imperfect: "The trouble is I have never been used to frankness. I go very rarely to confession, once every few years. I do not know how to do that and it seems to me afterwards that I was lying."[38] Even more, to hear a distinguished monk confess, "I think we are both grasping something important, that cannot be said. I have made far too many affirmations, and while I hold to them, they do not affirm what I have intended, and they cannot. I think that I have never reached my final choice or stated it. I will end up on your side in metaphysical torment."[39] Not making the "final choice" or stating it becomes commensurate, perhaps the sine qua non, of a serious and honest spiritual posture in the world. Yet the continued effort to press language closer to this ineffable truth that torments and eludes articulation remains unavoidable and irresistible. Milosz in Paris, surrounded by an intellectual communism dedicated to the existential proposition that "God is dead," felt even more alienated from that philosophy than from the doctrinal certainties of the Church. Letting go of a principle of divine origin entirely is an odious, repellent option for him, particularly for the consequences of such chaos and bleakness on art. Writing from Paris in 1960, Milosz, speaking from intense alienation, explains to Merton, "If I cling to such people as you, in spite of my weak faith, it is because I am revolted against that complete craziness one observes today in art and literature and which reflects a more general madness."[40]

Heaney, given his ambition to explore all the metaphysical options, the search on display in "Squarings," also rejects the "complete craziness" into which the relativism and fragmentation of modernism can ultimately devolve. His retention of form betrays this need to retain an ordering principle, one that hovers between the passionate indeterminacies of Stevens, yet still beckons toward romantic unities and the sublime form of Dante. In "Station Island" Heaney discovers how far he has traveled from his catechismic, obedient childhood. In "Squarings" he discovers how much he is still at home in the heart of that early belief, while never being reconciled fully in his head. Milosz echoes this continuous condition of believing and not being able categorically to affirm belief in "Hope," an early, frequently anthologized poem. Interestingly, faith in the existence of the world carries with it, through an aura bestowed by language, faith in a world beyond. It is like the mirror world that appears in Clonmacnoise and affirms the world we are in:

Hope is with you when you believe
The earth is not a dream but living flesh,
That sight, touch, and hearing do not lie,
That all things you have ever seen here
Are like a garden looked at from a gate.

You cannot enter. But you're sure it's there.
Could we but look more clearly and wisely
We might discover somewhere in the garden
A strange new flower and an unnamed star.

Some people say we should not trust our eyes,
That there is nothing, just a seeming,
These are the ones who have no hope.

They think the moment we turn away
The world, behind our backs, ceases to exist,
As if snatched up by the hands of thieves.[41]

This garden is poised delicately by the language between a real verdant place and an allegorical Garden of Eden. When human consciousness ceases to believe it is responsible for this creation, the entity that does not vanish is both biological and metaphysical. By asserting belief in the independence of this life, prior even to the prime mover of Coleridgean imagination, Milosz in fact shows a way to free the ordering principle of religious belief from Romanticism and its compensations for religion. Yet this is a poem in which poeticity in a way reminiscent of Mandelstam almost replaces consciousness, for the independent existence asserted is dependent on a perception that both affirms and denies its reality. Notice the end stop of the first line with the word "believe": "Hope is with you when you believe." The line structure almost makes hope dependent exclusively on a subjective experience. Then as the language unrolls into the next line it is as though the carpet itself has been whisked from under us and rolled up. The enjambment reads, "Hope is with you when you believe / The earth is not." This negation in turn is overturned as the second line continues: "The earth is not a dream but living flesh." The somersaults performed as the syntax unrolls, much like the multiple conversions from dream to reality in the *Tractatus,* simulate exactly the affirmations and negations necessary to the dialectical process of creating a faith, which does not banish reason but integrates it with intuition. Poetry in this register, balancing belief and skepticism but never suppressing the ache in the heart and glint in the mind (or is it the reverse?) for total affirmation provides a model for Heaney, who during this formative decade of his career, is also in "metaphysical torment."

Milosz, however, offers no easy answers to the dilemma of how poetry should address the moral atrocities of this century. Two accessible, chatty passages from his late collection of prose poems and reflections, *Road-side Dog,* make it clear that there are no simple options. To start from the pole of religion carries the risk of appearing to suffer less conflict and doubt than is the case: "Yet the religious content of my poems is not the result of design by a believer; it grew out of my doubts, turmoil and despair, as they searched for a form. . . . Thus my resistance to being squeezed into the rubric of the 'Catholic poet' was well founded."[42] To set out from the pole of a nationalism saturated with religiosity is even more falsifying, perhaps damning. Significantly, in describing this danger for the poet Milosz refers by example to Ireland: "It is understandable that there are those who prefer nothing to religion, especially religion with nationalistic baggage (Bosnia, Northern Ireland). There is ample experience to show that men envelope themselves in sublime goals, purity and the nobility of a highfalutin spiritual domain, in order to pretend they don't know what their hands are doing."[43] It may well be that, as Heaney claims, the success of "Incantation" is due to its emphatic privileging of life over literature, "that this poem was written by somebody who resisted the Nazi occupation of

Poland and had broken from the ranks of the People's Republic after the war and paid for the principal and pain of all that with a lifetime of exile and self-scrutiny."[44] Nonetheless, Milosz, according to the record of his six Eliot Norton Lectures in *The Witness of Poetry,* has no pat formula for a poetic beyond a rebuttal of a modernism inapplicable to the precise historical circumstances he inherits. He readily makes the analogy between what history wreaked on his country, his consciousness, and Dante's *Inferno:* "Thus one can say that what occurred in Poland was an encounter of an European poet with the hell of the twentieth century, not hell's first circle, but a much deeper one."[45] Milosz has just been describing in lecture 5, "Ruin and Poetry," the complete severance from an otherwise continuous link with European culture that the Nazi occupation and the Holocaust in Poland effected. It is a rupture that has limited but discrete similarities with the suppression of Irish culture under Cromwell and the continued trauma epitomized by the Great Famine. So Milosz easily assumes the morally beleaguered Dante's skin, as Heaney has. For, Milosz, too, however, the assumption of a Dantesque persona proliferates rather than solves problems. Heaney in "The Impact of Translation" makes the critical point for understanding his approach to Milosz and the Eastern European poets, that "Pound and Eliot and Joyce may have regarded themselves as demolitionists of sorts but from a later perspective they turned out to be conservationists, keeping open lines to the Classical inheritance of European literature."[46] Again, Heaney's tone is hard to decipher, especially around that word "conservationists." As a conservationist and an iconoclast both, Milosz points to the need for both continuity and disruption for poetry to do its work.

The place where Milosz most elaborates this nonformulaic, contrarian negotiation of tradition is in *The Witness of Poetry.* The series of lectures that constitute the book were given at Harvard in 1981–82. These were, as we have seen, crucial years for Northern Ireland and Heaney, being just prior to "Station Island." Heaney, who taught at Harvard for a semester in 1979, did not begin a five-year contract with the university until December 1982; therefore, he did not necessarily hear each Milosz lecture as it was delivered. It is unthinkable, though, that the Irish poet would not have read all of them as soon as possible, maybe before they assumed book form. Milosz, in the fourth lecture, "A Quarrel with Classicism," clearly registers a set of imperatives behind his hard-fought poetic that separates it from modernism on this central question of the relationship with the past, particularly the question of what past and whose past, does one emulate, if any. Of course, there is no single attitude toward the past held by modernists, a falsely homogeneous term. Kevin Whelan makes the distinction between left-wing and right-wing modernists, the former lamenting a breakup of tradition, the latter seeing this fragmentation as a freeing into style.[47] Milosz departs from both these political wings by not espousing that which links them: a foregrounded reflexiveness about language deriving from a dislocated, fragmented historical moment. For Milosz, such studied self-consciousness militates against what Heaney will call a "transitive" effect in poetry, the same value contained in Mandelstam's appeal to "transmutability." Despite the adversarial tone of Milosz's title, his essay far from urges a dismissal of classicism. It is a "quarrel" indeed, ongoing, tough, tense, poised between equally compelling poles. Milosz ends the essay by carefully weighing his position: "My aim here has been to indicate a contradiction that resides at the very foundation of the poet's endeavor. . . . Today it is difficult to escape the awareness of an internal tension between imperatives. Such tension does not invalidate my definition of poetry as 'a passionate pursuit of the Real.' On the contrary it gives it more weight."[48] As Milosz debates the respective merits of an adherence to classicism and a shift toward iconoclasm, he must weigh the necessity of inherited forms and conventions for reaching through to reality.

No easy answer is possible. Milosz is very aware of the inauthenticity of inherited forms. His guiding principle in this fraught argument is to be on the side of all that preserves the possibility for clarity, a classical value. Having said that he resided for a time in a lower circle of hell, he not only resorts to allusion and convention, but also points to the ineradicable, paradigmatic fictionality of Dante's hell. This observation is part of an extremely delicate, brave discussion of Holocaust poems:

> Next to the atrocious facts, the very idea of literature seems indecent, and one doubts whether certain zones of reality can ever be the subject of poems or novels. The tortures of the damned in Dante's *Inferno* were, after all, invented by the author, and their fictitious character is made apparent by form. They do not appear raw, as do tortures in documentary poems. On the other hand, because they use rhyme and stanzas, documentary poems belong to literature and one may ask, out of respect for those who perished, whether a more perfect poetry would not be a more appropriate monument than poetry on the level of facts.[49]

We are back to the dilemma Dante limns himself at the end of the *Inferno* about the failure both of sophisticated and untutored language to meet horror. Milosz even understates the fictionality of Dante's work, how dependent it is on convention, being spliced, as we have seen, with the *Aeneid* and, by implication, the entire genre of underworld literature, including the *Tractatus*. Milosz, at the other end of the spectrum, is basing his judgment about Holocaust poems on the work of Michal Borwicz, "a veteran of the Polish resistance."[50] In his book, *Les Ecrits des condamnes a mort sous l'occupation allemande,* on the literature of prisons and concentration camps, Borwicz, according to Milosz, shows how these writers "belong stylistically to the pre-war period, but at the same time . . . try to express 'the new' which cannot be grasped by any of the available notions and means of expression."[51] Resorting to his own metaphor, Milosz describes this poetry as reading "like a mute who tries in vain to squeeze some articulate sound out of his throat," a trope with postcolonial resonance.[52] Contrary to the expectations of some, an unmediated encounter with the too real can lead, according to Milosz, to expression that is highly mediated, indeed warped, by convention and cliché. The bind, therefore, is that convention both enables and hampers translation of the real, that distance both blurs and sharpens focus. On the whole, Milosz comes down on the side of time attentively used as a clarifier: "a glass wall of conventions rises between a poet and reality, conventions never visible until they recede into the past."[53]

This perception explains precisely the cultural, heuristic end served by the intertextual writing of Lough Derg. Not only does inherited form and convention appear to be needed to give full expression to the site, but time, detachment also from the former strategies employed, recognizing them for what they are. Milosz's long historical view enables him also to relegate to an ephemeral convention the dominant tone of pessimism in the poetry of our time. Yet it is not enough, however great the temptation, simply to cave in to the inevitable mediation of convention: "If this is so, then let us respect the rules of the game as adopted by consensus and appropriate to a given historical period, and let us not advance a rook as if it were a knight. In other words, let us make use of conventions aware that they are conventions and no more than that."[54] Fighting always the decadent lure of a "surrender to merely graceful writing,"[55] the ever-present temptation, incidentally, for a poet with Heaney's facility, Milosz teaches that a higher, purer purpose has to be kept steadily in view. He reminds us through Borwicz's work, albeit one man's scholarly research, that the only voices who succeeded in writing the Holocaust were children. Their expression displays "a realism naïve yet sober, and through its soberness, evocative."[56] It is important that unmediated reality can continue to correct high art, the conventions that come to define and calcify into classicism. Here, for example, children of the Holocaust are afforded the power to throw into doubt the great Dante's judgment about the articulacy of babes.

No one could be a better model for the magical combination of the childlike and the wise than Milosz, who does indeed have in his voice that mixed quality of the "naïve yet sober," the tone of these direct and simple but learned lectures, throughout which the theme of the child weaves in and out. The reader of Heaney can readily see how all these ruminations by Milosz would strike the Irish poet with such revelatory force. They drill down instantly into the core of his problems in constituting a poetic. Not only is there a great deal of common experience, primarily of being subject to the pressures of their respective histories, tragic to different degrees, but also there is the moral imperative to communicate these tragic truths particularized by history and geography to a world for whom they seem, for different reasons, invisible and marginal. Milosz begins his lectures with this poignant observation, that no one seems to know Poland and, most of all, to know that Polish poetry exists. Almost directly replicating the cultural nationalist efforts of the Irish in the nineteenth century, Milosz, earlier in his life, dictated (for the sake of expediency) his massive and learned tome, *The History of Polish Literature*, just to be sure the world would have such a record. He opens his first Eliot Norton lecture by observing that "the literary map of Europe, as it presented itself to the West, contained until recently numerous blank spots."[57] He maintains that the "white space" on the map of Europe to the east of Germany "could have borne the inscription *ubi leones* (Where the lions are), and that domain of wild beasts included such cities as

Prague (mentioned only sometimes because of Kafka), Warsaw, Budapest, and Belgrade."[58] *Ubi leones* might be another way of saying "beyond the pale," the expression that encapsulates the perceived barbarity of Ireland to English eyes.

Where Milosz's powerful reimagining of the European inheritance most touches upon Heaney's own concerns, however, is in this imperative to blend the childlike and wise, the private and public, the raw and the transformed, in proportions acceptable both to the demands of history and to the individual poetic conscience. When Heaney first encounters Milosz in Berkeley, the Irish poet has the highly mediated *North* behind him and has gone on to *Field Work,* with its greater tangibility and tucked away, "hutched" privacies, in contrast to the burden of public responsibility carried by *North.* These two buckets, of the poet's responsibility both to the rapt, honest child in the self and the vexed, skeptical adult, have been carried by Heaney for his whole career, leaning for a time more in one direction, then correcting his overall balance by leaning more toward the other. In 1980, therefore, with *Station Island,* with its thorough reevaluation, and the *Haw Lantern,* with its transformation of personal loss, ahead of him, we can only assume that Heaney must have been listening intently to Milosz as a guide.

Milosz treats as sacred the childlike predisposition in the self to believe; he sees this innocence, what his *Treatise on Poetry* calls "melody," as perhaps the most important asset for the poet to protect. Indeed, this is Hardy's song of the "darkling thrush," as highly prized as it is seen as threatened by Heaney. Indeed, Milosz's preserved accessibility to the domain of childhood (so similar to Heaney's with his youthful propensity for hiding in pea drills and the hollowed-out boles of trees) enables him to extol the need for a sense of protection throughout life, and to articulate the way in which poetry can provide it. Protection is the balm this century has eliminated: "The twentieth century is a purgatory in which the imagination must manage without the relief that satisfies one of the essential needs of the human heart, the need for protection."[59] It is this cruel weaning, beginning with the protection of childhood, that Heaney faces in his purgatory on "Station Island." What this return to a sacred site from childhood also elicits, however, is the dormant belief that once flourished in childhood. Milosz sanctions an honoring of this vestigial faith, however strenuously the adult must also interrogate it. Indeed, this faith, annihilated in tandem with the genocidal tragedies of this century, seems their only redress, because such faith returns the witness to a childlike state that can tell the truth as it sees it. Milosz states boldly that becoming civilized, the achievement that did not prevent genocide, seems to amount to a process of the child gainsaying his own instincts about truth. As evidence for this insight, Milosz relies on the Russian philosopher Lev Shestov. Shestov explains that, as a child is subjected to the basics of scientific education, learning for example that the sun does not revolve around the earth, the child is taught more deeply an axiom for adulthood: "to accept as truth only that to which our entire being seems false."[60] Not in a primitive or naïve way, the poetic imagination for Milosz exists to reverse this indoctrination. His example resonates in especially complicated ways for someone from a postcolonial culture where, history insists, all innocence is lost. The alienation from some idealized authentic self seems to make simplicity not just impossible but fraudulent. Heaney, however, has long appeared to have perceived the hegemony of postcolonial theory itself, of its insistence on a historical determinism that gives the individual imagination little latitude beyond the mimetic rendering of an echo chamber. Milosz, often faux naïf, offers an approach that is anarchic and iconoclastic, not least toward academic orthodoxies.

As a man of reason, too, accepting the laws of science up to a point, Milosz nonetheless does not automatically accept some of the predications for which these laws have served. For example, it is not hard for Milosz, with a nearly fundamentalist zeal, to stretch the theory of evolution out toward a point where the human being becomes a "statistical cypher" and where society becomes "indifferent to the fate of the individual"[61] as indifferent as the prodigal Nature upon which his Manichaean propensities are predicated. A moral poetry, therefore, in relation to unimaginable horror, involves for Milosz the rediscovery of a prescientific, childlike corner of the imagination. This is what Heaney is doing in Glanmore, as part not just of recovering from the systematic, relentless horror of Belfast but of preparing himself to confront it more adequately as a poet. Like Heaney, Milosz also confesses to an early immersion in a culture dominated less by religion than superstition. For Milosz the pagan is not a romanticization so much as a location in the believing part of himself, again a match with Heaney. Milosz, in glossing one of his poems, "Bypassing Rue Descartes," explains how in large part this pagan inheritance has meant that he has bypassed reason altogether in some part of himself. That poem ends with a memory of killing a snake: "I pushed a rock down on a water snake coiled in the grass."[62] The image of that act, while resisting, though lightly encouraging, allegorical interpretation as a Christian act of subduing evil, stands for Milosz as a betrayal of an earlier, much more powerful faith: "Because I come from Lithuania where the water snake was considered holy."[63] The crisscross pattern this earlier iconography inscribes on that of Christianity, a Sweeney moment, conditions Milosz from the beginning to the expectation of innate contradiction. So it can be that he explains the preponderance of religious concern, indeed theological cogitation, in his work by means of a memory of schooldays dominated by this arcane subject: "For several years I studied the history of the Roman Church and dogmatics from thick textbooks that have since been abandoned everywhere."[64] This cameo of Milosz's religious education might have predicted Heaney's middle-aged self-portrait: "For years and years bent over a *prie dieu*,"[65] a posture learned from his early education by priests and his reading of an early Irish poetry copied and composed by monks. By their troubled and oblique relationship with organized religion, both poets are essentially claiming not just spiritual autonomy but also agency for poetry.

As Heaney reveals in "Crediting Poetry," implying both giving credit to and believing in poetry, the recovery of some basis for faith is essential to both poets. For Milosz poetry offers a recovery of hope for countering the despair all intelligent human beings, especially witnesses, must feel at the spectacle of the twentieth century's atrocities. One of his most compelling arguments against the solipsism endemic to modernism emulates that of an opponent to the pre-Socratic Zeno: "that Greek who, upon hearing the argument . . . that movement is an illusion since an arrow in flight remains motionless, got up and took two steps." [66] For Milosz, the equivalent in fighting the absurdity and nihilism induced by the display of programmatic evil in our time is the guileless intervention of empathy: a common understanding of pain. This is precisely the intervention, as we have seen, accomplished in Irish culture by Kavanagh's "The Great Hunger." Milosz maintains, that "the twentieth century has given us the most simple touchstone for reality: physical pain"; [67] therefore, if the commonality of this experience can be trusted, so can other sensations, even the pleasurable stirrings of hope. Milosz's lament through all these lectures, one I believe Heaney has listened to and absorbed deeply, to the point of becoming more resolute in his nonmimetic approach to the pain of Northern Ireland, is that contemporary poetry is hampered most by its dreary, lifeless, despairing tone. For Milosz, not succumbing to the sin of despair is the single greatest religious imperative surviving his childhood, honored in his maturity.

Milosz's optimism has clearly been an inspiration to fellow Poles, obviously artists, but people in general as well. It can be useful, given Heaney's natural hostility to a demand to speak on behalf of a culture of violence, to see how the recruitment by Solidarity, the labor movement in Poland, of a then extant Milosz poem reveals the innate resistance of good poetry to reductionism, when a noble cause is in question. This Polish example, however, involves one work of art being mediated by another, not being exposed to raw consumption. In the opening scene to Andrzej Wajda's "Man of Iron," the great Polish filmmaker's dramatization of the Solidarity strike of 1980, we are in a radio studio listening to a woman read aloud the Milosz poem, "Hope," for broadcast. The time of the broadcast is presumed to be the very beginning, the first weeks, of the nationwide strike. The poem on the page, with all its ambiguity, of mode especially, ranging from realism to allegory, is both radically altered and reaffirmed by being heard in a highly political, specific context. Suddenly Milosz, the international émigré poet, is brought home and recruited on behalf of Justice, with a capital letter. Far from flattening the poem, this adoption only expands the promise for personal faith at the poem's center. It is being read for the benefit of ordinary people suffering under Soviet communism, therefore hungering not just for social justice but cultural nourishment. So while the poem can be enlisted as an assault on Soviet domination, the force that keeps Poles behind the gate looking at the far-off garden "you cannot enter," the philosophical and religious levels of the poem still resonate, if not with more force, given the added impetus from immediate reality. Milosz's poem not only resists religious cant but integrates politics with metaphysics.

More directly, in December 1980 a permanent monument was erected by Solidarity to commemorate the workers in the Lenin Shipyard who were killed by the police in 1970. The monument included as an inscription part of a poem by Milosz, his words literally carved in stone. The poem, "You Who Wronged" was written in 1950 and is from his book *Daylight* (1953), composed for the most part in Washington, D.C. His poem, in a translation by Richard Lourie, contains these lines: "Do not feel safe. The poet remembers. / You can kill one, but another is born. / The words are written down, the deed, the date."[68] Here Milosz, not unlike Yeats in "Easter 1916," serves as an articulate and honest witness of history. Both are sifting through the numbing complications of events to find some saving wisdom. Perhaps because Yeats is confronting a revolution about which he has ambivalence, and Milosz is confronting a totalitarian regime for which he has unequivocal disdain, the two poets handle their respective problems differently. Yeats rescues from a transcendent simplicity the complexity, multiplicity, and individuality of ordinary life. Milosz, on the other hand, takes the spurious complexity, the sophistry, of the communist propaganda he knows firsthand and recovers a moral rectitude and simplicity by which to judge it. The ending of "You Who Wronged," where his anger is as unswerving as Zeno's arrow, made sharper by irony and by contrast a honed directness, sends a shiver up the reader's spine: "And you would have done better with a winter dawn, / A rope, and a branch bowed beneath your weight."[69] Recommending suicide for others, Milosz risks his own soul. The crime that deserves courting such self-perdition is a tampering with an innocence that intuitively understands the difference between good and evil. Here the focus is not evil deeds but the official establishment rationalizations that make a blur of all morality:

> You who wronged a simple man
> Bursting into laughter at the crime,
> And kept a pack of fools around you
> To mix good and evil, to blur the line.[70]

Here, as in the entire book *Daylight,* Milosz is unafraid as a poet to assume the role of moral arbiter.

In that book, while individual poems sparkle with a moral certainty, the poems play off each other, much as Heaney's "Squarings" do, ratifying and negating, so that the final light shed is as turbid as his description of Kraków as a "horse-fleshed colored city in ruins,"[71] from "Mid-Twentieth Century Portrait." This is a book overcast by the disgust of total moral opportunism. The defined rainbow colors of belief and pure emotions seem completely annihilated by history. More than anything, Milosz implicates himself in this gray evasion and cynicism. "Child of Europe" is the poem where his dark night of the soul, that of a continent, is most revealed: all is equivocation, rationalization, betrayal, and some small vestige of honesty, the hope he never totally loses:

1.
Having the choice of our own death and that of a friend,
We chose his, coldly thinking, let it be done quickly.

We sealed the gas chamber doors, stole bread,
Knowing the next day would be harder to bear than the day before.

2.
Treasure your legacy of skills, child of Europe,
Inheritor of Gothic cathedrals, of baroque churches,
Of synagogues filled with the wailing of wronged people.

3.
Let your lips, proposing a hypothesis,
Not know about the hand faking the experiment.

Let your hand, faking the experiment,
Not know about the lips proposing a hypothesis.
. . . .

4.
Grow your tree of falsehood from a small grain of truth.
Do not follow those who lie in contempt of reality.

Let your lie be even more logical than the truth itself,
So the weary travellers may find repose in the lie.[72]

Rectifying the blurring of good and evil, Milosz, like a moral clockmaker, constructs the precision instrument of the poem bit by bit, precise discernment by discernment, wielding epigraphs but not succumbing to rhetoric alone, one of his satirical targets. Most of all the poem is saved from egotism, Heaney's moral goal in "Station Island," by the repeated pronoun "we," which makes the poet complicit, equally culpable. (Milosz uses pronouns as strategically as Devlin does). At the same time, the book defines a role for the poet that transcends his identity as a social being: the poet as detached observer, namer, and bearer of hope. The poem "A Nation" closes with lines again reminiscent of "Easter 1916" as they assign an active role to the poet as a witness and as a parental, nurturing presence, a protector of life: "Only the word passes from mouth to mouth and prophecy of poets / A man of that nation, standing by his son's cradle, / Repeats words of hope, always, till now, in vain."[73]

Pain, the brother of hope for Milosz, is almost always his answer to what propels the essentially Marxian, Heraclitan dialectic forward. (Curious that omnipresent pain is the one quality that according to Heaney, makes Eliot wary of Dante and makes him ascend to the more symbolist mode of the "Four Quartets" from the tangible, imaged pain of the "Wasteland.") Apart from Adam Mickiewicz, the canonic Polish poet whom Milosz admires most is sixteenth-century Jan Kochanowski. With an anti-Parnassian daring similar to Mickiewicz's,

Kochanowski broke with classicism through a deviation reminiscent of Dante's: he abandoned Latin and espoused the vernacular, a Polish still readable to the average Pole today. Further flouting classical conventions, Kochanowski departed from his hitherto impersonal lyrics to write a series of "Laments" about the death of his youngest daughter, Ursula, that vibrate even now with intense, immediate, personal pain. Heaney, with Stanislaw Baranczak, a professor of Polish literature at Harvard, translated Kochanowski's "Laments" in a little book that was published in 1995. Heaney's own *Haw Lantern,* which contained the sonnet sequence "Clearances" about the death of his mother, had been published in 1987. As the "Laments" revolutionized Kochanowski's work, so did "Clearances" for Heaney. His translating the "Laments" implicitly underlines not just this common history and Heaney's connection with Milosz but also, often by contrast, the strategies and achievements of "Clearances." Both sequences are born of eschatological meditations; both explore the effect that the intimacies of the parent-child relationship have on loss. Although Heaney's series is written from the point of view of a son after his mother's death and Kochanowski's of a father after his daughter's, so much shared material exists between the two, spanning centuries and cultures, that it is clear how translating the Kochanowski acted as an opportunity for Heaney to consolidate certain values and insights laid down by the *Haw Lantern,* and *Station Island,* its immediate predecessor.

Reading Baranczak's introduction to the volume (there are nineteen poems in the sequence, the last lament being several pages long), one can imagine further reasons for Heaney's attraction, but perhaps none more than the fact that up to this rupturing, extreme moment in Kochanowski's career, he was known, like Heaney, as a temperate man, a man with his own internal spirit level, produced as much by the training of his humanist education as by temperament: "His cast of mind was formed by a philosophy of the golden mean and moderation, and this in turn produced a quiet acceptance of whatever life might bring, a tendency to handle the vicissitudes of earthly existence in a rational and orderly way."[74] Then something happened to so topple this apparently unshakeable world view that he was left, for example, opening one of his laments, the fourth, with two words of absolute heresy, "Ungodly Death,"[75] reminiscent of Kavanagh's iconoclastic opening to "The Great Hunger": "Clay is the word and Clay is the flesh." All of Heaney's despair in "Station Island," which will resurface in the fitful nihilism of *Seeing Things,* filters through these words of translation. We can hear Heaney's horror of his own vanity as a poet in Kochanowski's registering the temptation to give up writing in response to the death of his child: "I must forego my rhyme and lute: / My soul is mute."[76] These lines almost corroborate Milosz's axiom that hope sustains poetry, as hope is precisely what Kochanowski has lost. "It is not just you / That I am burying, but my own hope too."[77] The Orphic impulse fails when hell exists on earth and the underworld is as devoid of song as mute grief. Kochanowski even asks for the location of what would have been Lough Derg. While not using this name, he expresses the desire to find the opening to hell and have the opportunity Orpheus lost: "Where is that gate for grief which, long ago, / Let Orpheus enter the dark realm below / In search of his lost love?"[78] This is the proverbial medieval cave at Lough Derg, and it can be easy to overlook the vast underworld of historical sadness, otherwise unspoken, which Lough Derg writers have brought to the surface, made conscious for Ireland. It is also compelling to consider the gender implications of the suffering Heaney enters through Kochanowski. His anguish is seen as a salutary gift from a patriarchal God to whom the grieving poet prays,

> Yet punish us as evil fathers do:
> 　Your wrath would burn us through;
> 　We'd vanish without a trace
> Like snow when warmed by the sun's piercing rays.[79]

Suffering with this male provenance paradoxically births the manly fortitude to sustain the worst challenges in life, above all to retain a faith too easily eroded by security. At the same time this punishing God must stop short of being the embodiment of Manichaean darkness: "Your mercy and goodwill / Would not let evil reign."[80] As this discriminating caveat discloses, the "Laments" are not simply despairing. They have their own dialectical energy, tracing a process of grief operating by means of opposites, which are suffered, weighed, ever evolving. The greatest of these opposites is that between the male poet composing the lament and the female who has died.

So it can be, that as in "Clearances," the very sense of emptiness, absolute barrenness, that predominates in the early laments can become the space out of which a renewed, if much more sober, faith emerges. In tackling this translation, Heaney, so intent on collecting surrogate father figures, so reluctant to include a full Beatrician radiance in "Station Island," is reinforcing the spiritual and stylistic revolution accomplished by "Clearances," where the focus is the radiant absence felt by a male after the death of a female. For Kochanowski his dead daughter may as well have been Dante's Beatrice, so much did his faith depend on her. Lament 8 begins with the quatrain:

> The void that fills my house is so immense
> Now that my girl is gone. It baffles sense:
> We are all here, yet no one is, I feel;
> The flight of one, small soul has tipped the scale.[81]

The desolation expressed here is reminiscent of that in the opening poem to "Squarings," where the void is evoked by "winter light in a doorway . . . a gazing out from far away, alone." Just as this representation by Heaney of an out-of-body perspective is the paradoxical harbinger in the poem of transcendent moments, so in the Kochanowski, the fact that a loss can weigh more than what one tangibly has is the beginning of belief in the soul. Without it sounding like hollow rationalization, Kochanowski convinces the reader that only through this loss did the vanity of earthly things drop away and leave him in the presence of faith. Most significantly, however, the arrival of this epiphany is marked by the appearance of his own mother in a dream, a tactic recalling the *Tractatus*. In the extended lament 19, because this is a dream narration, a different level of discourse and belief is found. Kochanowski's mother makes this Dantean point about the Beatrician Ursula: "You cannot see her as she is—your sight / Is mortal and sees things in mortal light."[82] It is the fact, however, that Kochanowski's mother appears holding her grandchild, Ursula, in her arms, that brings these lines so close to Heaney, particularly the later Heaney in "Squarings" 9, lying in the crook of his mother's arm and apprehending an existence beyond the earth.

Kochanowski and Heaney in their respective expressions of grief, however, differ in important ways, ways that must remind Heaney of important decisions reflected in "Clearances" and based in myriad specificities of temperament and history. The major difference is a departure in Heaney's poem from the idealizations and polarizations that mark Kochanowski's. A grief that questions the existence of God over most of the distance of Kochanowski's poem gives way in the final lament to an unequivocal affirmation of a higher level of faith. No such clear moment of affirmation exists in "Clearances," though in the last two sonnets a metaphysical breakthrough is glimpsed. It is the idealization of the other, however, the deceased, that is dramatically absent from Heaney, while being pronounced, straining credibility, in Kochanowski. Less from outright lying, even the forgivable exaggeration brought on by loss, than from adhering to the convention of hyperbole that goes with elegy, Kochanowski recalls his Ursula as a paragon of precocity and angelic goodness. Even though Ursula was, according to Baranczak, only two-and-a-half when she died, this prodigy is portrayed in the poem as not only capable of performing little household chores with unearthly obedience and delight, but of singing all day songs of her own composition. Kochanowski calls his lost daughter "my Slavic Sappho," attributing a preternatural poetic ability to the toddler—"With what sheer wit and verve / You fitted words together, song by song."[83] Although a certain narcissism seems a natural reaction to loss, by seeing the child as a mirror of himself—"little poet-heiress / Ghost owner of my goods"[84]—Kochanowski deprives the reader of a palpable, creditable Ursula whom we can mourn with the poet. While his subjectivity may consume his daughter's, what he gives us instead, grounding the poem in this world, is an uncensored record of his grief, speaking with no thoughts of impressing the reader:

> "You weep in vain," my friends will say. But then,
> What is not vain, by God, in lives of men?
> All is in vain! We play at blind man's bluff
> Until hard edges break into our path.
> Man's life is error. Where, then, is relief?
> In shedding tears or wrestling down my grief?[85]

Kochanowski decides to shed tears, risk opprobrium for this merely personal lapse. The result is that his freely flowing tears provide the movement out of a calcified convention of restraint and impersonality. They move a genre, the elegy, on. We hear a man speaking through the cry, "Help me to mourn my small girl, my dear daughter, / Whom cruel death tore up with such wild force."[86] Moreover, we hear an artist at this intersection, where a new convention is being formed, not knowing how to find a voice for this freer expression. Consider, in the light of previous discussions of the bearing of gender on poetics, how it is precisely a breaking with the manly stance of stoic containment that enables Kochanowski, in Milosz's assessment, to achieve the virile feat of surpassing convention. In doing so, however, Kochanowski confesses to a confusion, almost a fear, that such openness might mean regression, effeminacy. He essentially revives Dante's question of whether a child's voice might not better confront this material. The way Kochanowski puts the question is whether his task might not be easier if he were a writer of nursery rhymes, or lullabies, or jingles to soothe a fretful child. This involuntary response to the noncomprehension of death, reminiscent of being a child again, echoes Yeats's impulse in "Easter 1916." Trying to forget momentarily that the dead are dead, Yeats takes on the voice of a mother speaking the name of her sleeping child. Kochanowski is also lamenting his own loss of innocence. So identified is Kochanowski with the lost child that he is one with her and yet is not: he is still an adult who must grapple with these crosscurrents of anarchic feeling and find a poetic means to be true to them:

> The lullaby, to a grown man like me,
> Seemed far too childish; now the epitaph
> Looms like a cliff above some wild and rough
> Shore, where I'm cast by fate and where I sing
> Oblivious to my fame, to everything
> Except my grief.[87]

It is crucial for Milosz, however, that Kochanowski would not have been capable of such risks, such departures, were he not thoroughly disciplined by his classical training.[88]

Heaney's "Clearances" displays a similar paradox between form and content: traditional sonnets, to a degree subverted formally, but to a radical extent breaking with the traditional view of the Irish mother. From the initial invocation to the sequence proper, we appreciate that Heaney is trying to do something entirely new here, to crack open the truth at the heart of a relationship compacted over time and by the intensity of childhood intimacy, but also to crack open a convention, not simply elegy, but writings that construct the icon of the mother in Ireland. Above all he is inventing a way finally to address with both reason and intuition the eschatological questions begged by "Station Island." The invocation, almost visually resembling an epitaph, with the dates of his mother's life and death above the poem, "in memoriam M. K. H. 1911–1984,"[89] announces particularity. This poem, this brave investigation of the mother-son dyad, revives in Irish poetry the gender concerns of "The Heavenly Foreigner," and makes its own distinctive advances in the struggle. From the beginning, Heaney ascribes a powerful educational presence to his mother. The first tercet reads: *"She taught me what her uncle once taught her: / How easily the biggest coal block split / If you got the grain and hammer angled right."*[90] The poet goes on to explain, in the first sonnet, that stories handed down from one generation to the next, like the practical tip of how to split a coal block, are his inheritance, "instead of silver and Victorian lace."[91] This accumulated, earthed knowledge helps him find a way of addressing a grief rooted in a parent-child relationship with a very particular woman. The paradox of cracking open this most resistant, private material is that repressed cultural truths are equally exposed and the tradition advanced, though the poet's aim is always on the individual. He knows by now that this is the obliquely political angle required. The tool that will break open this recalcitrant subject is a steely honesty razor stropped in "Station Island." The simplicity of language used is also the product of those many self-administered chastisements for being too aesthetic. "Clearances" gives us a portrait of a woman and a relationship that is unidealized, particular, and for this reason universal. Honesty about his own grief similarly served Kochanowski. Heaney's focus, however, is less his grief than who his mother was and how they were together.

One of the temptations Heaney's sequence resists, and in doing so withstands the weight of centuries of convention in Irish literature, is to merge the actual mother with an allegorical one, emblematic of Ireland. History is invoked but serves as a context, a nest, like the crook of a mother's arm, in which the particular life of Marie Heaney rested. The first sonnet begins, "A cobble thrown a hundred years ago / Keeps coming at me, the first stone / Aimed at a great-grandmother's turncoat brow."[92] The phrase "the first stone" has a softly ironic ring, gently mocking the self-serving purpose of family lore like tribal tales, to ascribe the role of starting all the trouble ("The Troubles") to the other side. The poem, however, about his mother's grandmother, who was a Protestant and suffered a stoning as she and her Catholic husband went to mass, also implodes from within such pretensions to purity. Historical narrative even at the level of family is one of ineradicable otherness. It would have been easy to hand over the burden of untangling a complicated relationship to history and let those complications take the place of the interpersonal, but this displacement is staunchly resisted. Although the sequence returns to history again in the penultimate sonnet where the word "clearances"[93] finally appears, even there the seam explored is still resolutely personal. History is part of the large, compressed block of matter being opened up by the poem. So, though sonnet 7 ends with a quatrain that suggests a mysterious change in historical consciousness simultaneously with a shift in personal religious belief, history is but another concentric circle created by emanations out from the center of one of the most personal experiences possible, witnessing the death of one's mother:

The space we stood around had been emptied
Into us to keep, it penetrated
Clearances that suddenly stood open.
High cries were felled and a pure change happened.[94]

Dilations of painful historical memories are detonated by the poem. Achieving articulate, honest grief for one woman evokes and honors all the losses contingent historically on her being. The word clearances resonates along with this highly personal loss (one loss, like an atomic reaction, setting off all the others); and, as the loss of the mother's physical being is transformed into an apprehension of the possibility of her soul, so the burden of history is transformed, lightened by understanding. The poem reverses the usual way of approaching the subject of the mother, putting history and culture first. It radically revises Joyce, whose mother is a demonized caillach, a hag. Somehow, in Heaney all of the obscure and disturbing sexual musings of "Station Island" are vindicated by this honest confrontation with the issues of gender and power between mother and son. His wandering in purgatory searching for father figures is through; the poet has come home.

Eschewing the vast panorama of the mother and son against the backdrop of history, the most searing and poignant poems here go indoors. This is the same multivalanced space where the drama of the cracked mug took place. It is a feminine space, and these performative moments derive their power from the energy that rushes through the narrow seam of difference between mother and son. This voltage is never greater than when they are resisting the melding of identities typical of their *"Sons and Lovers* phase." These are usually liturgical moments, made magical by "cruet tinkle,"[95] which may go some distance to explain Heaney's Low-Church bias with regard to Eliot. The more believable, reliable kinds of experience that guide "Clearances" are ordinary and quotidian: peeling potatoes, folding sheets. In both these activities a "touch and go"[96] dynamic, a coming together and moving apart, dominates the narrative. It is the electrified space in between, like the space between Adam's finger and God's, a synapse across which intense energy fires, that compels Heaney. Only here, at this point in his oeuvre, that energy flows between male and female. "Clearances," a profoundly feminist poem, vindicates Heaney's gradual and painful stabilizing of a male identity, particularly from "Station Island" on. The profound revelation of the poem is that this space of unrelieved ambiguity and imperfect separation, psychic purgatory, is the same space in the end where "a pure change happened."[97] This is precisely the in-betweenness, which the site of purgatory offered Heaney in "Station Island." In other words, the "touch and go" relationship with his mother extends into a similarly ambivalent but no less intense relationship with the idea of the soul. The mother, outside patriarchy, outside the Church as a hegemonic institution colluding with hegemonic nationalism, offers Heaney a means to an individual and free exploration of faith. This is a faith, thanks to the mother, that bypasses the Rue Descartes of doctrinal

Catholicism. The rich ambiguities of the mother/son relationship become the rich ambiguities of "striving towards being."

This honesty about spiritual matters likewise is dependent on an honesty about emotion. The passion of this poem finds its source in a need for truth on every level, for a truth that does not eliminate feelings, which are not ideal, but unlocks them for their unorthodox energy. In those two sonnets (iii and v) about sharing physical work with his mother, doing in fact woman's work, the paradoxical foundation for a virile overturning of a genre, Heaney is not afraid to portray incipient violence. Mother and son folded sheets and the wide, sail-like expanses of fabric caught "in a cross wind" and "made a dried-out undulating thwack." The poet continues, "So we'd stretch and fold and end up hand to hand / For a split second as if nothing had happened." [98] This "nothing," which is clearly something, but left untranslated in an ellipsis, is not unrelated to the "one thing" [99] known at the end but not spoken. Whether that climactic moment of folding the sheets resonates with a frightening anger or love, it is this passionate attachment that produces the absence that floods with a sense of the soul. Similarly, the way in which the peeled potatoes dropping into a bucket are seen as "solder weeping off the soldering iron" [100] indicates this fluency between states of being and experience, liquid and solid, religious and secular. Those solder tears effortlessly and organically suggest the sorrow of Christ. Again, the energy required for such transformations comes from a space that crackles with an incipient violence. Consider this picture of the intimacy between a mother and son peeling potatoes: "Her breath in mine, our fluid dipping knives— / Never closer the whole rest of our lives." [101] When one sees and feels the electricity flowing through that narrow seam between two people who love, it is not farfetched to believe in a conversion of that energy into the purely spiritual. The wonder of sonnet 7, where Heaney's father launches into a consoling fiction for his dying wife about seeing her again, immediately after her death, in the very place where their relationship began, her father's house, is that the reader is taken by surprise, half-believing this will literally happen: "You'll be in New Row on Monday night / And I'll come up for you and you'll be glad / When I walk in the door." [102] The reader is almost fully prepared to believe there will be a mimetic replay of this history in another world. We have been prepared for such elisions and splicings in time and levels of being by temporal manipulations in the previous poems: from the "co-opted and obliterated echo" [103] of the hammer on the piece of coal in the invocation, a sound that catches the moment before and the moment after the striking, but not the precise, present moment, to the remembered behavior of a grandfather who came to the door before his daughter knocked, having a prescience that collapses time. A collapsing of identities, along with separate moments in time, threatens at every moment, hence the suppressed violence.

One of the most elaborate games of collusive fusion and passive-aggressive separation surrounds language, a mother who deliberately mispronounces fancy names, like "Bertold Brek," "as if she might betray / The hampered and inadequate by too / Well-adjusted a vocabulary"[104] is met by a son who reciprocates, mispronounces too, a practice that, like an accurate aiming of a hammer, both splits and joins them:

> So I governed my tongue
> in front of her, a genuinely well-
> adjusted adequate betrayal
> of what I knew better. I'd naw and aye
> and decently relapse into the wrong
> grammar which kept us allied and at bay.[105]

There is a doubleness in almost every twist of this utterance, for instance he "knew better" meaning both he was better educated and had better sense. The word that performs the most somersaults, however, is betray, always implying both to prove faithless and to reveal: "she might betray the hampered and inadequate"; he performs a "betrayal of what (he) knew better."[106] In this passionately close bond of two separate people, every minute word and act is a betrayal in both senses. One cannot imagine any vehicle other than poetry as adequate to this complexity, as able for this translation in two directions simultaneously. One also can understand how a poet, coming from such a bond and background, might, like his mother, be tempted in both senses not "to betray the hampered and inadequate," in other words, to be cosmopolitan and local at the same time. One can imagine almost believing in a childhood faith again not to betray this intimacy, and not believing in order not to betray oneself. In this sequence, Heaney forever entwines his faith in the deepest, most atavistic emotions of family ties. He also brings adequate language to that generative space between his life and theirs, where this kind of poetry happens.

In allowing his mother's death to make intimations of a soul manifest, Heaney is enacting a synoptic version of the gradual ascent to heaven performed by Dante, Beatrice being his portal to the divine. The difference with "Clearances," however, is that faith and its negation continue to oscillate in tight proximity. Yet this grief-stricken and ultimately exultant poem represents in Heaney's oeuvre the summit of Croagh Patrick reached after the long trudge, often appearing to be going in circles, at Lough Derg in "Station Island." That Heaney's movement is the reverse of Patrician mythology, the snakes being banished from the mountain to the lake, says everything about Heaney's revisionist achievement, not just in relation to Catholicism but to nationalism as well, and especially, diabolically, the fusion of the two.

Conclusion

A Bright Nowhere

THE POSTCOLONIAL is itself a purgatory. It is a state of in-betweeness where what appears to be solid may be a shade, from one's dearly held beliefs, to the landscape of one's birth, to the most familiar faces. Even one's own body can seem spectral, present and not present. A lack of ownership, a condition of being possessed by ideas and perceptions so long imposed from without that they seem one's own, pervades. There is a reason the colonist targets religion as the native cultural property, second only to language, to be razed. It is not just because transcendent ideas fuel political actions. For a reigning power, collective belief can be destabilizing, but perhaps even more so, like an atom being split, is the event of one person finding his or her own answers to the ultimate questions, or, even more disruptive, deciding what those questions are. Because Lough Derg is a totem of native religion, it became a rallying post for the colonized and a whipping post for the colonizer. Of course, given the dialectics of history, the endless flip-flops of position in the individual and collective mind, who the colonizer really is becomes as shadowy as the figures Dante met in purgatory, or as Denis Florence MacCarthy envisaged wandering the roads during the Great Famine. Given, however, this laser concentration on the shrine by apologists and debunkers both, those of a self-described Hiberno- or Anglo-, Catholic or Protestant point of view, Lough Derg is a place where a vast history is compressed. Buried away in remote Donegal, it has resided for centuries as latent, explosive energy. For the student of Irish cultural history, Lough Derg is where our still inadequate understanding of colonization may be advanced and tested. For the student of Irish literature, it is also the place where the linearity of history intersects with the timelessness of faith and doubt, the core of metaphysical poetry. To study modern Irish writing about Lough Derg, especially poetry, is to observe both the extent of colonization, be it by England or the Catholic nation, and, even more important, the limits of such hegemony on imagination.

Yet hegemony is real. Carleton views people who are as close to him as his own arms and legs from the interstellar distance of a Reformationist critic. Then,

Carleton's manly fight against the effeminate irrationality he associates with Rome is taken up by those who see themselves as staunch defenders of the Vatican and the Catholic nation, Alice Curtayne prominently. My study includes a litany of such historically determined ironies. For example, remaining with the extravagantly pious 1930s, the flip side of the more liberal climate in which Carleton found self-expression, Curtayne and Shane Leslie both adamantly maintain that a unified Catholic culture exists in an Ireland entering upon a Golden Age. Yet these advocates proceed from very different but collusive racial and religious premises: Leslie with his high-Romantic myth of a super race, Curtayne with her classical stoicism. Moreover, Curtayne's argument with the Leslie family over the ownership of Lough Derg is nothing less than a bitter reaffirmation of ownership of Ireland, as though literal independence were insubstantial. Perhaps the crowning irony with regard to these fraternal, not identical, twins, is that both possess voices implying they and they alone synthesize all the conflict embedded in the past, epitomize Ireland.

It is little wonder, therefore, that the search for truth devolves ultimately upon an art made over time to contain complexity and transform it into formal beauty: poetry. That this aesthetic transformation can be turned in the political mind into a conceit for the transforming dream behind violent resistance is yet another complication poetry must confront. Poetry can even convey how this penitential site, burdened with a myth of purity but resting on a foundation of sin, forces a recognition of unruly reality. For this reason, much of the largely dialogic poetry about Lough Derg is indebted to certain prose strategies, especially the use of many voices to narrate a many-layered story. To step even a measured distance away from the crazed dialectics of postcolonial identity creation is to acknowledge the impossibility of encompassing Lough Derg with one voice, a single stroke encircling this island symbol. Rather, there are many tangents crisscrossing its plot in both senses of the word, as place and as story. There is no one Lough Derg, as there is no one Ireland, and this is what polyvocal "Station Island" tells us. Heaney's parade of ghosts, all urging their divergent advice, underline with irony the clean, linear ascent enabled by Dante's ghosts, who inexorably lead that poet upward. Scrutiny of Lough Derg, like scrutiny of one's soul, consistently yields a sobering revelation: the intractability of paradox. One voice is always the sum of many voices; individual integrity is the product of a multitude of internalized others; the authentic is always implicated in the artificial. Heaney's truly catholic response gathers inchoate history into a nightmare vigil, where influences from Curtayne's fastidious asceticism to Carleton's slapdash pragmatism, echo and clash. All the ghosts, no matter how they identify themselves politically or religiously, are embedded in the poem like genetic programming.

The slow acceptance of this radically impure but fertile condition is the narrative spine of all the mini-episodes of the Lough Derg story, which uncurls from the womb of history with a biological imprimatur to attain maturity. Much of this potential for expansive growth stems from the paradox that this icon of stifling nativism is also a prime channel into the relative spaciousness of Europe. This constant pressure on the margins of atavistic, nativist fictions, of course, can be observed and felt closer to home, at Lough Derg, in the way that Saint Patrick, putative founder of the shrine, is claimed equally as the National Apostle by Catholic and Protestant Irelands. Above all, the Lough Derg story also relates how all these myths of continuity rest ironically on rupture. The entire edifice of Catholic-nationalist triumph built around the icon of Lough Derg, like the very basilica itself, rests on its Cromwellian razing by Bishop Spottiswoode. The very fact that such paradoxes stubbornly inhere in history is a lesson for the present and the future, especially for those of us intent on analyzing the phenomena Lough Derg handily presents for inspection. Postcolonial theory has had a salutary effect in correcting overweening myths of continuity, be they colonial or native, with evidence of rupture. Lough Derg, however, mixes this truth up, presenting us with both continuity and discontinuity. Lough Derg also fosters a newly inflected perception of the interconnection of the individual and culture. First of all, by paying for one's own sins one implicitly begins to free a nation that has systematically frustrated such individual reckoning. Beyond this, however, and most paradoxically in relation to an icon constructed by means of unholy fusions (church and nation, self and nation), Lough Derg enforces a degree of self-accountability that disqualifies any displacement of responsibility for suffering exclusively onto history. History comes to reside in each individual, finally the site where true change can occur.

All of the artists examined here have had this crusade in common: the search for self-possession, an autonomy they achieved, however, only by means of courting everything that thwarts it. The original conceit of Saint Patrick's Purgatory, that one can enter the underworld in life and view one's penance after death, is played out on a historical stage: the poet gets to descend into nightmare and discover the dues owed to the past. The penance is personal, the overall expiation cultural. The assumption of various masks and roles on this odyssey is essential, especially that of the culturally privileged priest. Point-of-view narration, the empathic entering into others, particularly by means of translation, allows one even to inhabit the soul of a saint, be it Heaney's John of the Cross or MacCarthy's Saint Patrick as conceived by Calderón. Through a process of identification and differentiation, individuation proceeds. Gender, perhaps more than any other shaper of identity, figures largely in the Lough Derg metamorphosis, which is almost always a journey through the liminal space between genders. This negotiation involves every provisional stance from the aggressive posturing of Carleton to the fraught worshiping of the female in Devlin. Moreover, the myth of the National Apostle's attachment to the site prompts the male pilgrim's search for a legitimate and legitimating paternal authority, one of the chief erosions of colonialism. This search in turn is contingent on a traditional fetishizing and idealizing of Ireland as female, epitomized by Lough Derg with its convenient memory of a cave. Once more, paradox abounds: Lough Derg is the site both of an unredeemed misogyny and of an evolved feminism. This change of perspective on women is most evident in

Heaney, culminating in "Clearances," where the Beatrician ideal of the woman as virgin is reinvested in and revised to embrace an actual mother. Both these movements, retrograde and retrospective as well as revolutionary and far-seeing, are made possible by poetry, where time is flexible and binary thinking rare.

Poetry is, of course, another purgatory, another state of in-betweeness. Practiced on this earth, it contains intimations of hell and heaven, everything from inert despair to transforming joy. Built upon the split but also doubly strong foundation of representation per se, it constructs itself by means of proliferating ambiguities. Its choicest building material is irreducibly double: metaphor, whose tenor is solid and whose vehicle is spectral. To enlist the variety of figuration words invite is to participate in just about all the arguments philosophers and theologians have conducted. The spectrum between metaphor and metonymy is the same line ranged across by Lough Derg apologists for visionary rapture or grounded penance. And metaphor conjures further paradox because the transformation it effects on things can be seen as redemption or as death, sensuous flesh or unregenerate matter. All this we learn from Heaney's "Squarings," his consummate intermeshing of poetics and metaphysics.

Poetry enables all these truths, antithetical and otherwise, to coexist as appropriate and salutary complication. By means of poetry, for example, in Kavanagh's "Lough Derg," the self-annihilating herd instinct remains a conformist pressure but also turns itself inside out into an empathy that reconciles self and community. Self-punishment remains destructive but also gives way to the balm of self-forgiveness. By recognizing as its stock-in-trade certain rhetorical ploys such as synecdoche, poetry is poised to deconstruct the manipulations achieved by propaganda, most perniciously the conflation of little Lough Derg with all of Ireland. Modernism, especially, has taught the poet to expose the machinery behind poetic magic. At the antipodes from this cool detachment, poetry is also the place where immersion in the earth of the self is experienced on all its tenebrous levels. Words can seem as much a part of the flesh as breath itself. Each word, like each breath, plumbs the abyss within, dredging up everything from memory to prophesy, all tangibly corporeal and sublimely verbal. This is Heaney's way with language.

When language is used with this kind of bodily integrity, it is grounded empirically in individual experience, making most theories, doctrines, and sweeping narratives suspect. Within the discrete sphere of the individual shivering on "Station Island," however, huge shifts in the architectonic plates on the globe of culture can begin. This process can start with the penitent sensing the frail flame of the ego buried under the rubble of history or lost within the engulfing conflagration of historical mass evil. Lough Derg promotes a view of where one's deepest privacies merge with public events. It is also the place for the poet where schools of poetry and intellectual movements are confronted head-on as specters, as such ideologies are the archaeological remains of past responses to historical circumstance. Romanticism and its descendant, modernism, are perhaps the aesthetics most rigorously challenged by Lough Derg. As Kavanagh discovered, Lough Derg is the place where one goes inside, out of sight of the blue dome and green fields, which make the "stony grey soil" of a hardscrabble existence endurable. All such consolation, the staple of Romanticism, vanishes when the pilgrim enters "prison." The consolation of nature, not just the linchpin of English Romanticism but also of Yeats's Celtic inflection of it, becomes obsolete when one assumes the mindset of Knight Owen, fasted and weak, enclosed in the cave of himself. In this fetal position, certain props of sophistication become obsolete—not just schools of thought, but quite possibly the refined pleasure principle, maybe even the artistic impulse itself, and the paradigms for what a poem is. Lough Derg is the place where poetry itself is shriven, the vocation of poet hauled over the coals. One may begin here to rely on other sources of comfort, such as the remembered common sense of ordinary people, such as the wisdom of folk culture.

With its soporific mantras, with its probings of the preverbal in the body, Lough Derg plumbs history in the core sample of the individual, making all the layers vibrate. The pilgrimage relies on credulity yet tempts one with belief, as crusty Sean O'Faolain's "Lovers of the Lake" reveals. The Lough Derg poetry we have read here is as close to prayer as it is possible for words to come while still retaining reason and avoiding the rote. These poems so nearly approach religious practice that the very doctrinal distinctions one might bring to bear to prove or disprove belief would snuff out the real, elusive thing. This tradition of writings, in a sense religious *Dindshenchas,* provide a neutral but formal zone where the individual's innate spirituality can express itself without crooking the knee to Church or nation. The miracle of the constantly self-shaping, self-generating poem, as Mandelstam defines it, replicates the Creation itself and plunges the poet into its primal mysteries. Perhaps this is the greatest Lough Derg irony: this place where human souls are corralled like cattle is also the place where they are granted the existentially terrifying isolation that both tests and prompts faith. Poetry, with its inherent ambiguity, its very lifeblood, keeps this steady pumping of alternating affirmation and negation going, keeps a spiritual life going both for the self and the nation.

Running counter to the radical movement down and into the self, to the point where one's mortality slips into whatever else there may or may not be, is a movement up and out into time—past, present, and future—perceived in a fresh way. Heaney, reaping the collective benefit of his Virgilian precursors in purgatory, effects on his emergence from his penitential vigil a shift in culture far greater than might seem possible for one man. This feat, which would in fact be impossible were he alone, nonetheless proves the subversive power lodged in a single freed conscience. Like Dante with his trusted guide, Heaney has especially learned from Kavanagh. It is the gruff Monaghan man who might have spoken, in his own inimitable voice, the kernel of reassurance Virgil offered Dante in hell: "Do not fear, for none can hinder our passage," a recognition not just of progress but also of the collaborative effort salvation requires. Heaney has enjoyed the brave example of

Kavanagh, who heard the lone "darkling thrush" and made it sing, especially in his later poems, despite the overwhelming evidence accrued in his earlier poems of causes for despair. What is more, Heaney's own sometimes difficult, evolving relationship with this elder has been like a journey through stop-and-start purgatory, where the example of Kavanagh has both retarded and enabled progress. Ultimately, however, Heaney's listening to Kavanagh's listening to what Milosz calls the "melody" of hope within, has led inexorably to Heaney's purging of himself and by extension of the culture. If one looks at the ending to his early essay on Kavanagh, "From Monaghan to the Grand Canal," one sees how reliant Heaney was in his youthful evaluation of Kavanagh on canonic standards for literary achievement laid down by Yeats. Heaney said, famously, even infamously by now, of Kavanagh, "When he had consumed the roughage of his own Monaghan experience, he ate his heart out."[1] The reason for this self-cannibalization, a further, nightmare extension of the Ugolino drama, is that Kavanagh allegedly lacked a sustaining myth, Yeats's staple. As Heaney expressed it then with distaste: "Without myth, without masters, 'No system, no plan,' he lived from hand to mouth and unceremoniously where Yeats—and Sydney—fed deliberately and ritually."[2] The gap in attitude and judgment between this early effort at assessing Kavanagh's legacy and Heaney's later essay, "The Placeless Heaven: Another Look at Kavanagh" is vast. For one, the oxymoronic title of that second effort is practically a synonym of the "bright nowhere" glimpsed as the destination of Heaney's mother's soul in "Clearances" 8. Indeed, in the second essay Heaney praises qualities in the elder poet's mature phase with words that might be applied to "Clearances": "weightlessness," "the luminous spaces within the mind," "the white light of meditation."

How this "pure change" happens for Heaney in relation to Kavanagh is not a facile Oedipal story, where the son fantasizes but resists actual patricide and then from the position of successful psychic separation renders a more just account of the father, for this is not just a psychological saga. Its deeper mysteries are religious and entwined with Heaney's poetic response to the death of his mother. With regard to Kavanagh, however, this process starts with Heaney's having to be tough about some hard problems stemming from a complex literary inheritance. Specifically, the first essay is less about Kavanagh than about Heaney preparing to confront a heterogeneous, often conflicting bequest. Of a different chronological and postcolonial generation than Kavanagh, Heaney at the onset of his career cannot afford, especially in the roiling reality of Northern Ireland, many of the binarisms the early Kavanagh permitted himself, such as being simply anti-Yeatsian. Heaney from the beginning is instinctively and honestly hybrid, incorporating Yeats's myths and masks. This is abundantly clear if we trace the arc from the extended conceit of *North* to the dramatis personae of "Station Island," when the actual North was at its worst. As a self-protective poet, too, Heaney understands the valuable lessons encoded in Yeats's artistic longevity and regards the privilege as no longer exclusive.

In "The Placeless Heaven," however, Heaney achieves a rare, fresh level of independence that, after incorporating hybridity, transcends it, acknowledging a hard-won simplicity in Kavanagh. It is critical that the symbol by which Heaney relates Kavanagh's religious experience to his own is the chestnut tree, the trope that crucially opens "The Placeless Heaven" and closes "Clearances," both musings on the possibility of the soul.

> Deep-planted and long gone, my coeval
> Chestnut from a jam-jar in a hole,
> Its heft and hush become a bright nowhere,
> A soul ramifying and forever
> Silent, beyond silence listened for.[3]

Contemplation, indeed acceptance, of loss leads to a new autonomy, which paradoxically rests on the assimilation of a double vision of the self, a lesson learned in purgatory, as both flesh and shade. Heaney, of course, knows that the chestnut tree is the same symbol that concludes Yeats's magisterial, eschatological poem, "Among School Children." At this point not just in his career but in cultural history, Heaney is free to claim, without the static of intertextual echo so omnipresent in "Station Island," this symbol as his own. He returns it to the public domain, sharing it with his self-elected father/guide, Kavanagh. In aligning himself with this autodidact's roughhewn religion, inhospitable to all orthodox naming, even mysticism, Heaney is revising both the hegemonies of English literature and the Catholic Church. He is calling attention to an independent lineage of metaphysical inquiry among poets and how an unlikely revolution in cultural givens can be achieved by meditation.

As Heaney's career soared in a metaphysical direction after his subterranean sojourn on "Station Island," so, I believe, Irish poetry generally has benefited from the expiation performed by this tradition of Lough Derg literature, two hundred years of painful but liberating meditation. Ireland is now enjoying a new era of religious poetry. By "religious" I emphatically do not mean Catholic, nor do I refer to any orthodoxy. Poets in Ireland are now free to use the innate resource of childhood religion to explore the complexities of personal and cultural maturity. I have tried to point this out in passing, especially as it converges with gender, in the poetry of Eiléan Ní Chuilleanáin and Medbh McGuckian. As both these poets demonstrate, religious instincts, lodged in the viscera of memory, become a key element in the safe exploration that can occur in the space of the poem. Perhaps, however, no contemporary poet after Heaney has confronted these first and last things with as much stamina, independence and ludic energy as Paul Muldoon. It is both ironic and logical that this most irreverent of poets is also one of Ireland's most religiously trenchant. Acclaimed perhaps more for his verbal tricks, high to low cultural allusiveness, and infinitely recessive reflexivity and intertextuality, he is also an unorthodox religious poet. One word that crops up repeatedly from his early to late poetry is "mystery." We have the postmodernist masterwork of "Madoc, a Mystery" and, at the start of his career, the limpid but opaque "Why Brownlee Left," which begins: "Why Brownlee left, and where he went / Is a mystery even now." The countless inadequate explanations for this disappearance encoded in this cryptic, elegant sonnet range from emigration to theological translation, a process more swift and complete even than ordinary death.

It should be no surprise, therefore, that Muldoon has his own, little-noted history as a Lough Derg writer. One of his earliest publications, *Knowing My Place* (1971), includes a poem, "The Island," that is about "Station Island." The poem, bearing the endnote, "Lough Derg, 1969," also tells us that the other poems collected here were written on that island. Muldoon refers to:

> A year that taught me nothing
> About God. Only that by wettings
>
> And dryings He shrank that Island
> To a summary of itself. A year that taught me nothing
> About verse. Only that these poems,
> Composed on that island, are guesses
> At the truth, summaries of themselves
> Like the miniature trees in an Oriental garden.[4]

With the near nihilism implied by the end-stopped and repeated word "nothing," Muldoon's response to the ordeal is in the key of "Vain My Visit to Lough Derg." Contemporizing that futility, however, he is also able to draw attention to the fallacy of Lough Derg as a synecdoche for Ireland. That various "wettings and dryings," conquests and rebellions, perhaps, have produced a need to oversimplify, to neatly summarize, is ironically cast as militating against complexity and truth, especially of a metaphysical variety. The beginning of the poem announces the theme of warped miniaturism that is echoed by the symmetrical ming trees at the end. The poem's first two lines are "The Japanese are expert / with that form the tanka." As though deliberately expanding the walls of the prison of "Lough Derg," Muldoon makes the sort of lateral move into a remote culture, a move we have seen so many of his Lough Derg predecessors perform. For Muldoon at this early stage, however, that sideways maneuver appears to be aesthetic in motivation, myopically focused on the fine points of a minimalist Japanese poetic form. A true subversion of essentialism, which reduces complexity to a dangerous island of idealization, has to wait for a much later poem. Here Muldoon executes another lateral move. Only now, much like Heaney's excursion into Dante, Muldoon occupies a context that expands complication beyond the bounds of human comprehension. Muldoon enters the Holocaust to reenter certain persistent questions in his work about the metaphysical implications of human oppression in its subtle and blatant forms.

Now, in Muldoon's latest collection *Moy Sand and Gravel,* we have "At the Sign of the Blackhorse, September 1999," which for one thing subverts Yeats as a metaphysical poet. Specifically, Muldoon executes a scathing rewriting of "A Prayer for My Daughter," interrogating above all its claim for the existence of "radical innocence." Beginning his revision and continuing the still unfinished task of reconstructing Irish male identity, Muldoon casts this poem as a prayer for his son. The newborn boy, safe in his pram, enjoys the high ground of the Muldoon home in Princeton, New Jersey, along the flooded Raritan Canal after Hurricane Floyd in September 1999. This flood becomes transformed into the flood survived by Noah and his family. The biblical parallel is enforced not least by the endless parallels of Muldoon's fantastic rhymes, a parade of often exotic animals lined up two by two and contained in the ark of this poem. While celebrating human resilience by the exuberance of its style, the poem also asks whether Mount Ararat, concretized in the here and now by the wooden house protecting Muldoon's nuclear family against the elements, really offers a new beginning. When, in the course of the poem, the punning author uncages the inevitable image of an actual rat from the name "Ararat," nothing less than Yahweh's covenant with a chosen people is thrown into doubt. By means of this rodent released by a flood in New Jersey, the reader scurries back into the Warsaw ghetto, where the starving ate anything. With his mordant word play, Muldoon allows us to glimpse the enormous span of his poem's ethical enquiry. "At the Sign of the Blackhorse, September 1999" ultimately fails to subscribe to a godless, unredeemed chaos or to one religion, one God, even *a* God. Rather, the poem presents us at a refreshingly simple level with one man, a father in a recognizably suburban setting, worrying about the safety and future of his child in the world he will inherit. This was also Yeats's posture in "A Prayer for my Daughter." The weather, too, was similar in Yeats's poem. There we have: "once more the storm was howling," "roof-leveling wind" and a "flooded stream"—evidence perhaps of a hurricane. More incisively, as he brings in specific lines from Yeats, Muldoon asks us to step back and consider whether Yeats's conceit of the storm fudges the issue of human responsibility. Or is it possible that the evil men do is as natural and inevitable as weather? Basically Muldoon is asking whether Yeats's wish for his daughter, a moral inviolability, is possible in the world that unfolded after 1919, the year when Yeats wrote his poem. This question became even more urgent after 1939, when Yeats died. Muldoon's poem indirectly asks whether those ironically exclusionary and double Irish and Anglo-Irish dreams of purity have any relevance for a family of irreducibly hybrid origins, the condition, after all, of any postcolonial scion. Muldoon takes Yeats's absolutist and elitist claim, echoing that of nationalists, and drags it through the alleyways and tenements of the Warsaw ghetto, questioning its veracity in the lurid hell of the Holocaust. This poem alone is a literary and cultural event that has been waiting to happen since the nativist posturing of post-independence, isolationist Ireland. It marks a true maturation, an arrival at a point where a self-identified suffering people can empathically enter the pain of those who have suffered more. This is exactly what Milosz has asked poetry to do.

Muldoon also, with his habitation of and subversion of form, offers both continuity with the past and correction of it, as Milosz advises in his "Quarrel with Classicism." For example, in his parody of Yeats, Muldoon reproduces the stanza structure of "A Prayer for My Daughter" (aabbcddc) through his rhyme scheme but undermines it by erratically varying his line lengths. Overall, however, in not just his modified adherence to but mastery of form, he inadvertently follows Milosz's prescription for the self-conscious use of literary convention in a post-Holocaust world: as a clarifier of the dark history from which it emerged. Muldoon meditates on what the evidence of history beyond Ireland has to say about good and evil, whether perhaps, as Milosz suspected, Manichaeanism is closer to the truth than the triumph of good is. Once again, in these deliberations Muldoon is both on his own and part of a collective effort. "At the Sign of the Blackhorse, September 1999" in its remote ramifications may also gesture toward and challenge Heaney, a healthy indication. Readers of the Irish poetic tradition will not forget, after all, that in "The Placeless Heaven" Heaney, inveterately hybrid, once more returns to Yeats as a model against which now to measure Kavanagh's success. As Heaney puts it, "I believe now that it would be truer to say that when Kavanagh had consumed the roughage of his early Monaghan experience, he had cleared a space where, in Yeats's words,

> The soul recovers radical innocence,
> and learns at last that it is self-delighting,
> self-appeasing, self-affrighting,
> And that its own sweet will is Heaven's will."[5]

Heaney appeals to the definition of poetry embedded in "A Prayer for My Daughter," the very playfulness Milosz links to a childlike innocence in need of protection.

The endless dialectics of Heaney's relationships with both Kavanagh and Yeats, and of Muldoon's with both Heaney and Yeats, add up to a truly blessed freedom, which allows emulation and revision of all predecessors. Heaney locates the place where such freedom begins to flex its newly discovered muscles when, as he puts it, Kavanagh "cleared a space." The historical irony behind the title "Clearances," that oppression and liberation are tragically linked, that the takeover of land also represents an annihilation of the familiar, a grim opportunity for new inquiry, is perhaps the final lesson to be learned from Lough Derg. In "At the Sign of the Blackhorse, September 1999" Muldoon has the ghost of one of his wife's ancestors angrily ask, on the occasion of their son's birth, "By which authority did we deny Asher a mohel? / By which authority did we deny Asher a rebe?" These two questions add up to the same question: why, having decided not to have Asher circumcised, did they deny him a traditional Jewish male start in life? The nub of the question is touched, however, in the phrase "by which authority." The projected speaker believes in authority, that of sacred text. The listener, who like Heaney in "Station Island" has invented his own ghosts, written his own text, is uncertain that any one central authority reigns in our centrifugal world. This can be the perverse legacy of any authoritarian state, the final abrogation of all authority beyond private conscience. That may be why religious poetry, above all, eventually thrives in a country where the hegemonic attempt has been made to conquer the individual soul. Muldoon, freed of the past sufficiently to set his poetry firmly in the futuristic present, encases his meditation in a context ruled by the new multinational imperialisms, which speak in a bloodless, peremptory language that micromanages hapless humans. For every parodied Yeatsian reference in "At the Sign of the Blackhorse, September 1999" there are half a dozen other signifiers from contemporary, ordinary life: from instructions on the highway—at tollbooths, gas pumps, intersections: "No Way Out," "Do Not Fill Above the Line," No Turn on Red," "Road Narrows," "Stop Ahead," "Do Not Drive in Breakdown Lane," "Keep Clear, All Directions"; to those in public spaces: "Please Use Tongs," "Please Use the Hammer to Break the Glass," "Please Leave the Window Ajar," "Do Not Litter," "Keep Out"; to those in the air: "Place Mask Over Mouth and Nose" or on the train, "Please Remember to Take Your Belongings When You Leave the Train."[6] This list hardly exhausts these inserted imperatives, but the last particularly, among a plethora that suggest human beings in transit, is poignantly evocative of the Jews under the Nazis being shunted from Eastern European cities like Milosz's Warsaw to concentration camps like Auschwitz. Muldoon suggests that we are all perpetually in transit, on pilgrimage, as it were. There is no longer, however, one, well-marked way. In "At the Sign of the Blackhorse, September 1999" he imaginatively follows a tandem path, not just that of his wife's ancestors but of his own, those "Irish schlemiels,"[7] scrappy emigrant laborers, who built the canal that flows in front of the comfortable house he still can barely believe he owns. After all, how can one own anything material when the concept of possession itself has been thoroughly gutted? Yet Muldoon thrives in, possesses the cracks made by competing histories. Following one track of history, one tradition is as impossible for him as imagining a child without two parents. And like every child ever born he "finds himself" in the space between. Both Heaney and Muldoon have made a virtue of historical disinheritance by staking a claim in their respective versions of a "bright nowhere." Heaney's metaphysical ambit hovers "beyond silence listened for." Muldoon's, less transcendentally, walks the length of that symptomatic line along the Raritan Canal: "between the preposterous two-path and the preposterous berm,"[8] the purgatory of now.

Notes

❧

Bibliography

❧

Index

Notes

Introduction

1. William Carleton, "The Lough Derg Pilgrim," in Carleton, *Traits and Stories of the Irish Peasantry,* ed. Barbara Haley, (Gerrards Cross, Bucks: Colin Smythe, 1990; facsimile of 1844 edition), 238.

2. Peter Harbison, *Pilgrimage in Ireland* (London: Barrie and Jenkins, 1991), 70.

3. Czeslaw Milosz, *A Treatise on Poetry* (New York: HarperCollins, 2001), 5.

4. Ibid.

5. Helen Vendler, "A Lament in Three Voices," *New York Review of Books,* 31 May 2001, 31.

6. Milosz, *Treatise on Poetry,* 1.

7. Ibid.

8. Ibid., 5.

9. Ibid., 1.

10. Jacques Le Goff, *The Birth of Purgatory* (Chicago: Univ. of Chicago Press, 1981), 193–201.

11. Patrick Pearse, "The Murder Machine," in *The Field Day Anthology of Irish Writing,* ed. Seamus Deane (New York: Norton, 1991), 2:291.

12. David Lloyd, *Nationalism and Minor Literature* (Los Angeles: Univ. of California Press, 1987), x.

13. Kevin Whelan, "The Regional Impact of Irish Catholicism, 1700–1850," in *Common Ground,* ed. W. J. Smyth and Kevin Whelan (Cork: Cork Univ. Press, 1980), 253–77.

14. Lawrence Taylor, "Irish Catholicism," *Archive des Sciences Sociales Des Religions,* 71, 35e anné, July-Sept. 1990, 98.

1. The History

1. Deirdre Purcell, *On Lough Derg* (Dublin: Veritas, 1988), 7.

2. Shane Leslie, *Saint Patrick's Purgatory* (London: Burnes Oates and Washbourne, 1932), 171.

3. Purcell, *On Lough Derg,* 76.

4. Leslie, *St. Patrick's Purgatory,* 138.

5. Julia Kristeva, *The Kristeva Reader,* ed. Toril Moi (Oxford: Blackwell, 1986), 161.

6. Pedro Calderón de la Barca, *Calderón's Dramas,* ed. and trans. Denis Florence MacCarthy (London: Kegan, Paul Trench, 1887), 248.

7. Jean Michel Picard, trans., *Saint Patrick's Purgatory: A Twelfth Century Tale of a Journey to the Other World* (Dublin: Four Courts Press, 1985), 63.

8. Ibid., 73.

9. From Thomas Carve, *Lyra; sive Anacephalaeosis Hibernica* (Sulzbach 1666).

10. Leslie, *St. Patrick's Purgatory,* 56.

11. Ibid., 62.

12. Ibid.

13. Ibid.

14. Ibid.

15. Ibid., 64.

16. Ibid., 80.

17. Ibid., 82.

18. Ibid., 113.

19. Victor Turner, *The Ritual Process* (Harmondsworth, U.K.: Penguin, 1974), 81. Turner explains: "The attributes of liminality or of liminal personae ('threshold people') are necessarily ambiguous, since this condition and

these persons elude or slip through the network of classifications that normally locate states and positions in cultural space."

20. Harbison, *Pilgrimage in Ireland*, 64.

21. Tadhg Ó Dúshláine, *Lough Derg in Native Irish Poetry* (Dublin: An Clóchóir, 1987), 1.

22. Ibid., 2.

23. Ibid., 3.

24. Thomas Kinsella and Seán Ó Tuama, *An Duanaire* (Dublin: Dolmen Press, 1981), 26.

25. Ó Dúshláine, *Lough Derg*, 9.

26. Samuel Dillon, *Sketches of the Scenery, History and Antiquities of the North-West of Ireland; including A Minute Account of the celebrated Lough Derg, & Patrick's Purgatory, in the County Donegal*, (Dublin: J. Jones, 1818), 21.

27. Rev. Philip Skelton, Rector of Fintona, *The Complete Works*, ed. Orobert Lyman (London: Richard Baynes, 1824), 5:16.

28. Ibid., 19–20.

29. Rev. Mr Reilly, *Hindooism in Ireland or, a succinct Account of the Celebrated Saint Patrick's Purgatory at Loughderg, and a similar Station, lately established, at Coronea, In the County of Cavan* (Dublin: Richard Moore Tims, 1826), 3.

30. Kevin Whelan, *The Tree of Liberty* (Cork: Cork Univ. Press, 1996), 100.

31. Carleton, *Traits and Stories*, 238.

32. Tess Hurson, *Inside the Margins: A Carleton Reader* (Belfast: Lagan Press, 1992), 11.

33. Seamus Deane, *A Short History of Irish Literature* (South Bend, Ind.: Univ. of Notre Dame Press, 1986), 109.

34. Ibid.

35. Denis Florence MacCarthy, *Poems* (Dublin: M. H. Gill and Son, 1882), 243.

36. Denis Florence MacCarthy, *Poets and Dramatists of Ireland: with an Introduction on the Early Religion and Literature of the Irish People* (Dublin: James Duffy, 1846).

37. *The Táin*, trans. Thomas Kinsella (Oxford: Oxford Univ. Press, 1969), xiv (e.g., "A strong element in the sagas is their directness in bodily matters: the easy references to seduction, copulation, urination, the picking of vermin, the suggestion of incest in 'How Cúchulainn was Begotten.' ")

38. Letter from Irish cardinal in Rome, 5 May 1882, *Irish Monthly*, May-June 1882, 445.

39. Daniel (D. Canon) O'Connor, *Lough Derg and Its Pilgrimages* (Dublin: Joseph Dollard, 1879), 197.

40. Shane Leslie, *Lough Derg in Ulster* (Dublin: Maunsel and Co., 1909), 1.

41. Charles Gavan Duffy, *Young Ireland: A Fragment of Irish History 1840–1850* (New York: D. Appleton & Co, 1881), 14.

42. *Collected Stories of Seán O'Faoláin* (Boston: Atlantic Monthly Press Book, Little Brown, 1932), 465.

43. Patrick Kavanagh, *The Complete Poems* (Newbridge, Ireland: Goldsmith Press, 1972), 124.

44. *Collected Poems of Denis Devlin*, ed. J. C. C. Mays (Dublin: Dedalus Press, 1989), 132.

45. Ibid., 135.

46. Denis Donoghue, *We Irish* (New York: Knopf, 1986), in the chapter, "Yeats: The Question of Symbolism," 34–51.

47. Duffy, *Young Ireland*, 14.

48. Seamus Heaney, *Station Island* (New York: Farrar, Straus and Giroux, 1985), 93–94.

2. William Carleton: A Poet, but Not a Fanatic

1. Carleton, *Traits and Stories*, 238.

2. Ibid., 251.

3. Ibid., 242.

4. Ibid., 255.

5. Whelan, *Tree of Liberty*, 141.

6. Carleton, *Traits and Stories*, xvi.

7. Ibid., 236.

8. Whelan, *The Tree of Liberty*, 59.

9. Kavanagh, *Complete Poems*, 14.

10. Kevin Whelan, *Tree of Liberty*, 59.

11. Carleton, *Traits and Stories*, xvi.

12. Ibid., 255.

13. Ibid., 255.

14. Ibid., 242.

15. Ibid.

16. Ibid., 255.

17. Ibid., 250.

18. Ibid., 251.

19. Ibid., 243.

20. Ibid.

21. Ibid., 241.

22. Ibid., 251.

23. Ibid.

24. Ibid.

25. Ibid., 253.

26. Heaney, *Station Island,* 64.

27. Carleton, *Traits and Stories,* 248.

28. Ibid., 249.

29. Ibid., xxii.

30. Ibid., 259.

31. Ibid.

32. Ibid., 261.

33. Ibid., 256.

34. Ibid., 358.

35. Ibid., 349–50.

36. Ibid., 355.

37. Ibid.

38. Ibid., 357.

39. Ibid., 351.

40. Ibid., 355.

41. Ibid., 361.

42. Ibid., 362.

43. Ibid.

44. Ibid.

3. Denis Florence MacCarthy: A True Irish Poet?

1. *Irish Ecclesiastical Review,* July 1882, 420.

2. Lloyd, *Nationalism,* 82.

3. Denis Florence MacCarthy, *Shelley's Early Life* (London: John Camden, 1872), vi.

4. Rev. Matthew Russell, SJ, *Irish Monthly,* January, 1903, 8.

5. Lloyd, *Nationalism,* 59.

6. Ibid., 71.

7. Ibid.

8. MacCarthy, *Shelley's Early Life,* xiv.

9. *Irish Monthly* 36 (June 1908): 344.

10. *Irish Monthly* 31 (June 1903): 9.

11. Duffy, *Young Ireland,* 293.

12. Lloyd, *Nationalism,* 101.

13. Duffy, *Young Ireland,* 297.

14. *Irish Monthly,* May-June 1882, 446.

15. *Irish Monthly* 19 (May 1891): 214.

16. W. B. Yeats, "The Celtic Element in Literature," in *Poetry and Ireland Since 1800,* ed. Mark Storey (New York: Routledge, 1998), 115.

17. "The Purgatory of Saint Patrick," *Calderón's Dramas,* 347–48.

18. Ibid., 350.

19. Ibid., 353.

20. *Poems of Denis Florence MacCarthy* (Dublin and Cork: The Educational Company, 1882), 1.

21. Charles Gavan Duffy, *Ballad Poetry of Ireland* (Dublin: James Duffy, 1845), xv.

22. Ibid., xlviii.

23. *Irish Monthly* 36 (June 1908): 343.

24. *Irish Monthly* 31 (June 1904): 11.

25. Denis Florence MacCarthy, *The Book of Irish Ballads* (Dublin: James Duffy, 1846), 26.

26. Ibid., 19.

27. Ibid.

28. Ibid., 16.

29. Ibid., 26.

30. MacCarthy, *Poets and Dramatists,* 16.

31. Ibid., vi.

32. Ibid., vii.

33. *Dublin University Magazine,* Dec. 1851, 711.

34. MacCarthy, *Poets and Dramatists,* 18.

35. MacCarthy, Denis Florence, trans., prefatory note to Calderón, *The Two Lovers of Heaven, Chrysanthus and Daria: A Drama of Early Christian Rome,* (Dublin: John F. Fowler, 1870), ii.

36. MacCarthy, *Poets and Dramatists,* 11.

37. MacCarthy, *Calderón's Dramas,* xii.

38. Ibid., x.

39. Ibid., viii.

40. Ibid., ix.

41. *Dublin University Magazine,* Apr. 1862, 447.

42. Ibid., 443.

43. Samuel Ferguson from *Dublin Magazine,* 1834, *Poetry and Ireland since 1800,* ed. Mark Storey (New York: Routledge, 1998), 42.

44. MacCarthy, *Calderón's Dramas,* 279.

45. Ibid.

46. Ibid., xii.

47. Ibid., 295.

48. Ibid., 308.

49. *Irish Monthly,* May 1891: 253.

4. O'Connor, Leslie, Curtayne, and O'Faoláin: Perfect Ease in Home Surroundings

1. Terence Brown, *Ireland: A Social and Cultural History, 1922 to the Present* (Ithaca, N.Y.: Cornell Univ. Press, 1985), 33.

2. Joseph Timoney, *St Patrick's Purgatory, Lough Derg: Impressions of a Pilgrim* (Enniskillen: Fermanagh Herald, 1926), 5.

3. Ibid., 8.

4. Brown, *Ireland,* 29.

5. D. Canon O'Connor, *St. Patrick's*

Purgatory, Lough Derg (Dublin: James Duffy and Son, 1931), v.

6. Ibid., v-vi.

7. Ibid., vi.

8. Ibid., xi.

9. Ibid., xii

10. Ibid., viii.

11. Ibid., vi.

12. O'Connor, *Lough Derg and Its Pilgrimages*, 2–3.

13. O'Connor, *St. Patrick's Purgatory*, 192–93.

14. O'Connor, *Lough Derg and Its Pilgrimages*, 2–4.

15. Ibid.

16. O'Connor, *St. Patrick's Purgatory*, viii-ix.

17. Ibid., ix.

18. Ibid., 12.

19. Ibid., 12.

20. Ibid., 84–85.

21. O'Connor, *Lough Derg and Its Pilgrimages*, 80.

22. O'Connor, *St. Patrick's Purgatory*, 21.

23. Ibid, 12.

24. Ibid. 12.

25. Ibid.

26. Ibid., 13.

27. Ibid., 12.

28. Ibid., 13.

29. Ibid., 56.

30. Ibid., 140–41.

31. Ibid., 132.

32. Ibid.

33. Ibid., 115–16.

34. Ibid., 191.

35. Ibid., 188.

36. Ibid., 189.

37. Ibid.

38. Ibid., 30.

39. Carleton, *Traits and Stories*, 270.

40. A. T. Lucas, *Penal Crucifixes* (Dublin: National Museum of Ireland, 1958).

41. O'Connor, *St. Patrick's Purgatory*, 241.

42. Shane Leslie, *Long Shadows* (London: John Murray, 1966), 39.

43. Ibid., 4.

44. Alice Curtayne, *Lough Derg* (Monaghan: R and S Printing, 1944), 95–07.

45. Ibid., 101.

46. Ibid., 106.

47. Ibid., 100.

48. Ibid., 98–99.

49. Ibid., 99.

50. Ibid., 99.

51. Ibid., 100.

52. Leslie, *Long Shadows*, 39.

53. Ibid., 4.

54. Ibid., 4.

55. Ibid., 4.

56. Ibid., 5.

57. Ibid.

58. Ibid.

59. Shane Leslie, *The Celt and the World* (New York: Charles Scribner's Sons, 1917), 203.

60. Shane Leslie, *The End of a Chapter* (New York: Charles Scribner's Sons, 1916) 17.

61. Ibid.

62. Ibid., 93.

63. Ibid., 94.

64. Leslie, *Long Shadows*, 118.

65. Ibid., 122–26.

66. Ibid., 152.

67. Leslie, *Celt and the World*, 88.

68. Ibid., 201.

69. Ibid., 199.

70. Ibid., 18–19.

71. Ibid., 163.

72. Ibid., 172.

73. Ibid., 177.

74. Ibid., 204.

75. Ibid., 143.

76. Ibid., 41.

77. Ibid., 1.

78. Ibid., 4.

79. Ibid., 20–21.

80. Ibid., 22.

81. Ibid., 73.

82. Ibid., 53.

83. Ibid., 46.

84. Ibid., 65.

85. Ibid., 82.

86. Ibid., 85.

87. Luke Gibbons, *Gaelic Gothic* (Galway: Arlen House, 2004), 10.

88. Ibid., 13.

89. Leslie, *Long Shadows*, 146.

90. Ibid., 147.

91. Ibid., 142. ("He is a real 'Playboy' with a tremendous twinkle and sudden quick impulsive gestures.")

92. Leslie, *Celt and the World*, 26.
93. Leslie, *End of a Chapter*, 125.
94. Ibid., 136.
95. Ibid., 133–34.
96. Ibid., 154.
97. Ibid., 69.
98. Leslie, *Celt and the World*, 111.
99. Ibid., 111.
100. Ibid., 8.
101. Leslie, *End of a Chapter*, 173.
102. Leslie, *Celt and the World*, 45.
103. Alice Curtayne, *A Recall to Dante* (1932; repr., Port Washington, N.Y.: Kennikat Press, 1969), 111.
104. Ibid., 108.
105. Ibid., 112.
106. Ibid.
107. Ibid., 113.
108. Ibid., 112.
109. Seamus Heaney, private conversation with author.
110. Curtayne, *Recall to Dante*, 50.
111. Ibid., 46.
112. Ibid., 30.
113. Ibid., 215.
114. Ibid., 215.
115. Ibid., 12.
116. Ibid., 12.
117. Ibid., 66.
118. Ibid., 156.
119. Ibid., 179.
120. Ibid., 79.
121. Ibid., 78.
122. Ibid., 79.
123. Ibid., 94.
124. Ibid., 95.
125. Ibid., 107.
126. Ibid., 68.
127. Ibid., 190.
128. Ibid., 109.
129. Ibid., 109.
130. Curtayne, *Lough Derg*, 33.
131. Ibid., 34.
132. Ibid., 35.
133. Ibid.
134. Ibid., 36.
135. Ibid.
136. Ibid. 35.
137. Ibid., 38.
138. Ibid., 37.

139. Ibid., 50.
140. Ibid.
141. Ibid.
142. Ibid., 54.
143. Ibid., Foreword.
144. Harbison, *Pilgrimage in Ireland*, 65.
145. Curtayne, *Lough Derg*, 6–7.
146. Ibid., Foreword.
147. Ibid.
148. Ibid., 11.
149. Ibid., 37.
150. Ibid., 12.
151. Ibid., 16.
152. Kavanagh, *Complete Poems*, 100.
153. Curtayne, *Lough Derg*, 1.
154. Ibid., 123.
155. Timoney, *St Patrick's Purgatory*, 5.
156. Brown, *Ireland*, 155.
157. Ibid., 73.
158. John Montague, "An Occasion for Sin," *Death of a Chieftain* (Chester Springs, Pa.: Dufour, 1967), 119.
159. Ibid., 115.
160. Ibid., 119.
161. O'Faolain, *Collected Stories*, 559.
162. Ibid.
163. Ibid., 569.
164. Ibid., 458.
165. Ibid., 462.

5. Denis Devlin: Clan Jansen

1. Devlin, *Collected Poems*, 264.
2. Ibid.
3. Ibid., 264–65.
4. Antoinette Quinn, *Patrick Kavanagh: Born-Again Romantic* (Dublin: Gill and Macmillan, 1993), 154.
5. Kavanagh, "The Great Hunger," *Complete Poems*, 90.
6. Devlin, *Collected Poems*, 271.
7. Ibid., introduction by J. C. C. Mays, 26.
8. Tim Armstrong, "Muting the Klaxon: Poetry, History and Irish Modernism," in *Modernism and Ireland*, ed. Patricia Coughlan and Alex Davis (Cork: Cork Univ. Press, 1995), 46.
9. Deane, *Short History of Irish Literature*, 231.
10. Armstrong, "Muting the Klaxon," 46.

11. Ibid., 71.

12. John Wilson Foster, "Irish Modernism," in *Colonial Consequences* (Dublin: Lilliput Press, 1991), 50.

13. Dillon Johnston, *Irish Poetry after Joyce,* 2d ed. (Syracuse: Syracuse Univ. Press, 1997), 168.

14. T. S. Eliot, *The Complete Poems and Plays* (New York: Harcourt, Brace and World, 1934), 6.

15. Devlin, *Collected Poems*, 260.

16. Ibid., 273.

17. Ibid., 262.

18. Ibid., 154–55.

19. Ibid., 262.

20. Ibid., 266.

21. Ibid., 268.

22. Ibid., 263.

23. Ibid., 274.

24. Alex Davis, *A Broken Line: Denis Devlin and Irish Poetic Modernism* (Dublin: Univ. College Dublin Press, 2000), 93.

25. Ibid.

26. Anne Fogarty, "Gender, Irish Modernism, and Devlin," in *Modernism and Ireland*, ed. Patricia Coughlan and Alex Davis (Cork: Cork Univ. Press, 1995) 223.

27. Medbh McGuckian, *Marconi's Cottage* (Oldcastle, Ireland: Gallery Press, 1991), 71.

28. Joseph Brodsky, "A Hidden Duet," *Times Literary Supplement,* 27 Aug. 1991, 16.

29. Ibid., 13.

30. Ibid.

31. Ibid.

32. Ibid., 14.

33. Ibid.

34. Ibid.

35. Ibid., 14.

36. Ibid.

37. Ibid.

38. Ibid.

39. Ibid.

40. Ibid.

41. Ibid.

42. Ibid.

43. Ibid.

44. Ibid., 15.

45. Devlin, *Collected Poems,* 132.

46. Ibid., 135.

47. Ibid., 132.

48. Ibid., 139.

49. Ibid., 132.

50. Ibid.

51. Ibid.

52. Ibid.

53. Ibid.

54. Ibid.

55. Ibid.

56. Ibid.

57. Ibid.

58. Robert Welch, "Language as Pilgrimage: Lough Derg Poems of Patrick Kavanagh and Denis Devlin," *Irish University Review* 31 (Spring 1983): 61.

59. Devlin, *Collected Poems,* 132.

60. Ibid.

61. Ibid., 133.

62. Ibid.

63. Ibid., 132.

64. Ibid., 133.

65. Ibid.

66. Ibid., 134.

67. Ibid.

68. Ibid.

69. Ibid., 134.

70. Ibid., 133.

71. Ibid., 134.

72. Ibid., 134.

73. Ibid., 134.

74. Ibid., 135.

75. Ibid.

76. Ibid.

77. Ibid.

78. Ibid.

79. Ibid.

80. Ibid.

81. Ibid.

82. Ibid.

83. Johnston, *Irish Poetry after Joyce*, 169.

6. Patrick Kavanagh: Compassion's Ecstasy

1. Antoinette Quinn, *Patrick Kavanagh: A Biography* (Dublin: Gill and MacMillan, 2001), 196.

2. Ibid., 193.

3. Marjorie Howes, *Yeats's Nations* (Cambridge: Cambridge Univ. Press, 1966), 20.

4. Quinn, *Patrick Kavanagh: Born-Again Romantic,* 139.

5. Ibid., 129.

6. Ibid., 135.

7. Ibid.

8. Ibid., 128.

9. Patrick Kavanagh, *Collected Poems* (London: Allen Lane, Penguin Books, 2004), 37.

10. Quinn, *Born Again Romantic,* 154.

11. Seamus Heaney, "From Monaghan to the Grand Canal," in *Preoccupations* (London: Faber and Faber, 1980), 126.

12. Seamus Heaney, *Redress of Poetry* (Oldcastle, Ireland: Gallery Press, 1995), 3.

13. Kavanagh, *Collected Poems,* 73.

14. Ibid.

15. Ibid., 73–74.

16. Ibid., 69.

17. Ibid., 70.

18. Ibid., 69.

19. Ibid., 80.

20. Ibid., 69.

21. Ibid., 74.

22. Ibid., 78.

23. Ibid., 76.

24. Ibid.

25. Ibid., 73.

26. Ibid.

27. Ibid., 71.

28. Ibid., 63.

29. Ibid., 68.

30. Ibid., 76.

31. Ibid., 70.

32. Ibid., 72.

33. Ibid.

34. Ibid.

35. Ibid.

36. Ibid.

37. Ibid.

38. Ibid.

39. Ibid., 68.

40. Ibid., 63.

41. Ibid., 66.

42. Ibid., 65.

43. Ibid., 80.

44. Ibid., 81.

45. Ibid., 224.

46. Ibid.

47. Ibid., 63.

48. Ibid., 85.

49. Ibid.

50. Ibid.

51. Ibid.

52. Ibid., 86.

53. Ibid., 80.

54. Ibid.

55. Ibid., 74–75.

56. Ibid., 67.

57. Ibid., 69.

58. Ibid., 76.

59. Ibid., 124.

60. Ibid., 46.

61. Ibid., 47.

62. Ibid.

63. Ibid.

64. Ibid., 48.

65. Ibid., 47.

66. Ibid., 58.

67. Ibid.

68. Ibid.

69. Ibid., 48–49.

70. Ibid., 45.

71. Ibid.

72. Ibid., 55.

73. Ibid.

74. Ibid., 44.

75. Ibid., 45.

76. Ibid., 53.

77. Ibid., 53.

78. Ibid., 50–51.

79. Ibid., 52.

80. Kavanagh, *Patrick Kavanagh: A Biography,* 81.

81. Ibid., 203–4.

82. Kavanagh, *Collected Poems,* 79.

83. Ibid., 51.

84. Ibid.

85. Ibid., 59.

86. Ibid., 63.

87. Quinn, *Patrick Kavanagh: A Biography,* 201.

88. Kavanagh, *Collected Poems,* 104.

89. Quinn, *Patrick Kavanagh: Born-Again Romantic,* 178.

90. Ibid.

91. Ibid.

92. Kavanagh, *Collected Poems,* 100.

93. Ibid., 102.

94. Welch, "Language as Pilgrimage," 56.

95. Kavanagh, *Collected Poems,* 90.

96. Ibid., 90.

97. Ibid.

98. Ibid., 91.

99. Ibid.

100. Quinn, *Patrick Kavanagh: A Biography,* 195.

101. Kavanagh, *Collected Poems,* 91.

102. Ibid., 93.

103. Ibid.

104. Ibid., 217.

105. Ibid., 93–94.

106. Quinn, *Patrick Kavanagh: A Biography,* 193.

107. Tom Stack, *No Earthly Estate: Patrick Kavanagh and God* (Dublin: Columba Press, 2002), 173.

108. Kavanagh, *Collected Poems,* 92.

109. Ibid., 206.

110. Ibid., 208.

111. Ibid., 207.

112. Ibid., 110.

113. Ibid., 92.

114. Ibid.

115. Ibid., 110.

116. Ibid., 102.

117. Ibid., 105–6.

118. *Selected Prose of T. S. Eliot,* ed. Frank Kermode (London: Faber and Faber, 1975), 255.

119. Welch, "Language as Pilgrimage," 56.

120. Ibid.

121. Kavanagh, *Collected Poems,* 90.

122. Ibid., 100.

123. Ibid., 101.

124. Ibid., 92.

125. Ibid., 96.

7. Seamus Heaney and the Politics of Poetics: Strumming a Harp of Unforgiving Iron

1. Carleton, *Traits and Stories,* 5.

2. Heaney, *Station Island,* 79.

3. Ibid., 80.

4. Ibid.

5. Ibid.

6. Seamus Heaney, "A Dream of Solstice," *Irish Times,* 21 Dec. 1999, 1.

7. Heaney, *Crediting Poetry* (Oldcastle, Ireland: Gallery Press, 1995).

8. Seamus Heaney, *Seeing Things* (London: Faber and Faber, 1991), 66.

9. Seamus Heaney, *Field Work* (London: Faber and Faber, 1979), 33.

10. Seamus Heaney, *The Haw Lantern* (New York: Farrar, Straus and Giroux, 1987), 31.

11. Helen Vendler, *Seamus Heaney* (Cambridge, Mass.: Harvard Univ. Press, 1998), 117.

12. Adrian Frazier, "Anger and Nostalgia: Seamus Heaney and the Ghost of the Father," *Eire-Ireland* (Fall/Winter 2001): 14.

13. Heaney, *Redress of Poetry,* 150.

14. Ibid.

15. Ibid., 158.

16. Heaney, *Station Island,* 83.

17. Ibid.

18. Ibid.

19. Heaney, *Redress of Poetry,* 149.

20. Ibid.

21. Ibid., 151.

22. Ibid.

23. Ibid., 159.

24. Ibid., 153.

25. Seamus Heaney, *The Spirit Level* (New York: Farrar, Straus and Giroux, 1996), 36.

26. Seamus Heaney, *North* (London: Faber and Faber, 1975), 32.

27. Heaney, *Field Work,* 12.

28. O'Connor, *St. Patrick's Purgatory,* 241.

29. Ibid.

30. Heaney, *Station Island,* 62.

31. Ibid.

32. Seamus Deane, "Heroic Styles: The Tradition of an Idea," *Field Day,* pamphlet no. 4 (Derry: Field Day, 1984), 5.

33. Heaney, *Station Island,* 87.

34. Heaney, *North,* 8.

35. Ibid.

36. Thomas Merton and Czeslaw Milosz, *Striving Towards Being: The Letters of Thomas Merton and Czeslaw Milosz,* ed. Robert Faggen (New York: Farrar, Straus and Giroux, 1997), 35.

37. Ibid., 115.

38. Heaney, *Station Island,* 75.

39. Ibid., 89.

40. Ibid.

41. Ibid., 89–91.

42. Ibid., 90.

43. Ibid.

44. Heaney, *Seeing Things,* 1.

45. Wallace Stevens, *Selected Poems* (London: Faber and Faber, 1953), 36.

46. Heaney, *Station Island,* 87.

47. Heaney, "A Dream of Solstice."

48. Ibid.

49. Vendler, *Seamus Heaney*, 94.

50. Heaney, *Haw Lantern*, 30.

51. Ibid., 26.

52. Heaney, *Station Island*, 94.

8. Heaney's Ghosts: And Maybe There's a Lesson There for You

1. Heaney, *Station Island*, 93.

2. Ibid., 93.

3. Ibid., 94.

4. James Joyce, *A Portrait of the Artist as a Young Man* (Harmondsworth, U.K.: Penguin, 1964), 31.

5. Ibid., 37.

6. Ibid., 38.

7. Ibid., 38.

8. Ibid., 37.

9. *The Collected Works of W. B. Yeats*, ed. Richard Finneran (New York: Scribner's, 1997), 1:162.

10. Merton and Milosz, *Striving Towards Being*.

11. Dante Alighieri, *The Divine Comedy*, trans. John D. Sinclair (New York: Oxford Univ. Press, 1961), *Purgatorio*, canto xxx, 397.

12. Ibid., 395.

13. Dante, *The Divine Comedy*, trans. John D. Sinclair, *Inferno*, v, 75.

14. Heaney, *Station Island*, 69.

15. Ibid., 75.

16. Ibid., 76.

17. Ibid., 75.

18. Ibid., 93.

19. Ibid., 75.

20. Dante, *Inferno*, canto ii, lines 127–32 (according to Heaney's note in "Station Island").

21. Ibid.

22. Heaney, *Station Island*, 76.

23. Ibid., 73.

24. Ibid., 75.

25. Ibid.

26. Ibid., 93.

27. Ibid., 67.

28. Ibid.

29. Ibid.

30. Heaney, "Mossbawn," in *Preoccupations*, 17–18.

31. Ibid.

32. Kavanagh, *Complete Poems*, 294.

33. Dante, *Divine Comedy*, trans. John D. Sinclair, 103, 105.

34. Heaney, *Station Island*, 82.

35. Ibid., 85.

36. Dante, *Divine Comedy*, trans. John D. Sinclair, 61.

37. Dante, *Divine Comedy*, trans. John D. Sinclair, *Inferno*, 51.

38. Ibid., 115, 117.

39. Dante, *Divine Comedy*, trans. John D. Sinclair, *Inferno*, 39.

40. Leslie, *Saint Patrick's Purgatory*, xvii.

41. Ibid., xxiii (Leslie quotes *Inferno* iv).

42. Picard, *Saint Patrick's Purgatory*, 33.

43. Seamus Heaney, conversation with author.

44. Stephen Greenblatt, *Hamlet in Purgatory* (Princeton, N.J.: Princeton Univ. Press, 2001). Chapter 2, "Imagining Purgatory," is the most up-to-date synopsis, not just of these other narratives but of the many extant versions of the *Tractatus*.

45. Picard, *Saint Patrick's Purgatory*, 60.

46. Heaney, *Station Island*, 69.

47. Picard, *Saint Patrick's Purgatory*, 64.

48. Ibid., 65.

49. Heaney, *Station Island*, 76.

50. Ibid., 72.

51. Picard, *Saint Patrick's Purgatory*, 63.

52. Heaney, *Station Island*, 89.

53. Greenblatt, *Hamlet in Purgatory*, 5.

54. Ibid., 84.

55. Heaney, *Preoccupations*, 41.

56. Greenblatt, *Hamlet in Purgatory*, 92.

57. Ibid., 82.

58. Ibid., 82.

59. Ludwig Beiler, *The Irish Penitentials* (Dublin: Dublin Institute for Advanced Studies, 1975), 123.

60. Greenblatt, *Hamlet in Purgatory*, 212.

61. Heaney, *Station Island*, 85.

62. Ibid., 78.

63. Seamus Heaney, *Opened Ground* (New York: Farrar, Straus and Giroux, 1998), 241.

64. Heaney, *Station Island*, 80.

65. Ibid., 81.

66. Ibid.

67. Ibid., 82.

68. Ibid.

69. Ibid.

70. Ibid.

71. Ibid., 85.

72. Ibid.

73. Ibid., 67.

74. Ibid., 81.

75. Ibid.

76. Ibid., 82.

77. Medbh McGuckian, "Horsepower Pass By! A Study of the Car in the Poetry of Seamus Heaney," pamphlet (Coleraine, Northern Ireland: Crannagh Press, 1999), 3.

78. Heaney, *Station Island*, 64.

79. Ibid., 65.

80. Ibid.

81. Ibid., 66.

82. Ibid.

83. Ibid.

84. Ibid.

85. Ibid.

86. Ibid., 74.

87. Ibid., 73.

88. Heaney, *Preoccupations*, 43.

9. Heaney's Guides: Do Not Waver

1. David Lloyd, "Pap for the Dispossessed," in *Anomalous States: Irish Writing and the Post-Colonial Moment* (Durham, N.C.: Duke Univ. Press, 1993), 14–19.

2. Heaney, *Redress of Poetry*, 159.

3. Ibid., 1.

4. Wallace Stevens, *The Necessary Angel* (New York: Vintage, 1951), 3.

5. Ibid., 3–4.

6. Seamus Heaney, *The Government of the Tongue* (London: Faber and Faber, 1988), 5.

7. Ibid., 4.

8. Heaney, *Opened Ground*, 272.

9. Heaney, *Crediting Poetry*, 20.

10. Dante Alighieri, *Purgatorio* trans. Dorothy L. Sayers (Harmondsworth, U.K.: Penguin, 1955) canto ii, 17–18, 81.

11. Heaney, "A Dream of Solstice."

12. Ibid.

13. Dante, *Divine Comedy*, trans. John D. Sinclair, *Purgatorio*, 69.

14. Seamus Heaney, "Envies and Identifications: Dante and the Modern Poet," *Irish University Review* 15 (Spring 1985): 12.

15. Sayers translates: " 'Whoso would ask my name, I'd have him know / That I am Leah, who for my array / Twine gradlands, weaving white hands to and fro. / To please me at the glass I deck me gay; / The while my sister Rachel never stirs, / But sits before her mirror all the day, / For on her own bright eyes she still prefers / To gaze, as I to deck me with my hands; / Action is my delight, reflection hers.' " Dante, *Purgatorio*, trans. Dorothy L. Sayers, 284.

16. Yeats, *Collected Works*, 1:183.

17. Heaney, "Envies and Identifications," 10.

18. T. S. Eliot, *Dante* (London: Faber and Faber, 1929), 48.

19. Ibid.

20. Heaney, "Envies and Identifications," 16.

21. Osip Mandelstam, *The Complete Prose and Letters*, trans. Jane Gary Harris and Constance Link (Ann Arbor, Mich.: Ardis, 1979), 415.

22. Heaney, *Station Island*, 33.

23. *The Prose of Osip Mandelstam*, trans. Clarence Brown (Princeton, N.J.: Princeton Univ. Press, 1965), 88.

24. Medbh McGuckian, *On Ballycastle Beach* (Oxford: Oxford Univ. Press, 1988), 57.

25. Mandelstam, *The Complete Prose and Letters*, ed. Jane Gary Harris, trans. Jane Gary Harris and Constance Link (Ann Arbor, Mich.: Ardis, 1979), 414, 399.

26. Medbh McGuckian, *Captain Lavender* (Oldcastle, Ireland: Gallery Press, 1995), 42.

27. Heaney, *Haw Lantern*, 31.

28. Mandelstam, *Complete Prose and Letters*, 409.

29. R. F. Foster, *Modern Ireland: 1600–1972* (London: Penguin, 1989), 209.

30. Heaney, *Station Island*, 94.

31. Heaney, *Spirit Level*, 28–30.

32. Heaney, *Field Work*, 62.

33. Dante, *Inferno*, trans. Dorothy L. Sayers, 271.

34. Ibid., 276.

35. Ibid., 275.

36. Ibid., xxxii, 31–32, 272.

37. Ibid., 278.

38. Heaney, *Field Work*, 62.

39. Ibid., 61.

40. Dante, *Inferno*, trans. Dorothy L. Sayers, xxxiii, 7.

41. Heaney, *Government of the Tongue,* 30.

42. Heaney, *Seeing Things,* 94.

43. Ibid.

44. Ibid.

45. Czeslaw Milosz, *The Collected Poems* (Hopewell, N.J.: Ecco Press, 1988), 434.

46. Heaney, *Seeing Things,* 66.

47. *Merriam-Webster's Third New International Dictionary,* s.v. "prolepsis."

48. Ibid., 60.

49. Ibid., 60.

50. Ibid., 61.

51. Ibid.

52. Devlin, *Collected Poems,* 85.

53. Ibid., 87.

54. Heaney, *Seeing Things,* 55.

55. Ibid.

56. Ibid.

57. William Wordsworth, *The Prelude: Selected Poems and Sonnets,* ed. Carlos Baker (New York: Holt, Rinehart and Winston, 1965). This and the five preceding quotations are from "I Wandered Lonely as a Cloud," 143.

58. Heaney, *Seeing Things,* 55.

59. Ibid.

60. Ibid.

61. Ibid., 56.

62. Ibid.

63. Ibid.

64. Ibid., 62.

65. Ibid.

66. Ibid.

67. Ibid.

68. Ibid., 63.

69. Ibid., 56

70. Ibid.

71. Ibid.

72. Heaney, *Station Island,* 62.

73. Ibid.

74. Ibid.

10. Heaney and Milosz: Striving Toward Being

1. Milosz, *Collected Poems,* 210.

2. Heaney, *Government of the Tongue,* 40.

3. Ibid., 38.

4. Ibid., 40.

5. Ibid., 38.

6. Ibid., 33.

7. Ibid., 39.

8. Dante, *Inferno,* trans. Dorothy L. Sayers, xxxii, 12, 271.

9. Ibid., xxxii, 4–9.

10. Heaney, *Government of the Tongue,* 38.

11. Ibid., 41.

12. Ibid., 40.

13. Ibid., 39.

14. Ibid., 44.

15. Seamus Heaney, *District and Circle* (London: Faber and Faber, 2006), 47–51.

16. Heaney, *Government of the Tongue,* 56.

17. Merton and Milosz, *Striving Towards Being,* 62.

18. Heaney, *Finders Keepers* (New York: Farrar, Straus and Giroux, 2002), 444.

19. Merton and Milosz, *Striving Towards Being,* xi.

20. Heaney, *Haw Lantern,* 31.

21. Ibid., 32.

22. Merton and Milosz, *Striving Towards Being* 62.

23. Ibid., 89.

24. Ibid., 84.

25. Ibid., 61.

26. Ibid., 61.

27. Ibid., 22.

28. Ibid., 30–31.

29. Ibid., 119.

30. Ibid., 61.

31. Ibid., 50.

32. Ibid., 44.

33. Ibid., 110.

34. Ibid., 28.

35. Ibid., 104.

36. Ibid., 26–27.

37. Ibid., 28.

38. Ibid., 44.

39. Ibid., 120.

40. Ibid., 63.

41. Milosz, *Collected Poems,* 49.

42. Czeslaw Milosz, *Road-side Dog* (New York: Farrar, Straus and Giroux, 1998), 77.

43. Ibid., 22–23.

44. Heaney, *Government of the Tongue,* 38.

45. Czeslaw Milosz, *The Witness of Poetry* (Cambridge, Mass.: Harvard Univ. Press, 1979), 79.

46. Heaney, *Government of the Tongue,* 42.

47. Kevin Whelan, "The Memories of the

Dead," *Yale Journal of Criticism* 15, no. 1 (2002), 64.

48. Milosz, *Witness of Poetry*, 75.
49. Ibid., 84.
50. Ibid., 67.
51. Ibid., 80.
52. Ibid., 70.
53. Ibid.
54. Ibid., 65.
55. Ibid.
56. Ibid., 68.
57. Ibid., 7.
58. Ibid.
59. Ibid., 53.
60. Ibid., 42.
61. Ibid., 43.
62. Ibid., 9.
63. Ibid.
64. Ibid., 5.
65. Heaney, *Crediting Poetry.*
66. Milosz, *Witness of Poetry*, 66.
67. Ibid.
68. Milosz, *Collected Poems*, 106.
69. Ibid.
70. Ibid.
71. Ibid., 90.
72. Ibid., 85–87.
73. Ibid., 92.
74. Jan Kochanowski *Laments,* trans. Seamus Heaney and Stanislaw Baranczak (London: Faber and Faber, 1995), vii.
75. Ibid., 9.
76. Ibid., 35, lament 16.
77. Ibid., 25, lament 12.
78. Ibid., 29, lament 14.
79. Ibid., 43, lament 18.
80. Ibid.
81. Ibid., 17, lament 8.
82. Ibid., 47, lament 19.

83. Ibid., 13, lament 6.
84. Ibid.
85. Ibid., 3, lament 1.
86. Ibid.
87. Ibid., 5, lament 2.
88. Milosz, *History of Polish Literature* (Berkeley: Univ. of California Press, 1969), 75.
89. Heaney, *Haw Lantern,* 24.
90. Ibid.
91. Ibid., 25, sonnet 1.
92. Ibid.
93. Ibid., 31, sonnet 7.
94. Ibid.
95. Ibid., 30, sonnet 6.
96. Ibid., 29, sonnet 5.
97. Ibid., 31, sonnet 7.
98. Ibid., 29, sonnet 5.
99. Ibid., 31, sonnet 7.
100. Ibid., 27, sonnet 3.
101. Ibid.
102. Ibid., 31, sonnet 7.
103. Ibid., 24.
104. Ibid., 28, sonnet 4.
105. Ibid.
106. Ibid.

Conclusion: A Bright Nowhere

1. Heaney, *Preoccupations,* 130.
2. Ibid., 129–30.
3. Heaney, *Haw Lantern,* 32.
4. Paul Muldoon, *Knowing My Place* (Northern Ireland: Ulsterman Publications, 1971).
5. Heaney, *Government of the Tongue,* 14.
6. Paul Muldoon, *Moy Sand and Gravel* (London: Faber and Faber, 2002), 74–87.
7. Ibid., 81.
8. Ibid., 90.

Bibliography

Armstrong, Tim. "Muting the Klaxon: Poetry, History and Irish Modernism." In *Modernism and Ireland: The Poetry of the 1930s,* edited by Patricia Coughlan and Alex Davis. Cork: Cork Univ. Press, 1995.

Beiler, Ludwig. *The Irish Penitentials.* Dublin: Dublin Institute for Advanced Studies, 1975.

Brodsky, Joseph. "A Hidden Duet." *Times Literary Supplement,* 27 Aug. 1991, 16.

Brown, Terence. *Ireland: A Social and Cultural History, 1922 to the Present.* Ithaca N.Y.: Cornell Univ. Press, 1985.

Calderón de la Barca, Pedro. *Calderón's Dramas.* Edited and translated by Denis Florence MacCarthy. London: Kegan, Paul Trench, 1887.

———. *The Two Lovers of Heaven, Chrysanthus and Daria: A Drama of Early Christian Rome.* Translated by Denis Florence MacCarthy. Dublin: John F. Fowler, 1870.

Carleton, William. *Traits and Stories of the Irish Peasantry.* Edited by Barbara Haley. Gerrards Cross, U.K.: Colin Smythe, 1990. Facsimile of 1844 edition.

Curtayne, Alice. *Lough Derg.* Monaghan: R and S Printing, 1944.

———. *A Recall to Dante.* 1932. Reprint, Port Washington N.Y.: Kennikat Press, 1969.

Dante Alighieri. *The Divine Comedy.* Translated by John D. Sinclair. New York: Oxford Univ. Press, 1961.

———. *Il Paradiso,* canto xxxiii, translated by Seamus Heaney, from a photocopy of a draft provided to the author by Seamus Heaney.

———. *Inferno.* Translated by Dorothy L. Sayers. Harmondsworth, U.K.: Penguin, 1955.

———. *Purgatorio.* Translated by Dorothy L. Sayers. Harmondsworth, U.K.: Penguin, 1945.

Davis, Alex. *A Broken Line: Denis Devlin and Irish Poetic Modernism.* Dublin: Univ. College Dublin Press, 2000.

Deane, Seamus. "Heroic Styles: The Tradition of an Idea." *Field Day.* Pamphlet no. 4. Derry: Field Day, 1984.

———. *A Short History of Irish Literature.* South Bend, Ind.: Univ. of Notre Dame Press, 1986.

Devlin, Denis. *Collected Poems of Denis Devlin.* Edited by J. C. C. Mays. Dublin: Dedalus Press, 1989.

Dillon, Samuel. *Sketches of the Scenery, History and Antiquities of the North-West of Ireland; including A Minute Account of the celebrated Lough Derg, & Patrick's Purgatory, in the County Donegal.* Dublin: J. Jones, 1818.

Donoghue, Denis. *We Irish.* New York: Knopf, 1986.

Duffy, Charles Gavan. *Ballad Poetry of Ireland.* Dublin: James Duffy, 1845.

———. *Young Ireland: A Fragment of Irish History 1840–1850.* New York: D. Appleton, 1881.

Dublin University Magazine, Dec. 1851, 711.

Eliot, T. S. *The Complete Poems and Plays.* New York: Harcourt, Brace and World, 1934.

———. *Dante.* London: Faber and Faber, 1929.

———. *Selected Prose of T. S. Eliot.* Edited by Frank Kermode. London: Faber and Faber, 1975.

Ferguson,Samuel. From *Dublin Magazine,* 1834. In *Poetry and Ireland since 1800,* edited by Mark Storey, 42. New York: Routledge, 1998.

Fogarty, Anne. "Gender, Irish Modernism, and Devlin." In *Modernism and Ireland,* edited by Patricia Coughlan and Alex Davis. Cork: Cork Univ. Press, 1995.

Foster, John Wilson. "Irish Modernism." Chap. 3 in *Colonial Consequences.* Dublin: Lilliput Press, 1991.

Foster, R. F. *Modern Ireland: 1600–1972.* London: Penguin, 1989.

Frazier, Adrian. "Anger and Nostalgia: Seamus Heaney and the Ghost of the Father." *Eire-Ireland* (Fall/Winter 2001): 14.

Gibbons, Luke. *Gaelic Gothic.* Galway: Arlen House, 2004.

Greenblatt, Stephen. *Hamlet in Purgatory.* Princeton, N.J.: Princeton Univ. Press, 2001.

Harbison, Peter. *Pilgrimage in Ireland.* London: Barrie and Jenkins, 1991.

Heaney, Seamus. *Crediting Poetry.* Oldcastle, Ireland: Gallery Press, 1995.

———. *District and Circle.* London: Faber and Faber, 2006.

———. "A Dream of Solstice." *Irish Times,* 21 Dec. 1999: 1.

———. "Envies and Identifications: Dante and the Modern Poet." *Irish University Review* 15 (Spring 1985): 12.

———. *Field Work.* London: Faber and Faber, 1979.

———. *Finders Keepers.* New York: Farrar, Straus and Giroux, 2002.

———. *The Government of the Tongue.* London: Faber and Faber, 1988.

———. *The Haw Lantern.* New York: Farrar, Straus and Giroux, 1987.

———. *North.* London: Faber and Faber, 1975.

———. *Opened Ground.* New York: Farrar, Straus and Giroux, 1998.

———. *Preoccupations.* London: Faber and Faber, 1980.

———. *Redress of Poetry.* Oldcastle, Ireland: Gallery Press, 1995.

———. *Seeing Things.* London: Faber and Faber, 1991.

———. *The Spirit Level.* New York: Farrar, Straus and Giroux, 1996.

———. *Station Island.* New York: Farrar, Straus and Giroux, 1985.

Howes, Marjorie. *Yeats's Nations.* Cambridge: Cambridge Univ. Press, 1966.

Hurson, Tess. *Inside the Margins: A Carleton Reader.* Belfast: Lagan Press, 1992.

Johnston, Dillon. *Irish Poetry after Joyce.* Syracuse: Syracuse Univ. Press, 1997.

Joyce, James. *A Portrait of the Artist as a Young Man.* Harmondsworth, U.K.: Penguin, 1964.

Kavanagh, Patrick. *Collected Poems.* London: MacGibbon and Kee, 1954.

———. *Collected Poems.* Edited by Antoinette Quinn. London: Allen Lane, 2004.

———. *The Complete Poems.* Newbridge, Ireland: Goldsmith Press, 1972.

Kiberd, Declan. *Inventing Ireland.* Cambridge, Mass.: Harvard Univ. Press, 1995.

Kinsella, Thomas, and Seán Ó Tuama. *An Duanaire.* Dublin: Dolmen Press, 1981.

Kochanowski, Jan. *Laments,* translated by Seamus Heaney and Stanislaw Baranczak. London: Faber and Faber, 1995.

Kristeva, Julia. *The Kristeva Reader.* Edited by Toril Moi. Oxford: Blackwell, 1986.

Le Goff, Jacques. *The Birth of Purgatory.* Chicago: Univ. of Chicago Press, 1981.

Leslie, Shane. *The Celt and the World.* New York: Charles Scribner's Sons, 1917.

———. *The End of a Chapter.* New York: Charles Scribner's Sons, 1916.

———. *Long Shadows.* London: John Murray, 1966.

———. *Lough Derg in Ulster.* Dublin: Maunsel and Co., 1909.

———. *Saint Patrick's Purgatory.* London: Burnes, Oates and Washbourne, 1932.

Lloyd, David. *Nationalism and Minor Literature.* Los Angeles: Univ. of California Press, 1987.

———. "Pap for the Dispossessed." In *Anomalous States: Irish Writing and the Post-Colonial Moment.* Durham N.C.: Duke Univ. Press, 1993.

Lucas, A. T. *Penal Crucifixes.* Dublin: National Museum of Ireland, 1958.

MacCarthy, Denis Florence. *The Book of Irish Ballads.* Dublin: James Duffy, 1846.

———. *Poems.* Dublin: M. H. Gill and Son, 1882.

———. *Poems of Denis Florence MacCarthy.* Dublin and Cork: The Educational Company, 1882.

———. *Poets and Dramatists of Ireland: with an Introduction on the Early Religion and Literature of the Irish People.* Dublin: James Duffy, 1846.

———. *Shelley's Early Life.* London: John Camden, 1872.

Mandelstam, Osip. *The Complete Prose and Letters.* Translated by Jane Gary Harris and Constance Link. Ann Arbor, Mich.: Ardis, 1979.

———. *The Prose of Osip Mandelstam.* Translated by Clarence Brown. Princeton, N.J.: Princeton Univ. Press, 1965.

McGuckian, Medbh. *Captain Lavender.* Oldcastle, Ireland: Gallery Press, 1995.

———. "Horsepower Pass By! A Study of the Car in the Poetry of Seamus Heaney." Pamphlet. Coleraine, Northern Ireland: Crannagh Press, 1999.

———. *Marconi's Cottage.* Oldcastle, Ireland: Gallery Press, 1991.

———. *On Ballycastle Beach.* Oxford: Oxford Univ. Press, 1988.

Merton, Thomas, and Czeslaw Milosz. *Striving Towards Being.* Edited by Robert Faggen. New York: Farrar, Straus and Giroux, 1997.

Milosz, Czeslaw. *The Collected Poems.* Hopewell, N.J.: Ecco Press, 1988.

———. *History of Polish Literature.* (Berkeley: Univ. of California Press, 1969.

———. *Road-side Dog.* New York: Farrar, Straus and Giroux, 1998.

———. *A Treatise on Poetry.* Translated by Czeslaw Milosz and Robert Hass. New York: HarperCollins, 2001.

———. *The Witness of Poetry.* Cambridge, Mass.: Harvard Univ. Press, 1979.

Montague, John. "An Occasion for Sin." *Death of a Chieftain.* Chester Springs, Pa.: Dufour, 1967, 119.

Muldoon, Paul. *Knowing My Place.* Northern Ireland: Ulsterman Publications, 1971.

———. *Moy Sand and Gravel.* London: Faber and Faber, 2002.

O'Connor, D. Canon (Daniel O'Connor). *Lough Derg and Its Pilgrimages.* Dublin: Joseph Dollard, 1879.

———. *St. Patrick's Purgatory, Lough Derg.* Dublin: James Duffy and Son, 1931.

Ó Dúshláine, Tadhg. *Lough Derg in Native Irish Poetry.* Dublin: An Clóchóir, 1987.

O'Faolain, Sean. *Collected Stories of Seán O'Faoláin.* Boston: Atlantic Monthly Press Book, Little, Brown, 1932.

Pearse, Patrick. "The Murder Machine." In *The Field Day Anthology of Irish Writing,* edited by Seamus Deane. New York: Norton, 1991.

Picard, Jean Michel, trans. *Saint Patrick's Purgatory: A Twelfth Century Tale of a Journey to the Other World.* (Dublin: Four Courts Press, 1985).

Purcell, Deirdre. *On Lough Derg.* Dublin: Veritas, 1988.

Quinn, Antoinette. *Patrick Kavanagh: Born-Again Romantic.* Dublin: Gill and Macmillan, 1993.

———. *Patrick Kavanagh: A Biography.* Dublin: Gill and MacMillan, 2001.

Reilly, Rev. Mr. *Hindooism in Ireland or, a succinct Account of the Celebrated Saint Patrick's Purgatory at Loughderg, and a similar Station, lately established, at Coronea, In the County of Cavan.* Dublin: Richard Moore Tims, 1826.

Skelton, Rev. Philip, Rector of Fintona. *The Complete Works.* Edited by Robert Lyman. Vol. 5. London: Richard Baynes, 1824.

Stack, Tom. *No Earthly Estate: Patrick Kavanagh and God.* Dublin: Columba Press, 2002.

Stevens, Wallace. *The Necessary Angel.* New York: Vintage, 1951.

———. *Selected Poems.* London: Faber and Faber, 1953.

The Táin. Translated by Thomas Kinsella. Oxford: Oxford Univ. Press, 1969.

Timoney, Joseph. *St Patrick's Purgatory, Lough Derg: Impressions of a Pilgrim.* Enniskillen, Ireland: *Fermanagh Herald,* 1926.

Turner, Victor. *The Ritual Process.* Harmondsworth, U.K.: Penguin, 1974.

Vendler, Helen. "A Lament in Three Voices." *New York Review of Books,* 31 May 2001.

———. *Seamus Heaney.* Cambridge, Mass.: Harvard Univ. Press, 1998.

Welch, Robert. "Language as Pilgrimage: Lough Derg Poems of Patrick Kavanagh and Denis Devlin." *Irish University Review* 31 (Spring 1983): 61.

Whelan, Kevin. "The Memories of the Dead." *Yale Journal of Criticism* 15, no. 1 (2002).

———. "The Regional Impact of Irish Catholicism, 1700–1850." In *Common Ground,* edited by W. J. Smyth and Kevin Whelan. Cork: Cork Univ. Press, 1980.

———. *The Tree of Liberty.* Cork: Cork Univ. Press, 1996.

Wordsworth, William. *The Prelude: Selected Poems and Sonnets.* Edited by Carlos Baker. New York: Holt, Rinehart and Winston, 1965.

Yeats, W. B. "The Celtic Element in Literature." In *Poetry and Ireland Since 1800,* edited by Mark Storey. New York: Routledge, 1998.

———. *The Collected Works of W. B. Yeats.* Edited by Richard Finneran. Vol. 1. New York: Scribner's, 1997.

Index

use of irony, 32, 35, 37–38, 40, 42; use of Lough Derg as symbol for Irishness, 32; on value of penitential exercises, 33, 36–37; water-walking episode, 35–36, 37
—*Traits and Stories of the Irish Peasantry,* 14, 16, 40
—"Wildgoose Lodge": affront to individuality in, 45–46; demonization of Catholic Ribbonmen, 44, 45, 46, 51; evocation of in "Station Island," 214; Heaney's allusion to, 200; on horrors of land agitation, 200; injections of realism in, 44, 45; plot of, 43–45, 46; representation of hell in, 46–47; theme of, 43, 45
Carolan, Turlough, 212
"Cassandra" (Heaney), 165
Catherine of Sienna, 88, 92
Catholicism: accolades for O'Connor's Lough Derg book, 70–71; assimilation of heresy into doctrine, 119; betrayal of Ireland, 181–82; Carleton's opposition to, 35, 41, 42, 113; censoring of "Father Mat," 138–39; colonization and feminization of individuals, 132; Cromwellian racialization of, 84; of Curtayne, 86; deconstruction of by artists, 33–34; as defense against nationalism, 65; Devlin's struggle with, 107, 109, 119–21; dispute over ownership of Station Island, 78–80; fusion with nationalism, 44–45, 128, 182, 203; Heaney's entry point into, 163; Heaney's position on, 182–99, 257; interconnectedness with nationalism, 166–67, 179, 239; international character of, 69; Irish identity and, xiv, 85–86; Kavanagh's discomfort with, 107; Kavanagh's portrait of, 128, 129–33; Leslie family heritage and, 81–82; as leveling force, 147; literary renaissance and, 67; literature of, 237; MacCarthy and, 19, 52, 56; Maynooth College and, xxi; McGuckian's employment of paradoxes of, 113; Milosz and, 237–38, 246; as Mother in "Station Island," 183; parallel to Lough Derg history, 71; poet's possession of words and, 187–88; racial purity and, 67; recovery of self-definition and, 67–68; reduced to routine and good manners, 103; relationship to nationalism, 51–52; renunciation of reason as requirement of, 201; sacrament of penance and Lough Derg, 11; separation

from nationalism, xxii; Skelton's view of, 14; "Station Island" as defiance of, 184–85; as substitute for deracinated urbanites, 101; subversion of in "Station Island," 212; threat of insanity in, 41; variable relationship with nationalism, 51–52, 181–82; vaulting of spatial, temporal and corporeal by, 113; vestigial power of over Carleton, 31; victory over skepticism, 41; World War I and, 82–83; wresting of artist from, xv, 166–67
cave symbol, 176, 178, 187
Celt and the World, The (Leslie), 78, 83
"Celtic Element in Literature, The" (Yeats), 55
Celticism, 21, 78, 82–84
censorship laws, 68
Charon (fict.), 189
"Chekhov on Sakhalin" (Heaney), 210
chestnut tree, 205, 264
Chiercati (papal nuncio), 9–10
"Child of Europe" (Milosz), 248
Christianity: allegory of triumph over paganism, 5; belief in good and evil, xix; Dante's sidestepping of, 207; Milosz's denunciation of love theology, 220; of Tsvetaeva's poems, 117. *See also* Catholicism; Protestants
Christian legend of Lough Derg, 5, 74–75, 76, 94–96, 181, 193
Churchill, Winston, 81
Clarke, Austin, 61
classicism, 242–43, 249–50
class issues, 96–97, 123
"Clearances" (Heaney): affirmation of, xv, 203, 251, 252; balance of truthfulness and metaphysics, 158, 159; central paradox of, 236; contribution to Lough Derg tradition, xviii; countermemory of emptiness, 230–31; decision made in, 252; doubleness of language in, 159, 205; on form of language, 211; gender concerns of, 255; gentle scold of, 178; historical irony of title, 267; history in, 254–55; honest emotions of, 256; image of chestnut tree in, 205, 264; language of, 254, 256–57; leap of faith in, 177; moment of final yielding in, 183, 252; paradox of form and content, 253; perspective on women, 260–61; place of mother's soul, 263; premise of, 172, 173; revisionism of, 253–57; transformation of personal loss, 245, 250
Cleary, Arthur, 107

150–51; Heaney's confrontation with, 168, 178, 179, 202; hobbling of nostalgia, 100–101; Kavanagh's negation of, 128; Muldoon's subversion of, 265

"Est Prodest" (Devlin), 110, 223–24

Estragon (fict.), 159

Europe: link to Ireland through Lough Derg, 7–11, 22, 55–56, 70–71, 175, 260; link to Ireland through monasticism, xxiii; pilgrims from, 98

existentialism, xix, 53

experimentalism, 107

Faggen, Robert, 235–36

Fairy Faith in Celtic Countries (Wentz), 4

faith: balanced with skepticism by Kavanagh, 135–36; Devlin on falling away from, 121–22; Devlin's questioning of justification of, 120; gender and, 114; as healer to rifts, 177–78; Heaney on, 240–41; Heaney's investigation of, 205, 255; Heaney's nonverbal spaces as, 197; impact on language, 24; as integration of reason and intuition, 241; Joycean rejection of, xx; Kavanagh's knowledge of need of, 130; light as vehicle for, 224; link to philosophy, 221–22; link to poetry for Milosz, xvi; loss as revealer of, 251; love as source of, 197; Milosz on, 236–38; misuse of by prolepsis, 222; need for childlike innocence of, 245–46; paradox as means to, 175; paradox of dialect of, 235; *Purgatorio*'s address of, 211; relationship to poetry, 237–38; renewal of through sacraments, 142–43; stripping of in "Squarings," 226; warning of "Station Island" about, 173; women as route to, 109. *See also* beliefs

"Faithless Wife, The" (O'Faoláin), 101–2

Fanon, Franz, xx

father figures, 178, 179, 180, 183, 199

Father Mat (fict.), 138–43, 148

"Father Mat" (Kavanagh), 107, 138–43, 148

Father Ned (fict.), 140, 142–43

"Feeling into Words" (Heaney), 202

feminism, 6, 88–89, 112, 184

Fenian legend of Lough Derg, 4, 5, 27–28, 98, 187

Ferguson, Sir Samuel, 17, 56, 63, 218

Field Day pamphlets, 171, 180, 220

Field Work (Heaney): "Glanmore Sonnets," xviii, 158, 159, 214; hutched privacies of, 245; poetic of, 154, 159; reference to *Inferno* in, 206; "The Strand at Lough Beg," 161; "Ugolino," 214–15, 216–18

Finders Keepers (Heaney), 235

Fionn MacCool (legendary character), 5, 14, 27–28, 188

"Fireman's Lift" (Ní Chuilleanáin), 88

Fitzherbert, Mrs. (supposed wife of George IV), 81, 82

"Flight Path, The" (Heaney), 212–16, 217, 218, 233, 234

Fogarty, Anne, 112

forgiveness, 27, 261

form: Calderón's use of *auto*, 18; of "Clearances," 253; "Clearances" on form of language, 211; emergence from language, 211; of *The Issa Valley*, 235; of Kavanagh's sonnets, 150–51; Milosz on, 243–44; Muldoon's subversion of, 266–67

Foster, John Wilson, 108

Foster, R. F., 212

"Four Quartets" (Eliot), 209, 249

Francis Hughes (fict.), 157

Francoise O'Meara (fict.), 100

fraud, 75

Frazier, Adrian, 160, 163

freedom of religion, xx

"From Monaghan to the Grand Canal" (Heaney), 168, 263

Gaelic Gothic (Gibbons), 84

Gaelicization, 68

Gaelic revival, 99

gender: Brodsky's perspective on in literature, 115–17; concerns of in "Clearances," 253–54, 255; concerns of in "Heavenly Foreigner," 117, 253; faith and, 114; Heaney's use of the feminine, 198, 199–202; implications of in "Lament," 251; Lough Derg narratives and, 6–7, 65, 260; McGuckian's manipulations with, 113; Milosz's use of as emblem, xvii; poetry and, 114–17, 253, 264; Reilly's link to Lough Derg legend, 14; unresolved puzzle of in "Station Island," 194–95. *See also* father figures; mother figure

George IV (king of England), 81

Gibbons, Luke, 84

Heaney, Seamus (works) (*cont.*)
poetic diction of, 224, 238, 248; refined doubt
of, xv; reinterrogation of, 203; rejection of
modernism and relativism, 240; revelation
of relationship to Catholicism, 240;
"Settings," 220; "Squarings" section of, 220;
style and structure of, 219, 220;
transformation of physical to metaphysical,
219; use of "phenomenal," 221–22; use of
"proleptic," 221, 222–23; world view of, 236
—*Station Island,* 158, 174–75, 245, 250
—"Station Island," 177–78; account of Lough
Derg experience, 32–33; allusions to in
"Squarings," 229; allusions to other
literature, 227–29; alter egos in, 138;
approach to, 168; benefit to Irish literature,
264–65; bird images, 198–99; blistered
cornfields imagery, 16; bridging of
differences in, 209; candle image, 197–98; as
capstone of investigations of Lough Derg,
27, 259; change in moral perspective, 165–66;
characters of, 168, 170; conformity to terza
rima, 212; confrontations with father figure,
178; confrontation with Carleton, 39,
199–201, 214; confrontation with Kavanagh,
201–2; construction of Lough Derg, xviii,
156, 168–69, 170; as core sample of Ireland,
168; Dante reflected in decisions of, 212–16;
despair in, 250; dominant narrative
paradigm of, 181; effect of perspectival
shifts, 226; enlistment of Joyce, 171, 178–82;
events surrounding writing of, 156;
examination of moral conduct through, xix,
146, 157–59, 238; father figures in, 178–79,
180–81, 183–84; as fine incision, 167; focus
of, 157, 180, 189, 238; force of lived
experience over book learning, 186;
fragmented images of, 176–77; heteroglossia
of, 259; illumination in, 172; identities of
poet in, 173; inflected feminism of, 178–79,
184; on jeopardy of artist's soul, 195;
McCartney's presence in, 208; moment of
integration in, 171–74; moral goal of, 249;
movements and mental gyrations of, 238;
mug symbolism, 172–74, 176–77, 230, 255;
Muldoon on, 265; on need for collaboration,
175–76; nonresolution in, 164–65; as part of
ongoing translation, 156, 218; as penitential
exercise, xv, 177, 203; as pivotal point in
Heaney's career, xv, 233, 254, 255, 257,

262–64; place of good thief's hearkening to
the promise, 164; political and personal
climate fostering, 154; political point of, 158;
presentation of sexual matters, 184–87, 191,
197–98, 201–2; questions posed by, 8, 154–55,
182, 197; reckoning with female sexuality, 6;
referentiality and intertextuality of, 153, 156,
157, 177, 182–99, 211; resemblance to *Hamlet,*
192–93; revelation of relationship to
Catholicism, 240; revisionism of, 200, 212;
revisiting of in "Flight Path," 212–16; self-
centeredness and reflexivity of, 26; on sense
of protection, 245–46; on separation of
Catholicism and nationalism, 166–67;
sidestepping Christianity in, 207;
significance of references to light, 185; on
sins of omission, 161; skepticism of
rapturous religion, 177–78; speed and moral
movement of, 208; spiritual and moral
hunger necessitating, 174; structure of, 157,
166, 179; theme of, 166, 168; transformation
from physical to metaphysical, 8, 168–69,
170, 172–73; translation of Saint John of the
Cross, 27, 56, 174, 175, 191, 194, 201, 260;
traversing of gender morass, 199–202;
urgings of ghosts, 182–83; use of alternative
identities, 128; weaning experienced in, 245
—"The Strand at Lough Beg," 161
—"Sunlight," 172
—"Sweeney Astray" (translation), 168, 170,
171–72
—"Terminus," 20
—"The Tollund Man," 28
—"Triptych," 167
—"Ugolino," 214–15, 216–18
—"Weighing In," 206
"Heavenly Foreigner, The" (Devlin): body seen
as route toward transcendence, 111–12;
gender concerns of, 117, 253; hint of
Mariolatry in, 109, 110; organization and
imagery of, 104, 110; paradox of, 111;
promise extended by woman, 114; sketch of
civil servant, 104–5; style of, 125; theme of,
110–11; use of repetition in, 111; writing of,
107
"Hedge School, The" (Carleton), 43
hell, 46–47, 60
Henry of Saltrey, 7–8, 92, 94, 190, 191, 193
Herbert, Zbigniew, 163
herd instinct, 43

178–82; Heaney's view of, 223; invitation to freedom, 28; on self-reflexive allusions, 124; modernism and, 203; mother figure of, 255; pilgrimage to Dante, 205; renunciation of Lough Derg, 2; as unnamed character in "Station Island," 178–79, 180–81, 192, 201–2, 212; use of "whinge," 196; *Opened Ground*, 196; *Portrait of the Artist as a Young Man, A*, 181–82

"Joy or Night" (Heaney): argument with modernism, 163; comparison of Larkin and Yeats, 160, 203; comparison of Larkin to Beckett, 204; Heaney's affinity with Yeats and, 162, 171

Juan de la Cruz. *See* John of the Cross, Saint

justice, 129–30

Kavanagh, Patrick (general): acceptance of Maguire, 138; attempt at integration, 106; career of, 135–36; compared to Devlin, 97–98, 106, 137; concept of love, 147; context for poems of, 70; first sexual encounter, 141–42; focus on Mary as healer, 140; Heaney's assessment of, 205, 262–64; identification with needs of the people, 146–47; life of, 168; Lough Derg experiences, 146; as Lough Derg writer, xiv; management of conflict in writings of, 127; modernism and, 105–6; poetic of, xviii, 128; precursor to, 200; preparation for spiritual breakthrough, 136–38; programmatic debasement of self, 142; protection of manly rectitude, 178; restoration of repose and confidence of, 151–52; on spiritual poverty of 1940s, 13; stimulation of Christ's suffering for, 133–34; strategy of, 21, 106, 146, 149; struggle for self-realization of, 20, 138, 144–45; style of, 24, 106, 134, 139, 143–44, 150; subversion of idealizing example of Yeats, 107; as unnamed character in "Station Island," 179, 201–2; view of mortification of flesh, 26; view of provincial and parochial positions, 210; voice of in "Station Island," 192

Kavanagh, Patrick (works)
—"Canal Bank Walk," 135, 187–88
—"Father Mat," 107, 138
—"The Great Hunger": acceptance of Maguire, 138; balancing of skepticism and faith in, 135–36; characterization in, 104, 105, 128,

129, 130–31; cottagers' view of visitors, 96; effects of choices made in, 137–38; empathy of, 247; examination of Catholicism, 129–33; as exploration of culture from inside, 148; exploration of pedophilia, 142; fusion of narrator and character, 133; on imagination, 134; indication of moments of transcendence in, 134, 139; opening words of, 250; as preparation for "Lough Derg," 131–34; as preparation for spiritual breakthrough, 136–38; realism of, 153; religious and symbolist energy of, 106; reparation of idealization of Ireland, 127–28; request of, 136; on suffering and compassion, 134–35; test for survival of religious vision, 129; theme of, 155; use of alterity of Maguire, 128; voice of the people in, 129–30; writing of, 107
—"The Hospital," 146–47
—"Lough Derg": characterization in, 145–46, 149, 151; conflict in, 145; culminating paradox of, 143; description of the site, 148–49, 261–62; empathy with self-annihilating herd instinct, 261; events surrounding writing of, 155; evocation of Famine scenes, 32; key to delight in, 148; language of, 22; moments of radiance in, 143; perspective of, 156; prayer sonnets at end of, 143–44, 147, 150–51; precursor to, 138; Quinn's assessment of, 144; reception of, 22; religious and symbolist energy of, 106; revision of history, 149; as shadow play behind "The Great Hunger," 131–32; sociological analysis of the ritual, 32; style of, 143, 150; transformation from physical to metaphysical, 23; use of secrets in, 151; Welch on, 145; writing of, 107
—"Pilgrims," 128–29
—"Prelude," 147
—"Why Sorrow," 107, 148; writing of, 138–43
Kiberd, Declan, 127, 153, 220
Kinsella, Thomas, 11, 218, 233
Knight Owen legend, 7–8, 73–74, 91–92, 190, 193, 194
Knowing My Place (Muldoon), 265
Kochanowski, Jan: background of, 250; break with classicism, 249–50; honesty of, 254; lament of loss of innocence, 253; response to death of child, 249–53; "Laments," 250–53

Lough Derg (O'Connor): accolades earned by
first edition, 70–71; approach of, 168;
foreshadowing of patriotic piety, 68, 69;
homogenization of attacks on Lough Derg,
75–76; on origin of name of Saint Patrick's
Purgatory, 74; perspective of, 70, 157, 158;
publication of, 69; revisionism of, 71, 200; on
Saint Patrick's role in Lough Derg, 76
"Lough Derg Pilgrim, The" (Carleton): account
of Lough Derg experience, 30–31, 33, 36–37;
attacks on Lough Derg, xxi; background of,
1, 14–15; blistered foot imagery, 15–16, 71;
Catholicism equated with disease, 35;
ceding of authority to Otway and Jones, 29;
comparison of Lough Derg to Rome, 30;
complex personality of, 14–16; connection of
impressions and occurrences with inner
vibrations, 41; on corruption of Lough Derg,
13, 14; cosmopolitanism of, 26; description
of characters in, 38–40; description of
experiences at Lough Derg, xiii, 40–43;
dormant grief of, 40–41; events surrounding
writing of, 155; experience at Lough Derg,
30–31, 33; gender confusion in, 31; Heaney's
allusion to, 199; heteroglossia of, 127;
identity crisis of, 31; interrogation of value
of penitential exercises, 33, 36–37;
intertexuality of, 201; introduction of
cultural interrogation, 34; introspection of
pilgrims, 36; irony in, 32, 35, 37–38, 40, 41,
42; Lough Derg as symbol for Irishness in,
32; on mortification of the flesh, 29–30, 37;
narrative strategy of, 16–17; as only
literature on Lough Derg for significant
time, 149; outlook of, 37; paradigm for
inquisition of pentitentiary, 33, 34; pilgrim
mistaken for priest, 35; portraiture in, 31,
38–40; presentation of self, 30; Protestant
dissent in, 14; realism of, 34–35, 37, 39;
revelation of individual psyche as site of
nightmare of history, 32; revisionism of, 33;
sartorial ruse in, 138; simony of priest, 31,
35; spiritual hunger in, 201; struggle for self-
realization, 20; style of, 38; suicidal leap of
boy, 30–31, 137; transformation of material
reality, 25–26, 34–35, 41–43; two crones, 31,
39–40; view of mortification of flesh, 26;
water-walking episode, 35–36, 37
Lough Derg publicists, 21
Lourie, Richard, 248

love: Dante's infant sucking trope, 206–7, 230;
Dante's revelation of in Beatrice, 183;
differentiation of divine from human, 172,
173; Heaney's attempt to describe the ideal,
230; imagery of maternal love in "Station
Island," 178; MacCarthy's confession of, 19;
as means to healing pagan-Christian divide,
185; as means to salvation, 103, 109, 185;
Milosz on failure of, 220; as source of faith,
197, 229; Tsvetaeva's view of, 184–85; two
sides of represented in "Station Island," 184;
unity and knowledge thwarted by, 176
"Lovers of the Lake" (O'Faoláin): hint of
Mariolatry in, 109; Lough Derg's temptation
to believe, 262; perspective of, 70; plot of,
102; revelation of author's attachment to
Holy Ireland, 22; setting of, 101
"Love Song of J. Alfred Prufrock, The" (Eliot),
109–10, 122, 137
Lucas, A. T., 77
Lucy (fict.), 64
Luis Enius (fict.), 19, 63–64, 158
lust of eye, 40, 42, 111
Lynch, John Joseph, 70
lyre-harp image, 170–71, 176

MacBride, Sean, 179
MacCarthy, Denis Florence: anxiety about
fidelity, 233; assault on English language,
61–62; background of, 18; on ballads and
songs, 57–58; beginning of transformation
through language, 7; biography of, 17, 47,
53; on Calderón's religious vision, 65; chief
tactic of, 55; contradictory image of, 49,
53–54; cosmopolitanism of, 26; as dark horse
of Irish Lough Derg writers, 57; death of, 49,
66; description of figures of Great Famine,
258; on discovering unknown poem by
Shelly, 50; erection of barrier between pagan
and Christian Ireland, 82; eulogies to, 49, 63,
66; events surrounding translation, 155;
excavating fervor of, 55–56; life of compared
to Carleton's, 18; linking of Europe to
Ireland, 55–56; as Lough Derg writer, xiv;
management of conflict in writings of, 127;
medieval narratives of Lough Derg revealed
by, 19–20; obituary of, 20; personality of,
53–54; position on pre-colonial past, 59–60;
problems solved through translation, 60–62,

Other titles in Irish Studies

Anglo-Irish Autobiography: Class, Gender, and the Forms of Narrative
   Elizabeth Grubgeld

Contemporary Irish Cinema: From The Quiet Man *to* Dancing at Lughnasa
   James MacKillop, ed.

Gender and History in Yeats's Love Poetry
   Elizabeth Butler Cullingford

Irish Orientalism: A Literary and Intellectual History
   Joseph Lennon

John Redmond and Irish Unity, 1912–1918
   Joseph P. Finnan

Joyce and Reality: The Empirical Strikes Back
   John Gordon

Joyce and the City: The Significance of Space
   Michael Begnal, ed.

The Long War: The IRA and Sinn Féin, Second Edition
   Brendan O'Brien

Reading Roddy Doyle
   Caramine White

Sengoídelc/Old Irish for Beginners
   David Stifter

Two Irelands: Literary Feminisms North and South
   Rebecca Pelan

Twentieth-Century Irish Drama: Mirror up to Nation
   Christopher Murray

Women Creating Women: Contemporary Irish Women Poets
   Patricia Boyle Haberstroh

Yeats and Artistic Power
   Phillip L. Marcus